TSP^{SM}—Coaching Development Teams

TSP^{SM}—Coaching Development Teams

Watts S. Humphrey

♦♦Addison-Wesley

Upper Saddle River, NJ • Boston • Indianapolis • San Francisco
New York • Toronto • Montreal • London • Munich • Paris • Madrid
Capetown • Sydney • Tokyo • Singapore • Mexico City

CarnegieMellon
Software Engineering Institute

The SEI Series in Software Engineering

Many of the designations used by manufacturers and sellers to distinguish their products are claimed as trademarks. Where those designations appear in this book, and the publisher was aware of a trademark claim, the designations have been printed with initial capital letters or in all capitals.

CMM, CMMI, Capability Maturity Model, Capability Maturity Modeling, Carnegie Mellon, CERT, and CERT Coordination Center are registered in the U.S. Patent and Trademark Office by Carnegie Mellon University.

ATAM; Architecture Tradeoff Analysis Method; CMM Integration; COTS Usage-Risk Evaluation; CURE; EPIC; Evolutionary Process for Integrating COTS Based Systems; Framework for Software Product Line Practice; IDEAL; Interim Profile; OAR; OCTAVE; Operationally Critical Threat, Asset, and Vulnerability Evaluation; Options Analysis for Reengineering; Personal Software Process; PLTP; Product Line Technical Probe; PSP; SCAMPI; SCAMPI Lead Appraiser; SCAMPI Lead Assessor; SCE; SEI; SEPG; Team Software Process; and TSP are service marks of Carnegie Mellon University.

Special permission to reproduce portions of "TSP process materials," © 2005 by Carnegie Mellon University, in this book is granted by the Software Engineering Institute.

The author and publisher have taken care in the preparation of this book, but make no expressed or implied warranty of any kind and assume no responsibility for errors or omissions. No liability is assumed for incidental or consequential damages in connection with or arising out of the use of the information or programs contained herein.

The publisher offers excellent discounts on this book when ordered in quantity for bulk purchases or special sales, which may include electronic versions and/or custom covers and content particular to your business, training goals, marketing focus, and branding interests. For more information, please contact:

    U.S. Corporate and Government Sales
    (800) 382-3419
    corpsales@pearsontechgroup.com

For sales outside the United States, please contact:

    International Sales
    international@pearsoned.com

Visit us on the Web: www.awprofessional.com

Library of Congress Cataloging-in-Publication Data
Humphrey, Watts S., 1927-
    TSP : coaching development teams / Watts S. Humphrey.
        p. cm. — (SEI series in software engineering)
    Includes index.
    ISBN 0-201-73113-4 (hardcover : alk. paper)
  1. Capability maturity model (Computer software) 2. Software engineering. 3. Teams in the workplace. I. Title. II. Series.

    QA76.758.H8627 2006
    005.1'068'5—dc22

                                  2006001143

ISBN 0-201-73113-4
Text printed in the United States on recycled paper at Courier in Westford, Massachusetts.
First printing, April 2006

I dedicate this book to my colleague, Jim Over.
He, more than anyone else, has been responsible for SEI's
success in demonstrating the power and effectiveness
of the methods described herein.

CONTENTS

PREFACE

Teamwork is required for most development projects. Although some small jobs can be handled by individuals, the scale of modern systems is such and the demand for short schedules is so great, it is physically impossible for one person to do the entire job. Development work is a team activity, and the effectiveness of this teamwork largely determines the quality of the team's work. The quality of the team's work, in turn, largely determines the success of the entire project.

A team is more than just a group of people who happen to work together. Teamwork takes practice and it involves special skills. Teams require common processes and agreed-upon goals, they need effective leadership, and to be most effective, they must have coaching. Since development teams need as much guidance and support as any other kind of team, the Software Engineering Institute (SEI) has developed a framework and a process for building and guiding development teams. We call this the Team Software Process (TSP).[1]

While the book title refers to development teams, the material is much more general than this would suggest. Except for a few of the examples and some of the discussion about quality management, all of the material in this book can be applied to almost any kind of professional team. For example, the TSP process

---

1. Team Software Process and TSP are service marks of Carnegie Mellon University.

has been used by testing teams, for requirements work, by a senior management group to run a business, and to guide a process improvement effort.

In describing various coaching situations, I use many examples throughout the book. While I don't name any organizations or people, these examples are all based on real situations with practicing TSP teams. These cases are drawn from the hundreds of teams the SEI has worked with while researching, developing, and deploying the TSP methods into industrial practice. It is my hope that, as more people gain experience coaching such development teams, they will publish their experiences and findings so that we can build the base of reference literature needed to properly grow and enrich the field of coaching for development teams.

Who Should Use This Book

This book is designed to be used by several kinds of readers. Senior managers and executives could find the four chapters in Part I a brief but complete overview of the issues involved in modern system development teamwork. Managers who are considering using the TSP to improve their development organizations should review Parts I and II. Those aspiring to be TSP coaches should read the entire book. It addresses many of the issues you will face in assembling and building development teams, in motivating and guiding these teams, and in helping the team leader and team members do superior work.

Even though the book's principal focus is on TSP teams, knowledge of the TSP and Personal Software Process (PSP) is not required. The methods are quite general and can be understood without prior knowledge of any process or method. However, to gain full advantage of the methods described, it is suggested that you and your teams learn the PSP and use the full set of TSP process materials to guide the development work. You can get additional information on the PSP and TSP from SEI's Web site (www.sei.cmu.edu/tsp).

What You Will Learn from This Book

In developing modern complex systems, any single mistake can have devastating consequences. Thus, everyone on the development team must do high-quality work. Such levels of consistently high performance are possible only with effective coaching and leadership. This book describes how to recognize quality work and how to guide teams in consistently doing such work. It also discusses how to recognize when the team's work does not measure up and how to motivate the developers to improve.

The team coach monitors team performance and assists the team members to improve. This book also shows coaches how to cooperatively support the team leader and how to work with that leader to build, guide, and motivate the entire team.

The Contents of This Book

While a great deal could be said about teamwork in general, this book concentrates on the coach's role in guiding a development team. It is organized in five parts.

Part I—Team Formation

The four chapters in Part I provide overall background and context for the entire book. The principal topics in Part I are development teams, team behavior, coaching principles and methods, and teambuilding. The sample LAU script in Chapter 4 illustrates TSP process concepts and methods. However, like all useful processes, the TSP process changes as we learn more about teams and as we evolve the TSP process to capitalize on this knowledge. Therefore, it is suggested that you get updated copies of the TSP scripts when you need them. For information about obtaining these scripts, contact the SEI or its transition partners (www.sei.cmu.edu/tsp/).

Part II—Launching a TSP Team

Part II describes how the TSP builds effective, productive, self-directed development teams. Such teams are especially well suited for creative development work. The 12 chapters in Part II review the TSP launch process and suggest how to coach and support the team and team leader in conducting an efficient and effective team launch.

Part III—Coaching a TSP Project

Part III concerns guiding the team through the many problems commonly faced in doing development work. Its four chapters describe how to coach the team after the TSP launch and how the team can maintain its plan, manage quality, and conduct a project postmortem.

Part IV—TSP Extensions

There are many types of teams and it is important to adapt the TSP process to the particular project and team involved. The four chapters in Part IV discuss the issues of team type and size and explain how the TSP can be adapted to handle them. Functional teams typically support a functional activity such as product maintenance or system test. The developers in such teams typically work alone or in groups of two or three. Multiple and distributed TSP teams are used either for large projects or where a project includes multiple different disciplines like hardware, software, systems, or test. It is also used when the work is performed in multiple locations. Very large projects generally have unique needs and require customized processes. The final chapter in this section discusses ways to adapt the TSP to address the needs of very large integrated development projects.

Part V—Maintaining a TSP Team

The final four chapters of the book deal with the more subtle topics of teambuilding and the nature and rewards of coaching development teams.

TSP Prerequisites

Before developers can practice the TSP, they must be properly trained. They need to know how to plan and track their work, how to measure and manage quality, and how to follow a defined process. They must understand the importance of quality work, and they must have learned the discipline of recording their task time and the defects they inject and remove. These methods are all taught in the PSP course.[2] Because there is so much material to cover, the PSP course is typically offered in universities at the senior or graduate level and it usually takes a full quarter or semester. The industrial PSP course requires about 100 to 120 hours of a developer's time, generally spread over two weeks with some homework.

Although PSP training is intensive and takes considerable time, competent software professionals have no trouble completing it. Many developers receive PSP training during their college education and many others have been PSP trained by their organizations as part of TSP introduction. Since the PSP and TSP

---

2. This course is described in the book *PSP^{SM}: A Self-Improvement Process for Software Engineers,* Watts S. Humphrey, Addison-Wesley, 2005.

methods are language- and tool-independent, they have long-term value and can be used with any of the languages or tools that developers typically use. Many thousands of developers have now been PSP trained, and the data from these courses show that this training substantially improves their ability to deliver quality products on their planned schedules. The SEI has established a PSP certification program to assist organizations in identifying qualified PSP professionals.

Acknowledgments

This book has grown from my work at the SEI. When I joined the SEI some years ago, I had established the personal goal of transforming the world of software engineering. While some would call this an outrageous objective, I have found it liberating and exciting. This goal has guided my work in the years since I retired from IBM.

I decided to pursue this goal because software-intensive systems play an increasingly important role in modern society. As software has become important for many products and services, it also has become a principal constraint in achieving many business objectives. In fact, the poor state of development practice continues to limit advances in many areas of business and science. Our inability to build quality products on predictable schedules and for reasonable costs severely inhibits the application of modern technology to the service of humankind.

Although it may seem outrageous to attempt to change the world, with the help and support of the SEI and the TSP project team, we have made a good start. Teamwork is a fascinating subject, but it is not a subject one can pursue alone. SEI's TSP team has generously contributed its time and efforts in support of this work. I particularly thank the members of this team for their help and support over the years. They are Dan Burton, Kim Campbell, Anita Carleton, Noopur Davis, Marlene MacDonald, Jim McHale, Julia Mullaney, Bill Nichols, Jim Over, Marsha Pomeroy-Huff, Jodie Spielvogle, and Alan Willett.

I am also deeply indebted to the SEI management team. For their generous support and encouragement, I particularly thank Bill Peterson, the Director of the Software Process Management Program; Clyde Chittester, SEI's Chief Operating Officer; and Paul Nielsen, the SEI Director. Without their help and support, this work would not have been possible.

In writing this book, many people have offered help and encouragement. While I could not possibly thank all of the many team members who have provided me with marvelous examples of effective teamwork, I do want to acknowledge those who have directly helped me with this book. They are Linda Alexander,

Dan Burton, Bob Cannon, David Carrington, John Ciurczak, Noopur Davis, Don McAndrews, Jim McHale, Bill Ommert, Jim Over, Hans-Peter Pfister, Marsha Pomeroy-Huff, Dan Reese, Dan Roy, Jeff Smith, Rafi Syed, Rob Tonneberger, Jim VanBuren, Dan Wall, and Alan Willett. I also want to thank my brother, Phil Humphrey, for his many insightful comments.

Finally, I dedicate this book to Jim Over, the leader of SEI's PSP and TSP project, for his leadership and energy. He, more than any other person, has been responsible for turning the ideas described in this book into effective and practical methods that can be used by modern industrial development teams. I have worked with Jim for over 15 years and have found him to be an insightful and caring team leader, a creative technical contributor, and a good friend.

PART I

Team Formation

Most of us understand coaching and its purpose because of our early experiences on athletic teams. Although few of my early coaches were especially memorable, Coach Umbach was truly amazing. He wasn't a particularly impressive guy: only about 5 feet, 6 inches tall and 158 pounds. But no matter how big you were, if you ever got on a wrestling mat with him, you would never forget it.

Throughout my high school education, I had enjoyed sports but was never much good. This was frustrating because I was willing to practice and work out, but somehow my natural talents did not include ball games. My dad had been a wrestler in college and had enjoyed it, so when I got out of the Navy and went to college, he urged me to try out for the wrestling team. Since I was the only light heavyweight who tried out, I made the cut and was told to show up for practice. As we waited for the coach the next day, I got to know my teammates and it turned out that none of us had ever wrestled before. No one knew what wrestling practice involved or that coach Arnold W. "Swede" Umbach was a truly extraordinary coach.

When the coach arrived, we started with a brief warm up and then a two-mile run, with the coach in front. Then he paired us up and had us work on a few basic holds. The coach took turns wrestling with each of us. After an hour and a half, when we were all pretty beat, we ended with another two-mile run, again with the coach in front. The workouts were so tough that the matches seemed easy. By the end of the year, several of us were undefeated, the team took the 13-state championship, and we were campus heroes. All of this from a ragtag bunch of inexperienced recruits. It was Coach Umbach who made the team.

Our coach's dedication, commitment, and energy were amazing, but what I found most inspiring was that he really cared about how each of us did. I have always remembered how he made a small band of raw recruits into a championship team and how he fostered the kind of cohesive team spirit that made losing simply unthinkable. I remember on my second match, after completing the regular three rounds, I was laying flat on my back, so exhausted that I knew I couldn't even get up for the final two tie-breaker rounds. All I could hear was Coach Umbach whispering in my ear that the other guy was every bit as beat as I was. All I had to do was get in there and "explode." To this day, I don't know how I did it, but I did, and I won.

When writing this book, I learned that I was on the first Auburn team Coach Umbach coached and that, in his 27 years at Auburn, he had 25 Southeastern Intercollegiate Wrestling Association Championship teams, 127 conference champions, and 4 national champions. In 282 competitive meets, his teams only lost 28. "Swede" Umbach was an inspiring coach then and he has been an inspiration to me ever since.

This book is about coaching. While it provides lots of tips, hints, and guidelines, the key thing to remember is that your attitude and commitment to the team and its members will largely determine how quickly your team turns into an effective working unit and how rapidly the members grow and develop their skills and capabilities. While you share the responsibility for the team with the team leader, your dedication and commitment to the team and every one of its members is critically important to their performance. Part I of this book provides the context for all that follows. Its four chapters cover various aspects of teams, teamwork, and team coaching.

Chapter 1 discusses what teams are, the nature of self-directed teams, and why such teams are particularly important for development work. It also describes the importance of teamwork in developing modern large and complex computer-based systems as well as the teamwork issues involved in doing creative and innovative work.

Chapter 2 discusses team behavior, how teams work, and the various kinds of teams. It also discusses the conditions required to make teams effective along with the various styles and personalities exhibited by teams. This chapter describes a few of the most common team types and the methods that are most effective for coaching them. Several examples illustrate key aspects of team behavior and help explain the team characteristics to consider as you coach a development team.

Chapter 3 covers your responsibilities as a TSP coach, what you do, and how your role changes as your team and team leader gain experience. The chapter also discusses how you can support the team and its leader in becoming self-sufficient and in learning how to be fully effective. The chapter closes with a discussion of your relationship with the team leader.

Chapter 4 describes the teambuilding process, various teambuilding approaches, and how the TSP launch builds teams. The chapter also reviews the need for team involvement in the launch process and provides guidelines to help you obtain team members' participation in that process. It also discusses why observers are excluded from most of the TSP launch meetings and provides examples of what typically happens when visitors are permitted.

1

Development Teams

This chapter discusses why teams are needed, the innovative nature of development work, and the conditions required for teams to do such work. It then describes what a team is, the distinction between teams and work groups, and the various kinds of teams. Finally, the chapter discusses how to build and run high-performing teams, together with an overview of how you, the team coach, contribute to these activities.

Before starting the team and team-working discussions, it is important to first briefly describe the Team Software Process (TSP). This is because much of this book describes how to coach teams that are using the TSP to guide their work. While the coaching concepts and methods described will apply equally well to other types of teams, the TSP is a powerful process and, by using it to guide your teams, you will find it easier to be an effective coach and to produce "winning" teams.

1.1 TSP Overview

The TSP process is designed to guide development teams while they design and develop software-intensive systems. While it will work for many other kinds of

5

teams, its initial focus was on software development work and that is where it has been most widely used.

The TSP process guides development teams and their management in planning and developing quality products on predictable schedules. It provides detailed guidance and its process scripts lead the developers through launching and operating their teams. During the initial launch process, the team first learns the product requirements and project goals from management. It then produces a plan to meet these objectives. At the end of the generally four-day launch, the team meets with management to agree on the team's plan and delivery commitments.

Following the launch, the TSP process guides the team and team leader in working as a self-directed team. As described later in this chapter, a **self-directed team** defines its own strategy and process, produces its own plan, and negotiates it own commitments with management. Experience shows that when the members of such teams are properly trained, led, and coached, they typically deliver quality products on schedule. They also find their work more productive and much more rewarding. For more information on the TSP process, the required training, and the benefits of using the TSP, see the books *Winning with Software: An Executive Strategy; PSP^{SM}: A Self-Improvement Process for Software Engineers;* and *TSP^{SM}—Leading a Development Team* (Humphrey 2002; Humphrey 2005; Humphrey 2006).

1.2   Why Teams Are Needed

Modern systems are becoming increasingly complex. Aircraft, automobiles, computer printers, television sets, and even electric razors contain software—often lots of software—and the amount of software in these products has been rapidly increasing over time. The design of such systems is vastly more complex than it was only a few years ago. Although there are still many relatively modest-sized systems, the trend is for the software content of just about every product to increase by about ten times every five years. As shown in Figure 1.1, this trend has more or less occurred for decades, and it appears likely to continue for the foreseeable future.

Today, many development projects simply cannot be handled by an individual. Most jobs are just too large for one person to complete in a reasonable time. Time-to-market is the critical performance measure in many industries, and the speed with which organizations form and deploy teams has been the single most important factor in determining competitive success.

Teams also have a range of talents and capabilities. Some jobs are so complex and involve so many different specialties that one person could not possibly

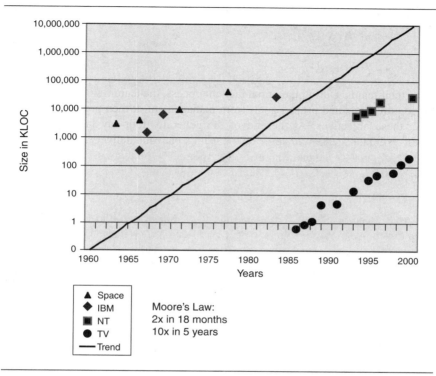

Figure 1.1 Program Size Growth

handle them: No single person could know enough or have a broad enough range of experiences. With a team, the members can specialize on parts of the job and concentrate on those tasks that best fit their abilities. Reasonably sized teams contain a mix of talents and, when these talents are fully utilized, such teams can achieve better performance than any of their individual members could achieve alone.

Participation on a team also improves individual performance. Members often have complementary skills and can learn from each other while providing mutual help and support. Examples of such support are product inspections, group design sessions, and one-on-one assistance. By working with more experienced developers, novices can learn more quickly than they could alone. When properly formed, led, and coached, teams can provide a rich and stimulating environment for building development talent.

1.3   What Are Teams?

A team is a group of people who share a common goal. They must all be committed to this goal and have a common set of practices to guide them as they work to achieve that goal. The definition that best describes a TSP team is one that I have adapted from Dyer (Dyer 1984, 286).

- □ A team consists of at least two people.
- □ The members are working toward a common goal.
- □ Each person has one or more specific roles.
- □ Completion of the mission requires interdependency among the members.

Every one of these elements is important. For example, it is obvious that a team must have more than one member. The need for common goals, however, is more subtle. When groups of people work together without a common goal, they have no need to interact or to support each other. Without some mutual goal, people do not strive—they just put in their time. Then they can have no common group focus and there can be no team. Even if the goal seems simple, such as processing all of today's orders before quitting time, common objectives energize teams.

A principal requirement for team membership is that all of the members have a common set of working guidelines and practices. For example, on sports teams, they must all play the same game. While the reason seems obvious in athletics, it is not so clear in development. However, unless everyone follows consistent guidelines and practices, their work will be unrelated and it will be difficult, if not impossible, for them to cooperate. For a team to work cooperatively and effectively, the members must have a common set of working practices and strive to meet a common team goal.

The reason that team members need roles is not as obvious. Roles provide a sense of ownership and belonging, and they guide the members in doing their work. Roles also ensure that someone is assigned to handle each of the team's important tasks, and they help to spread project management responsibilities across the team.

A further important aspect of team performance is cooperation and interdependence. Each team member must depend to some degree on the performance of the other members. With a common goal and strong team-member interdependence, teams develop the trust and cohesion required to jell. DeMarco and Lister define a jelled team as follows (DeMarco 1987, 123).

A jelled team is a group of people so strongly knit that the whole is greater than the sum of the parts. The production of such a team is greater than that of the same people working in unjelled form. Just as important, the enjoyment that the people derive from their work is greater than what you'd expect given the nature of the work itself.

1.4   Kinds of Teams

In sports, there are different kinds of teams. For example, a basketball team has a high degree of interdependence. Conversely, wrestling and track teams have individual competitors who support each other emotionally but not interactively. Baseball team members have relatively static positions or roles, but they all must work cooperatively for the team to win. While tennis doubles partners may dynamically switch their roles, the quality of their play depends on how well they cooperate and support each other.

Development Teams

In development work, there are also different kinds of teams. **Project** teams often behave much like baseball and basketball teams. They may have multiple specialties, like hardware design, systems integration, software implementation, and test. However, all of these specialties must work closely together to produce a quality product in the shortest possible time.

On systems maintenance and enhancement teams, the developers are often relatively independent, much like wrestling and track teams. Maintenance activities are often handled by what we call **functional** teams, while development groups are called **project** teams. Although the TSP supports both types of teams, the discussions in this book principally concern project teams. Most of this discussion will apply equally to both project and functional teams; some of the special considerations for functional teams are covered in Chapter 22.

Team Size

Teams cannot have fewer than two members, but there is no clear limit on how big they can be. While teams presumably could be of almost any size, high-performance groups tend to be quite small. This is because when teams have more than about 10 to 15 people, they lose the intimacy that makes them effective. This is true in sports, the performing arts, research, and development.

The upper limits on TSP team size are set at around 12 to 15, although we typically say that TSP teams can have up to 20 people. When teams get much larger than about a dozen members, the recommended practice is to break them into multiple, smaller teams and use the multi-team process (TSPm is described in Chapters 21 and 23). The TSPm process preserves the benefits of small team size while retaining many of the advantages of a single overall project team.

Small, Large, and Mega-Teams

Team characteristics and structure change with team size. At the low end with two developers, the members can work together informally and the more structured communication and coordination mechanisms needed for larger teams are unnecessary. Even though two-person teams can use a much less formal process, the TSP principles and the full range of TSP launch activities are still needed to define goals, produce plans, and negotiate commitments with management.

The basic TSP process has been designed for teams with about 3 to 15 members. This is where it works most effectively. These basic or unit teams each have a single team leader who directly supervises all of the team's work. As team size grows, it becomes increasingly difficult for the team leader to closely monitor the work of all the members. Depending on the team leader, the needs of the team members, and the nature of the work, large teams should be handled as multiple teams, with a separate leader for each unit team. These leaders directly supervise the team members, while the overall program manager supervises the team leaders through what is called the **leadership team**.

A single multi-team process can handle teams of up to a few hundred members. As the number of unit team leaders grows, it soon becomes impractical for a single program manager to directly supervise all of the unit team leaders. One way that program managers deal with this problem is to break the overall team into several multi-teams, each headed by an assistant program manager. A second approach is to form a program office, with an associate program manager to share the workload. A third approach is to form a program manager staff to handle many of the program manager functions. When team size grows beyond about 1,000 or so members, the issue of team structure becomes one of organizational design. Using the TSP with such mega-teams is discussed in Chapter 24.

1.5   The Nature of Self-Directed Teams

For development work, it is important to have motivated and energetic teams. On such teams, the members sense what is needed without being told, pitch in to help, and do whatever is needed to get the job done. This is their job, they own it, and they intend to finish it. This is the characteristic behavior of what we call **self-directed teams**. Self-directed teams stick together to the end of the job. Typically, employee turnover on such teams is zero. The members may know that the team will be dispersed, the organization disbanded, or the contract transferred, but this is their project and they will do their utmost to see it through. Their principal commitment is to the team, not to the project or the organization.

While a self-directed team would be useful for any kind of job, such teams are essential for complex and creative development work. This kind of work requires everyone's wholehearted participation. If the team members are not committed to the project and dedicated to its goals, they will not strive to do a quality job. Quality work is not done by mistake; it is done by thinking, caring, and motivated people. Self-directed teams have some special properties that set them apart from all other teams. The following are the six properties of self-directed teams.

☐ A sense of membership and belonging

☐ Commitment to a common team goal

☐ Ownership of the process and plan

☐ The skill to make a plan, the conviction to defend it, and the discipline to follow it

☐ A shared commitment to honest, truthful, and respectful behavior

☐ Dedication to excellence

Membership and Belonging

The members of a self-directed team are part of a cohesive and distinct group, and there is no question who is on the team and who is not. All of the members share a common bond of membership, and they seem to have a special way to communicate. They are so familiar with the job and with each other that they can almost speak in shorthand. The most impressive aspect of a self-directed team is the way that its members work together. Cooperation is the essence of teamwork and, when team members do not cooperate, they cannot build the trust and spirit required for effective teamwork. Self-directed teams are close-knit and cohesive, and every member is a valued contributor.

Cohesion is the bond that knits the members together. Cohesion requires contact and close association. The team members must share a common work-space, see each other regularly, and communicate freely and openly. You can't legislate cohesion; it is a consequence of the team's working context. Cohesion is a fundamental property of a self-directed team.

Team cohesion is strengthened by the support the members provide to each other. Human beings are social animals, and few like to work entirely by them-selves, at least for very long. Team membership provides a comfortable human environment and a source of mutual commitment, support, and motivation. All of the members of such teams make a special effort to meet their obligations to their teammates.

When a team does not have clear boundaries and its members seem to ran-domly drift on and off the team, the members cannot rely on each other. This is the principal problem with part-time team members. When developers are simultaneously assigned to several projects, they have split loyalties, and their teammates cannot count on them for support and assistance.

While it is normal for developers to have demands from prior projects, these must be the exception, and every developer should have a principal project assignment. Teams with a substantial number of part-time members rarely jell. When management is unwilling to commit a developer to a project, that developer is not likely to feel fully committed to that project or make the kind of effort that produces superior results.

Commitment to a Common Goal

Self-directed teams share a commitment to a common goal. The importance of the goal, however, is not so much because of its value to the organization as it is to the team. The team members' motivation comes from the common commitment that the team has made to meeting the goal. This is what the members have decided to do, and they will do their utmost to bring it off.

To maintain this commitment, the team must receive feedback on its work. Whoever heard of a winning team that didn't know the score? To be motivated, teams must know when they are ahead and when they are behind. They must see progress every day. Only then can teams continue pushing to achieve their goals. For example, studies have shown that to achieve high personal and team performance, feedback is the single most important ingredient.

> Goal tracking and feedback are critically important. Effective teams are aware of their performance and can see the progress they are making toward their goals. In a study of air defense crews, those with frequent and precise feedback on goal performance improved on almost every criterion. This compares with the stable, unimproving performance of crews that did not get feedback. (Humphrey 2000, 21)

Owning the Process and Plan

Another property of self-directed teams is a sense of ownership. This is not just *any* job these teams are doing; it is *their* job. They feel responsible for it and have decided just how to do it. Such teams speak of their work with a special pride. To feel this sense of ownership, teams must define their own processes, produce their own plans, and track and report on their own work. The members must be solely responsible for doing this job, and they must know that nobody else will do it. This responsibility provides a sense of personal importance and a feeling of self-respect.

Finally, when a team has a defined process and a detailed plan, the members will know what to do. While this seems obvious, it is also fundamental. When a group is unsure about what to do and doesn't know where to get guidance or help, it cannot jell. It is merely a group of confused people looking for direction. Under these conditions, the members will work to different priorities and not effectively support each other. Following a process and a plan provides stability and builds the team's motivation and energy. To be self-directed, teams must have a common goal, they need a defined and understood process, and they must have a detailed plan.

Skill and Discipline

Self-directed teams are especially well-suited for development work. They define the process and the plan for doing the work, they believe in and will defend that plan, and they have the discipline to follow the plan. Discipline, in fact, is what separates the experts from the amateurs in any field. Their willingness to rehearse, to practice, and to continually improve is what makes them experts and what makes superior work so natural that they can devote their energies to being creative. Studies have shown that the principal distinction between world-class performers and those who finish in the middle of the pack is their disciplined behavior (Gawande 2002).

Honest, Truthful, and Respectful Behavior

The essence of teamwork is trust: Do the members all trust each other to do their jobs? While trust is a nebulous concept, most of us know it when we see it. In fact, learning about trust is a big part of growing up. Most of us start life as trusting dependents: Without even thinking about it, we trust our parents to take care of and support us. However, those of us with siblings soon learn that other people are not always trustworthy—they take things we want and do things that we don't like.

Depending on our personal backgrounds and experiences, we may or may not be naturally trusting people. What is even more important, we may or may not be trustworthy people. While many people feel that the key to a truly superior team is finding the right teammates, that is not the case. The real key is to *be* the right teammate. To have a truly rewarding team experience, every team member must be trustworthy. That means that all of the members must be trustworthy and respect the rights and needs of their teammates, deal honestly and openly with all team members, and respond rationally to the guidance and leadership of the coach and team leader.

A Dedication to Excellence

The final property of self-directed teams is their dedication to excellence. For teams to work cooperatively and to maintain their energy and motivation, all members must strive to do more than just their share. Everyone volunteers for the tough assignments, pitches in, and contributes to the best of his or her ability. The spirit and energy of such teams depends, however, on the quality of everyone's work. If one member does sloppy work, makes frequent mistakes, and causes excessive rework, it wastes everyone's time. If this happens often, everyone will know why and resent it. Poor work by any team member can quickly destroy the team's spirit.

1.6   The Team Leader and Coach Roles

While all of the steps of teambuilding, training, goal setting, and feedback are necessary, they alone will not produce high-performance teams. That takes leadership and coaching. The team leader and coach are both essential in team formation and operation. The coach role is, in fact, the subject of this entire book. Figure 1.2 provides a conceptual view of the various aspects of team leadership and coaching, and how they relate in building and supporting teamwork.

Your role in building and maintaining effective teamwork is the topic of this book. After you have read this book, you will understand the conditions for effective teamwork, and you will know how and why to establish these conditions. This will prepare you to build and coach a self-directed development team.

1.7   Coaching Workload

Coaching is a full-time job. While one coach can generally support several TSP teams, there are periods, particularly with new teams, when the coach must be available full time to support just one team. Even after teams have been coached through several months of a project, they must still be monitored to ensure that they are performing the process properly and that they are effectively gathering and using their data to both guide their work and to improve their performance.

The amount of time required to coach a development team can vary widely. It depends on the TSP experience of the members, team size, the nature of the work, and the business environment. However, one coach should generally be able to support three to five teams of six to twelve developers each. Since there will be periods when one of these teams will occupy the coach full time, it is

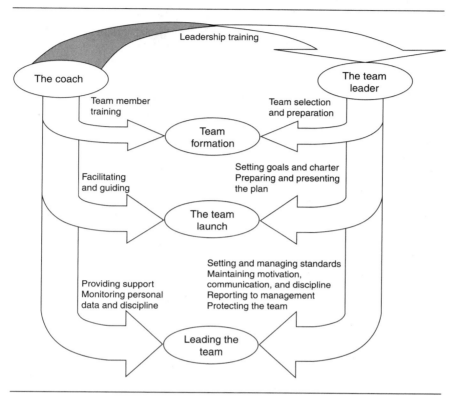

Figure 1.2 The Team Leader and Coach Roles

always desirable to have at least two coaches in any organization, even if there are only two teams.

1.8   Summary

Today, many development jobs are so complex and involve so many different specialties that they simply cannot be done by any one person. Teams are needed for most jobs and, when the members are fully and effectively utilized, these teams can achieve better results than any individual member could produce alone. By participating on a team, developers both improve their personal performance and learn from their peers.

In sports, there are different kinds of teams. Basketball teams have a high degree of interdependence, whereas wrestling and track teams are composed of individual competitors who support each other emotionally but not interactively. In development work, maintenance projects are like wrestling and track teams, and they are often handled by what are called *functional* teams. Development groups generally behave more like basketball teams and they are called *project* teams.

A team consists of at least two people who share a common goal and who have specific roles. They also need an agreed-upon strategy, a common process, and a shared plan. The team members must communicate freely, they must be committed to the job, and they must know their status as they do the work. The TSP process provides a defined framework for building and sustaining self-directed teams that have these properties.

While all of the steps of teambuilding, training, goal setting, and feedback are needed to produce a high-performing team, they alone are not sufficient. The final key ingredient is leadership and coaching. The team leader and coach are essential to team formation and effectiveness. Your role as a TSP coach is the subject of this book.

References

DeMarco, Tom, and Timothy Lister. *Peopleware: Productive Projects and Teams.* New York: Dorset House Publishing Co. 1987.

Dyer, Jean L. Team Research and Team Training: A State-of-the-Art Review. *Human Factors Review.* The Human Factors Society, Inc. 1984, pp. 286 and 309.

Gawande, Atul. The Learning Curve. *The New Yorker.* January 26, 2002, pp. 52–61.

Humphrey, Watts S. *Introduction to the Team Software Process[SM].* Boston: Addison-Wesley. 2000.

Humphrey, Watts S. *Winning with Software: An Executive Strategy.* Boston: Addison-Wesley. 2002.

Humphrey, Watts S. *PSP[SM]: A Self-Improvement Process for Software Engineers.* Boston: Addison-Wesley. 2005.

Humphrey, Watts S. *TSP[SM]—Leading a Development Team.* Boston: Addison-Wesley. 2006.

2

Team Behavior

This chapter provides background on teams and teamwork and gives examples of team behavior. It also describes the kinds of behavior that are most effective for various teamworking situations. When you understand a team's behavior, you can guide its members to most effectively handle the situations they face.

During formation, teams go through several well-known phases. Once the team is formed, it may be effective or not, depending on its circumstances and the way its members work together. The team may also face an external threat or have internal problems. Teams also adopt various working styles, and each style type is most effective for a different kind of situation. By understanding these phases, problems, and styles and where they are most effective, you can better help your teams be most effective.

While development teams occasionally have technical problems, most project failures are caused by the way the development team was formed, coached, and managed. Once you understand these problems, you can help your organization build and launch successful teams and help these teams focus on solving their technical and business problems. The chapter concludes with a discussion of the reasons for team failure and suggestions on how the material in this and the remaining chapters of the book can help you to address these problems and to get your team working productively.

2.1   The Team Life Cycle

As teams are formed, they go through a natural life cycle (Morgan 1993). In the pre-forming phase, the members are identified and trained. Next, they progress through the forming, storming, and norming phases, during which they struggle to become an effective team. Next comes the performing phase where the team does the job it was formed to do. The final step is team dissolution, when the job is completed and the team is disbanded or reassigned.

The Forming Phase

During team formation, the members are recruited and trained, and they officially join the team. They learn their mission and objectives; the team leader is identified; and they define their procedures, processes, standards, and plans.

For the team members, this is generally a confusing period. They often don't know what the job is, understand their role on that job, or even know the team leader and many of the team members. Since uncertainty causes stress and stress can impact one's effectiveness, it is important to quickly clear up these uncertainties and explain what lies ahead. Until you have watched a team struggle through the various phases of team development, it is hard to appreciate what you could face. Jeff's team provides a helpful illustration of these steps.

At the beginning of the TSP launch, Jeff's project was typical of this **forming** phase. Most of the developers were new to the company, and they had all completed PSP training. They knew they were starting a new job, and a few of them had already been involved in its early planning. However, this was a new product, there was no clear definition of its functions, and no one had a plan for doing the work. This team was to use the TSP process, but they didn't know what the TSP process was or how it would work. They didn't even know that, in the TSP launch, they would define their own process and plan.

The first launch step was a meeting where management described the project objectives. The entire team attended the management briefing. The development director briefly described why a new product was needed, and then the marketing manager discussed the desired product functions. He also emphasized that the company faced severe competition, and that this product had to be completed in nine months. Although the developers all knew that the nine-month schedule was very aggressive, nobody said anything.

During this forming phase, it is not unusual for new teams to be passive until they know each other and understand the project. After they have worked together, the members will usually develop self-confidence and become more outspoken. In the opening meeting, however, it is normal for the team members to be quiet and to let management, the team leader, and the coach do all the talking.

The Storming Phase

Teams next go through what is called a **storming** phase. This is often an emotional period where the developers react to the new assignment and to the seemingly impossible challenges. Teams often have no idea how to attack the job and feel threatened by the many unknowns. The requirements are usually ill-defined or unavailable, and the demanded schedule is often impossibly short. No one knows what they are supposed to do, the members often do not know each other, and they may even have a new and unfamiliar team leader. Finally, the developers may have to use a new process or work with unfamiliar tools and technologies.

While even an experienced team would be threatened by any one of these conditions, most new teams face all of these challenges at once. Often, their first reaction is to get emotional. They may challenge the assignment, object to the launch process, or vent their anger and frustration at any convenient and non-threatening target. The coach is often just such a target.

Although the team's reactions in the storming phase are generally emotional, their concerns are real. The project description is often totally inadequate and the schedule is usually impossibly tight. In the storming phase, teams struggle through the painful process of discovering that they must attack their problems logically. Once they start to focus on how to solve their problems, they will quickly establish an effective way to work together and to get the job done.

Jeff's team is a good example of the storming phase. When he and his team gathered after the opening management meeting, the only people in the room were the coach, the software and hardware development team members, and Jeff, the team leader. There were no other managers and no observers.

Several developers immediately started to argue with the coach. A similar previous project had taken two years and been a disaster, so the nine-month date was clearly impossible. Another developer objected to making a plan. "We don't even know the requirements, so how can we possibly make a plan?" Others were concerned with the launch schedule. "Without data, how can we possibly make a plan in only four days?" The coach took the time to address each of these issues.

First, he asked what management meant when they said that the job had to be finished in nine months. No one answered. The coach then asked what would happen if they produced the product in six months? Would management accept it? They all agreed that they would. Then he pointed out that what management really had said was, "We want this job done as fast as possible, and the fastest we think you can do it is nine months." They all agreed.

Next, the coach asked how long they thought the job would take. "After all," he pointed out, "in most negotiations, people don't usually accept the first bid. Management has made an initial nine-month bid. Now you should make a counteroffer. However, if you merely guess at a date, you won't be able to defend it. Then management will insist on their own nine-month guess." He told the team members that they must produce a plan that they could defend. If the plan was longer than nine months, they would know why and be able to defend it.

The team members again objected. "How can we make a plan when we don't even know the requirements?" The coach responded with another question. "You do have to make a commitment, don't you?" They agreed that they did. "Then you had better make a plan. You can't make a realistic commitment without a plan to meet that commitment."

The developers then argued that they could not make an accurate plan. Most of them were new to the job, and many had just joined the company. They didn't have any historical data, so they could not possibly know enough to make an accurate plan. The coach responded that a plan will always be more accurate when you have more information about the job. For maximum accuracy, the best time to produce the plan is at delivery time. Then they would know the most about the job, but then they would least need the plan. Right now, their plan would necessarily be inaccurate, but *now* was when the team most needed a plan.

The team's final argument was that they didn't have time to make a good plan. "How can we possibly make a plan in just a couple of days?" The coach asked how long it would take to make a good plan if they had historical data. They agreed that, under those conditions, planning would not take very long. "Now, without data," he asked "what do you have to do?" The developers thought for a few minutes, and one of them answered, "Guess." They all agreed that it should not take very long to guess. Then the team got to work to make a plan.

The key to coaching teams during the storming phase is to let the members vent their anger and frustration, then deal with their concerns. Don't rush teams through this phase, but help them understand and address their frustrations. Once they see that they have no choice and that the problem will not go away, they will agree to produce a plan. Once they do, they will want to get started right away.

The pressure to get to work will be greatest if the developers know that they will have to work into the evening whenever the launch falls behind schedule. The general guideline is to tell teams that, in the TSP launch, they work half days: from 8:00 AM until 8:00 PM. If they get right to work, they will likely finish early. Then they can leave at a reasonable hour!

The most effective way to move teams through the storming phase is to put them to work solving problems rather than just complaining about them. The TSP launch is designed to do just that.

The Norming Phase

In the **norming** phase, teams start to address their problems. They establish goals, define roles, determine strategies, and produce plans. In the norming phase, Jeff's team produced a plan. The developers first created a product conceptual design and agreed on the development strategy. They defined the development process and estimated the sizes of the major product components. Finally, they made an overall estimate for the total job.

With the help of the coach and the TSP process, the team accomplished this work in only three days. While the developers had originally thought that they could not find any data, they quickly found useful information about several prior projects. Based on these and their own PSP data, they concluded that the job would take them 18 months instead of the 9 months that management had requested. They were confident that their plan was realistic and were ready to defend it.

The Performing Phase

Finally, in the **performing** phase, the team members presented their plan to senior management and the marketing executives. After a rather heated session, they convinced the group that their plan was realistic, and that it was the best that management could expect. By following the TSP process, teams can rapidly work through the forming, storming, and norming phases. Then they are prepared for their first real challenge: to sell their plan to management.

After some debate, management accepted the team's plan and the team started on the job. The project was a resounding success: the team finished a few weeks ahead of the 18-month schedule, and the overall hours were within 10% of their original estimate. The finished product had even higher quality than the team had planned.

Coaching Suggestions

Every team is different. Some teams struggle through the storming phase and others have little or no trouble. The ease with which a team works through these formative steps is a function of the members' personal skill and discipline, the team's maturity, team leadership, and coaching skill.

While developers generally get considerable technical guidance in their work, they get little or no help on building and running teams. There is considerable evidence that team effectiveness requires that developers be both technically proficient and capable of working together cooperatively (Morgan 1993). The problems that teams face in the forming, storming, and norming phases are not new, and teams should not have to struggle through them unaided. By following the TSP launch process, you can help the teams you coach to work through these phases smoothly and efficiently.

During forming, get the developers to voice their concerns. This will help them to understand the project's business and marketing objectives, and it will better equip them to make their plan. However, caution them in advance to be positive. They should keep an open mind and not prejudge the plan before they make it. In the initial management meeting, if they complain about the short schedule, they will give a negative impression. Management could then get the idea that they will not try to meet the organization's business needs.

Be positive! The entire team must strive to meet management's needs. Say, "If that's what you need, we'll do our utmost to bring it off." After all, that is what the team is paid to do. If the developers can't do what management wants, they should show that they really tried. There will be plenty of time to argue about the schedule after the team has produced a plan. Until then, the developers should not debate the schedule with management. They should ask questions and clarify the issues, but they should not start the schedule argument until they have produced a plan that they can defend.

Storming helps the team members vent their frustrations. It gets their concerns on the table and allows you to deal with them openly and rationally. If a member has raised an issue, do not dismiss it; it is, by definition, a valid concern. Until the members all believe that their concerns will be addressed, they will not be prepared to make a plan.

In the norming phase, the team members agree that they must produce a plan. They have also agreed to estimate a job that they know very little about. Now they can start planning. This is where the TSP launch process is most effective. The team is emotionally ready to produce a plan, and the developers are prepared to find any relevant data that might help them to make accurate estimates. An indication that teams have reached this point is that the members start thinking about where to find useful data. Once teams are prepared, they will produce a plan they believe in. Then they will defend that plan and do their utmost to meet it.

Finally, in the performing phase, the team has jelled, knows what to do, and does it. The objective of the teambuilding process is to build teams that can smoothly and efficiently perform their assigned tasks.

2.2 Kinds of Groups

By definition, a team is a group of people. Berne has classed groups into three kinds: the **work group** concentrates on the job, the **process group** is focused on internal dynamics, and the **combat group** is fighting an external threat (Berne 1996). An understanding of these three group types can help you to assist your team overcome the group-related problems that could limit its performance.

The Work Group

The work group is usually easy to recognize. The members concentrate on doing the job and they focus on task-related activities. Take, for example, Jeff's team.

During its storming phase, the developers were concerned about the lack of data. However, once they started to make the plan, they began to think about where to find relevant information. One developer realized that a major component was similar to part of a previously developed system. On the evening of the first day, she got a copy of the source code and measured that component's size. Another developer knew someone in the Swedish laboratory who had worked on a similar system. Early the next morning, he called his colleague and found out more about that kind of work.

In working groups, team members volunteer for jobs; they don't jockey for position or worry about who has the most to do. They don't complain about unreasonable management, and they don't simply listen to the team leader and the coach. As they think seriously about how to do the job, they can be very creative. This is how teams get committed, and it is a necessary step in producing a sound plan.

The Process Group

The process group[1] is concerned about the team's internal structure and behavior. The developers often have no defined roles and have not established a pecking order or agreed on how to work together as a cooperative team. The group's energies are concentrated on internal issues. They are not yet ready to get to work.

When teams do not get right to work, it usually means that one or more members are uncomfortable or unclear about their roles or assignments. Get these issues on the table and deal with them directly. With small teams, such problems can usually be handled quite quickly. On larger teams, however, it usually takes a great deal longer. This is both because there are more people involved and because there are often several subteams with separate team leaders. If any subteam leader has a role or responsibility concern, those issues must be resolved before their teams can become work groups. Once the team leaders are in agreement, their subteams can start to resolve their internal issues.

Process issues concern responsibilities and roles. The best way to deal with these issues is to have a team assign specific role responsibilities to its members and to develop detailed plans. When all team members have assigned role responsibilities and when the team has made a detailed plan for doing the work, the process issues will generally go away. This approach will handle most, but not all, process issues. For a further discussion of team process problems, see Chapter 25.

---

1. While the name *process group* may be a little confusing to those who have worked with software engineering process groups (SEPGs), this terminology has been used for many years by those who study the behavior of groups.

The Combat Group

The combat group is fighting an external threat. This threat is typically perceived as an attack on the team's mission or responsibilities. The team may think that its very existence is at stake. Mack's team was working as a subcontractor on part of a large project. His group was in a separate department from the larger group, and all the developers in this department worked for him. Mack's people were just finishing one job and there was no other immediate next job for them to do.

The project manager wanted Mack's entire staff transferred to his department. However, Mack's management wanted to keep them as a separate development group. Mack was in a difficult political position. While he was committed to doing the subcontract, he knew that his management wanted his group to remain separate from the larger central development group.

Mack was a developer and didn't like politics. He started sending an alternate to the weekly project management meetings and began to deal very formally with the rest of the project. When Mack's team made a major change in its development strategy, Mack decided not to make a new plan. This made status hard to measure and progress almost impossible to track. The program manager became concerned about Mack's dependability and raised the issue with senior management. When rumor of this escalation leaked out, Mack's team felt even more threatened.

Combat groups are often difficult to deal with. They feel threatened and often behave illogically. This generally makes the situation worse, and may actually increase the threat. As the threat increases, the team members submerge their internal process issues and concentrate on defending the team. It is then almost impossible to find out what bothers the developers. They are concentrated on repelling the perceived attack and will view any outsider as part of the threat. Even the coach will have trouble helping teams that are in combat mode.

The best way to deal with a combat group is to identify the perceived threat and to deal with it directly. Either get management to make the feared change or demonstrate that the team's fears are unfounded. The unknown is generally more frightening than the known, so by confirming a team's fears you will actually reduce the threat. This converts an unknown and potentially frightening risk into a known and specific issue to be addressed. By confirming the team's fears and working with the team on a plan to handle those fears, you can show that the situation is not as bad as the team had feared.

Coaching Suggestions

When a team is behaving like a process or a combat group, it will not work effectively. Its energies will be largely devoted to addressing the perceived internal or external threat. While the team may seem busy and focused, the members will be uneasy. They will know that the team is not performing effectively. Examine the group's behavior and talk to the members, both individually and as a group. Try to understand what troubles them and then, together with the team leader, directly address their concerns.

2.3 Team Styles

Even when they are working effectively together, teams can adopt various working styles. There is no right or wrong style, and each team style is appropriate under different conditions. By understanding these styles, you can guide your teams to adopt the working styles that best handle the situations they currently face. Larry Constantine defines the four styles of team behavior as the *open group*, the *random group*, the *closed group*, and the *synchronous group* (Constantine 1993).

These four styles are the extremes. Real team styles generally occur in combination, as shown in Figure 2.1, and it is rare to have a team behave purely in a closed style with no synchronous, open, or random characteristics. Typically, teams will operate in some position nearer to the middle of this figure. The general characteristics of these four group styles are as follows.

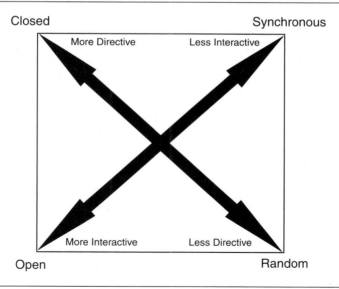

Figure 2.1 Team Styles

The Open Group

In the **open group**, the members are all capable of doing the various team tasks. They flexibly adjust their behavior to support or assist each other as needed. When Mary's team was in the early stages of product planning, it was a good example of an open group. The developers were estimating the size of the product they were going to produce. The design manager first outlined the conceptual design and then briefly described each component's function. He then asked who had worked on something similar and could provide data to help them make a size estimate.

The developers all participated in the discussions, and although their individual estimates varied widely, the team quickly arrived at a consensus estimate for every component. The entire estimate was completed in less than an hour, and the total size was estimated at about 100 KLOC. When the project was completed over a year later, the team found that their original estimate was within 20% of the final product's size.

Although the conclusions reached by open groups are often sound, when one or a few team members have special knowledge, they can bias the results. One team, for example, followed a similar size-estimating procedure, but Craig had much more experience than the others. He dominated the estimating discussion and his views were generally accepted by the group. Since Craig had written a great many programs and had already worked on the exploratory design and proposal for this project, his views were given considerable weight. However, it turned out that Craig was not a very good estimator. He generally opted for the lowest estimate, and this estimate ended up being less than half the final size of the product.

When one member dominates the team in any activity, the team will start operating as a closed group. If a different style would be more appropriate for addressing the current task, help the team and team leader move the team to a more appropriate style. If this doesn't work, consider breaking the group into two or three subgroups and have each of them address the topic independently. Then have the entire group reconvene to combine the subgroups' results.

The Random Group

The **random group** style is a brainstorming style for finding a creative solution to a difficult or controversial problem. When meetings are well run, with a precise schedule and agenda, people are often reluctant to disrupt the proceedings. More chaotic meetings are much less intimidating. Since random group meetings are purposefully chaotic, it is easier for people to speak up.

While random groups often involve considerable contention, there is usually a free flow of ideas. The objective is to take full advantage of everyone's knowledge and experience. There is also often a requirement that the group reach consensus on the final result. When random groups are given the time to fully explore a topic, they generally reach consensus on a conclusion, and their conclusions are normally sound.

An example of a random group is Sally's team. While the team was discussing project risks, Sally stood at the front of the group and asked the members to randomly suggest risks, which she listed on the board. She let the team members discuss whatever risks they thought of, but she prevented them from evaluating or comparing any items. She asked that they hold any discussion for later so that they could initially focus on ideas. She kept the team in brainstorming mode until everyone had run out of ideas. When all of the risks they could think of were listed on the board, Sally led the group in an open-group evaluation of each item. At this point, the group efficiently eliminated duplicate items and ranked the remaining risks for likelihood and impact. By consciously switching the team's working styles, Sally quickly led the team through the risk assessment process and ended up with team consensus on the result.

The Closed Group

The **closed group** is essentially managed from the top down. It has a specific job to do and a clearly defined way to do it. There is little need for discussion or creativity, and the challenge is to get the job done as quickly and efficiently as possible. Sally's team is also an example of a closed group. After it had completed TSP launch planning and was preparing the presentation to management, Sally needed help in producing the materials. As team leader, she had decided to make the entire presentation but had little time to prepare. She outlined the presentation, listed the tasks to be done, and assigned each task to a team member. If any member did not know how to handle that task, she gave it to someone who did. There was no debate, the tasks were clear, and the assignments were made quickly and efficiently.

Groups often fall into the closed style when there is a crisis or some specific task that needs to be done in a hurry. Closed groups can be very efficient for relatively brief and well-understood tasks, but this style should be limited to short-term and fully defined activities. Otherwise, teams can degenerate and cease behaving as creative and thinking teams. They then lose their commitment to delivering quality products and stop behaving like self-directed teams.

The Synchronous Group

The **synchronous group** consists of relatively independent individuals who each have a job to do. They have the skills and resources to do their own tasks, and they have little need to interact with the other team members. They each operate essentially alone, only calling for help when they need it. An example of this type of group is Sally's team during the production of the management presentation materials. The developers each had specific assignments, and they carried them out independently. While all of the pieces had to fit together into the final presentation, that was Sally's concern, and there was no need for the developers to interact with each other. This allowed them to produce the required materials in the limited time available.

2.4   Why Teams Fail

There are many reasons for teams to be ineffective, but the most common problems fall into one or more of these four categories.

- ☐ **Inadequate resources.** Teams cannot be effective when they have too few members, or the members have inadequate training, poor support, or improper skills.

- ☐ **Leadership problems.** Lack of clear and consistent leadership will waste a team's time and sap its energy.

- ☐ **Impossible goals.** When teams have unrealistic schedules or wildly optimistic objectives, they often behave irrationally in a frantic effort to succeed. Such behavior always damages a project and often leads to total failure.

- ☐ **Morale problems.** When team members are concerned about evaluations, promotions, salary, or job security, they cannot concentrate on their work.

By itself, any one of these conditions could cause a team to be ineffective or even to fail. Unfortunately, such problems often come in combination. For example, inadequate resources and goal problems tend to go together. Leadership shortcomings also lead to morale problems. To address a team's problems, it is necessary to understand their causes and then know how to deal with these causes.

Inadequate Resources

A team of six developers was told to plan their next project. Only one developer was assigned full-time to the job, and she was acting as temporary team leader. The other five developers each had another full-time job, and two were working on two other projects. A new team leader had just been hired and would start in a week. This wasn't really a team. Since management had not committed them to this project, the members didn't feel committed to it either.

To cut expenses, senior management had stopped all hiring. Rather than face the resulting developer shortage, however, the managers double- and even triple-assigned the few people they had. They could then pretend that every job was staffed, but the jobs all quickly fell seriously behind schedule. Projects were only fully staffed when they became crises. As delivery dates neared, management would pull people off the jobs with later delivery dates to staff the current crisis. While the hot projects ultimately got done, they were always late and the customers were always irate. This happened on *every* project. As each crisis project finished or died, another project became hot and was handled in the same way.

When organizations do not realistically address their resource problems, their projects are always in trouble, and they stay in trouble either until new management is brought in or the company goes out of business. To get a job done, management must dedicate developers to the work. Then, these developers will know that the job is important and be able to ignore almost everything else. When management does not make such priority decisions, the developers must decide for themselves which projects to work on. Since they can't do everything they are supposed to do, they must establish personal priorities. The result is conflicting job priorities and a very inefficient use of development resources.

The TSP launch process is designed to address this resource problem, and it has proven to be very effective in doing so. However, the TSP is not magic and TSP teams do occasionally make serious underestimates. Also, projects sometimes do have critical end dates, resources are often very tight, and management may be unwilling to face these issues in time to do anything about them. The important point to remember is that some problems really can't be solved and to work with management and the team to rationally decide what to do. That is always better than sticking your head in the sand and hoping that things will get better. However, in addressing these issues, proceed with caution and remember that bearers of bad news are often the first to be shot. For coaching suggestions, look at the discussions in Chapter 14 on the launch closing management meeting and in Chapter 25 on principled negotiation.

Leadership Problems

When teams have leadership problems, they lose the excitement and energy that produces superior products. One example is Ken's team. Ken had extensive management experience and was the logical choice to lead the next TSP team. He had all the right technical qualifications, but he did not believe that the TSP would improve his team's performance. Ken participated in the team's TSP launch, but he soon made it clear that he did not believe this process would be helpful. His behavior essentially told the developers not to bother tracking their time or defects, to stop doing product reviews, and not to hold any team inspections. As he said, "We're in a hurry and don't have time for that stuff." When the coach told management about the problem, Ken argued that his team was following the process. Nothing changed, however, and management was reluctant to take stronger action.

When Ken's product was completed, the results were disappointing. Every other TSP team had sharply reduced test defects and cut test time, but Ken's team was very late and spent over half of the schedule in test. After reviewing the added testing and rework costs, management found that Ken's attitude had cost the company over $1 million. They could no longer afford to use Ken as a team leader. He soon left the company.

Leadership problems will disable a team or severely damage its performance. As a coach, you will occasionally encounter problems of ineffective leadership. They are the most sensitive topics you will face. Ways to deal with them are discussed in Chapters 17 and 26.

Impossible Goals

Another common cause of team failure is impossible goals. What makes impossible goals so damaging is that teams generally strive to meet them, and then they make counterproductive decisions in a panicked attempt to do the impossible. If they had recognized that the goals were impossible and ignored them, they would have been better off. The most common situation is an unrealistically short development schedule. When teams work to impossible schedules, they often race through the requirements and design work so they can start coding. However, with poor requirements and incomplete designs, the schedule problems will only get worse.

Jeff's team is a good example of how to handle this problem. This was the first team in the company to use the TSP, and it had just completed the first launch. Management had demanded an impossible 9-month schedule, but the team plan showed that the work would take 18 months. When Jeff presented this plan in the final launch meeting, management was very upset, and the marketing executive was downright angry. Jeff explained that the prior similar project had taken 24 months, and he felt that the team was very aggressive in proposing an 18-month plan. The marketing executive was not satisfied. "This will sink the company," he said. "The competitor is in the market right now with a better machine, and we cannot wait for a year and a half for a replacement." This was undoubtedly true, but the team knew that there was no way they could produce the new product in 9 months.

At this point, the coach spoke up. He asked the marketing executive when he thought the competitor had started to develop their better product. The executive did not know. "It was probably a year or two ago, wouldn't you think?" he asked, and the executive agreed. "Well then," asked the coach, "why didn't *you* start then? After all, if you only start developing a better product when the competitor already has one on the market, you will always be late, and there is nothing these developers can do to catch up. Your job is to anticipate the market, not just to react to it." The marketing manager had never thought about the problem this way. Although he did not agree, he did not know how to answer. The meeting soon concluded, and management accepted the team's plan.

In spite of the apparent success of the management meeting, the marketing manager did not give up. He and a few of his people met with Jeff and his team again the next week to grill them on the plan. After a several-hour discussion, the marketing manager scratched his head and said, "You really do have a lot to do, don't you?" Marketing soon recognized that the new product design was truly superior, and by showing their customers the team's design strategy, they managed to avoid losing any of their key accounts.

While things do not always work out this well, thorough planning, responsible commitments, and quality work will generally pay off. The key is for teams to make plans that they are willing to commit to and to then vigorously defend their plans.

Morale Problems

There are many causes for morale problems, and most of them stem from the problems already discussed. When developers are frustrated about their jobs, think that the project is badly managed, or are unable to do quality work, they get upset and their performance suffers. On Gloria's team, the developers had worked for more than a year on an important project. They had followed the TSP process, tracked their weekly work, and consistently reported their progress.

One key team measure was **task hours**, the hours that the developers spend on scheduled project tasks. Task hours do not include time for meetings, classes, helping coworkers, taking breaks, dealing with e-mail, or any of the myriad other things that developers must do. Task time is only the time that actually contributes to the project's planned tasks. With considerable effort, Gloria's developers had improved their weekly task hours from around 10 to nearly 17. However, the project had started more slowly than planned, and it was still behind schedule. Management realized that in order to get the project back on schedule, the developers needed to increase their weekly task hours to around 20. They told the team to put in whatever overtime was needed to average 20 task hours every week.

The company had also been secretly negotiating a merger with another company, and for legal reasons, they would have to divest some operations. The same week that management announced the required overtime, they also announced that this project's division was to be divested. Morale took a nose dive. As shown in Figure 2.2, the team's weekly task hours had an initial jump due to the overtime, but then it started to drop.

When developers are worried, they cannot be fully productive. These developers were now afraid of losing their jobs. Most had worked for this company for

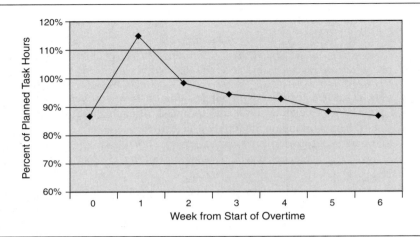

Figure 2.2 Team Task Hours

many years, had children in school, and could not afford to miss a paycheck. With problems like these, team performance will always suffer. In fact, project performance declined so sharply that the customer cancelled the contract and the team was disbanded.

Coaching Suggestions

As the team coach, your principal responsibility is to maximize team effectiveness. To be effective, however, you need to help the team address any resource, leadership, goal, and morale problems. To do this, you must help the team satisfy the following four conditions.

☐ The team must have adequate resources, training, and support.

☐ Team leadership must be involved and effective.

☐ The team must have challenging—but realistic—goals, and a detailed plan for meeting these goals.

☐ The developers' morale must be high, and they must be committed to doing the job.

Your job is to show the team members how to use the TSP to establish these conditions. This chapter and much of the rest of the book describe how, with the TSP, you can guide the team and its members through the steps of building a cohesive and effective team.

2.5 Summary

When groups of people start working together, they go through several well-known evolutionary phases: forming, storming, norming, and performing. These phases are described together with suggestions on how you can use the TSP launch process to accelerate the team's progress through these phases and to quickly start them working on the job they have to do.

Once a team is formed, it may be effective or not, depending on its circumstances. These circumstances concern whether it is faced with an external threat, has internal problems, or is working effectively. Your job as team coach is to understand the group's behavior and to help your teams become fully effective, regardless of their circumstances.

Teams also have various working styles. These styles are of four types: open, random, closed, and synchronous. Since each style is best suited for different kinds of tasks, you should understand these styles and know how to guide your team to the particular style that is most effective for the task it currently faces.

This chapter concludes with a discussion of team failure and some of its more common causes. The reasons that these problems make teams ineffective are each explained together with suggestions for how to address these problems.

References

Berne, Eric. *The Structure and Dynamics of Organizations and Groups.* New York: Grove Press. 1966.

Constantine, Larry L. Work Organization: Paradigms for Project Management and Organization. *Communications of the ACM.* Vol. 36, no. 10 (1993), pp. 35–43.

Morgan, Ben B. Jr., Eduardo Salas, and Albert S. Glickman. An Analysis of Team Evolution and Maturation. *Journal of General Psychology.* Vol. 120, no. 3, July 1993, pp. 277–291.

3

The Coaching Job

This chapter discusses the coaching job and what it means to be a coach. It covers issues you will face when you coach a team launch or relaunch and when you work with a TSP team. The chapter also discusses the issues you will likely face in guiding teams and in helping the team leader. The topics covered in the chapter are:

- ☐ Coaching principles
- ☐ Launching a TSP team
- ☐ Coaching the team
- ☐ Coaching experienced teams
- ☐ Coaching the team leader
- ☐ The TSP checkpoint

3.1 Coaching Principles

As a coach, you have many responsibilities and must deal with a wide array of situations. The following paragraphs review some of the basic principles you must follow to be an effective coach.

Build talent. Your principal job is to build talent, and then to help and support this talent in meeting the team's goals. An important first step is to study the team members, to learn about their potentialities, and to see how to help them improve. Tailor your approach to the needs of your team and its members, and dynamically adjust your coaching approach based on what each team member needs and wants at each point in time.

Set high standards. Teams have needs, and these needs change, often very quickly. Since these changes are unpredictable, you must work from a firm set of principles. You must know what superior work looks like and understand the practices and methods that produce it. You must recognize when work is below standard and understand what caused the problems. You must also know precisely what each team member did or failed to do that caused these problems.

Coaching does not mean inventing methods on the fly. It means recognizing where and how proven methods can be used and then helping the team members to use these methods consistently. When people fail to meet expectations, motivate and guide them to do better the next time.

Focus on success. When teams lose in the Rose Bowl, there is no chance to redo a bad play. The game is over and they lost. In software, we have opportunities that most other teams do not have. When a task is done poorly, we can do it over. Software teams have another important difference from athletic teams. In sports, one team plays many games, so the coach can concentrate on winning the next game, even if the team loses this one. With software teams, there is generally only one game. While the team may stay together for the next project, there are usually enough changes to make it a different team. Thus, your focus must be on succeeding with this project and this team.

Focus on improvement. Because the team's focus must be on this job, you want the members to see how well the job can be done. You also want them to know how much better they could have done if they had followed the process a little better. Help the members learn from this project and motivate them to follow the process even better the next time. Focus on gradual improvement. After all, if a team is doing better work than it has ever done before, that is cause for celebration. It is not the time to discuss where they failed or how they could have done better. You want the developers excited about this achievement, and you also want them motivated to do even better the next time.

Improve in steps. While you should demand that the team members do the best work they are capable of doing, you cannot insist on perfection. Building capable teams means working with the team that you have and developing its skills and talents. While insisting on quality work is important, use judgment. Consider what the members are capable of doing right now. Remember that the team's objective is to produce a product, so be pragmatic and don't ask for things that will not contribute to that job. While the members will support the idea of improvement, their focus must be on developing a quality product on its committed schedule and for its planned costs.

Celebrate every step. Software is a tough business and, to do superior work, we must do everything right. But nobody does everything right the first time, and we are constantly falling short. This can be discouraging, so focus on the improvements the members have made and cheer every achievement, no matter how small. Remember that the better the developers feel about this job, the more likely they are to improve. While you may know that they fell far short of their potential, they probably also did better work than before. Remind them of that and focus on how far they have come, not how far they have to go.

3.2   Launching a TSP Team

The chapters in Part II of this book describe how to coach the TSP team launch. There are, however, some important points to consider while launching TSP teams. The ostensible reason for the TSP launch is to produce the team plan and to get management's agreement to that plan. The less obvious, but well-understood, second reason for the launch is to build the TSP team. Beyond this, there is even a third reason for a TSP launch. It is to build the team's ability to produce plans and to sell those plans to management. The last and fourth reason for a TSP launch is to build the team's confidence in their ability to do quality work, even in the face of severe pressure and stress.

This fourth reason is most important. As a result of the TSP launch process, you want the team members to understand that when they act professionally, they have the power to control their own commitments. Here, acting professionally means that the team produces a detailed plan before starting on the job. Then the team presents that plan and its supporting evidence to management. Next, the team convinces management to accept that plan. Finally, the team follows its process and plan to do the committed job.

The team should always be willing to negotiate resource or project content changes, but it must insist on working to a plan that the members understand and believe is realistic. Although the PSP methods and the TSP launch process are important, they are only tools. The power that you seek to develop is the team's power to act professionally, even under pressure. Once teams learn the power of professional behavior, they can handle almost any situation and still produce quality results. Your ultimate goal is to have the team members learn that they have a power they did not know they had. That is the power of being professional.

The Power of Cohesive Teams

Teams don't generally realize what a strong position they are in. If the team leader tells an executive that the demanded schedule cannot be met, that is only the team leader talking, and he or she can be quickly replaced. Many developers would like to be team leaders, so if the executive wants a more pliable leader, one can almost always be found. However, if the entire team insists that the plan is the best that they can do, the executive is in a much more difficult position. Experienced and competent teams are not that easy to find and there probably aren't any waiting to do this job. Further, with the entire team in agreement, the executive might begin to realize that the team is right.

The team will almost certainly win any schedule debate if it has made a thorough and detailed plan, the team leader properly explains this plan, and the team members all support the plan. Since the executives cannot possibly know how long the job will actually take, they will have to bluff. If they call for an independent assessment, that would be even better. The team has the facts and no impartial party can find otherwise. So convince the team members to hang in and to not weaken. They have the strongest hand and will almost certainly win.

3.3   Coaching the Team Members

Teams have hidden talents, and a logical and rational coaching strategy can help them to use these talents most effectively.

> Take the example of Maurice Greene, who broke the world record for the 100 meters in Athens on June 16, 1999. While he had always been a fast runner, he had not been winning races and was becoming discouraged. Then he went to see coach John Smith in Los Angeles. Smith videotaped Greene doing a sprint, and then broke Greene's ten second run into eleven phases. He analyzed each phase and showed Greene how to maximize his performance in every one. This became Greene's defined and measured personal running process. After several months of coaching, Greene started winning world records and, for several years, he was known as the fastest man alive. (Humphrey 2005)

Think about how to capitalize on this team's talents and how to help the members understand and improve their own capabilities. For the first couple of months after you have launched a new team, try to spend some time every week with each team member. Find out what they do best and where they have weaknesses. Learn about their interests and what they most like to do. One of your objectives is to monitor the processes that the developers follow, see how well they follow these processes, and determine how effectively they are gathering and using their data. While this is relatively easy to do, it involves several sensitive issues.

First, at no time should you imply that you, the team leader, or management do not trust the team members. You trust them to do good work. You are merely monitoring their work to help them understand how they work and to use their data to build their personal skills and abilities. After the launch, tell the team members that you will meet with each of them at least every week for a few weeks and then at least once a month. You will look at their data, examine their plans, and check the granularity of their tasks. Then you will help them to see how they can use their data and adjust their personal practices to improve their performance.

Second, point out that your objective is to help each team member perform at his or her best. You need their data to do this, and these data must be complete and accurate. Without the data, you cannot understand what they have done or offer helpful advice.

Third, the reason for gathering process data is to help the team and its members, not to do an audit or to report to management. While you will evaluate the data, you will not provide any of their personal data to anyone. Your objective is to help the team members. While no one is likely to ask if you will provide their data to management, many will suspect that you will, almost regardless of what you say. So demonstrate by your behavior that you mean what you say. Do not give anyone any personal information on any of the team members.

When one or more team members do not follow the process or properly use their data, you have a problem. Your first step should be to motivate them to do a better job of gathering and using data. Most developers will follow the process and gather their data, particularly if they know you will regularly look at their data. You will also need the team leader's help in stressing the importance of gathering and using the process data.

If, in spite of everything you do, some team members will not follow the process or properly gather and use the TSP data, consult the discussion in Chapter 25 on developing teamwork. But even then, do not compromise that team member's personal data. While you may want to show management the data to describe this developer's problem, that is rarely necessary. Competent team leaders do not need process data to identify their difficult members.

3.4 Coaching Experienced Teams

The first time that you deal with an experienced TSP team is in that team's first relaunch. The TSP relaunch is described in Chapter 16, but there are a few more points that need to be made. These developers have now worked together for several months. They know each other and have developed a strong set of associations. They also appreciate each other's strengths and weaknesses. The relaunch can be more efficient than the original launch, and the team members are more likely to speak out and to contribute.

The second major difference is that the team members have learned how to use the PSP and TSP methods. They have data on the tasks they have done and know the task hours they can expect to achieve. They also have data on what they have accomplished in these task hours. With a seasoned group of professionals, your focus can shift from just getting people to properly use the process to using the process and process data to enhance product quality and to improve the efficiency and effectiveness of their work.

Using a Defined Process

As teams get more experienced, you can pay more attention to process fidelity. When teams learn to explicitly follow a defined process, they can start to coach themselves. Now the members can use their process data to see what their peers have done and to identify any methods that could help them improve their own performance. However, to do this, the team must faithfully follow its process.

Establishing Benchmarks

Another way to help experienced teams, particularly after they have completed one or more projects, is to use their prior performance as a benchmark. If the team has conducted a thorough postmortem, maintained its project notebook, and produced a final report, this is a good starting point. Then, in a subsequent launch or relaunch, discuss the team's prior quality, productivity, and planning performance and use these data to set new goals. Finally, have the team define the process or plan changes needed to reach these goals.

3.5   Coaching the Team Leader

Since leadership problems will generally disable a team, they are a critical coaching concern. While some team leaders will quickly see how to lead a TSP team, others will not. The TSP and the self-directed teams it produces are major departures for most organizations and, without guidance, many managers and team leaders will not know how to behave. Not only is TSP leadership a new experience, but when the TSP is first introduced into an organization, there will be no successful leaders to emulate. Some issues that you will face in coaching new team leaders are illustrated by the following examples. Each example is followed by a discussion of how the coach could have handled the problem more effectively. The five cases are

☐ The newcomer

☐ The designer

☐ The wimp

☐ The autocrat

☐ The hard-head

The Newcomer

After the coach for this team was told that it was fully prepared for the TSP launch, she did not check further. However, in launch meeting 2, the team told her that the most experienced team member had been designated the acting team leader. The permanent team leader was Larry, and he would not start work until next Monday. The launch was completed as planned, but management was upset that the team plan did not support a customer demonstration the following August. The earliest date the team would commit to was in January. After some debate, the team's schedule was finally approved with the January date.

When Larry started work the following week, the coach gave him a private briefing on the PSP and TSP. Larry next met with his manager and the company president. They told him that the company had to have software support for the customer demonstration in August. Larry agreed that his team would provide the needed support by August.

When Larry described this meeting to his team, the developers felt betrayed. In spite of their arguments, however, Larry insisted that the August date was sacrosanct. He had not participated in the launch and did not understand the team's plan, so he did not realize that the team should now have produced a new plan. Since the developers felt that Larry had betrayed them, no one explained the need for a new plan or offered any suggestions on how to produce one.

Without a new plan, the team continued to work to the old plan and to essentially ignore Larry. In every team meeting, Larry talked about the August date and emphasized its importance. While the developers listened politely, they did not say anything. Finally, in early July it was obvious that the team could not make the August date. When Larry told management that the team could not support the demonstration until January, the company president was very unhappy.

Coaching the Newcomer

As is clear from this example, the first thing a coach must do before agreeing to a launch is to check that the entire team is prepared and trained. On finding that Larry would not participate in the launch, the coach should have deferred the launch until Larry had arrived and was PSP/TSP trained. Once the launch had been done without Larry, it was too late to recover. Larry did not understand the plan and was not committed to the team.

If Larry had participated in the launch, he would have realized that the plan was not his to change. He would also have known that, to meet the August date, the team needed a plan to meet that date and that all the developers must agree with that plan. The coach should have explained to Larry that, if management wants a better date, he should certainly strive to meet that date. However, before committing to the date, the team must make a plan that meets it. Without a plan, Larry should not have committed to any new date. If he had been properly trained and participated in the team launch, he would almost certainly have realized this.

The second problem was that the team ignored Larry and continued to follow their prior plan. While this is not surprising considering the circumstances, it is not the right way to run a project. The coach should have advised Larry that if the team had to work toward the August date, he and the team would have to produce a new plan. Since the only plan that the developers had was for the January date, they had no choice but to work toward that date. By making an empty promise, Larry not only undercut his team, but he disappointed management and inconvenienced the customer.

The third problem is that the team had originally tried to develop a plan for the August date but had not been able to do so. So why should Larry do any better? While he probably could not have produced a plan to meet that date, he could have led the team through another planning cycle to examine all of the alternatives. For example, they could have considered a minimum-function demonstration or explored a special prototype. They might have considered adding staff or modifying some prior demonstration system. If the August date was truly impossible, then Larry would have understood why and had the evidence to convince management to accept the team's plan.

Larry was not the problem. He had not been TSP trained, and he could not be expected to know what to do. The real problem was coaching. The team was launched without the team leader, then when the new leader arrived, he was not trained. Finally, the coach did not guide either Larry or the team in producing a new plan that management and the team would accept. It is not surprising that this team failed.

The Designer

Nora was leader of a large team, but she was also the chief designer. She understood the design better than the other developers, so she decided to also personally lead the design work. While the launch was successful, Nora was badly overloaded. She was involved in all of the design work and she had many management commitments. Nora finally realized that she could not both be an effective team leader and lead the design work. There simply were not enough hours in the day. Nora then arranged for one of the developers to take over as design manager.

Coaching the Designer

While Nora's situation worked out reasonably well and the project was ultimately successful, this is a common problem. Most team leaders have been the team's lead developers and they are often the product experts. They are therefore the "natural" choices to lead the design work. While this is rarely desirable, this arrangement may make sense with small teams. With a large team like Nora's, it is generally a mistake.

When team leaders are also technical leaders, they usually have considerable technical experience and are most comfortable doing technical work. As a result, they will often concentrate on their technical work and not devote enough time to their leadership responsibilities. Conversely, they generally have little leadership or management background and are not as comfortable assessing the team's overall needs and providing team support. Since few people can be effective team leaders and lead designers at the same time, they should choose to be one or the other.

Many team leaders fail to realize that, by being team leader, they do not have to stop doing all technical work. While they will not have time to manage the design details, they can still guide the overall design. Assuming that there was at least one other competent designer on the team, Nora should have initially turned over the design leader's job to that developer and then participated in the key design meetings and reviews. While she would not know all of the design details, she could still guide the overall design.

Don't try to get team leaders to completely back away from all technical work. By having another team member act as the design manager, they can still stay technically involved. This will also build the team's design capabilities and it will provide the team leaders with the necessary time to handle their leadership tasks. The team leader will also discover that, even though the design leader handles the design details, he or she can still be involved in design decisions and can still guide the design strategy.

The Wimp

Peter had not been a developer and he was uneasy about his lack of software experience. Peter's project had been successfully launched but, as the work progressed, Doug, one of his developers, refused to use the process or gather any data. The other developers were concerned because they were carefully following the process and tracking their work. After several developers complained, Peter decided to tell Doug to follow the process. However, Doug refused. He said that he was the most experienced developer on the team and that using the process and gathering data would slow him down.

While Peter argued with Doug, he did nothing further and Doug continued to ignore the process. Some months later, Peter was replaced by a new manager who learned that Doug's code had so many problems in test that the team had fallen three weeks behind schedule. By this time, the other developers were even more upset about Doug's behavior and team performance was beginning to deteriorate.

Coaching the Wimp

Some developers will refuse to follow the process. They may not understand how a defined process can help them or they could just be resisting any kind of change. However, if everyone else is following the process and striving to do quality work, they will resent people like Doug. This is the critical test: is this leader truly in charge? Since the organization decided to use the TSP process and has invested time and money in training the team, following the process is part of Doug's job. If he won't follow the process, the team leader should either get Doug assigned to a different project or tell him to get another job.

Leaders must maintain standards. When employees refuse to do their jobs the way that management directs, they either do not understand what management wants or they are refusing to take direction. First make sure that the team leader agrees, and then advise him or her to talk to the personnel department and to understand how to handle discipline or termination discussions. The team leader should then meet with Doug to resolve the issue.

When employees are told to either do their jobs correctly or to find another job, they almost always do their jobs as directed. If the team leader is unwilling to take a strong position, point out that the other team members will likely start acting like Doug. If you can convince the team leader to take a strong stand right away, however, this will generally prevent later trouble.

The Autocrat

Mary ran her small team like a military operation. Everyone participated during the team launch, but once the coach had left, Mary took charge. The weekly meeting was a command exercise. Everybody reported their weekly results, but other than that, Mary did all the talking and there was no discussion.

As long as the team worked to the original plan, Mary's management style did not cause problems. After a few weeks, however, Mary decided to change the project strategy. She told the developers about the change, but she didn't think a new plan was needed. *She* knew what everybody had to do, so she didn't see why a plan was needed. Without a plan they understood and believed, however, the developers could only do what they were told.

The team coach came to visit this organization every month or two. When he found out what was happening, he talked to Mary's manager and to the laboratory director. He did not have time to fix the problem remotely, so he asked Mary's manager to counsel Mary on how to run a project. Over the next week, the manager and laboratory director had several telephone conference meetings with the coach about Mary's problems. After the second call, the coach realized that these managers were not going to counsel Mary; they planned to fire her. It took several more phone calls before the coach could convince them not to fire Mary.

Coaching the Autocrat

The coach made several mistakes. First, when it became clear that Mary was not an effective team leader, the coach should have first talked to Mary. Then, when he understood the problem, he could have decided what to do. If Mary was truly opposed to the process and refused to follow it, then perhaps reassignment or dismissal would be necessary. Second, since Mary may not have known how to lead her team, the coach should have taken the time to guide her on how to be a more effective leader. Since Mary had already been through team-leader training, however, this approach might not have worked.

When senior managers see problems, they often look for blame and then fire that person and get a replacement. It is often difficult for managers to realize that most project problems are process problems. With proper guidance and support, most people can follow well-designed processes. While the coach did need management's help, he should have talked to Mary first. Then, when he understood the problem, he could have developed an improvement plan. With this plan, he could have met with Mary's managers, reviewed the improvement plan, and gotten their agreement to implement it. Since Mary's managers did not know how to devise an improvement plan, they assumed that the problem was Mary and that the best way to fix the problem was to replace Mary.

While getting rid of Mary might have been the right answer, there are several reasons not to be hasty. First, Mary was a competent and experienced developer who could probably become an effective team leader. Second, firing Mary would almost certainly frighten the team. Although management might ultimately have had to fire Mary, they should not do so if they could avoid it. Firing some manager for not using the process would get everyone's attention, but it would be a risky step to take, at least until the managers understood the process and could clearly explain their actions. This usually requires that the organization have experience with several successful TSP projects.

The Hard-Head

Ken did not believe the TSP was worthwhile, but his management told him to use it. While the coach knew that Ken's team was not gathering data or following the process, he could not convince Ken to do anything about it. When he talked to senior management, they would not replace Ken or tell him to get his team to use the process.

When Ken's team finished the project, the coach looked at the results. He found that Ken's team had taken almost four months longer to complete testing than any other TSP project. When he showed senior management the data and explained how much Ken's behavior had cost the company, they removed Ken from his job. He soon left the company.

Coaching the Hard-Head

If the team leader does not agree with the process or does not require the team to follow it, find out why. Assume that the leader wants to do the job properly but is confused or needs guidance. Then provide whatever help you can. If, however, the leader really does not intend to follow the process, you must talk to senior management. Your objective should be to enlist their help in changing the team leader's attitude, not in getting him or her reassigned, disciplined, or dismissed.

When it is clear that you cannot turn the team leader around, urge management to promptly name a new team leader. Occasionally, as in Ken's case, the senior managers are hard to convince, and it may take some time to get them to take action. Usually the real problem is that these senior managers do not really understand the business benefits of properly performing TSP teams. Once they do, Ken's performance and that of the other team leaders like him will be obvious and the leadership problem will be easier to address.

3.6 Coaching Management

Development organizations typically have hierarchical management structures. Development teams have leaders, these leaders report to managers, the managers report to even higher-level managers, who in turn report to more senior managers or executives. Each of these managers has goals and objectives to meet and must set priorities and establish plans to meet them.

Since most people know that their immediate manager's opinion of their performance is the single most important factor in determining their salary and advancement, they are responsive to their manager's wishes. Therefore, if you want to change someone's behavior, the single most important consideration is the immediate manager's view of that change. If the manager believes the change is important and is willing to say so, getting the employee to change should be relatively easy. If not, it could be very difficult or even impossible.

One example of how a coach handled this issue was before the first team launch in a department. The coach met with Pete, the manager, and offered to prepare the presentation he was to make to the opening launch meeting. Then the coach worked with Pete to understand his priorities and to explain how, by following the TSP process, the team could most rapidly and economically address these priorities. After Pete's presentation in the opening launch meeting, the team understood what Pete wanted and was able to establish personal and team goals and plans to do superior work. This approach can be very effective, but it is also important to have Pete then periodically review team performance against these goals to demonstrate that they really are important to him and to the organization.

3.7 Summary

This chapter discusses what coaching is and what it means to be a coach. As a coach, your principal job is to build talent and to help and support this talent in meeting the team's goals. To be an effective coach, you must know what superior work looks like and understand the practices and methods that produce it. You should also help your team members learn from their current projects and use their data to gradually improve their development capabilities.

The ostensible reasons for the TSP launch are to produce the team plan, to get management's agreement to that plan, to build the TSP team, and to build the team's ability to produce plans. A fourth and less understood reason for the TSP launch is to build the developers' confidence in their ability to do quality work, even in the face of severe management pressure.

Once you have launched a new TSP team, spend some time with each team member every week for the next few weeks. Thereafter, try to meet with them at least once a month. You are monitoring their work to help them develop and maintain their personal skills and abilities. Most developers can be convinced to follow the process and to gather their data, particularly if they know that you will frequently look at the data. You will also need the team leader's and management's help in stressing the importance of gathering and using the process data.

While some team leaders will quickly see how to lead a TSP team, others will not. Team leader problems will generally disable a team, and they must be one of your highest-priority concerns. If the team leader does not agree with the process or does not require the team to follow it, find out why and provide whatever help you can. Once your teams are properly following the process, your job changes to one of guiding them in using the process and process data to improve their performance and to produce superior products.

Reference

Humphrey, Watts S. *PSP^SM: A Self-Improvement Process for Software Engineers*. Boston: Addison-Wesley. 2005.

4

Teambuilding

This chapter discusses teambuilding, why it is needed, and how it works. It covers the launch process from the point of view of the coach and it describes your objectives, some of the things you should think about, and how to act as you guide the team through the launch process.

The chapter starts with a brief summary of the factors that make teams successful. It then covers teambuilding, the purpose of the TSP team launch, and how the launch builds teams. Next, it discusses the two basic principles behind the launch process: to build the conditions for a team to jell and to get team-member involvement. It also explains why no observers or visitors are permitted during most of the launch process. The chapter concentrates on the principles of the TSP launch process. Subsequent chapters discuss the issues you will likely face in each step of the team launch.

4.1   What Makes Teams Successful?

While jelled teams must embody all of the right traits, just establishing these conditions is not enough. Successful teams also need a mission that is compelling,

49

that the team believes is achievable, and that all of the members are committed to accomplishing. Even the best teams cannot be successful if they have a mission that they think is impossible. Also, successful teams need suitably trained resources and proper guidance and support. If any single condition is lacking, the team may jell, and it may even strive valiantly, but it is not likely to succeed. To establish all of these conditions, you need a teambuilding process, and you need a team leader who is capable of acting like a leader and is willing to work under your guidance and support. Your job as coach is to work with the team leader to establish all of these conditions.

4.2   Teambuilding Approaches

From the earliest cave dwellers, humans have always banded together. Just to survive, people have lived in groups, hunted in groups, and fought in groups. Banding together under stress is normal, but the conditions for producing coherent and effective group behavior when lives are not in danger are not as obvious or natural.

Teambuilding Exercises

Some common teambuilding approaches take advantage of the natural trait of people to seek support when threatened. One technique is to put a group into a stressful situation. Then, as the members instinctively react to the situation, they become a cohesive group. These strategies generally work. For example, various outdoor experiences take groups on river-rafting expeditions or up treacherous mountains. Some of these adventures are downright dangerous, and they are all stressful. They require considerable personal stamina and a willingness to put up with hardship and privation.

The Problems with Teambuilding Exercises

These common teambuilding approaches have one fundamental shortcoming: they are not done in the working environment. The people who lead and participate in the team exercise are often strangers who will have no further association with the team or its members. Thus, even though the team may bond and some members may become lifelong friends, the experience has no connection to the working group, and the participants return to a work situation that is essentially unchanged.

Even if the teambuilding exercise was very successful, when the members return to their jobs, they will still face all of the conditions that had blocked effective team behavior. Thus, while the teambuilding experience may have been exciting and the participants may even see how rewarding teamwork can be, they will not have the tools, methods, or support systems needed to use these methods on the job. The net result is that, when teambuilding is disconnected from the working environment, it will be an exciting memory with no connection to the job. Therefore, such exercises generally do not have a measurable effect on the way the participants subsequently work together.

4.3 The TSP Teambuilding Strategy

The principle behind off-site teambuilding exercises is that by showing people the benefits of close teamwork and putting them through a convincing and effective teambuilding exercise, they will somehow translate this experience into their working lives. However, teambuilding is a nontrivial activity, and few people have the time or skill to devise an effective teambuilding process, particularly one that will work in a complex and high-pressure development environment. That is what the TSP is designed to do.

The TSP establishes the conditions for jelled teams by using the job that management wants this team to do. With the TSP launch process, you guide and support the team leader as you jointly lead the team through determining its goals, selecting team-member roles, and making plans. Once the team members have built their plan, you help the team and team leader conduct an effective management meeting. Here, they address the most common cause of team failure: the inability of development teams to rationally negotiate their commitments with management. Finally, after the launch, the team and team leader continue to work together, and you continue to provide guidance and support.

4.4 How the Launch Builds Teams

The TSP launch is a multiday process that guides teams through planning a project. While the launch process ostensibly produces the team plan, the principal launch objective is to establish the conditions needed for the team to jell and to develop the skills and relationships to continue working together as a cohesive group. Then, given proper leadership and coaching, the team will almost certainly jell at some point in the future. Think of the launch process as a teambuilding activity.

Most important, recognize that the launch will not be successful unless you produce a cohesive team that is ready to jell.

If the team produces all of the required launch products but has not become a cohesive unit, the launch was not successful. When teams are not cohesive, they are not likely to make effective use of the materials they produced during the launch. Conversely, even if the launch does not produce all the required launch products, a jelled team can produce the remaining products in short order. Jelled teams are the most powerful tool humankind has devised for doing challenging work. That is what you want to build; all else is secondary.

The TSP Launch Process

The TSP launch process is shown in Table 4.1 and Figure 4.1. The steps in this sample script describe the contents of the meetings shown in the figure. By walking

Table 4.1 TSP Team Launch—Script LAU

Purpose	To guide teams in launching a software-intensive project				
Entry Criteria	• The launch preparation work has been completed (PREPL, PREPT). • All team members and the team leader are committed to attend launch meetings 1 through 9 and the launch postmortem, and management and marketing representatives are prepared and available for meetings 1 and 9. • An authorized launch coach is on hand to lead the launch process.				

General	Schedule	Day	1	2	3	4
		Timing	8:30– 6:45	8:00– 5:00	8:30– 5:30	8:30– 4:30
		Meetings	1, 2, and 3	3 (cont.), 4, 5, and 6	6 (cont.), 7 and 8	9 and PM

Step	Activities	Description
1	Project and Management Objectives	Hold team launch meeting 1 (script LAU1). • Review the launch process and introduce team members. • Discuss the project goals with management and marketing.
2	Team Goals and Roles	Hold team launch meeting 2 (script LAU2). • Define and document the team's goals. • Allocate team roles among team members.

Table 4.1 (continued)

Step	Activities	Description
3	Project Strategy and Support	Hold team launch meeting 3 (script LAU3). • Produce a system conceptual design, and, if needed, a fix list. • Determine the development strategy and products to be produced. • Define the development process to be used. • Produce the process and support plans.
4	Overall Plan	Hold team launch meeting 4 (script LAU4). • Develop size estimates and the overall team plan.
5	Quality Plan	Hold team launch meeting 5 (script LAU5). • Develop the quality plan.
6	Balanced Plan	Hold team launch meeting 6 (script LAU6). • Allocate work to team members. • Produce bottom-up next-phase plans for each team member. • Produce a balanced next-phase plan for the team and each team member.
7	Project Risk Analysis	Hold team launch meeting 7 (script LAU7). • Identify and evaluate project risks. • Define risk assessment checkpoints and responsibilities. • Propose mitigation actions for near-term, high-impact risks.
8	Launch Report Preparation	Hold team launch meeting 8 (script LAU8). • Prepare a launch report for management.
9	Management Review	Hold team launch meeting 9 (script LAU9). • Review the launch report with management. • Discuss project risks, responsibilities, and planned actions.
PM	Launch Postmortem	Hold team launch postmortem meeting (script LAUPM). • Gather launch data and produce a launch report. • Put the launch report in the project notebook. • Assess the launch process and prepare PIPs.
Exit Criteria		• The launch is completed with documented team and team member plans. • Team roles, goals, processes, and responsibilities are defined. • Management agrees with the team plan, or resolution actions have been identified and responsibilities assigned. • The launch data are in the project notebook (NOTEBOOK specification).

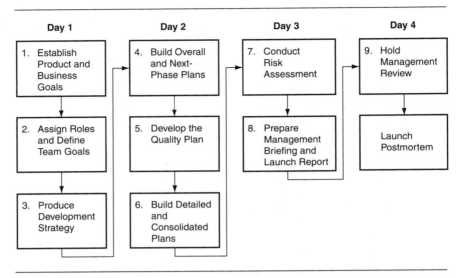

Figure 4.1 TSP Launch Meetings

through this process, teams will generally produce a realistic plan, and they are likely to jell into a cohesive and effective working unit. To jell, however, all of the team members must be committed to the plan and, to be committed, they must all have been involved in producing that plan. Thus, in addition to leading the team through the TSP launch process, you must make sure that all of the team members are actively involved and that they all agree with the resulting plan. The principal topics of this chapter concern the methods for getting team-member involvement in the launch process.

It is not easy to involve all of the members in producing a complete and realistic team plan. There are several reasons why team-member involvement is not normal or natural.

- ☐ **History.** In most development organizations, managers have always done the planning.
- ☐ **Experience.** The managers and lead developers know much more about the job than do most of the developers. Therefore, it would seem reasonable for the managers and lead developers to produce the plans, not the developers.
- ☐ **Pressure.** When everyone is in a hurry, nobody wants to make waves, so why not let the boss and the lead developers do the planning?
- ☐ **Knowledge.** Often, most of the team members have limited knowledge of the product and would prefer to have experts give them the plan.

If the objective of the launch was to produce the best possible plan, these arguments might have some validity. Remember, however, that is not the objective. The principal objective, and the absolute top priority of the launch process, is to have all team members cooperate in producing the team's plan. Then they are all likely to agree with the plan and be committed to meeting it.

Even if you could somehow magically get a plan that all of the team members accepted as the most accurate representation of the job they were about to do, that plan would not replace the need for a team launch. For example, there are tools that use historical data to generate plans. These tools can produce reasonably accurate plans when they are properly used, and all you need to do is to plug in a size estimate for the total job. The tool will then spit out a complete plan with detailed estimates for every phase. Such tools can produce helpful after-the-fact benchmarks, but teams should produce their own plans first. Only then will you have a team that understands the plan and is committed to meeting that plan's commitments.

4.5   Getting Involvement

On most teams, there are a few experienced developers and several who are relatively new and inexperienced. The newcomers are often unsure of their roles, so they are reluctant to speak up or to voice opinions. If you let them, they will just watch. However, these silent members will not really be part of the planning process, the team will not get the benefit of their judgment, and the team will not have their full commitment at the end. Overcoming the team members' reticence and getting them all involved can take a great deal of effort and patience. Some techniques that can help are

- □ Ask, don't tell.
- □ Play dumb.
- □ Frequently check for agreement.
- □ Sense unspoken concern or disagreement.
- □ Don't let anyone monopolize the discussion.
- □ Manage the experts.
- □ Coach the team leader.
- □ Keep the focus on facts and data.
- □ Allow no observers.

Ask, Don't Tell

Try to get everyone involved in all of the team discussions. One way to do this is to ask leading questions. For example, in defining the team's process, ask the members what they would expect to do first, and then second, and so forth. This will be hard at first, but the developers will soon loosen up and start contributing.

Keep asking and probing. For example, when a design is to be completed, ask about what should come next. Should they inspect the design, review the design with the customer, or start test planning? Bring up relationships with other groups such as hardware, systems, or test, and make sure that the team considers various ways of doing the job. Most products are designed in parts, so think about prototypes, multiple versions, or incremental builds. Ask how many parts there will be, the order in which they will be designed, and the sequence for their implementation and test.

Walk the team through each step in the development process. To truly represent what the members will do, the process must consider the many details and relationships that are likely to be forgotten during the job. Only then will the process be useful for detailed planning, and only then will it be used while the developers are doing the work. When everyone is included in developing this process, it will incorporate their ideas and be most likely to meet their needs. The team is then most likely to follow it.

While this sounds fairly easy to do and you will quickly learn to do it, the launch process is actually much more complex. Your objective is not a one-shot launch experience but a major behavior change. You want the team leader and all of the team members to learn how and why to involve every team member in the launch process and in all other important team activities. Only then will they continue to involve all their members in the key strategy, design, and planning decisions that the team will make every week.

Play Dumb

When the coach is an expert on the subject the team is addressing and the team members know this, it is often difficult to get them to participate. For example, in defining the team's process, Fred was the organization's process expert. He was the coach and he was leading the team through defining the project process. He knew a great deal about the organization's process, and everyone recognized him as the expert. When Fred asked about the process they would use, none of the developers said anything. After a few moments, he started to write down a proposed process as the suggested starting point. He was the only person talking, however. No one agreed or disagreed; they just watched.

This approach is a mistake. At the end, Fred might get a very sound process, and it might even be an excellent process for the team to use, but it would have been

Fred's process, not the team's. The objective is to get the team members to think through how they will do the job. During the team launch, the team members select standard roles, and one of these roles is the process manager. Fred should have had the team's process manager lead the process discussion. Then he should have guided the process manager in asking questions until the team produced a suitable process. This approach is important because, unless the process manager involves everyone in contributing to the process, it will be the process manager's process, not the team's. Unless the team members believe that they have the right process, they will not use it, at least not consistently. Without a sound process, the team's plan cannot be very good, and if the plan is not very good, the members won't follow it in doing the work. Under these conditions, the team members will continue working much as they have in the past.

Think about the process this way: What you want is a process that will work for this job, not a standardized framework that was defined by someone else. For example, there are now many organizations that have fully defined processes and many would be willing to give you a copy. Suppose you got a copy of such a defined process and gave it to the team. Would that be useful? Probably not. While there would probably be useful things to emulate in this process, the real need is to have the team members think through the work they plan to do, debate each step of the job, and then agree on how to do it.

The members need to do this before they produce the plan. If they don't, they will get so involved in estimating that they will not think through how to do the work. While they might get a reasonable estimate, the tasks will be in big chunks and many steps will not be defined. Such plans do not provide much help in doing the work. A defined process specifies how the work is to be done. Once the process is defined, the products named, and the product sizes estimated, it is relatively easy to estimate how long it will take to do each step of the process, particularly when the developers have historical data on similar work.

Frequently Check for Agreement

Watch the team and notice who is talking and who is not. When someone has not said anything for a while, ask for his or her opinion and get the team leader and anyone else who is leading the team discussion to do the same. Don't make the question threatening by asking for specific answers like, "How big do you think this is?" Instead, ask what this person thinks. While you might expect the quiet types to duck the question and not give much of an answer, you will almost always be surprised. These are very bright people, and just about every time I have asked a quiet team member for an opinion, I have been surprised at how much he or she had to contribute.

So watch for the quiet ones. Frequently they are quiet because they are listening and thinking. They often have a good deal to say when given the chance. It almost always will be pertinent, and it will frequently be an important and useful contribution. But even if they have nothing new to add, just asking their opinion will help to get them involved. Help the team to treat every contribution with respect and to make the contributor feel good about having spoken up. Then, after you have asked them a few times, they will generally start to speak on their own.

After the first day or two, the team leader and some other team members should start asking each other for agreement. If they don't, discuss the subject with them and have them take responsibility for getting everyone's agreement.

Sense Unspoken Concern or Disagreement

Another useful technique is to watch for disagreement. While some members will be outspoken when they disagree, others will indicate that they have a problem by an expression or some other nonverbal signal. Examples would be frowning, pushing away from the table, or acting nervously. While these signals are generally subtle and you have to watch for them, they are almost always detectable. After all, they are really signals and they are meant to be received. So, you can invariably tell when silent members disagree just by how they act. In such cases, ask a question such as, "Barbara, what bothers you about this?" Barbara will invariably have a good answer, and it will often be something that nobody else has thought of.

Another way to tell when there is disagreement is that nobody volunteers. For example, while one TSP team was reviewing its support plan in launch meeting 3, the coach suggested that someone check with the other TSP teams to see what support tools they were using. The idea was that this would suggest useful tools for this group to consider. When none of the team members volunteered to do this, the team leader was about to assign someone. However, the coach interrupted to ask the members if there was some reason that his idea wouldn't be helpful. They were clearly reluctant to tell the coach that he had made a dumb suggestion, but one finally explained that this was a C++ team and that the other teams were all using Java. None of their tools could be used by this team. When developers on a self-directed team agree that an issue is important, someone will invariably volunteer to handle it. When no one volunteers, find out why.

Don't Let Anyone Monopolize the Discussion

Occasionally, a team will have one member who talks more than anyone else. He or she is invariably the first to break in with a comment that turns into a monologue. The monologues then often drag on without adding measurably to the subject at hand. This situation can be difficult to handle for three reasons. First, neither you nor the team leader should be heavy-handed and autocratic in controlling the meeting, since that will destroy the informal and freewheeling environment required for team participation. It is also likely to cause everyone else to think twice before opening their mouths. Second, it is important to cut the monopolist off because he or she is wasting precious time, but do it diplomatically to avoid upsetting the rest of the team. Third, this person is a member of the team and his or her contributions and commitment are important.

You or the team leader can deal with such people either overtly or subtly. The overt approach is to use the rest of the team to help. When this speaker (say, Jed) has just finished a point and is about to continue, interrupt and say, "Jed, thanks, but before you go on, I would like some other opinions on this." Then return to the subject that the team is addressing and ask specific team members for their views. When Jed tries to break in again, politely say you are not done yet and ask another team member for his or her views. Let Jed speak from time to time, but break in periodically, either to get other opinions or to return to the subject at hand.

Often, these "Jeds" do not stay on the subject, and it is relatively easy to say, "Jed, thanks. While you have a point, we need to continue with the process. Let me write your point on the board and we can return to it later when there is time." Then write down the idea on a list at the side of the room and get on with the launch process.

Another and more subtle approach is nonverbal. As you or the team leader lead the discussion, walk around the room. If you are effectively leading the meeting, everyone will be talking with you and not holding private discussions. Thus, people will have trouble talking without making eye contact with you and being recognized. By standing directly behind Jed, he will have trouble talking without twisting around. This not only makes it difficult for him to talk, it makes it difficult for the rest of the team to hear him. Under these conditions, it is relatively easy to make eye contact with the other team members and ignore Jed without seeming to be impolite.

Above all, don't lose the Jeds. They are team members, and they frequently turn out to make valuable contributions. Usually, they just have some insecurity that makes them crave attention. Be polite and do not turn them off, for they can be helpful. In fact, you can sometimes convert them into assets by asking for their help, possibly as the meeting recorder, for posting notes, or in maintaining a list of open questions and issues.

Manage the Experts

Experts generally have information that the team needs. The problem is that just one expert can seriously hinder team communication. Much like Jed, the experts will have opinions on many topics, but they often do not have the patience to listen to other people's views.

One expert, Derrick, had been invited to help the team understand the planned product's technology. When he arrived, he opened with the comment, "Unless you have delivered a major project, you can't really know anything." Of course, this was a direct slap at almost every member of the team. While the team was largely composed of junior people, they were very bright, many had advanced degrees, and most had several years of experience. Not surprisingly, Derrick was not interested in anyone's views and he quickly antagonized the entire group. The coach soon broke up the meeting and reconvened later without Derrick. The group then quickly completed their conceptual design, but they had not been able to capitalize on Derrick's considerable experience.

Experts are often difficult to handle and you may have to occasionally treat them as Jeds. When these experts are members of the team, you cannot exclude them from the launch meetings or other team activities. One approach is to try to get the expert to help you handle the problem. Find a convenient time to have a private chat and ask for help. Point out that, as the expert, the rest of the team is likely to treat his or her opinion as the last word and feel unqualified to make further comments. Ask the expert to hold back and not state opinions too soon. Emphasize that while you need his or her views, you would appreciate getting them *after* the rest of the team has had a chance to speak. By taking a positive approach, you will usually get the expert's cooperation.

For example, in estimating and planning sessions, it is often possible to focus the expert's comments on how a product might work or what similar products the organization has developed. Then, get the team members to be the first to state size estimates. The principal problem is that the expert often will be outspoken on his or her views about the size estimate. Try to get other opinions, but don't turn off the experts. After all, they could be right.

If the experts are not team members, it is generally a good idea to keep them out of the working meetings. Start by having them meet with the group, state their views, and answer questions. Then let them leave with profuse thanks. Not only will this permit your team to jell as a working group, it will actually flatter the experts and save them the annoyance of sitting through long meetings and listening to people whose opinions they do not value.

You might also ask the experts to look over the team's final strategy, process, or design and to make comments or suggestions. Do not ask for comments on the team's plan, however, for experts are usually technical experts and not planning experts. They tend to make bad estimates, just like everybody else. In fact, they often feel that complex products are a lot simpler than they really are and they will tend to bias the team estimate to be much smaller than it otherwise would be.

Finally, experts are not always difficult, and some can be downright charming. In graduate school, I once went to a seminar where another student was describing his research work. Harold Urey, the Nobel Prize-winning chemist, came into the room and sat next to me. All conversation stopped until Professor

Urey said, "Please continue." The speaker continued and Dr. Urey occasionally asked a question. It was soon clear that the professor was genuinely interested in what was being discussed and was there to learn. By this time, the speaker had gotten over his initial shock and the meeting continued. We were all enormously impressed. I have always felt that this was the best example of expert behavior I have ever seen. Most experts are very nice people and many are quite modest about their accomplishments, so don't hesitate to use them whenever you and the team think they could be helpful.

Coach the Team Leader

While most team leaders will participate in the process along with the other developers, some cannot help acting like managers. As with experts, team leaders can end up dominating the team meetings. For example, Otis was leading his team during load balancing. All of the developers had completed their detailed plans for the next phase and several of them had much more work than they could possibly do in the available time. However, several others had relatively little to do. Otis was very concerned, so he immediately jumped up and started reassigning work among the developers. As he tried to mastermind the workload for the entire team, the developers just sat and watched. This was a large team and it was soon clear that Otis did not know enough to assign every task.

At this point, the coach suggested that they take a break. Then he met privately with Otis and suggested that he tell the team the basic schedule requirements for the load balancing work. Then the two of them would step out of the launch meeting and allow the team to do the load balancing. Otis agreed and, after the break, he told the team what was needed and said that he wanted to meet separately with the coach. The team members all participated in the load-balancing process and soon had a balanced plan that they all understood and accepted.

Keep the Focus on Facts and Data

One important reason to use data is to make sound team commitments and to convince management that the team has a sound and aggressive plan. Also, a focus on facts and data will increase team member involvement. It levels the playing field. While experts will have lots of opinions, they rarely have a monopoly on the facts. By emphasizing the importance of data, you make it clear that no one knows all the answers and that everyone is equally capable of providing useful input. When the team members realize that one fact will trump a dozen expert opinions, the estimating process becomes less threatening, and the less experienced members are more likely to participate.

Allow No Observers

There are three problems with having outsiders observe the launch process. First, they inhibit the team's discussions. Second, the observers may participate in the launch when they should not. Finally, the observers could react prematurely to the team's plan.

Carl's team was involved in a large system project and several groups insisted on participating in the launch. The manager of the requirements groups had several people working on this project, so he decided to personally represent his function. Similarly, the test manager had not yet assigned people to the job, but he had to plan the testing workload and needed to be involved. The process group manager also asked to be there because her people were fitting the TSP process into the organization's standard process and needed to understand how it worked. Finally, the quality assurance manager argued that with all of these other groups represented, it was unreasonable to exclude him.

When the team met to discuss goals and select team roles, there were more observers than team members. The coach started by asking the observers not to talk. They were quiet while the coach explained the meeting procedure and while Carl reviewed management's stated goals. However, when Carl started to discuss the customer's desires, the requirements manager interrupted to clarify several points. As the meeting progressed, the observers spoke up whenever they felt that the team had made a mistake or needed guidance. The bulk of the discussion during this launch meeting was among the team leader, the coach, and the observers. The developers remained pretty quiet and spoke only when they were asked to.

Even if the observers do not talk, their mere presence will inhibit team discussion. It will then be almost impossible for the team to communicate freely and openly. Until the team members start to communicate freely and openly and to take positions and negotiate disagreements, the team cannot jell.

A more subtle message that observers send is, "We don't trust this team to work without management oversight." This problem is illustrated by the example of Peter's project. This team had started on the job before the TSP launch. The final delivery date had already been committed, and management insisted that the date was not negotiable. Peter and his team had decided to introduce the TSP, and everybody had been PSP-trained. When the launch was about to start, management insisted on having some representatives observe the launch process.

The launch started properly and the management observers didn't say anything. Most of the developers were initially reluctant to speak up, but the coach finally got some of them to contribute. The team got through the conceptual design and size estimates with little trouble, but the size estimate turned out to be substantially larger than previously planned. Next, the team started on the total estimate for the overall job. They first estimated the remaining requirements work and then the high-level design tasks. Then they started to estimate the detailed design phase. When the team broke for lunch, it was clear that the early project phases would take much longer than management had expected.

During lunch, the observers met with the program manager and told him what they had heard. He then called in Peter, the team leader, and told him to abort the launch and to continue the project according to the original plan. While the management observers had not interrupted during the launch meeting, they could see where the launch was headed, and they judged that the team's plan would probably be unacceptable. Even before the team had finished planning, management reacted to the assumed plan and canceled the launch.

What is most interesting about this story is that the team did finish the detailed design when they had estimated, and they did follow their PSP practices while doing their work. At the end of detailed design, they were several months behind management's schedule. Management was in a panic, but the developers' work was of such high quality that they finished coding and testing much faster than management had expected. The team actually delivered the product ahead of schedule. Without the observers, the team would have had the time to produce a complete plan and to show management how they could spend more time in the design phase but still complete the job on schedule.

Since the story had a happy ending, you might think that this behavior didn't really cause any problems, but it did. According to the original plan, the design was to be done in December when a customer design review was planned. If the team met this review date, there was to be a substantial bonus payment. If management had known that the design would not be completed until April, they could have either renegotiated the design review date with the customer or arranged for the team to produce some early higher-level design documents in time for the December review. Since the developers didn't know about management's problems, they could not help solve them. Management forfeited a substantial award fee and as a consequence considered the TSP project to have failed.

4.6 Summary

This chapter reviews the purpose of the TSP launch, how the launch builds teams, and the principles of the launch process. To get a team to jell and to get the team members commitment to a plan, they must all be involved in the launch process. There are several reasons why team-member involvement is not normal or natural. First, in most development organizations, managers have always done the planning. Also, the managers and lead developers know much more about the job than most of the team members. It therefore seems reasonable for them to produce the plan.

Generally, few developers know how to make plans or are willing to take the time to produce one, so they naturally let the boss and lead developer do the planning. Finally, most of the team members have limited knowledge of the product and would prefer to have someone give them the plan. Since the principal objective of the launch process is to have the team members believe in and be committed to the plan, their participation in producing that plan is essential.

Some techniques that can help to overcome the team members' reticence and to get them all involved are to ask questions, play dumb, and involve everyone. Also, frequently check for agreement, look for unspoken concern or disagreement, and don't let anyone monopolize the discussion. In addition, you must be sure to manage the experts and to keep the team leader from dominating the meeting. It is also important to keep the focus on facts and data and not to allow any observers.

Finally, your objective is not only to launch and to build the team, but to help the team leader build his or her leadership skills. This means that the team leader should continue following these same teambuilding principles during team operation, and that you should guide and support the team leader in learning how to lead a self-directing team. The launch process is an ideal place to begin this coaching.

PART II

Launching a TSP Team

Tim, the coach, had briefed Brad, the general manager, on the importance of management support. Brad had done an excellent job of explaining the importance of the project in meeting 1 and had told Tim and Valery, the team leader, to call on him if they had any problems. Then, later in the afternoon of the first day, he stuck his head into the meeting room to see how everything was going.

While Tim had been able to get Brad's conference room for the opening and closing management meetings, he was only able to arrange for a small conference room for the rest of the week. When Brad looked in, he noticed that Tim, Valery, and her team of twelve developers were crammed into a tiny room with barely room for their chairs and practically no working space.

While the team was doing its best under the circumstances, Brad could see that the space was totally inadequate and told the team he would get them a better room. However, no better rooms were available so he rearranged his own schedule and moved the team to his personal conference room for the rest of the week.

Management support is critically important in motivating and building superior teams, and Brad's thoughtfulness and consideration made a big impression on the team. As you prepare your team for a launch, make sure to brief senior management on their role in the launch process and on the importance of their support. It can have a big effect on the team's performance.

Part II of this book describes the principal considerations in launching a team project. Its 12 chapters cover various aspects of preparing for and launching

TSP team projects. The sample scripts shown in the book will give you an idea of how a properly defined process can guide a team's work. For information on using the TSP, see the SEI or an SEI transition partner (www.sei.cmu.edu/tsp/).

Chapter 5 describes launch preparation, including when to launch a project, team scope, team selection, and team preparation.

Chapter 6 discusses the team's charter and the job management wants this team to do. Unless the team members all know what their job is and why it is important, they will not likely do their best work or complete the job on the planned schedule. In the first TSP launch meeting, management describes its goals directly to the team.

Chapter 7 covers team goals, why goals are important, and the importance of having measurable goals. It also reviews various kinds of goals and some of the coaching considerations involved in setting and managing the team's goals.

Chapter 8 addresses team member roles. In the TSP, all team members take responsibility for one or more roles. These role assignments both ensure that key team issues are addressed and provide the team members with control over their working environment. Team members consistently say that the ownership and responsibility provided by the role assignments are one of the parts of the TSP process that they like the best.

Chapter 9 covers the initial steps of the TSP planning process. The principal topics are product conceptual design, development strategy, process definition, and support plans.

Chapter 10 describes the steps involved in producing the team's resource and schedule plan. This chapter also addresses the key coaching considerations involved in team planning.

Chapter 11 covers the TSP quality strategy, the quality plan, the importance of the quality plan, and some of the key issues to consider in producing this plan.

Chapter 12 is about detailed planning. It explains why detailed plans are important, how they are produced, and how they are used. It also covers many of the issues that you are likely to encounter during detailed planning.

Chapter 13 covers risk management and how the team handles risks, both during the launch and as the project progresses.

Chapter 14 describes how to obtain management support. It explains why it is important to warn management in advance about major issues and how to demonstrate the team's capabilities and dedication. Finally, the chapter discusses how to handle some of the typical management problems that you are likely to face during a TSP launch.

Chapter 15 deals with the launch postmortem, the key data to gather during the postmortem, and how these data can be used. It also discusses the Process Improvement Proposal (PIP) and why it is important.

Chapter 16 describes the TSP relaunch, when to hold a relaunch, and how the relaunch process differs from the launch process.

5

Launch Preparation

When forming a TSP team, you must decide when to hold the launch and determine who will be on the team. Training is also critically important. All of the involved managers must either have participated in the TSP executive strategy seminar or received TSP management training. The team members must also be properly trained. Finally, once all of the team members are prepared, it is time to launch the project. The formal part of the teambuilding process starts at this point. This chapter discusses when to launch a team, team scope, team selection, team preparation, common preparation problems, and the launch preparation checklist and script.

5.1   When to Launch a Project

Before starting launch preparation, make sure that the organization has or will have all of the needed tools, license permissions, and support systems needed for the TSP launch. Then, in preparing for the launch, you will likely be asked some of the following questions.

"How can we launch before we have the signed-off requirements?"

"We're right in the middle of design. Wouldn't it be best to wait until the design is completed before we launch?"

"We have a critical design review with the customer in only four weeks. Should we launch before or wait until the review is completed?"   .

"Implementation is nearly done and we are just starting integration and system test. Isn't this too late to hold a TSP launch?"

While every case must be decided after considering all of the relevant facts, the general rules on launch timing are as follows.

1. Launch as soon as you can, even before the requirements are signed off. In fact, if you can, launch at the beginning of the requirements work and involve the developers in producing and reviewing the requirements documents.

2. Do not wait for some phase to complete before holding a team launch. Project phases rarely have a clean end point: there is always some work to be completed. Launch as soon as you can and have the developers include the remaining prior-phase tasks in their new plans.

3. It is generally a mistake to launch in the middle of a crisis. When everyone is focused on performing some critical task, it will be hard to get management's attention. You will also likely have team members pulled off during the launch to handle some critical assignments.

4. Launching a team when the project is nearly completed will not produce the benefits of a more timely launch. However, the TSP can be very helpful during the testing process. For example, one TSP team decided that whenever a defect was found in test, they would review or inspect the modules involved. Even though the code had already been released to test, they found and fixed many defects in a fraction of the time it would have taken if they had waited for those defects to be found in test.

5.2 Team Scope

Ideally, everyone who will work on the project should participate in the launch. However, in determining team membership, it is important to consider each person's level of commitment to the project, the timing of their assignments, the integration of related project groups, and the team's TSP experience.

Commitment

Since teambuilding is an interesting subject and since many people would like to see how teambuilding is done, you may have to restrict participation in the launch meetings. Except for launch meetings 1 and 9, only the team members, the team leader, and the coach should be in the room. Teambuilding is a participative process and the presence of visitors or observers will disrupt that process. It is essential to restrict team membership to those people who will work essentially full time on this project. While developers often have other obligations, this job should be their principal responsibility.

In addition, sometimes even full-time project participants should not be included in the team. This would be the case, for example, for support or administrative personnel who will not be directly involved with the developers' work or be able to participate in planning for that work. However, all such team members must be trained in the PSP planning, measurement, and tracking methods. If there are many such people, put them on a separate support team, and use the multi-team TSPm process described in Chapters 21 and 23.

There could also be several related groups that insist on being "represented" on the team. The key word here is *represented*. The only people who should be included in launch meetings 2 through 8 are the members of the core development team. This must not include representatives.

Assignment Timing

While many people may work on the project in later phases, a launch should not include people who will not be directly involved in the current work. One important purpose of the TSP relaunch is to incorporate new members into the team. When people will be involved later, include them in the team launch or relaunch only for the phases in which they will actually start working on the job.

Integration of Related Functions

As long as the team can be kept to fewer than about ten to fifteen members, plan to include in the team all of the groups that will actively work on the project during the immediate next project phase. This should include hardware and software developers, test engineers, requirements or systems people, application specialists, and even customer representatives. However, if there are more than one or two people from any of these specialties, consider forming them into one or more separate teams and using the multi-team TSPm process. This topic is discussed further in the section Team-Member Selection.

Experience

The final consideration is the team's and organization's TSP experience. If you are launching a team for the first time, start with a single team that is developing the product. Larger or mixed groups that will use the TSPm process should be guided by an experienced TSP coach who is qualified to lead a TSPm launch. At least some of the team leaders and members should also have previously used the TSP.

5.3 Team-Member Selection

While you generally will not be involved in team selection, you often will be asked for advice on team scope and membership. To work together efficiently, teams must share a common understanding of the job to be done and they must have a common set of processes, methods, and terminology. For example, in forming a ball team, you would not pick players from different sports. While they might all be outstanding athletes, a ball team of football, baseball, basketball, and soccer players will not likely win many championships. They would not have the common language, mutual goals, agreed-upon rules, or supportive skills to cooperate effectively. Just as on a ball team, TSP team members need a shared process, common terminology, and the ability to work in an interdependent team environment.

In selecting team members, first consider the job to be done. What is the principal objective and what specialties must be involved in achieving this objective? Once you have determined the required specialties, consider the relationships among these specialties. This leads to the next question. Should all of these specialties be on the same team? The simplest way to answer this question is again to consider the ball game analogy. Are the members all playing the same game? When two specialties have different objectives, separate processes, and independent technologies, communication will be difficult. Then it will be almost impossible to mold this disparate group into a single cohesive team.

One group that had three requirements people and five software developers is a good example of the problems with mixed teams. Since they were all assigned full time to the project, it seemed reasonable to include them in a single team launch. However, in the goals discussion in meeting 2, it was soon obvious that the two groups had different points of view, terminology, and objectives. These differences made it hard for them to agree on a common set of team goals and objectives. Such mixed groups will generally have trouble jelling into a single cohesive team. If the specialty teams have more than one or two members, try to form them into separate teams and have them coordinate their work using the TSPm multi-team process.

With large multi-team projects or where the development work is done by largely independent software and hardware groups, each team is formed of common specialties. For example, the application programmers would be on one team, the system programmers on another, testers on a third, and the requirements analysts on a fourth. Then, each software team would have a member who was responsible for coordinating with the requirements team and another with the test team. Similarly, the requirements team should have a member who coordinates with each software team and so forth. The coaching and leadership issues for these multi-teams are described in Chapters 21 and 23, as are the leadership team's and coach's responsibilities and activities.

5.4 Preparation Topics

In forming a TSP team, the key requirement is that all of the team members be able to follow the agreed-upon processes and understand the principles behind the TSP methods. They must know how to plan and track their work, and be able to measure and manage the quality of the products they produce. The PSP engineer training course has proven to be very successful in providing these skills. The team leader, senior management, and any nonsoftware team members must also be trained in process methods and practices. This is done with a personal process course and TSP management training. The major topics that all team members must understand and be able to handle are the following.

- ☐ Planning
- ☐ Project reporting
- ☐ Measurements
- ☐ Quality
- ☐ Design
- ☐ Process
- ☐ TSP tool support

These topics are discussed in the following paragraphs.

Planning

The ability to make a plan is a fundamental requirement for any kind of sophisticated development work. Thus, for the TSP process to work, the team leader and all of the team members must know what plans are and how to make them. The principles behind this planning process are taught in the PSP engineers course and are illustrated in Figure 5.1 (Humphrey 2005, 63). In principle, these steps are the same for individuals and for teams. The basic planning topics developers need to understand are the following.

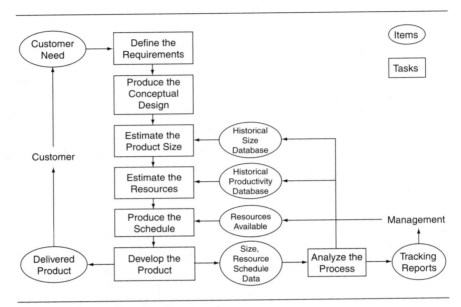

Figure 5.1 Project Planning Framework

Requirements. Before a team can commit to do a job, its members must make a plan to meet that commitment. The more information they can get about the commitment, the better. However, if all they know is a simple one-sentence requirements statement, they must either make a plan or tell management that they cannot make a commitment until they know more about the job. Since the requirements are the basis for planning, the better they are, the better the plan will be. If teams must make a commitment, however, they must make a plan and they need all the information they can get before they start planning.

The conceptual design. If you ask developers how long it should take to produce the conceptual design, they should answer, "An hour or two." If they talk about days or weeks, they do not understand the purpose of the conceptual design. The conceptual design is needed solely to guide planning, and the developers need to know how to produce a simple conceptual design rather quickly.

Product size. TSP team members need to understand size measures and the elements of size measurement. They also need to understand size accounting and the meaning of base, added, deleted, added and modified, total, reused, and new reusable size. They must also know how to select size measures for those cases where LOC measures are not appropriate. All TSP team members must be able to estimate product size, either with the PROBE estimating method or by analogy to other products of known size (Humphrey 2005, 85). They also must know how to measure the size of a product so that they can measure existing products to get data to guide their estimates.

Resources. Once the team members have estimated the sizes of the products they are to develop, they need to estimate the time needed for the development work. To make accurate estimates, developers must know how to use historical (or any other available) data to make resource estimates. They must also understand that, when they have better data, they can make better estimates and plans.

Schedules. Once the team has made its resource and task estimates, it is relatively easy to produce the product schedule. This, however, is not trivial; it requires a good tool and knowledge of available weekly task hours, earned value, planned value, and task size.

The PSP for Engineers and Introduction to Personal Process courses provide the background and basic skills needed in all of these areas.

Project Reporting

While TSP project reporting is not difficult, and though available TSP tools will handle much of the required work, precise status reporting is a new experience for most first-time TSP team members. The principal items that the developers need to understand are why weekly reports are needed and how to produce them. These topics are briefly addressed in the TSP scripts and in more detail in Chapter 13 of *TSP^{SM}—Leading a Development Team* (Humphrey 2006). Even when the developers are properly trained, it is a good idea to check that they regularly report on their work.

Measurements. Measurements are fundamental to the TSP process. To measure their work, the developers must all use the same defined process, know how to measure that process, and consistently measure it. If they do not, their measurements will be inaccurate, inconsistent, and largely useless. The principal measurements required for the TSP are the same as those introduced in the PSP course (Humphrey 2005). Since these measures are thoroughly covered in PSP engineer training, there is generally no need for briefings or special coaching. The only measurement-related coaching issues concern whether or not the developers completely and accurately report their data and whether or not they properly enter that data in a TSP support tool. These topics are covered in more detail in Part III of this book.

Quality. Because of the importance of quality in product development, developers must complete the PSP engineers course before they start a TSP project. When developers do not know how to plan, measure, and manage the quality of the products they produce, they generally spend a great deal of time in test and still produce poor-quality products. The PSP course provides a thorough grounding in quality fundamentals, but it does not address the more significant topics of quality management and quality control. These are introduced with the

TSP and are covered in detail in the books *Winning with Software: An Executive Strategy* and *TSP^SM—Leading a Development Team* (Humphrey 2002; Humphrey 2006). It is particularly important that the team leader and all involved managers be familiar with this material.

Merely ensuring that the developers understand quality principles is not sufficient. As a team coach, you must be directly concerned with the quality of the developers' work. Your job is to ensure that the team prepares an aggressive but realistic quality plan, and the team leader's job is to make sure that the developers work hard to meet that plan. This topic generally requires close attention, both during the launch and relaunches and in the weekly team meetings. These topics are covered in Chapter 11 on the quality plan, in Chapter 18 on maintaining the plan, in Chapter 19 on managing quality, and in Chapter 25 on developing teamwork.

Design. The kind of preparation required for design and design methods depends on the type of work the team is to do. However, all of the developers will need a solid grounding in design principles and methods. In addition, the developers must understand design verification methods, have experience with the principal verification techniques, and consistently use such methods in their work. This material is included in the PSP engineers course and also addressed in some design courses.

The second aspect of design preparation is the developers' familiarity with the design methods the team will use. If the developers have not used these methods, they must be trained or they cannot be expected to produce quality designs. It generally takes considerable time for developers to become fluent with a new design method. If they are not trained in these methods, their design work will take much longer and the quality of their designs will almost certainly suffer. While this subject is usually addressed during the launch, it is then often too late to conveniently arrange for the needed design training. It is highly desirable to identify and address the design training problem before the launch, if possible.

Process. PSP engineer training provides the needed understanding of process basics. Most developers complete the PSP course with a solid appreciation of what processes are and how a defined process can help in planning and managing their work. The areas in which developers often need help are in developing processes of their own and in tailoring selected elements of the TSP process. There generally is little need for the entire team to know how to develop processes as long as at least one developer has such skills and is willing to be the process manager. If not, the process manager may need special coaching. Chapter 13 of *PSP^SM: A Self-Improvement Process for Software Engineers* contains a complete discussion of this topic (Humphrey 2005).

TSP tool support. Teams should not attempt to use an unsupported TSP process. Tool support is essential for the effective and efficient use of the TSP. Except for very small projects, there is far too much data to record manually. Once the data are recorded, the task of sorting, tracking, and reporting these data is simply too complex and voluminous to handle without automated support. Therefore, it is assumed that your team is using a tool to support the TSP process.

For best results, the tool the team uses should support the full range of activities performed by TSP teams. The SEI provides an example of such a tool, and vendors also offer such support. Some organizations have also found it helpful to develop proprietary tools for their particular development environments and business systems. Integrated tools are generally easier to use and are more likely to be used consistently and properly.

Both you and the developers must be familiar with whatever TSP tool the team is to use. They may obtain this familiarity from training or through coaching and assistance. A brief course is generally desirable and will save the developers time when they start on the project. Tool training will also reduce the number of errors that developers typically make when they begin to enter process data into a new and unfamiliar tool. In addition, most teams find that it is helpful to be familiar with spreadsheets and simple database programs.

5.5   Common Preparation Problems

When developers are not properly prepared before the TSP launch, there are almost always problems. One example is a group that was in such a hurry to start on the project that they insisted on conducting the TSP launch before their people were PSP trained. Management had urged the group to use the TSP and Jim, the team leader, had reluctantly agreed. He also promised to get the developers PSP trained immediately after the launch.

The opening launch meeting went reasonably well. Management explained the project objectives and marketing described the needed product. They also discussed what was required, when it was needed, and the competitive situation.

Immediately after this first meeting, the developers started launch meeting 2. During the goals discussion, Jim argued that they already had their goals. Management had told them what to develop and when, so what was there to discuss? The developers all agreed, and the coach saw that nothing could be achieved by pursuing the goals discussion further. Role selection was no problem, even though the developers did not understand why they needed to have roles. However, they were willing to follow the process and the roles were assigned in a reasonably short time.

Meeting 3, the first planning meeting, was much more difficult. When the coach tried to get the team to discuss the conceptual design, nobody knew what he was talking about. The team members disagreed with even discussing design before they had a set of documented requirements. The coach asked them how they could possibly make a size estimate if they didn't have a conceptual design. At that point, Jim objected to making a size estimate. After all, he said, management had already decided how long the project would take, so why worry about a size estimate?

Then Jim wrote a schedule on the board. It was one that he had produced before the launch and it showed the team delivering the product on the date that management had requested. He was convinced this schedule was achievable, and the developers quickly agreed. Even if it was an aggressive schedule, they were committed to it, so they saw no advantage in debating the issue.

Jim's plan had eight checkpoints but no other details. All of the developers agreed with the schedule and thought the plan was good enough for their needs. None of them was willing to spend any more time discussing the plan. At this point, the coach gave up and aborted the launch. This team never did get the developers PSP trained, and the project continued with the organization's normal crisis-driven process. Not surprisingly, the project was months late and way over budget.

If the managers are not properly trained and if the developers do not know how and why to make a plan, there is no point in holding a TSP launch. It will not work. Without PSP training, developers will not be able to make a plan or know how to participate in the planning process. The team's plan will then be produced by the team leader and project manager. Not only will this produce a simplistic and poor-quality plan, but there will be no way to track progress against it. Most important, the developers will not have been involved in producing the plan and will have no personal commitment to meeting its dates. The principal message of this story is that if you want to change a project's outcome, you must change the way the developers on that project work. However, unless the developers are properly trained, it will be almost impossible to change the way they plan, track, and manage their personal work.

Of course, there are many special situations. For example, when all but one of the developers is PSP trained, teams usually can get through the launch process. This assumes that the team has at least five developers and that the lone untrained developer is willing to follow the process. If the team leader has not been trained, it is a mistake to do a TSP launch, even if all of the other team members have been trained. Team leader (and management) training can generally be completed in a few days, so it should always be possible to complete it before the launch. Generally, it is most desirable to complete management training before the developers are PSP trained. Then the managers can ensure that the developers complete their PSP course work before the launch.

5.6   Launch Preparation Steps

After the team members have been identified and trained, you are ready to prepare for the TSP launch. In preparing for a TSP launch, the following steps are particularly important.

1. Make sure that someone is appointed to be the launch coordinator and that this person will handle all of the details of launch preparation. There is a lot to do and someone must be responsible for doing it.

2. Get the team members identified as quickly as possible. They must all be available for the entire launch period and they must all be given enough notice so that they can plan to be at the launch every day and to stay late on several evenings.

3. Make sure that the executive and marketing participants are identified and trained, and that they are willing and able to attend launch meetings 1 and 9. They should know well in advance what they are supposed to do during those meetings. If they need help in preparing, either offer to help or arrange for some knowledgeable person to do so.

4. Make sure that all of the launch participants have the appropriate launch preparation materials at least a week before the launch begins.

5. Personally talk to the team leader, team members, and management participants to make sure that they understand their roles during the launch and to answer any of their questions.

6. Arrange for the necessary computer and support facilities and make sure that the team has adequate meeting space for the entire launch.

With proper preparation, the TSP launch process works surprisingly well, so make sure that all of the launch preparation items have been properly handled and that all of the launch participants are trained and prepared for the launch workshop.

5.7 Weekly Launch Preparation Status Meeting

To ensure that the launch or relaunch preparations are properly made, hold meetings with the team leader and launch coordinator every week for at least a month before the launch. If the preparations are proceeding properly, the meetings can be brief. But if the preparations are not proper, you need time to correct the problems. Otherwise, you could be forced to cancel a launch on short notice.

5.8 Summary

In forming a TSP team, management and all of the team members must be properly trained. Before anyone can participate on a TSP team, they must be able to plan and manage their work. The topics that all team members need to understand are planning, project reporting, and process measurement. These skills are covered in the Introduction to Personal Process course. In addition, the product developers need to understand quality management and product design. These and the planning topics are covered in the PSP engineers course. Since tool support is essential for any TSP project, the team must also have a suitable support tool that all of the team members know how to use.

When developers are not properly prepared before the TSP launch, there will almost certainly be problems. If the team leader has not been trained, it is a mistake to do a TSP launch, even if the developers have been trained. Generally, it is best to complete management training before the developers are PSP trained. Then the managers can ensure that the developers complete their PSP course work before the TSP launch. When many of the team members have not been PSP trained, there can be serious problems. These untrained members will not have the skills to participate in the launch and they will not know how to make plans. Either you will have to provide these developers with substantial coaching or they will simply not use the process.

References

Humphrey, Watts S. *Winning with Software: An Executive Strategy.* Boston: Addison-Wesley. 2002.

Humphrey, Watts S. *PSP^{SM}: A Self-Improvement Process for Software Engineers.* Boston: Addison-Wesley. 2005.

Humphrey, Watts S. *TSP^{SM}—Leading a Development Team.* Boston: Addison-Wesley. 2006.

6

The Team Charter

This chapter describes the opening management meeting, what it is, and why it is important. It also describes some of the topics to consider as you coach the team, the team leader, and management on preparing for and conducting this meeting. The topics covered in this chapter are

- ☐ The team charter
- ☐ The opening management meeting
- ☐ Starting with a positive attitude
- ☐ Issues and considerations

The TSP launch process consists of a series of ten team meetings. While management will participate in meetings 1 and 9, you will work with only the team and team leader in the other eight. As with all TSP launch meetings, the first steps are to select the meeting timekeeper and recorder roles, to provide a brief overview of the meeting agenda, and to describe the products to be produced in the meeting. At the start of every meeting, including meeting 1, make sure that team members agree to handle the recorder and timekeeper roles.

6.1   Establishing the Team Charter

The team's charter is the basis for everything the team does. Management has established this team for a reason, so everything that the members do should be directed toward that result. If this objective is important to the organization and if management can convince the team members that it is important, the developers will be motivated to do what management wants. The charter also defines the team's goals, and these goals establish the end objective for the team's strategy. In turn, the team's strategy forms the framework for the team's plan, which then guides the developers in doing their work. Without a clear and compelling charter, the team will not make a sound plan or work as energetically as it otherwise would to meet management's needs.

The team's charter provides the basis for the launch process and for all of the work that follows. Because the charter is so important, it is essential to have the senior manager who decided to do this project actually tell the team why it is important. It is also desirable to have this or some other senior manager provide as much of the business and marketing context as possible. This will help the team to understand what is to be done and why.

6.2   The Opening Management Meeting

The opening management meeting is the first step in the TSP launch process. Generally, the team leader or some other manager should open the meeting with a brief welcoming statement and then turn it over to you, the coach. You will then give a brief presentation on the TSP process, the schedule for the next several days, and the content of each of the launch meetings. You will then turn the meeting over to the management and marketing representatives. Their objective is to explain why this project is important to the organization and to motivate the team members to do their very best to make it a success.

Assuming that they have been given the launch preparation materials sufficiently in advance and that you have properly prepared them, the management and marketing executives will generally have no trouble handling their parts of this meeting. The senior manager describes the business need for the project and any critical cost, schedule, or quality concerns. The marketing manager's objective is then to describe the product to be developed, how it is to be used, and the key competitive issues that might impact the product's design. While the TSP process has the senior manager speak before the marketing executive, they could talk in whichever order they prefer.

At the end of the management and marketing discussions, ask for any questions or comments. While few team members will say anything at this point, it is important that you and the team leader make sure that all of the team members understand what is wanted and that they have had an opportunity to ask questions. The team should understand the following key items:

☐ The characteristics of the desired product and a clear definition of what is essential, what is optional, and why

☐ What management will view as a successful team result and management's criteria for determining success

☐ The degree of the team's flexibility with the project schedule, team staffing, and product features

6.3 Start with a Positive Attitude

Suggest that the team members put themselves in management's shoes. The question in the back of management's mind is, "Will this team really try to do what we want?" Management cannot know whether these developers will truly try to meet their requested date or if they will come back with a relaxed schedule. While the team will almost certainly strive to meet the shortest possible schedule, how could management know this? This is a question of trust. At the end of the meeting, will they believe that this team will really try to meet their needs? Conversely, will they feel that the members are starting with a negative attitude and will come back with a safe but unacceptable schedule?

Management's most important single consideration in deciding whether or not to trust the team's plan is their perception of the members' attitude. Did they start by trying to meet management's goals, or were they convinced that the goal was impossible? The impression that the team members make in the opening meeting will have a greater influence on this point than anything they say in the final meeting—that is, unless they happen to meet management's desired schedule!

Suppose, for the sake of argument, that in the opening meeting some team member complains about management's date. Perhaps someone says that this schedule is insane, that it allows less time than they spent developing the last product, and that this is a much more complex job. After that opening, management will expect the team to come back with a later date than they requested. They are then likely to bore into the team's plan to try to find the slack they are convinced is in the schedule.

Ideally, the team members will all leave the opening meeting with a positive attitude. Their objective is to meet management's goals. While they don't know whether or not they can, they will give it their best shot. If that is the way the team members start the launch, and if that is how they acted in the opening meeting, management will likely believe that they tried to meet the business' needs. So, coach the team members to start out believing that there is some way to do what management wants and then search for that way. If, in the last analysis, they cannot succeed, they will know that they did their best and will be able to convince management that they did. A positive attitude is the key to establishing the team's credibility.

6.4   Issues and Considerations

When TSP projects get into trouble, the problems often start in the first management meeting. The following paragraphs discuss some of the more common issues and some of the things you can do about them. Some of these issues are

- ☐ The missing executive
- ☐ No shows
- ☐ Untrained people

The Missing Executive

Since this team only had four developers and it was just developing a small enhancement for the company's major product, the team leader did not feel that senior management needed to attend the opening and closing launch meetings. He decided to handle these meetings himself. In the opening meeting, he did his best to explain the project's objectives and to convince the team members that the job was important. However, it was clear to everyone that this was an unimportant assignment and that it would likely be killed the moment something more important came along. Not surprisingly, the project was not a success.

While you will not be able to get a senior manager or executive to attend the opening and closing meetings for every small TSP project launch, it is important to have some manager other than the team leader attend these meetings and describe what management wants. It could be the team leader's immediate manager, someone from the requirements or systems groups, or even the manager of the process improvement program. However, whoever comes should be familiar enough with the project to make a convincing and informed statement of management's desires.

No Shows

While a team member might have an unexpected family emergency and miss one or more of the launch meetings, do not tolerate other kinds of absences. If some team members don't show up or the senior manager is delayed, don't start the launch without them. If the executive or other launch participants are unexpectedly unable to attend, reschedule the launch for a time when everyone can be there.

While management might object to your doing this, the launch must be a priority event. If management does not think it is important enough for everyone to attend, especially a senior management representative, the launch will not be successful. If the project really is small and not worth a senior executive's time, a lower-level manager could represent senior management. However, the team leader should *never* act as the senior management representative. If you are unable to get this condition accepted at the outset, the TSP will not succeed and there is no point in starting.

Untrained People

On several occasions, coaches have launched or tried to launch TSP teams that were not properly prepared. In one case, management had deferred PSP training until after the launch and in another case the team leader had not been able to attend TSP manager training. Another case was where a new team leader had just been hired but would not start work until the Monday after the team launch. While two of these launches were actually completed, in every case the projects failed.

As soon as you find that the team, the team leader, or a key manager has not been properly prepared, reschedule the launch for a time when everyone will be ready. You will almost certainly get an argument, but if you cave in, the launch will not be a success and the project will not get off to a good start. If the participants could not be trained before the launch, it is highly unlikely that management will make training a high enough priority afterwards. The launch is your principal bargaining chip. Use it wisely.

6.5 Summary

The first step in the team launch is the opening management meeting. This is when senior management explains what they want this team to do and why. It is also when a marketing executive describes the customer situation and the market-place need.

This chapter describes the management meeting and explains why both a senior manager and a marketing executive should personally meet with the team. To do a superior job, the developers must understand what kind of product is desired and why those particular characteristics are important. They also need to know the kind of flexibility they have in developing a plan and in designing the product. But, most importantly, by showing up for the launch meetings, senior managers demonstrate that the team has an important job to do.

The chapter also explains why it is important for the team leader, the coach, and all of the team members to maintain a positive attitude both during this opening meeting and throughout the launch process. The chapter concludes with a discussion of some common problems with the opening management meeting and offers suggestions on how to handle them. In general, when the team or team leader is not properly prepared or when all the necessary people are not trained and available for the launch meetings, it is best to defer the launch until they are.

7

Team Goals

This chapter reviews team goals and the topics to consider as you guide teams through the goal-setting process. It also discusses the various kinds of goals, why goals must be measurable, and the importance of goal feedback. Finally, it reviews some of the leadership and coaching issues associated with setting and managing team goals.

7.1 What Goals Are

The dictionary defines a goal as "the result or achievement toward which effort is directed" (Random House 1983). Goals concern results and efforts, but most importantly they concern direction. Goals provide direction and focus for our efforts. They clearly define the end that we desire and establish a priority for the required work.

Goals also imply several other things. For example, you need to know whether you have achieved the desired result and where you are along the way. Are you winning or losing and are your efforts likely to be successful? All of these—the result, direction, measurement, and effort—are involved in setting and achieving goals.

Why Goals Are Important

Goals are useful for individuals. Few would argue that, without a goal, it is impossible to strive. Without some objective, all the effort seems pointless and a waste of time. After all, if the effort doesn't get you anywhere, why bother? Thus, a goal concerns a destination, and this destination must be some place or some state that you really would like to achieve. This could be losing weight, getting a higher score, or delivering a product, but the goal provides a concrete objective toward which to strive.

Another way to think about goals is in the negative. A key reason given when the presumed better competitor loses in boxing, track, or any other sports competition is that he or she did not want to win badly enough. Similarly, in building products, it is widely accepted that when people don't strive to build quality products, they generally won't. In fact, they really cannot. Challenging goals are not achieved by mistake. If you don't consciously strive for them, you almost certainly will not achieve them.

So, goals are not just an invention of management, they actually satisfy a fundamental human need. The goal defines our purpose: why we are here, why we are working, or what we intend to achieve. Simply put, without a goal, you cannot succeed and, if you cannot succeed, why try?

Goals are the motivators for human endeavor. They energize our lives and our work. They give us purpose. Achieving a goal provides a sense of achievement and satisfaction. Goals are important to people and they are even more important for teams.

Why Teams Need Goals

Teams need goals for all of the same reasons that individuals do. In addition, goals provide a common working framework for the team. The goal is something that everyone agrees on and can cooperatively work to achieve. The goal helps to resolve issues. Does this activity move the team toward the goal or would something else be more effective? If some action does not help to achieve the goal, why bother doing it? After achieving a goal, the team members have something to celebrate. It was hard work but they brought it off. It was a team achievement and everyone shares in the celebration and in the credit.

Without a common goal on which all members agree, you have a loose collection of individuals who share only a common trait or facility; you cannot have a team. It would be hard to imagine an athletic team where the members did not all share a common goal, agree on precisely what that goal was, and know exactly what the score was at every point in the play. In addition, precise and timely feedback on goal status is an essential prerequisite for high-performance teams.

7.2   The Importance of Feedback

Who ever heard of a winning team that didn't know the score? Team performance requires knowing where you stand and how you are doing. Since the primary reason for having a goal is to achieve it, the goal must be measurable, at least in concrete enough terms to know whether or not the goal is being achieved. In fact, there is considerable evidence that when teams have measurable goals and when they know precisely where they stand against these goals, they perform substantially better than teams that do not have such feedback. This requires that the team's goals be measurable, that they be consistently measured, and that the team regularly see the results of these measurements. Only then can the team members see where they are succeeding or falling short. They can then adjust their efforts to resolve problems and make a special effort to achieve the objective.

7.3   Goal Priorities

When you consider goals, you must also think about priorities. After all, the purpose of the goal is to motivate, and if a team had twenty-eight critical goals, it is hard to see how any of these goals could provide much motivation. So a goal implies a priority, and it implies that there is one top priority. There may also be one or two second-level goals, as well as a host of other important things to remember as the team does the job. However, teams should only have a few high-priority goals.

As an example of defining a project's high-priority goals, consider a new web-based inventory management system that was planned to replace an existing system. Marketing and senior management defined the principal requirement as having the new product ready to ship to customers in one year. Clearly, this established the highest priority goal as a one-year schedule.

The next question concerned the product. What must it do? Marketing required a transparent replacement for the current system, plus a broad range of new competitive features. This defined one important secondary goal of providing an upward-compatible system with a defined list of competitive features.

At this point, either management or marketing should address the question of quality. Unfortunately, these managers had not yet learned to think about quality in any but the simplest terms: the system either worked or it did not. They should have required that it have better quality than the current system, have fewer defects in test, or cost less to maintain. In coaching management before the opening launch meeting, suggest that they make the team's quality goals important and provide some guidance on how they will measure performance against these goals.

In setting goal priorities, it is important to distinguish between the various goal categories. For example, the balanced scorecard approach views business strategies as having four dimensions: financial, business process, customer, and learning and growing (Kaplan 1996). By using this framework to think about goals, teams are likely to consider all the important aspects of their project.

7.4   Measurable Goals

To make goals meaningful, they must be specific and quantified. This means that they must be measured. Since establishing goal measures is often difficult and time consuming, teams should only establish measures for a few of the highest priority goals. Once teams have done that, if the members want to establish measures for a few more goals, that would be reasonable, but they should not measure too many things. In fact, I suggest starting with just three or four basic goals: cost and schedule, product capability, quality, and team performance. Once the team has experience with these, if they want to define more goals, they would have an informed basis for doing so on the next project.

Measuring goals is sometimes simple, but often not. To be measurable, a goal must be specific and precise. Teams must know exactly what they wish to achieve, and they need a way to tell whether or not they did it. In sports, measuring the result is generally straightforward. The winning team made the most points, had the fastest time, or achieved the highest mark. However, in development work, goals are much harder to measure. Frequently, there is one very simple goal, such as delivering on time. Often, however, there are a host of other, less-clear objectives, such as providing usable functions, producing a maintainable system, or releasing a fully compatible version. In product development, quality goals are also important, but are rarely explicit or measurable. However, with the TSP, quality is an important part of the goal-setting process.

An orderly way to consider goal measures is in terms of the goal-question-metric (GQM) framework (Basili 1984). Kaplan and Norton, for example, follow this strategy by stating a question for each of the balanced scorecard dimensions, then establishing objectives or goals to address that question. Then they call for measures for each goal, goal targets, and actions to achieve these targets. The four balanced scorecard questions are as follows (Kaplan 1996).

- □ Financial: "To succeed financially, how should we appear to our shareholders?"

- □ Business process: "To satisfy our shareholders and customers, what business processes must we excel at?"

☐ Customer: "To achieve our vision, how should we appear to our customers?"

☐ Learning and growth: "To achieve our vision, how will we sustain our ability to change and improve?"

While your team will almost certainly want to rework these questions to focus on cost, schedule, quality, process, and technology, the balanced scorecard provides an orderly framework for doing so.

7.5 Kinds of Goal Measures

A goal measure can be categorized as objective, judgmental, or opinion. Each of these is discussed in the following paragraphs.

Objective Goals

The most obvious and simplest goal measures concern the values of key indicators. With schedule performance, it is easy to tell whether or not you made the date. Other examples include performance, such as a required response time or a particular transaction volume.

While measurable goals often appear to be simple, they rarely are. For example, with schedule performance, there are often many considerations. Suppose the final delivery date was three months later than planned, but the customer had added some requirements and agreed to the new date. Did this meet the goal or not? Most people would argue that it did.

The arguments about goals are rarely simple, however. Suppose, for example, that the developers said they needed a three-month schedule delay but the customer had agreed only to a two-month change. Was the goal met or not? The customer and management would probably say no but the developers would likely disagree. The same considerations concern performance, reliability, or installation time measures. In every case, the decision is complicated by questions about what should be measured and the conditions under which these measures should apply.

The problem with complicated measures is that the more complex the measurement, the less useful it is as a motivator. With a complex measure, team members cannot readily tell where the project stands or how their efforts will impact the result. All of the calculations involved in complex measures delay and confuse the feedback. So, the team members cannot easily determine whether or not they are achieving the goal. To effectively motivate, feedback must be immediate and easy to understand.

Judgmental Goals

The second kind of goal measure concerns personal judgments. These generally pertain to such product characteristics as usability or maintainability. With these, the general view is, "I can't tell you how to measure it, but I'll know it when I see it." Unless these judgment calls can be connected to criteria, they will not be very useful. This means that if the team members use such measures, they should plan to define the measurement criteria. Then, the team must make sure that the criteria are reviewed and that they are used to evaluate performance against the goals.

Judgmental measures suffer from the feedback problems mentioned before, so they are generally not useful in motivating team performance. However, they are important in tracking the quality of the team's work and they should be considered in the TSP goal-setting process.

Opinions

The final type of goal measure concerns opinions. While opinions are much like judgments, they are generally more casual and harder to treat as facts. To determine whether or not opinions can be useful, consider the source of the opinions, how the opinions will be measured, and how they will be used. If, for example, you measure users' opinions of product usability, customers' opinions of customer satisfaction, or the maintainers' opinions of maintainability, these opinions are likely to be useful. The questions, then, are whose opinions you want, how to measure these opinions, and how to use them.

At IBM, we ran periodic customer opinion surveys. The same measures had been taken for all of the company's major large-system products, and they had been tracked for many years and for literally thousands of customers. These opinions were analyzed and correlated with product changes, and the results were used by the product managers to manage product improvement plans.

The opinion-survey measures were called CUPRIMD, for *capability, usability, performance, reliability, installability, maintainability,* and *documentation.* By the time I retired from IBM, the company had conducted many surveys, and there were substantial historical data. After each survey, we were besieged with requests for the results. These results were first reviewed with the product managers, then presented to the development executives, and finally released to the market planning groups. Product managers who had one or more customers with a "very dissatisfied" rating knew that they would be severely criticized if they had not personally visited those customers and established an action plan to fix the problems. While one could argue that opinion cannot be measured, it usually can be, and the effectiveness of the measures depends entirely on how the data are gathered and used.

To use opinion measures, have the team identify the items to be measured and the people whose opinions will be used. Then suggest that the team members construct a questionnaire to gather these opinions. Since the questionnaire design can influence both the results and the response rate, suggest that they get professional help in constructing, using, and interpreting any opinion questionnaires.

7.6 The Problem with Measurements

While measurements are potentially very useful, they can also be misused. The problem is that all measures are simplistic approximations of complex conditions or events. Each measure produces a value for a parameter regarding an event or situation. While these measures are certainly real and they may represent what they purport to represent, their interpretation usually involves an implied model.

For example, consider a simple measure, such as lines of code (LOC). LOC is often used to measure the size of a program and, in general, the number of LOC produced per hour is a simple measure of productivity. Thus, the higher the LOC per hour, the more productive the team or developer is judged to be. However, this is only a very crude approximation of the real situation. For example, when written to identical specifications, program sizes vary widely, even for competent programmers. Suppose that one developer wrote a 1,000 LOC program in 100 hours and another developer produced the identical function with 600 LOC and took 75 hours. Even though the second developer wrote a more sophisticated but smaller program in less time, he or she would be viewed as less productive by the simplistic LOC-per-hour measure. This would be the case, even though the second design was superior and cost less.

Developers have no trouble understanding this point. However, consider how the second developer's performance would change if the organization evaluated each programmer's performance based purely on the LOC-per-hour measure. Suppose the company had established a standard that every developer had to produce at least 10 LOC per hour. The developers with lower rates would receive a poor evaluation and probably get a reduced salary increase—if any at all. Under these conditions, any smart developer would produce a program of at least 750 LOC for every 75 hours worked. The problem here is not with the LOC measure, but with how it is used, particularly if it is used to measure people's performance.

The general rule with measures is that if they are used to evaluate people, they are likely to cause some undesirable behavior. While a great deal could be said about this subject, and books have been written on the matter, the message to remember is that quantitative goals should be used to motivate people but not to rate or punish them (Austin 1996). When simplistic measures are used for performance evaluation, sooner or later the goals will motivate undesirable behavior.

This will generally happen much sooner than later. For a discussion of how to evaluate and appraise people, see Chapter 17 in *TSP^{SM}—Leading a Development Team* (Humphrey 2006).

7.7 Kinds of Goals

In guiding a team through the goal-setting process, start by describing the various kinds of goals. These include

- □ Stated goals
- □ Imposed goals
- □ Implied goals
- □ Internal goals

Stated Goals

Stated goals are generally represented by what management said in the opening launch meeting. The typical example is, "We need this product delivered in nine months." While there may be other stated goals, cost and schedule are the most common—and generally the most explicit—goals the managers will define.

Imposed Goals

Imposed goals are usually a subset of the stated goals, and they are the goals that management insists be met. While most of these goals concern fundamental business issues such as cost controls, personnel policies, or product safety specifications, managers also often impose schedule or process goals. While these sometimes are appropriate, often they are not.

The problem is that many imposed goals are based on historical experience and have been established to prevent a recurrence of some prior disaster. Think of imposed goals as a kind of scar tissue. They represent an often crude and inflexible response to prior damage. They are invariably based on historical experience, rather than derived from a thoughtful appraisal of future risks and exposures. While the team you are launching may have to abide by the imposed goals, it is generally a good idea to question them, particularly if they conflict with sound development practices. Under these conditions, however, suggest that the team members first produce a plan that conforms to the imposed goals if they can.

Next, suggest that they produce an alternate plan that better fits the technical situation. Then they can use this plan to show how a change in the imposed goal would improve the plan.

Imposed goals must be addressed, but they should be addressed intelligently. When teams provide management with a logical story on why such goals should be changed, management will usually see the implications and be able to make a logical decision. Occasionally, however—and particularly with contract work—the imposed goals are a condition for doing the job and management may not have the ability to change them.

One example of a mindless response to an imposed goal was a software group working under a U.S. Department of Defense edict that all new programs be written in the Ada programming language. This group was writing a program for an application that could have been easily handled with a commercially available spreadsheet program. Simply because of the Ada edict, they had started a very expensive project to reproduce many standard spreadsheet functions in Ada.

Implied Goals

Implied goals are not stated, often because they are so obvious. For example, does the product have to work? While everybody knows that the product must work, how well must it work? Can it have defects? If so, how many defects? Other implied goals might relate to documentation, usability, maintainability, compatibility, installability, and a host of other "understood" things that the team must consider in its work.

It is usually a good idea to have teams list the important implied goals, both because such goals are not always obvious, and because all team members will rarely agree on exactly what these "obvious" goals mean. Some of these implied goals are likely to be very important, so teams should measure and track at least a few of them. It is also a good idea to explicitly describe these implied goals so management can understand them and know how the team plans to handle them.

Internal Goals

The external goals are intended to meet management or business objectives, and the internal goals serve to meet personal or team needs. An internal goal might be to learn a new skill or to build a successful product that the team members can all be proud of. These goals typically relate to the learning and growth dimension of the balanced scorecard (Kaplan 1996). Most developers seek a rewarding experience, and we all want the satisfaction of contributing to something important. Internal team goals are similar. A goal of most teams should be to help the team to jell and to establish a smooth and efficient way to work. Other goals might be to have fun, be more productive, or have a better life. Such goals might be to work a real 40-hour week or to get home late no more than one night a month.

While internal goals are rarely stated, even in close-knit groups, one of the principal objectives of the TSP is to align management's stated and implied goals with the developers' and team's internal goals. Then, the work will be most rewarding for the team members, management, and the organization. During goal setting, your job is to help the team to do this.

7.8 The TSP Goal-Setting Process

Goal setting is difficult for organizations and it is difficult for development teams. The principal problem is not with devising the goals, but with understanding how to connect these goals to the business objectives. If your organization has established a clear set of goals, the next step is to refine these goals so that they connect to the employees' work. Only then will the developers know how their behavior affects the attainment of the organization's goals. Under these conditions, team goal setting can be quite straightforward.

The problem is that few organizations have explicitly stated their goals. The principal reason is that the methods for establishing meaningful goals are not simple (Kaplan 1996). A comprehensive goal-setting process can take considerable time and effort, and it must be led by senior management. These topics are discussed in *Winning with Software: An Executive Strategy* (Humphrey 2002).

Assuming that your organization has not developed such comprehensive goals and refined them down to the working environment, the team will have to set the goals on its own. While this can involve some guesses and assumptions, it is important that the team agree on what it is trying to do and on what success would look like. Then the developers can use these goals to guide them during TSP planning and product development.

When you guide a team through the goal-setting part of the TSP launch, you will have just completed the opening management meeting. Management and marketing will have explained what they want the project to accomplish, and their statements will provide the principal basis for the goal-setting work. In addition, the team should consider any other organizational goals, such as mission statements or corporate instructions. The steps in the TSP goal-setting process are as follows.

1. Meeting overview
2. Review management's stated goals
3. Implied goals

4. Team goals

5. Goal tracking

The following paragraphs review the coaching considerations for each of these steps.

Meeting Overview

The principal need in the meeting overview is to explain to the developers why they need defined goals. Describe the importance of explicit goals and why the team members must agree on what they are trying to do. Also, discuss the importance of an explicit goal statement that the team leader can review with management. Point out that this statement could be used as a basis for resolving issues and justifying team plans.

Review Management's Stated Goals

In meeting 1, management will probably have stated some very explicit goals. These must be the basis for team planning, and it is essential to state these goals in operational terms that the team can measure and track. Then, when the team restates these goals and measures to management, management will know that the team members understood what was wanted and tried to meet their needs.

Implied Goals

In establishing the implied goals, the team defines both the stated and unstated conditions that would characterize a successful project. The challenge for the coach is to help the team and team leader think broadly about the business, the customers, and the users. They should also think about the product, their management, and other important stakeholders. How should the product relate to other products? Should it be an architectural foundation for a new product line or is it to be a one-shot prototype? Also consider the process: What would superior work look like, how should it compare with prior experience, and what kind of capability do you want to build for the organization?

Team Goals

When teams have too many important goals, they typically act just the way they would with no defined goals at all. Don't let your teams get carried away with setting dozens of goals. Get them to decide which one, or at most two, primary goals are really important and to then define a very few additional goals. Although all the goals may be important, one and occasionally two must have top priority. The big issue is priority. Don't ignore the secondary goals, but the team must agree on the one or two key measures that will characterize success. Get the team to focus on the few key things that will make the difference between a superior project and an ordinary one. Then, help them set and strive to meet these goals (Basili 1984; Kaplan 1996).

By using Kaplan's balanced scorecard framework and the GQM paradigm, lead the team through the following goal-setting steps.

1. Agree on the basic questions for each of the several dimensions of the balanced scorecard. Kaplan's questions on pages 88 and 89 should suggest ways to do this.

2. For each of these questions, help the team identify one or two goals.

3. Define a way to measure each goal.

4. For each of these defined measures, establish a quantified team objective, and the point in time when that objective will be met.

5. Establish the actions required to track and manage this goal and the team member responsible for tracking it.

7.9 Goal Tracking

To track a goal, you must measure it. However, there are two reasons why this is rarely simple. First, many goals are not directly measurable. Second, even with measurable goals, it is not easy to set numerical objectives. This is generally because few teams have relevant historical data and few organizations have quantified the benefits of reaching their goals. This means that the actual values established for the goal measures will be arbitrary. While a goal of having a defect level of fewer than 0.5 defects/KLOC in system test would certainly be challenging, why pick that number?

In setting goal measures, help the team devise a rationale for picking the value. One rationale for picking a system-test defect goal of fewer than 0.5 defects/KLOC could be that systems with such defect levels generally have few if any customer-reported defects and negligible maintenance costs. Another could be that other teams have reached that level so this team should be able to do so as well. While the team may not currently have the data to support their rationale, it should state the logic for picking the selected values and then verify these assumptions once the project has been completed.

The last step in goal tracking is to assign tracking responsibility to one or more team members. In assigning these responsibilities, the team should consider the team roles. For example, the test defect levels could be tracked by the test or quality managers, and requirements change activity could be tracked by the customer interface manager. Since the team members typically select their roles after they have assigned the goal-tracking responsibilities, they generally revisit this topic after completing the role-assignment steps described in Chapter 8. In tracking performance against team goals, the team member with tracking responsibility is also charged with periodically reviewing goal status and noting how team performance compares with the objective. Also, whenever the team members consider some activity that will affect the goal, they should remind the other developers of the established goal and discuss how the proposed activity would affect that goal.

The team leader must ensure that the team periodically tracks its performance against its primary goals. Your job is to help the team and team leader decide on the tracking frequency and the ways to ensure that every goal is regularly assessed and reviewed during every team relaunch. Some goals, such as schedule and quality, should be checked weekly.

7.10   A Goal Measurement Example

To see how a team might establish goal measures, consider the example described in the earlier section on goal priorities. There, the financial goal was to deliver the product within one year and a customer-related goal was to produce an upward-compatible product with competitive functions. The business goal was to minimize test time, and the team set a learning and growth goal of obtaining complete data on the project. The following paragraphs discuss how to establish measures for these goals.

For the financial measure, the team's question was: "What must the team do to make the project a financial success?" While the team tried to meet management's schedule goals, the members agreed that their goal would be to deliver on or before the team's planned date. The planning manager was made responsible for tracking and reporting every week on the team's performance against this goal.

For the customer measures, the team's question was: "For the customers to view this product as a success, what characteristics must it have?" In this case, the first goal measure was to achieve 100% success at running the functional tests for the prior system. Second, the team defined a list of important new product functions with a percentage coverage goal. One goal was to provide 50% functional coverage with the first release, 85% with the second release, and 100%

with the third release. The team then agreed that the customer interface role manager would work with the requirements and marketing groups to define how these ratings would be measured.

For the business process goal, the team agreed on the following question: "To be consudered a superior job, what characteristics should this project have?" To do this, the team decided on two basic goals: to reduce final testing time to less than 15% of the development schedule and to cut product maintenance costs by five times. While they did not have internal data to support these goals, they agreed that achieving a system-test defect level of under 0.5 defects/KLOC would probably be adequate. The team members then agreed to make this a goal for their quality plan and to have the quality manager track their performance every week against this plan.

For learning and growth, the team agreed on this question: "To significantly improve the team's capability for the next project, what actions should the team members take?" Here, the team members decided that the most important thing they should do was to gather complete and accurate data. Then these data would help them see where and how to improve in the future. They further agreed that the quality manager would be responsible for tracking the team's data-gathering performance and reporting to the team on a weekly basis.

7.11 Summary

A goal is the result or achievement toward which effort is directed. Goals provide direction and establish priorities. A goal must also include a destination, and this destination must be some place that the team would like to reach. The goal defines the team's purpose: why it is here, how it intends to work, and what it intends to achieve. Goals are the motivators for human endeavor. They energize our lives and our work. They give us purpose. Achieving a goal provides a sense of achievement and satisfaction. Goals are important to people, and they are even more important for teams.

Goals provide a common objective for the team. They are something that everyone agrees on and they help to resolve issues. Team performance requires that the members know where they stand and how they are doing. Since the primary reason for having a goal is to achieve it, the goal must be measurable, at least in terms concrete enough so the team will know whether or not the goal is being achieved. To effectively motivate, the feedback must also be immediate and easy to understand.

In setting goal measures, guide the team through the goal-question-metric strategy and help the members define measures against the four dimensions of the balanced scorecard. It is also important for the team to state why any particular measurement value is selected. As teams gather more data, this process will become easier. Then they can select goal measures either to be better than prior products or to meet stated business objectives. Without historical data, teams must make assumptions, but they should clearly state them. They should also describe how they intend to verify and assess their assumptions once the project has been completed.

References

Austin, Robert D. *Measuring and Managing Performance in Organizations.* New York: Dorset House Publishing. 1996.

Basili, V., and D. M. Weiss. A Methodology for Collecting Valid Software Engineering Data. *IEEE Transactions on Software Engineering.* Vol. SE-10, No. 6, November 1984, pp. 728–738.

Humphrey, Watts S. *Winning with Software: An Executive Strategy.* Boston: Addison-Wesley. 2002.

Humphrey, Watts S. *TSP^{SM}—Leading a Development Team.* Boston: Addison-Wesley. 2006.

Kaplan, Robert S., and David P. Norton. *The Balanced Scorecard.* Watertown, MA: Harvard Business School Press. 1996.

Random House Dictionary of the English Language. New York: Random House. 1983.

8

Team-Member Roles

This chapter discusses the TSP roles. The objective is to provide the background you need to guide a team in role selection and to help the team members handle their role responsibilities. The book *TSP^SM—Leading a Development Team* contains a more detailed discussion of the specific objectives and responsibilities of the TSP roles (Humphrey 2006). This chapter describes why the TSP roles are needed, the role-selection process, and some suggestions about coaching the role managers.

8.1   What Roles Are

A role is defined as "the rights, obligations, and expected behavior patterns associated with a particular social status" (Random House 1983). All of the elements of this definition are important.

By holding a team role, the developers have certain rights. They are active participants in managing the project. They do not just do what they are told—they develop their own plans, manage and track quality, and lead the design work. The TSP roles cover all aspects of team management, from customer interface issues to testing, and from process management to quality control. Thus, TSP team members own their processes and plans, decide how they will work, and control how their project is run.

The role managers are responsible for carrying out their roles and they are expected to act accordingly. They are active and thinking team members. When they see a problem, they get it fixed. When they anticipate problems, they address them, either personally or by alerting the team member with the appropriate role responsibility. This is the most important aspect of the TSP roles: team members feel responsible for the success of the team and they take that responsibility seriously.

Finally, the ownership of a TSP role confers status. When team members have role responsibilities, they know that those responsibilities are theirs and that no one will object or interfere when they handle them. This gives them the authority to speak out on role-related issues. Nobody will ask why they are concerned; it is their responsibility. They are expected to be involved, even if it means taking the issue to senior management or to the customer. While they must keep their team and team leader informed, they are expected to be proactive.

8.2   Why Roles Are Needed

While we don't question the reasons for athletic teams to have playing positions, it is not as obvious why development teams need roles. The reason is that roles provide a defined and accepted working framework. With roles, members can specialize and focus on specific objectives. Roles help teams to divide the work and they allow the members to concentrate on specific aspects of that work. With roles, each member can handle a defined subset of the overall job so nobody else needs to worry about doing those tasks. To be fully effective, however, each team member must not only know his or her personal role but be thoroughly familiar with all of the other roles.

It is hard to imagine a baseball, basketball, hockey, rugby, or cricket team where the positions have not been defined and the players assigned to positions before the play begins. Similarly, with the TSP, the standard roles divide the principal team responsibilities among all of the members. They ensure that a team member is assigned to cover each key area, and they ensure that the normal issues of running the team are handled expeditiously and effectively. Roles are needed because they fill a basic human need, help to accomplish necessary team tasks, and accelerate teambuilding.

To Fill a Human Need

Humans are social animals. We need the association of others, both in our work and in our personal lives. People need membership in groups; this satisfies the basic human need to belong and to be accepted. By agreeing that a member can have a defined role, the group signifies its acceptance of that member and demonstrates its confidence that he or she will handle the assigned role responsibilities.

To Handle Necessary Team Tasks

For teams to operate smoothly and efficiently, the members must handle a wide range of tasks. When team members do not have assigned roles, these tasks either do not get handled or the team leader attempts to handle them all. This has two unfortunate consequences. First, because there are so many tasks, the team leader will not be able to handle them all and many will not be done. Second, when the team leader is fully occupied trying to handle these role responsibilities, he or she will not have time for the true leadership tasks of motivating the team, monitoring process fidelity, resolving issues, and managing the team's external relationships.

As a result, many important team-management tasks end up not being addressed, at least not until they become crises. Plans are out of date, project status is not tracked, and the team's standards and procedures are not defined or followed. When the team leader is distracted by all of the team's operational details, he or she will not have the time to be an effective leader. Team performance then suffers.

To Accelerate Teambuilding

The TSP roles also accelerate teambuilding. They do this by allocating responsibilities and by giving the team members specific tasks to do. This helps to overcome the negative and defeatist character of the storming phase and is an important part of building a self-directed team. As noted in Chapter 2, the first sign that a team is getting through the storming phase is when the members start resolving issues rather than merely complaining about them. The TSP roles help to focus the team on addressing its problems and establishing the plans and actions needed to accomplish the assigned mission.

8.3   Selecting Team Roles

Team-member role selection is done in launch meeting 2. The team members must be involved in selecting their own roles and they must agree with the selections. While the team leader may influence the role selection process and can lobby for particular developers to fill certain roles, a big part of your job as team coach is to ensure that the team members get the roles they want and that they agree with the roles they are ultimately assigned. Generally, the developers will know the roles for which they are best suited, and the coach and team leader need not do more than facilitate the role selection process.

The team depends on the quality, process, and planning managers to maintain process fidelity and to manage the team's plan. The design, customer interface, and support managers are concerned with product development and management, while the implementation and test managers ensure that the team is properly prepared for the implementation and test activities. All of the team roles must be handled efficiently and effectively or the team will almost certainly have problems. That is why you and the team leader need to jointly ensure that all of the team roles are assigned to members who can handle them and that they actually do carry out their role responsibilities.

In one case, for example, a team was relaunching its project at the end of the requirements phase. Evelyn, the team leader, was not satisfied with how the quality manager job had been done, and she wanted to make a change. Fortunately, the previous quality manager did not want to continue in that role. Evelyn had identified Jerry as the developer she wanted to take the quality manager role but, when she tried to convince him to do so, he was reluctant. Jerry felt that it would take a lot of his time and that he would not be able to do his development work. Evelyn asked the coach for help, and the two of them finally convinced Jerry that the quality manager role was essential and that he was the best person to handle it. When the role selection process started and Jerry put his name down for the quality manager job, the others agreed that he was the right person for that role and no one else selected it.

8.4   The TSP Roles

The TSP process defines ten standard team roles. These are the team leader, the team member, and the eight role managers. The role-manager roles are

- □ Customer interface manager
- □ Design manager
- □ Implementation manager
- □ Test manager
- □ Planning manager
- □ Process manager
- □ Quality manager
- □ Support manager

These roles cover much of the management work that must be done by the team. The objective of the roles, however, is not to do everything implied by each role, but rather to provide a team focus and leadership for that activity. By providing consistent attention to the roles, the role managers can ensure that all of the relevant issues and concerns are identified and handled in a timely way.

While there are many possible ways to define each of these roles, when they first use the TSP, most developers will need help in determining what the role managers are supposed to do. You and the team leader should provide whatever guidance you can, but the best way for them to learn is to have them start, and then for the team and team leader to define one or two specific things for each role manager to do during the next couple of months. Do this for each role and then work with the team leader and role managers to help them do these tasks. The following paragraphs briefly describe each role's principal responsibilities and list some of the questions the team and team leader might ask the various role managers to address. Your focus should be on ensuring that each role manager knows his or her responsibilities and is handling them properly. The scripts describing the role responsibilities are in Appendix A of *TSP*^{SM}—*Leading a Development Team* (Humphrey 2006) and in the TSP process materials the team will use in the TSP launch.

Customer Interface Manager Responsibilities

The customer interface manager is responsible for the team's relationships with its customers. Since every group to which the team provides work products could be considered a customer, it is important to be precise in defining the particular customers the team and team leader want the customer interface manager to handle. The most common definition is the end user for the products the team is developing together with any groups that represent or speak for that user community. This could, for example, include systems groups, requirements groups, the marketing people, contract negotiators, or actual end users. Some of the questions the team and team leader might ask the customer interface manager are the following.

□ Are we being responsive to customer requests?

□ Are we properly handling customer requests?

□ Is every requested change being evaluated, planned, and approved before being implemented?

□ Is the interface between the developers and the requirements and/or systems people working properly? If not, what should the team do to improve this interface?

□ Is development being delayed by the requirements work?

□ Is the quality of the requirements documentation sufficiently good to guide the development work?

□ Are the right people reviewing and approving the requirements?

□ Do all team members understand the environment in which the system will be used?

□ Are there any other customer-related issues that the team should be aware of?

Design Manager Responsibilities

The design manager is responsible for the quality of the team's design work. He or she should track the design work and ensure that all appropriate design standards are being met and that the designs are properly recorded. The design manager may be able to get help from other team members, but it is generally not practical for this role to get assistance from outside the team. Some sample questions the team and team leader might ask the design manager are the following.

□ Are the team's design methods and notations capable of producing a quality design?

□ Do all team members understand how to use these design methods?

□ If some team members are not fluent with the design methods, what remedial action do you recommend?

□ Is the team's design work of high quality?

□ Has a sound system architecture been produced and documented?

□ Is the architecture properly controlled and maintained?

□ Does the architecture consider future product evolution?

□ Does the design conform to the architecture?

□ Is the design properly documented and maintained?

□ Are the interfaces and other design dependencies with other related teams properly identified and managed?

□ Are there any other design issues that the team should be aware of?

Implementation Manager Responsibilities

The implementation manager is responsible for the overall quality of the team's implementation work. For example, he or she should be concerned with the adequacy of the design being produced during the design phase. The implementation manager is also responsible for any required implementation standards as well as the degree to which these standards are followed. For example, the implementation manager should ensure that the coding and commenting standards are proper and that they are being followed. The team should also clarify whether the implementation or test manager will verify the adequacy of the unit test plans and the completeness of unit testing. Some sample questions the team and team leader might ask the implementation manager are the following.

- ☐ Are all of the team members fluent in the languages to be used?
- ☐ If any team members are not fluent with these languages, what remedial actions do you recommend?
- ☐ Have the proper implementation standards been developed and adopted?
- ☐ Are the implementation standards being consistently used?
- ☐ Are the team members taking advantage of shared and/or reused code where they can? If not, what improvement actions do you recommend?
- ☐ Are there any other implementation issues that the team should be aware of?

Test Manager Responsibilities

The test manager is responsible for the quality of all the testing and test-related work for the project. This includes testing standards, test plans, test procedures, and the degree to which the testing work is done in accordance with the team's and organization's plans and standards. Some sample questions the team and team leader might ask the test manager are the following.

- ☐ Are test plans being produced when the process requires them?
- ☐ Are these test plans complete and thorough?
- ☐ Do the developers understand how to produce suitable test plans? If not, what remedial actions do you recommend?
- ☐ Are the system test plans being reviewed when the requirements are reviewed, the integration plans when the design is reviewed, and the unit test plans when the implementation is reviewed?
- ☐ Are sufficient test facilities planned for integration and system testing?
- ☐ Are the needed test tools available?
- ☐ Do the developers know how to use the test tools? If not, what remedial actions do you recommend?
- ☐ Are there any other test issues that the team should be aware of?

Planning Manager Responsibilities

The planning manager is responsible for maintaining the team's plans, reporting on plan status, and supporting the team with any plan-related issues. Some sample questions the team and team leader might ask the planning manager are the following.

- □ Is each developer's plan sufficiently detailed?
- □ Do these plans accurately represent the work that the developers are currently doing?
- □ If any of the developers' plans do not represent their current work, what actions do you recommend?
- □ Is the team's workload reasonably well-balanced? If not, what actions do you recommend?
- □ Is the workload with any cooperating group or team reasonably well balanced? If not, what actions do you recommend?
- □ Are dependencies within the team and with other related groups known, properly planned for, and tracked?
- □ Are there any other planning issues that the team should be aware of?

Process Manager Responsibilities

The process manager is responsible for ensuring that the team's processes and procedures are properly defined, that they are used as defined, and that team members who have problems or suggestions submit PIPs on their suggestions. The process manager is also responsible for handling the PIPs. Some sample questions to ask the process manager are the following.

- □ Do the teams have defined processes for their principal activities? If not, what processes do you recommend be defined and by whom?
- □ Do these processes reasonably represent the way that the work is currently being done? If not, are PIPs being submitted to correct the processes?
- □ When team members raise process-related issues, do you encourage them to submit PIPs and how many have they submitted?
- □ Are the developers following the processes that they have?
- □ Is management providing the support needed to get the defined processes followed? If not, what remedial actions do you recommend?
- □ Do you have a defined process for handling the team's PIPs? If not, what is your plan?

Quality Manager Responsibilities

The quality manager is responsible for ensuring that the team members are recording their data, examining these data, and helping the developers properly follow the process. While the team leader can help in analyzing the team's data and in motivating developers to follow the process, the review of individual developer's data should generally be left to the quality manager or to the team coach. The quality manager should review all of the team's quality data on a weekly basis and alert the team and team leader to any work that is not of high quality. Some sample questions to ask the quality manager are the following.

- ☐ Are the developers properly recording their defect data?
- ☐ Do they record the defect data as they do the work or after the fact?
- ☐ Are the defect data complete and of sufficient quality to permit analysis? If not, what remedial actions do you recommend?
- ☐ Are the developers using their defect data to assess the quality of their work?
- ☐ Do the developers use their defect data to regularly update their review checklists?
- ☐ Do the developers' defect data indicate that the work is of high quality? If not, what remedial actions do you recommend?
- ☐ Are the developers holding team inspections of the requirements, design, and implementation products and are these inspections being done properly?
- ☐ Are the developers conducting personal design and code reviews and are these reviews being done properly?
- ☐ Is component and/or module quality being reviewed before integration and system test?
- ☐ Does the quality of all the components and modules meet the team's quality guidelines before integration and system test? If not, what is being done to fix the quality problems?
- ☐ Do you need further support from management or the team leader in assuring quality work?
- ☐ Are there any other quality issues that the team should be aware of?

Support Manager Responsibilities

The support manager's job is to ensure that every team member has the proper tools and support and knows how to use these materials correctly. The support manager also makes advance plans for the development environment and establishes and administers the team's configuration management system. Some sample questions the team and team leader might ask the support manager are the following.

- ☐ Does the team have suitable tools to support its work? If not, what additional tools do you recommend?
- ☐ Are all team members fluent with the available development tools?
- ☐ If any team members are not fluent with these tools, what remedial actions do you recommend?

□ Does the team have adequate tool support for the configuration management process? If not, what actions do you recommend?

□ Is the change control board working effectively?

□ Are all changes to baselined products being managed through the configuration control system?

□ Have all products that should be baselined been baselined?

□ Are there any other support issues that the team should be aware of?

8.5   Other Team-Member Roles

During the launch process, the team should think about the special issues of the project and identify any additional roles that might require attention. When any of these additional roles are assigned, make sure that the selected role managers define their role responsibilities and review these responsibilities with the entire team for agreement. Often, when some additional responsibility is identified, it could logically be added to an existing role. However, in making the choice about adding responsibilities to an existing role, be sure to consider what else that role manager has to do. In addition to those defined by the TSP, many other roles are possible. Examples of additional roles are the following. The roles listed in parentheses are those standard TSP roles that might reasonably be expanded to cover the particular additional role or take this role in addition. However, when the added role is considered especially important, it should be the only role handled by the selected developer.

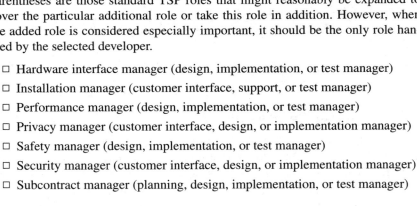

□ Hardware interface manager (design, implementation, or test manager)

□ Installation manager (customer interface, support, or test manager)

□ Performance manager (design, implementation, or test manager)

□ Privacy manager (customer interface, design, or implementation manager)

□ Safety manager (design, implementation, or test manager)

□ Security manager (customer interface, design, or implementation manager)

□ Subcontract manager (planning, design, implementation, or test manager)

8.6   Roles and Team Size

Role selection is relatively straightforward when there are eight or more team members. Then one member can take each role and the leftover members can act as alternate role managers. The team could also add one or two additional roles if that seemed appropriate. One selection approach is to have each team member privately decide on a first and second role choice, and then make a table on a whiteboard or flipchart with the eight team roles across the top and the team members' names down the left side as shown in Figure 8.1. After entering the team members' first and second choices, several of the roles usually have only one volunteer and can be assigned immediately. After eliminating the other choices for these team members, several more roles can be assigned. Ultimately, there will only be a couple of unselected roles left and the involved team members can generally agree on how to assign them. Then, to select the alternate role managers, the members' second choices will generally provide sufficient guidance so that the alternates can be quickly selected.

For smaller teams, the following general guidelines will help you to coach the role selection process.

☐ The planning manager role generally takes the most work and should be assigned as the only role for one team member.

☐ The quality manager role can also take a substantial amount of work, but only if the role manager understands what is needed and is willing to take the time to do the job properly. This should be a single role assignment for a team member or it could be merged with the process manager assignment.

	Customer Interface Manager	Design Manager	Implementation Manager	Test Manager	Planning Manager	Process Manager	Quality Manager	Support Manager
Team Members								

Figure 8.1 Role Selection Matrix

☐ Depending on the status of the project, it might be possible to assign some or all of the customer interface, design, implementation, and test manager responsibilities to a single development manager. However, in the early requirements phase, the team would probably need a separate customer interface manager and, in the final test phase, it would need a separate test manager role.

☐ The support and process manager roles could be combined and handled by a single team member or the team might ask for help from a member of the SEPG.

☐ Similarly, during the design and implementation phases, a member of the test department might be made a full-time team member, included in the team launch, and asked to handle the test role for the team.

The key to selecting and guiding the team roles is for the team and team leader to be clear on what they want the role managers to do.

8.7 Coaching the Role Managers

Some of the TSP roles have relatively obvious responsibilities, whereas others are not so clear. Make sure that the developers know that their job is to think broadly about their role responsibilities and to act as if they were running the project for all issues that relate to that role.

The role managers for each phase should be concerned with the quality of the phase input, the team standards for the work done in that phase, and the quality of the phase output. For example, the implementation manager should be concerned with the adequacy of the design being produced in the design phase, as well as with any implementation standards. He or she should also be concerned with the degree to which the implementation standards are being followed. The customer interface, design, and test managers have similar responsibilities.

Similarly, other role managers also have broad responsibilities for the team's activities. While the planning manager job is pretty obvious and quality management is discussed more fully in Chapter 19, the support and process manager roles are not as clear. Briefly, the support manager is concerned that every team member has the proper tools and facilities and knows how to use them correctly. The support manager also makes advanced plans for the development environment and establishes and administers the team's configuration management system. Likewise, the process manager is responsible for ensuring that the team's processes and procedures are properly defined, that they are used as defined, and that the team members who have problems or suggestions submit PIPs on their suggestions. The process manager is also responsible for handling the PIPs.

One of your principal jobs as team coach is to help the team members understand their responsibilities as role managers. In a nutshell, the role job involves acting as the team's conscience in the particular area involved. Without consistent coaching and periodic review, however, the role managers will often let their role responsibilities slide. Make sure to ask about the role responsibilities when you talk to the developers and suggest that the team leader review the role activities in the weekly team meetings.

8.8 The Role Manager Commitment

When team members take on a role assignment, they make a commitment to the team to handle the issues covered by that role. To do this, they will have to commit some time to handle these responsibilities. However, the amount of time need not be excessive, particularly if the organization has process, support, quality, and testing groups. The role managers should make a practice of asking such support groups to handle as many of the role tasks for them as possible. This can reduce the role manager job to monitoring the role-related issues and ensuring that someone is handling them for the team.

For some roles, the role managers will not be able to delegate much of the required work. This is particularly true for the planning manager, the design manager, and the quality manager. Generally, when the planning manager is overloaded, the team leader or one of the other team members are the only people who can help. Anyone from outside the team would not generally know how to offer much assistance.

You might offer to help the quality manager in examining the team's quality data or in helping the developers to better follow the process. While the team leader can help in analyzing the data and in motivating developers to follow the process, the review of individual developer data should generally be left to the quality manager with your help or that of another available TSP coach.

The design manager should also get help from other team members when they have the knowledge and skill to help. Also, particularly for projects that are part of larger systems, it is often possible to get help from members of the architecture or systems design groups.

8.9 Summary

This chapter discusses why TSP roles are needed, describes the role-selection process, and gives suggestions for coaching the TSP role managers. The TSP roles cover all aspects of team management, from customer interface issues to testing and from process management to quality control. TSP team members own their processes and plans, decide how they will work, and control how their project is run. Roles help to accelerate teambuilding and to handle necessary team tasks.

The TSP process defines the eight role-manager team roles. These are the customer interface manager, design manager, implementation manager, test manager, planning manager, process manager, quality manager, and support manager. The objective of these roles is not to do everything implied by each role, but to provide a team focus for that activity. The team members must select their own roles and agree with these role selections. Generally, the developers will know the roles for which they are best suited and the coach need not do more than facilitate the role selection process.

In addition to the standard TSP roles, other roles are possible. Examples are installation manager, hardware interface manager, performance manager, privacy manager, safety manager, security manager, and subcontract manager.

Some of the TSP roles have relatively obvious responsibilities, whereas others are not so clear. Make sure that the developers know that their job is to think broadly about their role responsibilities and to act as if they were running the project in all respects relating to that role. One of your principal jobs is to help the team members understand their responsibilities as role managers, which is to act as the team's conscience in the particular area involved.

References

Humphrey, Watts S. *TSP^{SM}—Leading a Development Team*. Boston: Addison-Wesley. 2006.

Random House Dictionary of the English Language. New York: Random House. 1983.

9

Team Planning

This chapter describes the TSP planning process and some of the more common planning issues to consider as you guide the team and team leader through the planning process. The topics covered in this chapter are

- ☐ The TSP planning process
- ☐ Launch meeting 3
- ☐ The conceptual design
- ☐ Team strategy
- ☐ The products to be produced
- ☐ The development process
- ☐ Process and support plans
- ☐ CCB membership
- ☐ Launch meeting documentation

9.1   The TSP Planning Process

The overall logic for the TSP planning process is much like that used in designing a system. In design work, the designer first visualizes the structure of the final product and then devises a strategy for designing the product's principal parts. In planning, the strategy is much the same: break the total job into parts or phases and then make detailed plans for each phase. The LAU script in Table 4.1 follows this same strategy.

TSP planning starts in launch meeting 3 (step 3 of the LAU script). The team first produces the project strategy, and it then defines the process and support plans. These steps are described in this chapter and they provide the context for the plan. Next, the team produces the overall plan (step 4, described in Chapter 10), which establishes the overall project resource needs and the development schedule from the present to project completion. In launch meeting 5 (step 5), the team produces the quality plan. This meeting is described in Chapter 11. In launch meeting 6 (step 6), each team member produces a detailed personal plan for the next project phase. The team then combines these plans and balances the team workload. Launch meeting 6 is covered in Chapter 12.

9.2   Launch Meeting 3

Launch meeting 3 starts the planning process. The first steps are to assign the meeting roles and for you, the coach, to give the team an overview of the meeting and what the team is to accomplish. At this point, it is important to describe why a conceptual design is needed and how it will be used in developing the team's strategy and plan. Also ensure that all of the team members know what a conceptual design is and how it differs from the actual design they will later produce.

9.3   Product Conceptual Design

The conceptual design is produced in launch meeting 3. Its purpose and the way it is used in planning was briefly mentioned in Chapter 5 and is covered more completely in Chapter 4 of *PSP^{SM}: A Self-Improvement Process for Software Engineers* (Humphrey 2005). However, there are several issues that teams often encounter in generating and using the conceptual design. These issues generally are of two types.

1. The conceptual design is too detailed and the team spends too much time debating it.
2. The conceptual design is too vague to be useful for planning.

It is generally a good idea to have one or more developers produce a draft of the conceptual design prior to the launch. However, don't involve more than one or two people since committees tend to produce poor designs. Then, during the launch, these designers can present their conceptual design to the team. Assuming that the team agrees with the design, it can be used to make the size and resource estimates.

Too Much Detail

It is usually helpful to have the conceptual design produced in advance, but doing so can lead to problems. The most likely problem is that described in point 1 above. That is, the group producing the conceptual design produces so much detail that it takes them many hours just to describe it. For teams of less than a dozen or so members, plan to cover the conceptual design in one or two hours at the most. However, for larger multi-team projects, you may have to take a full day or longer to review the conceptual design and to make the size estimates. In these cases, you should extend the launch process by a day or more.

If you spend too much time on the conceptual design, the team will likely confuse it with the real design. When that happens, the members will generally start debating requirements issues or get embroiled in design detail rather than thinking at a conceptual level. Remind them that the sole purpose of the conceptual design is to help them to develop a team strategy, to make a size estimate, and to produce a plan.

If one or two developers produce the conceptual design before the launch, make sure that they stay at a conceptual level. One way to do this is to place limits on the level of detail produced. For example, a modest-sized product should have about 10 to 20 components. This should provide a sufficiently detailed system structure for making the size estimate and plan. One trick that will help limit the detail in the conceptual design is to set a tight time limit for producing it. As long as the right people do this design work, the result should be a clean and useful conceptual structure.

Insufficient Detail

The problem of insufficient detail often results from no one having thought about the conceptual design in advance or from having little or no information on the product's requirements. Then, in the conceptual design discussion, the design manager will be forced to dream up a plausible design structure. When produced with little information or with no prior analysis, such designs will likely be superficial and the team will have little confidence in the resulting size and resource estimates. The team is also likely to realize the design problems part way through planning and either be forced to start over or to live with an estimate they no longer trust.

In cases where there is essentially no information on the product's requirements, the team will not be able to make an informed size estimate. Therefore, it should focus on making a plan to define the requirements. If management insists that the team produce a plan and a schedule for the entire job, the best strategy is to list the prior similar products developed by the organization together with their actual costs and schedules. Then indicate the range of the team's guesses for where this proposed new product would fall within this range. The team must make it clear that this is a guess and that the members cannot make a better plan until they have a better definition of the requirements.

9.4   Team Strategy

The team strategy is produced after completing the conceptual design. To select from the several possible development strategies that are usually available, the team should consider all the special needs for prototypes, demos, early test versions, and the like. For a general discussion of development strategies, see Chapter 10 of *PSP^{SM}: A Self-Improvement Process for Software Engineers* (Humphrey 2005). For large projects and for any projects that are developing parts of a larger system, suggest that the team consider the architectural principles discussed in Chapter 24 in this book while they select a development strategy.

The basic strategic questions concern how to subdivide a system into parts that can be separately developed, how to put these parts together to produce the finished system, and then how to test the completed system. In the simplest sense, one could design and build the entire system in one piece. This is called the "big-bang" or waterfall strategy. Basically, the developers design and build all of the system's parts and then put them together to see if they work. If the system is reasonably large, this strategy is almost always a disaster. It generally takes much longer to find and fix the system's defects than it would have taken to follow a more orderly incremental strategy.

Except for the big-bang approach, the various development strategies concern alternate ways to build a system in steps. These steps or versions progressively add enhancements to ultimately produce the complete system. The strategic questions concern the number of versions, the functional content of each version, and how these versions are integrated and system tested. While there are many considerations in making these decisions, it is impossible to make a project plan until the team agrees on a strategy.

The Gross Size Estimate

To produce a sensible strategy, the team must have some idea of how big the total product will be and of how the total job can be subdivided into small parts that one or two members could develop. This is the only reason to make a gross size estimate at this time. This estimating discussion might proceed as follows.

1. How big does the team think the total product will be? The fastest way to attack this question is to consider prior products the organization has developed and judge roughly where this new product would fit in that spectrum. Conversely, the team could choose to make the complete size estimate now rather than in launch meeting 4. For guidance on doing this, see the size estimate discussion in Chapter 10.

2. How does the team want to subdivide this total job? Generally, the choices are between the component and the functional enhancement strategy.

   a. With the component approach, the team members develop and test each separate system component and then assemble and test them one at a time until they have the final working system. Each component is developed as a full-function unit.

   b. The functional evolution approach would start by developing and testing minimum-function components and then integrating them all into an initial minimum-function system. The second and subsequent versions would then functionally enhance, integrate, and test some or all of these components.

   c. A mixed strategy might start with a core central component and then add one or two minimum-function components. For successive versions, the team would progressively add and functionally enhance more of the components. Alternatively, the team could start with a minimum core central system and progressively enhance it as well.

3. In selecting among the strategic choices, the team should identify the various components of the conceptual design and roughly estimate how big each is likely to be. Similarly, it should consider the likely functional enhancements and how big a job each enhancement appears to be.

With this information, the team should be able to settle on a development strategy. The team members should recognize, however, that when they produce the overall system design, they will know a great deal more about the system, so they should revisit the strategy to see if it is still appropriate.

Selecting the Development Strategy

Fundamentally, the development strategy must be based on the nature of the product. Is this a new system or an enhancement to an existing one? For an enhancement, the strategic issues are often established by the structure of the prior product and the nature of the desired enhancements. The base system is already there and the job of this project is to develop one or more enhancements. While these enhancements could be incorporated all at once or in several stages, the fundamental strategic questions of whether to enhance and how to do so have already been made.

In developing a new system, the basic strategic question is whether to build a small "kernel" system first and enhance it, or to build the entire system in one big step. The considerations here concern how much the team knows about this system, the experience they have with building similar systems, the quality of the developers' work, and the complexity of the system.

In general, it is a good idea to build new systems in as many small stages or versions as practical and then to carry each of these versions as far through the development process as possible. For all but the smallest systems, there are usually overall design or performance issues that cannot be fully understood until a basic system version has been built and tested. By building the system in multiple versions, the team can identify these system-wide issues early and address them while there is still time to make major design changes.

A second benefit of an incremental development strategy is that it is almost always faster to enhance an existing system than to build a new system from scratch. When teams start with a working system base, many of the interface, security, and performance issues can be resolved quickly. A further advantage of such an incremental strategy is that the team can often get early user feedback on system performance and function and more easily produce a usable and attractive product.

Incremental development strategies involve a quality trade-off. Unless program quality is exceptionally high, it can take a long time to test each product version. When each version of a poor quality product completes test, it will likely contain many remaining defects. Then testing each subsequent version will find problems in the prior versions as well as in the new enhancements. Since program size increases with each version and since defect find and fix times generally increase rapidly with product size, overall testing time often grows with each successive version. However, if the team follows the TSP process with reasonable fidelity, product quality will be high and testing time will not significantly increase with successive versions.

While the actual development time with an incremental strategy is likely to be shorter than with a big-bang or waterfall strategy, that is generally hard to prove. The reason is that teams that follow the big-bang strategy do not generally plan sufficient testing time. Then, when they get into trouble, they attempt to ship a reduced-function product at or near the originally scheduled date. The larger the system, the more likely it is that the system will ultimately be shipped in versions. Therefore, with larger systems, it is always a good idea to plan to build the product in increments. Then, even if the original schedule is not met, the initial version is more likely to be acceptable. This suggests, however, that the development strategy initially focus on the functions that the customer views as most important. The team should then plan these functions for the initial product versions.

9.5 The Products to Be Produced

After choosing the development strategy, the next step is to produce a comprehensive list of all the products the team will produce. Even though the team members may not think that all of these products are important, each will require development time and this time must be accounted for in the team's plan. With complex systems, there are generally many products. System code is needed, as are manuals, reports, test suites, training programs, installation guidelines, and so forth. By starting with a list of the required products, the team is most likely to produce a comprehensive process and a complete plan. It is also much less likely to overlook something important.

9.6 The Development Process

The team next defines its development process. The reason to define the process before making the plan is that **process definition** and **product planning** are two views of the same activity. In process definition, the team thinks about how to do the work. The developers consider the products they will produce, how they should do the work, and the issues they will likely encounter. The focus in process definition is on how to do the job in the best and most efficient way. This is also the point where the team should consider the lessons it and other teams have learned from prior projects and incorporate them into their process for this job.

Conversely, during product planning, the focus is on resources and schedules. The team members unconsciously think about whether or not they can do the job in the time management has requested. In this step, the team's estimates are most likely to be biased by schedule pressures. By defining the process before making the plan, the team decides how to do the job before it makes the plan. This both produces a better plan and simplifies the estimating job. When the team members know the process steps, it is much easier for them to estimate the time required for each step.

Build on the Organization's Process

If the organization has a standard process, the team should consider it as the starting point for the team process. Carefully walk through this process to ensure that it covers all of the activities needed to follow the team's strategy and to produce the desired products. Also, make sure that the steps are small enough to produce a suitably detailed plan.

It is also important for the team to define its own process. As noted in the example in Chapter 4, when Fred, the coach, led the team in producing a process definition, he essentially told the team what their process should be. This is a mistake. Try to run the process-definition meeting as an open discussion and ensure that everyone is involved. It is important for all team members to understand the process and to believe that it makes sense for the job they have to do. This is only possible if all of the members participate in the process definition work.

A Process Definition Example

In one launch, the team's laboratory had a highly capable development organization and it had a fully defined organization-wide process. When the team got to step 6 in launch meeting 3, the coach suggested that they review their existing process to see if they could use it. When they reviewed this process, however, they found that the many pages of text described what they were to do but not how to do it. While they agreed to do everything in the organization's process definition, they needed more specific guidance before they could make detailed plans.

The team's process manager then connected his computer to the conference room projector and started to produce a process script. The team members first agreed on the entry criteria: that they had completed the launch and that management had approved their plan. Then they started to define the process steps. It was a lively discussion with many interruptions and lots of questions like "Shouldn't we do a review before this inspection?" and "Where do we produce the test materials?" Within about 90 minutes, the team had produced a development process of 138 steps. In fact, during the team relaunch, they even refined this process to well over 200 steps. While this might seem like a lot of detail, it was exactly what the team needed to make detailed estimates and plans and to precisely track their work. The process manager then agreed to clean up this process script and to put it in the team's intranet folder that afternoon.

Process Consistency

While it is essential to have a team process that fits this team's needs for its current project, there are also reasons to have process standardization across development organizations. To prepare yourself to address this issue during the launch, meet with your organization's software engineering process group (SEPG) before the launch to discuss process consistency.

The key things to consider are standard cross-team measures, process reporting requirements, process documentation standards, and the availability of standard processes the team could possibly use. Also determine the SEPG's willingness and ability to support the team in developing any new process elements that are needed. Examples might be a configuration management process, a change control procedure, an inspection process, a product release process, and the like. With proper advance preparation, the SEPG can provide valuable support for the teams you coach.

9.7   Process and Support Plans

Next, the process and support managers lead the team in producing the process and support plans. Once the team has produced the process, the process manager should document it. While this script may be quite large, it is an important reference for planning and it will provide a foundation for later review and enhancement. There are also likely to be other process items to develop, such as coding and size counting standards and configuration control procedures. Make sure that someone is identified to handle each of these items.

This is also the time to consider the team's support needs. Is the development environment adequate? Are there suitable design and implementation tools? Are databases or other facilities needed? Is any special training required? While these needs may not require immediate attention, they often take considerable time to address and the team should think about them in advance. Make sure that the team discusses these questions and ask the process and support managers to lead these discussions. Again, have the team define the work to be done for the next project phase and identify who will do it. Each person must then put this work into his or her personal task plan.

In producing the process and support plans, use any available support groups in the organization. For example, if a software engineering process group is willing and able to handle any of the process definition tasks, that could save the team time. However, to be helpful, they would have to have been PSP-trained. Similarly, the resources of any other support groups should be used whenever they are suitably skilled and available.

9.8   CCB Membership

After the team has produced the conceptual design, decided on its strategy, listed its planned products, defined its development process, and produced its process and support plans, lead the members in identifying the membership of the team's change control board (CCB). While many groups defer CCB discussions until much later in the project, it is important to establish a CCB as soon as possible. The team's plan, its defined process, and any needed standards and procedures should be baselined and retained. It is also important to define and baseline a standard version of the team's development environment as soon as it is selected and available. While there should be relatively little CCB activity at the beginning of most projects, it is important to get the procedures established and the board functioning before the workload grows.

9.9   Launch Meeting Documentation

In concluding launch meeting 3, first check to ensure that the team has completed all of the necessary steps. Next, have the meeting recorder read each of the pending actions from the meeting, make sure that someone is responsible for each one, and find out when that task will likely be completed. Have the recorder note these facts in the meeting report, check that there are no other outstanding actions, and ensure that everybody agrees with what they are supposed to do. Finally, make sure that copies of the meeting documentation are put in the team's project notebook together with copies of the documentation from launch meetings 1 and 2.

9.10   Summary

This chapter describes the overall TSP planning process as well as the initial planning work done in TSP launch meeting 3. The first step is to develop the conceptual design. The team then produces the project strategy. In doing this, the basic strategic questions concern the number of product versions, the functional content of each version, and how these versions are to be integrated into a total system and tested.

In defining the development process, the team starts with a review of what that process is to produce. It then builds on the organization's standard process, if there is one. Once the team has produced the process, the process manager documents it. This is also the time to consider the team's support needs. Once the team has produced a product list and the defined process, it creates the process and support plans. The final steps of launch meeting 3 are to define the membership of the change control board (CCB), review any outstanding action items, and gather the launch meeting records for inclusion in the project notebook.

After completing launch meeting 3, the team is ready for launch meeting 4 where it produces the top-down plan. This includes a complete resource plan and schedule that extends all the way to project completion. This work is described in Chapter 10.

Reference

Humphrey, Watts S. *PSP^{SM}: A Self-Improvement Process for Software Engineers.* Boston: Addison-Wesley. 2005.

10

The Overall Plan

This chapter describes how the team makes its overall plan and some of the common issues you will face as you guide teams through this next part of the TSP launch. The three reasons for producing an overall plan are to determine the project schedule, to define the work to be done in the next phase or cycle, and to provide the basis for making the quality plan. The topics covered are

- ☐ Launch meeting 4
- ☐ The size estimate
- ☐ Determining project tasks
- ☐ The overall resource estimate
- ☐ Resource availability
- ☐ Generating and assessing the overall plan
- ☐ Optimum staffing

Again, for large projects and for teams developing parts of a larger system, suggest that they consider the architectural issues discussed on pages 337 and 338 during their overall planning.

10.1   Launch Meeting 4

As with all TSP launch meetings, the first steps are to select the meeting time-keeper and recorder roles, to provide a brief overview of the meeting agenda, and to describe the products to be produced in this meeting. This is also a good time to see if any of the team members have questions about what they have done so far in the launch.

10.2   The Size Estimate

After defining the team's strategy and process in launch meeting 3, the next step is to produce the overall plan. In making this plan, the team starts by making the size estimate. This estimate should take advantage of the high-level size estimate produced in meeting 3. Once the team has produced a product list and the defined process, the team has the information it needs to make the size estimate.

If the conceptual design is sufficiently detailed (about 10 to 20 component parts), the size estimating process should be relatively straightforward. The design manager leads the team through reviewing the conceptual design and making a size estimate for each of its major parts. In coaching this meeting, ensure that the team understands each part and that each member has a chance to ask questions or to state opinions.

If there is any serious disagreement on any estimate, ensure that the team takes the time to discuss it and to arrive at a consensus decision. One effective approach is to have the team make two or more estimates for each disputed part and decide on the criteria for selecting the one to use. One criterion could be to compare the part with the sizes of known similar products. The team could later measure these parts and decide which estimate to use. In the interim, proceed with planning but have the team pick one estimate—generally the larger—to use in making the plan. When teams make alternate estimates, they generally find that the differences among them are not enough to significantly affect the overall plan.

The planning manager should record the size of each part and the meeting recorder should note any open estimating issues, the criteria for settling these issues, and the names of the team members who will get that information. Once the size estimate has been produced, have the team compare it with the known sizes of completed products to see if it is reasonable. If not, the team should review the estimate to identify any significant errors or omissions.

10.3   Determining Project Tasks

Before starting to define the tasks in the overall plan, the team should consider the quality of the available requirements documents. Teams frequently find that their initial requirements materials are either incomplete or otherwise inadequate and must be substantially reworked. This work generally takes a good deal of time and few teams make adequate allowance for it. Make sure that the team considers this issue at the beginning of overall planning and allows sufficient time to review the requirements materials and to get any needed corrections made.

In producing the task list, the team needs time estimates for every development phase of every product element that is included in the overall estimate. For example, if the overall estimate has ten major components, the team will need times for every development and test phase for each of these components. This includes high-level design, detailed design, and coding, as well as the needed inspection, review, compile, and test steps. These times are needed to make the quality plan. If there are many components, this estimating process can take a substantial amount of time. That is why it is important to keep the number of components in the conceptual design to the minimum needed to estimate the size of the job and to allocate the tasks among the team members.

The principal issues to watch for during overall planning are that the team covers all of the elements of the job and that the tasks are estimated in sufficient detail. For the overall plan, the only steps that need to be estimated in detail are those for the immediate next phase. It helps to have the entire team walk through these next-phase steps and make the overall resource estimate for each step. Then, when the developers estimate their personal parts of the work in launch meeting 6, they can use these values as a guide. For the later process phases, it is generally adequate to make an overall estimate for the total job.

This overall estimate can often be made by using estimating rules of thumb. For example, a LOC-per-hour rate could be used to calculate implementation time, or an hours-per-page rate could be used for the documentation activities. Then, using available data, the team could divide these total hours into the various process phases. In doing this, the TSP planning assumptions shown in Table 10.1 can help in allocating time to each process phase. However, note that these are general guidelines, and that teams should use their own data as soon as they can get it.

The estimating factors will be useful for the implementation phase but, unless the team has considerable historical data, such factors will not be as useful for requirements or high-level design. For these phases, teams should estimate the tasks based on their experience and any available data. For the test estimates, rules of thumb can be helpful, but the principal testing time consideration is product quality. The suggested approach is to start with an estimate of the defect-free

Table 10.1 The TSP Planning Guidelines

General	• If your team does not have historical data, use these guidelines as standard planning factors. • Use these initial criteria until you have historical TSP data and can develop your own. • In all cases, use your judgment. If some guideline does not fit your case, use your best estimate instead.
TSP Plans	• Overall plan: produced first by the total team and later adjusted to conform to the balanced plan. • Bottom-up plan: produced by each developer for the next phase • Balanced plan: the next phase plan after load balancing
Requirements	• The requirements process depends heavily on the nature of the project, so no general guidelines are given. • In general, expect that all input materials will have to be inspected and substantially reworked.
Requirements Inspections	• The QUAL guideline provides a general factor to use in determining the time needed for the requirements inspection. • If this number is unrealistic for your project and situation, use your best estimate.
High-level Design	• No general guideline can be given because the high-level design process is highly variable, but the time required is principally a function of the size, complexity, and general nature of the system. • Without prior data, most teams substantially underestimate the time required for high-level design.
Implementation Phase	Implementation covers detailed design through unit test. • Calculate total implementation time from size/hour rates. • New or large modifications: about 10 LOC per hour • Small changes to large systems: about 5 LOC per hour • Pick a number that seems appropriate for your project. • Maintenance fixes: 5 to 20 hours per fix depending on complexity and degree of testing
Implementation Allocation	To estimate the implementation phases, make an overall estimate of implementation based on a size/hour rate, then use the following percentages to calculate time allocated to each phase. • Detailed design: 22.1% • Detailed design review: 11.1% • Detailed design inspection: 8.8% • Coding: 20.0% • Code review: 10.0% • Compiling: 3.4% • Code inspection: 8.8% • Unit test: 15.8%
Integration and System Test	For these phases, estimate the defect-free test time, then add 5 hours per defect in integration test, and 10 hours per defect in system test.

test time and then add a fix-time allowance based on the number of defects the team estimates will be found. If the quality plan indicates that the test times should be changed, then the plan should be adjusted. Quality planning is discussed in more detail in the next chapter.

10.4 The Overall Resource Estimate

Since detailed plans can involve a large number of tasks and since few of these tasks need to be defined right away, teams often find it best to only make detailed estimates for a few of the highest-level major components. This both limits the amount of time required for detailed planning and it simplifies the later planning steps. This is important because the developers' detailed plans will break the work into steps of ten hours or less. If there are detailed estimates for too many components, the number of tasks can easily become excessive.

The suggested approach is to make high-level estimates for all the components and then to break each of these estimates into detail shortly before starting work on that part. The developers will then have a detailed planning task as the first step in developing each component part. This approach not only reduces planning time during the launch, it also reduces the replanning work whenever the team's plans must be revised.

10.5 Resource Availability

After completing the effort estimates, the team determines its resource availability. This is often where teams have problems. For example, they may be understaffed and be promised more people at a later date. Under these conditions, the team should make a plan based on doing the job with no additional people. Then it should produce an alternate plan to show the schedule with the additional people required to meet management's desired date and when these people must be trained and available. Emphasize that the team leader is responsible for working with senior management to get the required resources and that the team members are responsible for specifying the required resources and effectively using these resources to do the job.

In calculating available team resources, the team members must estimate how many task hours they expect to have available each week. While these numbers will vary considerably from organization to organization, the team members should each strive to reach 15 or more task hours per week. However, since few teams achieve this rate, at least at the beginning, suggest that they start with a conservative task-hour rate and strive to increase it over time. Then, as they gain experience, they will have the data to establish realistic task-hour targets.

First-time TSP teams also often have problems getting started and accomplish very little in the first one or two weeks after the initial launch. There are many possible reasons for this, but the most common ones concern tool problems, planning misunderstandings, crises on prior projects, and the like. Whatever the cause, unless this start-up problem is recognized and allowed for in the team plan, the team will start off behind schedule and struggle for several months to catch up. Until they have TSP experience, urge your teams to consider this problem in their initial planning.

Generally, if the organization plans to make an external commitment based on the team's plan, suggest that this commitment be based on a conservative number of task hours. Initial numbers between 12 and 15 task hours per week would be reasonable—but aggressive—for most organizations. The team could later establish a more aggressive plan based on the results obtained during the project's first few weeks of work. While teams should strive to meet an aggressive task-hour plan, they should only commit to such aggressive goals after they have several months of data and can see whether or not the rate is realistic.

The most common reason for TSP teams to fall behind schedule is that they were overly optimistic in setting the initial task-hour rate and were unable to reach it. Remind the team members that, if they stay on schedule, they will be viewed as successful. However, if they fall behind schedule for any reason, they will not be considered successful, almost regardless of anything else they do.

After the team has estimated its available resources, the planning manager can generate the overall team plan. The team should then examine this plan to ensure that it is realistic and that all of the necessary work has been included. At the end, check to see that all the support and process development work has been included in the plan and that any needed requirements review and clean-up tasks are adequately covered.

Explain to the team that the overall plan is the most optimistic plan for the job. It assumes that all of the members can handle any part of the job and that their work will be completely balanced at all times. While teams can often come close to this ideal, that is not guaranteed and it generally takes periodic workload rebalancing and replanning.

10.6   Generating and Assessing the Overall Plan

Once the team has made the size, task, and resource estimates, the planning manager generates the overall team plan. While this should be a relatively mechanical process, there can be problems, particularly if the team members have not previously used their TSP support tool. It is also advisable to generate a Gantt chart for the overall schedule, both to help the team assess the plan and to use in explaining the plan to management.

Once the planning manager has produced the overall plan, the team leader leads the team in assessing it. They check that the plan includes all of the work needed to produce all of the required products. If not, any oversights should be corrected and a new plan generated. The team should also check that the plan is reasonable and that there are no significant errors. One way to do this is to multiply the team's weekly task hours by the total planned weeks to see if the total estimated task hours are reasonable. Also, have the members check that the overall estimated size per hour rate times the total task hours is close to the total estimated product size. They should also check that the times for the various project phases are close to the planning guidelines and that they look reasonable.

Once the team is satisfied that the plan properly represents its best judgment, compare the result to management's desired schedule to see if there is a problem. Since it is normal for managers to ask for very aggressive schedules, the plan will likely show a later completion date than desired. If so, the team should make one or more alternate plans to show what they could accomplish with more resources and when those resources must be trained and available. The team should also consider other alternatives such as delivering in multiple product versions or reducing the functional requirements. In producing alternate plans, it is important to consider the project's optimum staffing profile and when and if additional team members could help to accelerate the schedule.

10.7 Optimum Staffing

Staffing problems often make no economic sense. The cost of doing a job is not changed by its staffing level. Within rather broad limits, 10 developers working for 30 months will cost no less and probably a bit more than 15 developers working for 20 months. A 30-month project takes more management, support, and overhead than does one of only 20 months. In fact, if the project was committed to a 20-month schedule, staffing it with 10 developers would probably lead to panic, excessive rework, and increased costs. While fully staffing all the projects would increase quarterly expenses, most executives understand that it is unwise to cut costs so far that they jeopardize customer commitments.

Understaffed projects generally cost more than properly staffed ones. For example, if a project was estimated to take 96 development months, 8 developers could do it in 12 months. With 1 team leader and 1 support person, that would be 24 people-months of management and support. However, if the project was staffed with 12 developers, they could produce the 96 development months of work in 8 calendar months. The development months would still be 96, but management and support would be reduced by 33% to 16 months. Similar savings would accrue for the quality, test, administrative, and any other staff groups. In short, time is money.

Up to some limit, you can generally add development staff and reduce the schedule. This limit is the optimum staffing point. Beyond this level, adding staff would not shorten the schedule and could even lengthen it. However, the optimum project staffing level changes during the project. During the requirements phase, it is generally not productive to assign very many developers, particularly if they are not familiar with the application or with prior similar products. However, since there are usually prototypes to develop, standards to define, and tools to obtain and install, teams can usually use a few more members than the minimum number needed to work on the requirements. It is also helpful to involve the designers, test developers, and other knowledgeable people in the requirements reviews, both to take advantage of their skills and knowledge and to give them an early start on learning about the job.

During design, the number of developers who can constructively work on the job is largely determined by the nature of the system, the number of independent components, and the availability of skilled designers. Usually, only a few developers are needed for the overall system design and architecture work. Additional developers will usually cause confusion and delay the work. The greatest risk of overstaffing during the design phase is the natural inclination of many developers to start implementing before enough design work has been done (Brooks 1995). As has been amply demonstrated, this produces error-prone designs, extended testing, and extensive schedule delays.

Once the overall design is reasonably well advanced and detailed designs are being produced, it is usually practical to add developers for the implementation work. The feasibility of doing this, however, depends on the quality and completeness of the detailed design. When TSP teams use the PSP design templates or other suitably precise design methods to document their designs, and when the implementing developers have been PSP trained, this will not be a problem. Increasing staff at the beginning of implementation will then accelerate most TSP projects.

During planning, suggest that the developers consider the optimum team size for this project and make an alternate plan with that staffing level. While it is desirable to do this at an early point in the project, teams rarely know enough about the job to make accurate optimum-staffing estimates until they have completed the requirements and understand the high-level design. During a launch or relaunch, the best time to do this is after the team has produced the overall plan in meeting 4. At that point, ask the team members where additional staffing would accelerate the work. Then construct alternate plans with this and any other appropriate staffing levels. While making alternate plans, also consider any realistic variations in product content.

10.8 Summary

After teams have completed launch meeting 3, they will have produced a development strategy and a conceptual design. They also have a defined team process. Their next step is to make the overall team plan. This chapter describes how a TSP team produces its overall plan during launch meeting 4.

In making the overall plan, the team estimates product size, produces a complete resource plan, and develops a project schedule. This schedule extends all the way to project completion. If the schedule does not meet management's goals, the team should produce one or more alternate plans to show, if possible, various ways to meet management's objectives.

Reference

Brooks, Fredrick P. *The Mythical Man-Month, Anniversary Edition.* Reading, MA: Addison-Wesley. 1995.

11

The Quality Plan

TSP teams make quality plans for the systems they develop. This chapter describes the steps used in making a quality plan and the issues you will likely face when you coach meeting 5 of a TSP launch. The following topics are discussed in this chapter.

- ☐ The importance of quality
- ☐ Quality goals
- ☐ The cost of defects
- ☐ Measuring software quality
- ☐ Percent defect free (PDF)
- ☐ Making the quality plan

11.1   The Importance of Quality

When customers are willing to accept poor-quality products, that is what they will get. Many software users naively assume that the software they buy will work as advertised and that if it doesn't, the supplier will fix it. However, users are increasingly finding that this is not the case. It is unfortunate that people have to be personally injured by defective software before they realize that quality is important. Software is used for increasingly critical tasks, and unless software quality practices improve, we can expect many more people to suffer in the future. However, even when people are concerned about quality, the situation will not improve measurably until some suppliers start to produce better quality products.

The U.S. automobile industry is a good example of what could likely happen to the current software industry. Automobile quality had been a problem in the U.S. for many years, but customers did not have any better alternatives. Then the Japanese started offering cars that were more economical, had attractive features, and had much lower defect levels. Once customers realized that these cars were better, they quickly switched their loyalties. It took the U.S. auto companies several years to recognize that they had a problem and, even after a 20-plus year quality-improvement effort, they are still losing market share to the Japanese.

It is not clear how the software quality scenario will develop. However, if history is any guide, quality must first become important to the users. Once it is, competitors will start emphasizing quality. Then, as these higher-quality suppliers gain recognition, they will begin to take business from the leading suppliers. Once the leading suppliers understand why they are losing substantial business, they will launch effective quality programs. The longer they wait, the harder it will be for them to recover.

There are already signs that this is happening. Software is a very attractive business that requires little capital investment and can provide employment for large numbers of highly skilled and well educated but low-paid people. Many countries have established a goal of building a competitive software industry, and some have already become major factors in this business. While cost savings is often the initial motivation for moving software work offshore, quality is an important element in all of these countries' strategies. Unless the established software suppliers react, their market position is likely to be exposed.

The Importance of Quality to You

The reason quality is important to you and to the teams you coach is that it is likely to affect all of our jobs. While development groups that produce poor-quality products have survived—and often for many years—they have ultimately either learned to manage quality or they have gone out of business. It will take time for this to happen to software companies but, sooner or later, the poor-quality suppliers must either change their practices or fail. The world is increasingly competitive, and software is an attractive business. While many developers feel that quality is not their problem, it really is. The software developers are the only ones who can personally affect the quality of the products they produce. Your job as the team coach is to motivate them to do so. Quality is a development responsibility, and unless the development teams manage it, no one else can.

11.2 Quality Goals

Before making a quality plan, teams should agree on the quality issues that are important to their customers and to their businesses. The quality of a product is that set of properties that users find desirable. Conversely, a poor-quality product is one that either does not have these desirable properties or has properties that make the product undesirable or less useful. In determining the product's quality, it is important to consider the various quality categories.

The first quality category is product function. When ranking products, users generally consider its functions as most important. However, functions are unique to products. Thus, while it may be desirable to measure functional quality, there is no general way to do so. Functional quality must therefore be considered during the requirements and development phases, not in quality planning.

The second quality category concerns the product's properties. The principal software properties are the following.

☐ Compatibility

☐ Documentation

☐ Installability

☐ Maintainability

☐ Performance

☐ Reliability

☐ Safety

☐ Security

☐ Usability

Depending on how the software is to be used, these properties will have varying importance. Again, however, their relative importance is specific to the product so there is no general way to define them. Therefore, these properties must also be considered during product development, rather than during quality planning.

The third and final quality category concerns the product's defects. Defects are important to users only when they impact other important product properties. For example, a highly defective product is likely to have reliability, installation, performance, safety, or security problems. Such products often lose records, destroy data, or fail at inconvenient times. They could even kill people. Defects are important to users, but only because they block or reduce otherwise attractive product properties.

The principal reason to consider defects during planning is because product defect levels significantly affect the development organization. When programs have large numbers of defects, testing costs increase, schedules lengthen, and commitments are missed. High defect content also increases maintenance costs, often even above the development costs. That is why the TSP quality focus is on defects. It is also why the team's quality objective must be to produce defect-free products. Because developers are human, there is no way to guarantee that all defects have been eliminated, but they can be managed. Furthermore, by effectively managing a product's defect content, the development process becomes both more predictable and more efficient and it produces substantially higher-quality products.

11.3   The Cost of Defects

Because software organizations generally do not know how much defects cost, they do not manage defects. There are many different ways to determine defect costs, and the following paragraphs give examples of the costs some organizations have encountered.

The Teradyne Experience

While few organizations have data on the costs of defects, one laboratory in the Teradyne corporation had gathered such data for nearly ten years (Musson 1999). They found that after unit test, their products had an average of 20 defects per 1,000 lines of code (KLOC). While there were some fluctuations, the value generally fell between 19 and 21 defects per KLOC. These defects were found during system integration, functional testing, system testing, engineering field tests, customer acceptance testing, and operational use.

Teradyne also found that the time to find and fix each defect averaged 12 development hours. Thus, for every 1,000 lines of code developed, Teradyne developers spent an additional 240 hours finding and fixing its defects. By using the TSP, Teradyne reduced the defect content of its products to 1 defect per KLOC. This 20-times reduction in defects saved 228 development hours per KLOC. Teradyne estimated that these defect-repair savings amounted to $5.3 million in 2 years.

While the cost savings are significant, developers are usually more impressed with comparisons of testing and development times. With the PSP, the typical time required for a developer to design, implement, and unit test 1,000 lines of code is about 50 hours. Because industrial software projects often involve many uncertainties and complications, the development time for one KLOC could take 100 to 200 hours, but still much less than the 240 hours needed for testing. Thus, unless developers carefully manage the defects in their programs, they will spend at least as much time finding and fixing their defects as it took to develop the program. They could even spend twice as long.

When developers spend a modest amount of time doing design and code reviews, they can find most of the program's defects. Then, if their teammates inspect these same programs, they will find most of the remaining defects. A few hours spent finding defects early in development will save hundreds of hours both in systems testing and in maintaining and repairing the delivered products.

The Time Required for Testing

The calendar time required to find and fix defects during testing is best illustrated by system test data from the Jet Propulsion Laboratory (JPL) (Nikora 1991). As shown in Figures 11.1, 11.2, and 11.3, JPL tracked the defects removed during the system testing of three spacecraft. While these were relatively small software systems—with only 17 to 22 KLOC—the JPL developers found a lot of defects in test.

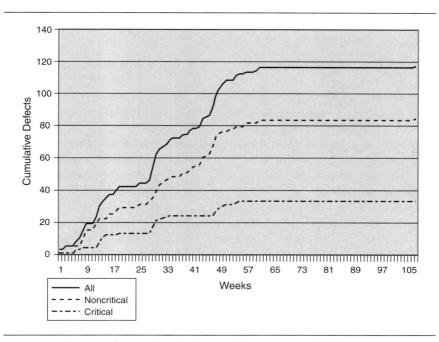

Figure 11.1 Voyager System Test Defects

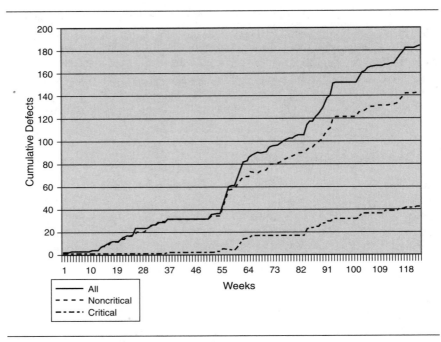

Figure 11.2 Magellan System Test Defects

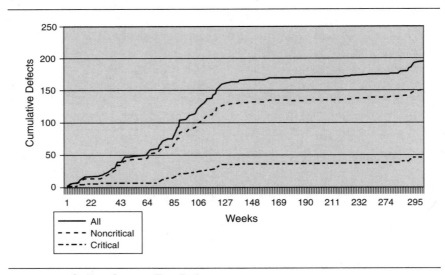

Figure 11.3 Galileo System Test Defects

As shown in Figure 11.1, Voyager testing took well over a year. The tests appear to have been reasonably complete since the mission was relatively trouble-free. For the Magellan spacecraft in Figure 11.2, system testing took more than two years and the system still had many remaining defects. Figure 11.3 shows that Galileo system testing took nearly six years. Some of this time was caused by the delays in the satellite launch schedule, but JPL was still finding defects after five and a half years of testing.

In another example, Microsoft developers found 30,000 defects while system testing the 6 million LOC first release of the NT system (Zachary1994). Two hundred and fifty developers spent an entire year finding and fixing these defects in system test. Assuming they only worked 40-hour weeks, this would be an average of about 16 hours per defect. The obvious conclusion is that a test-based quality strategy can waste a lot of testing time, increase product costs, and produce poor-quality products.

When developers have been properly trained and when they use sound quality methods, they can sharply reduce testing times. As shown in Figure 11.4, Boeing developers used the TSP to reduce system testing time by 94%. The TSP team at Hill Air Force Base also cut testing time by 88%. The test time was reduced from 22% to 2.7% of the development schedule (Webb 1999). Similarly, Teradyne developers spent nine months in the engineering and customer-acceptance testing of a prior product and only five weeks with the much larger product they developed with the TSP.

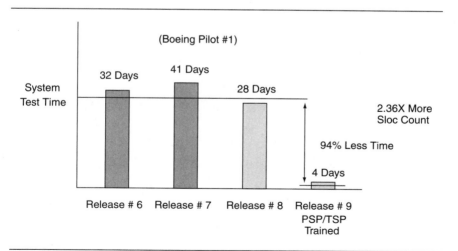

Figure 11.4 TSP Test Benefits

Maintenance Costs

While there is little published data on the cost of software maintenance, I remember the maintenance costs IBM incurred in the years before I retired. We spent about $250 million per year on customer problem management. For each of the many thousands of annual software service calls, customer service personnel had to report the problem, localize that problem, repair the defect, and distribute and install the fix for all affected customers. In addition to these costs, there were also development costs for incorporating defect fixes in product releases, testing the releases, and distributing the updated product versions.

Software maintenance costs are directly related to the quality of the developed product. Furthermore, product quality is a direct consequence of the quality of the development process. As shown in Figure 11.5, IBM found a direct relationship between defects repaired during development and those reported by its customers (Kaplan 1994). The high correlation indicates that the number of defects found in development test is a good predictor of the number of defects the customer will later report. This clearly demonstrates that the cost of software maintenance is directly controlled by the quality of the development process.

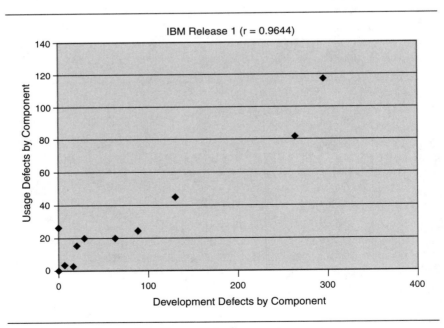

Figure 11.5 Development vs. Usage Defects

11.4 Measuring Software Quality

To produce quality products, the developers must both plan for quality and measure the quality of the products they produce. The quality plan is the first step in this strategy. It starts with the team setting quality goals. As described in Chapter 7, the members initially do this in launch meeting 2. Now, in meeting 5, they review the compatibility, installability, usability, and other quality properties described in section 11.2 and decide which are important to their customers and to management. Next, they define measures for these quality properties. While most will not be directly measurable, some can be measured with opinion surveys and others with special tests or focus groups. The team then plans to measure and track only the most important of these measurable properties.

For defect measures, the ultimate TSP quality objective is to consistently produce defect-free products. While few TSP teams can do this with their first projects, most can make substantial quality improvements. A reasonable goal for an initial TSP team would be to produce a product that has substantially lower defect levels than prior non-TSP products. Where historical data are available, a minimum goal of five or more times improvement would be realistic.

Where data are available on prior TSP projects, look at the best component quality levels achieved and urge the teams you coach to strive for average quality performance equal to the prior team's best performance. This is called **learning from variation**. Look at what worked best before and try to make that best performance normal in the future. This strategy has two advantages. First, since the prior team reached this quality level, everybody will know that it is achievable. Second, this kind of goal introduces a healthy element of competition. However, make sure that the team members set quality goals that they are willing to strive to meet.

11.5 Percent Defect Free (PDF)

The percent defect free (PDF) quality measure is used to characterize the quality of a software-intensive system. For example, if a product had 100 modules, and 38 of these modules had no defects in system test, then you would say that the PDF in system test was 38. The PDF measure can be used for each phase of the development and testing processes as well as during product use.

The PDF measure is easy to understand and it motivates sound development practices. When developers use the PDF measure, they soon see that they should measure quality for the smallest practical product element and at the earliest possible point in the process. For a given number of defects, measuring at the module level will maximize the PDF value. Similarly, by looking at PDF data early in the process, developers will quickly see where to concentrate their efforts most effectively to improve the PDF value.

11.6   Making the Quality Plan

The quality-planning process started in meeting 2 when the team established its quality goals. Now, in meeting 5, the quality manager leads the team in planning the steps required to meet these goals. In making the plan, many teams will not have historical data. In that case, they should use the quality guidelines shown in Table 11.1. While the values in this table are challenging, other teams have achieved them on their first TSP projects. Most teams can meet these goals by carefully following the TSP process and consistently measuring and tracking their work. The first step in making the team's quality plan is to determine the defect content that results from the overall development plan. Next, the team compares these defect levels with its goals. If the plan does not meet the goals, the team adjusts the overall development and quality plans.

Estimate Defects Injected

The team first estimates the number of defects it expects to inject. While there are many ways to estimate the defects injected in each process phase, TSP quality planning uses defect injection rates. This is because the quality plan is a model of what actually happens during development. As developers design and develop products, they inject defects and, the longer they work on any task, the more defects they are likely to inject. While PSP training reduces the developers' defect injection rates, these rates are relatively stable. Data on over 13,000 PSP class exercise programs show that the defect injection rate in detailed design declines by 8.3% from program 1A to program 10A. Similarly, the injection rate during coding declines by 34.6%.

While there are substantial PSP data on the numbers of defects injected per hour during detailed design and coding, there is less material available on injection rates during requirements and high-level design. Teams should use the rates in Table 11.1 with care and replace them with their own data as soon as suitable data become available. Once the plan is generated, have the team review the numbers of defects injected in each phase to see if they seem reasonable. For example, compare the total defect numbers with the team's PSP data for total defects injected and compare the estimated defects injected by phase with the members'

PSP data on defect distribution. Have them adjust the injection rates until these numbers look reasonable.

Estimate Defects Removed

To estimate the defects removed, the TSP uses yield data. With historical data, it is relatively easy to estimate the defect-removal yield for each phase. Without data, you can again use the guidelines in Table 11.1. The reason TSP uses yield to estimate defect removal is that the team members should be able to estimate the yields of their reviews and inspections from their historical PSP and team data. It is also possible to use defect-removal rates to make the quality plan, but because defect find and fix times are generally influenced by the project type and the development environment, that is not recommended.

Produce the Quality Plan

Once the team has estimated the defects injected and removed by phase, the defects/KLOC removed in each phase can be calculated. This calculation completes the quality plan. However, before accepting this plan, the team members should examine it to see if it meets their quality goals and is self-consistent. To make the consistency check, have them compare the quality levels in each test phase with the quality guidelines. Point out that test defect-removal yields vary with the defect density. For example, with high-quality products, testing yields generally improve. Check that the yield values used for each test phase are consistent with the defect rates planned. Again, the quality guidelines in Table 11.1 can be helpful.

It is not known precisely why test yields improve with product quality, but there are two likely causes. First, by considering the extreme case of an infinite number of defects, yield will be essentially zero, regardless of how many defects are found. Conversely, with only a few product defects, yields will be much larger, even if only a few of them are found.

Another likely cause for test-yield improvement with quality is that testing is like peeling an onion. As can be seen in Figures 11.1, 11.2, and 11.3, defects appear to be removed in waves. That is, it appears that many critical defects are masked by other defects. Thus, until some number of defects is removed, testing cannot find the remaining ones. Until the outer layers are removed, the remaining defects will remain hidden. When testing starts with the defect onion peeled, more of the defects are exposed and testing will find a higher proportion of them more rapidly. If testing were continued until all defects were found, this onion-peeling phenomenon should not change testing yield. However, with poor-quality products, testing is invariably truncated prematurely, causing a lower yield.

Table 11.1 TSP Quality Guidelines

General	• If your team does not have historical data, use these guidelines as standard planning factors. • Use these initial criteria until you have historical TSP data and can develop your own. • In all cases, use your judgment. If some guideline does not fit your case, use your best estimate instead.

Measure	Goal	Comments
Percent Defect Free (PDF)		
Compile	> 10%	
Unit Test	> 50%	
Integration Test	> 70%	
System Test	> 90%	
Defects/KLOC		
Total defects injected	75–150	If not PSP-trained, use 100 to 200
Compile	< 10	All defects
Unit Test	< 5	All major defects (in source LOC)
Integration Test	< 0.5	All major defects (in source LOC)
System Test	< 0.2	All major defects (in source LOC)
Defect Ratios		
Detailed design review defects/ unit test defects	> 2.0	All major defects (in source LOC)
Code review defects/compile defects	> 2.0	All major defects (in source LOC)
Development Time Ratios		
Requirements inspection/ requirements time	> 0.25	Elicitation in requirements time
High-level design inspection/ high-level design time	> 0.5	Design work only, not studies
Detailed design/coding time	> 1.00	
Detailed design review/detailed design time	> 0.5	
Code review/code time	> 0.5	
Review and Inspection Rates		
Requirements pages/hour	< 2	Single-spaced text pages
High-level design pages/hour	< 5	Formatted design logic

Table 11.1 (continued)

Measure	Goal	Comments
Detailed design text lines/hour	< 100	Pseudocode ~ equal to 3 LOC
Code LOC/hour	< 200	Logical LOC
Defect Injection and Removal Rates		
Requirements defects injected/hour	0.25	Only major defects
Requirements inspection defects removed/hour	0.5	Only major defects
High-level design defects injected/hour	0.25	Only major defects
High-level design inspection defects removed/hour	0.5	Only major defects
Detailed design defects injected/hour	0.75	Only design defects
Detailed design review defects removed/hour	1.5	Only design defects
Detailed design inspection defects removed/hour	0.5	Only design defects
Code defects injected/hour	2.0	All defects
Code review defects removed/hour	4.0	All defects in source LOC
Compile defects injected/hour	0.3	Any defects
Code inspection defects removed/hour	1.0	All defects in source LOC
Unit test defects injected/hour	0.067	Any defects
Phase Yields		
Team requirements inspections	~ 70%	Not counting editorial comments
Design reviews and inspections	~ 70%	Using state analysis, trace tables
Code reviews and inspections	~ 70%	Using personal checklists
Compiling	~ 50%	90+ % of syntax defects
Unit test at 5 or less defects/KLOC	~ 90%	If high defects/KLOC use 50–75%
Integration and system test at < 1.0 defects/KLOC	~ 80%	If high defects/KLOC use 30–65%
Before compile	>75%	Assuming sound design methods
Before unit test	> 85%	Assuming logic checks in reviews
Before integration test	> 97.5%	For small products, 1 defect max.
Before system test	> 99%	For small products, 1 defect max.

A further possible reason for higher test yields with improved product quality is that every defect-removal method is better at finding some kinds of defects than others. Reviews and inspections, for example, quickly find some defects that would take very long to find in testing. Similarly, testing will quickly find some defects that would be very hard to find with reviews and inspections. By properly using all defect-removal methods, defects can be removed much more efficiently and the time spent in defect removal will be minimized. The yields of the later defect-removal phases will also be significantly improved.

Regardless of the cause, with the TSP, the developers' personal reviews and the team's peer inspections remove most defects before testing. Test yields are then substantially higher, product quality is improved, and test times are sharply reduced. If careful reviews are not done, however, or if these reviews had relatively low yields, too many defects would remain. In that case, test yields would be low and testing times would be extended.

It is important for the team to check the defect levels planned for each test phase to ensure that they are appropriate. The defect level in system testing should be about 0.5 defects/KLOC or lower. If the quality plan shows significantly higher numbers, suggest that the team determine the reason for these higher levels and devise some actions for achieving more acceptable levels.

Perhaps the most important aspect of quality planning is showing the developers how many defects they are likely to inject and remove. When they review their quality plan, team members are often surprised at how many defects there are. Once they understand how many test defects they could have and how much time it would take to find and fix them, they generally appreciate the importance of doing careful reviews and inspections.

11.7 Summary

This chapter describes the issues teams face when they make a quality plan. The topics discussed are the importance of quality, quality goals, the cost of defects, measuring software quality, and making the quality plan.

While many developers feel that quality is not their problem, it really is. Software developers are the only ones who can produce quality products, and an important part of your job is motivating them to do so. Quality is the team's job. All of the team members must manage the quality of the products they produce; no one else can do it for them.

Before making the quality plan, the team should agree on the quality issues that are important to its customers and to its business. The quality of a product is that set of properties that users find desirable. Conversely, a poor-quality product is one that either does not have these desirable properties or has properties that make the product undesirable or less useful.

The TSP quality focus is on defects, and the quality objective is to produce defect-free products. Because developers are human, defects cannot be eliminated but they can be managed. Furthermore, by effectively managing a product's defect content, the development process becomes more predictable and efficient and produces better products. To manage defects, teams must understand defect-removal costs. The calendar time required to find and fix defects during testing can be excessive. However, when developers have been properly trained and when they use sound quality methods, they can sharply reduce test times. Software maintenance is also expensive. Because maintenance costs are directly related to the quality of the developed product, the cost of software maintenance is directly controlled by the quality of the development process.

To produce quality products, teams must both plan for quality and measure the quality of what they produce. The quality plan is the first step in this strategy. In making their quality plans, teams first use defect injection rates to estimate the defects injected in each phase. The defects removed are estimated by judging the yield values for each defect-removal phase. When they do not have historical data, teams should use the TSP quality guidelines to make these estimates. Once teams have made their defect-injection and yield estimates, they can calculate the defects to be found in each phase. This completes the quality plan.

References

Kaplan, Craig, Ralph Clark, and Victor Tang. *Secrets of Software Quality: 40 Innovations from IBM*. New York: McGraw-Hill, Inc. 1994.

Musson, Robert. Presentation at the Software Engineering Symposium. Software Engineering Institute. September 1999.

Nikora, Allen P. Error Discovery Rate by Severity Category and Time to Repair Software Failures for Three JPL Flight Projects. Software Product Assurance Section, Jet Propulsion Laboratory, 4800 Oak Grove Drive, Pasadena, CA 91109-8099. November 5, 1991.

Webb, Dave, and Watts S. Humphrey. Using the TSP on the TaskView Project. *Crosstalk*. Vol. 12, no. 2, February 1999, pp. 3–10.

Zachary, G. Pascal. *Showstopper!* New York: The Free Press. 1994.

12

Detailed Planning

The logic of the TSP planning process was described in Chapter 9 and the steps required to produce the overall team plan were covered in Chapter 10. Chapter 11 covered the quality plan, and this chapter discusses the issues to consider as you coach the individual team members through making their own personal detailed plans. There are two reasons for making detailed plans.

- ☐ Detailed plans allow the team members to precisely track their work. When all team members have detailed plans, teams can see which steps have been completed and tell whether they are meeting the plan or falling behind. Then they can measure their project's status to within a few hours.

- ☐ Detailed plans guide the developers in doing their work. When developers complete one task, the plan tells them what to do next.

Even high-level plans can generally provide these benefits, but more detailed plans are more accurate, provide more precise measures, and give better job guidance. While there are many types of plans, this chapter only covers detailed plans. The chapter's topics are

- ☐ How far out should teams plan?
- ☐ How detailed should plans be?
- ☐ How plans can improve efficiency

☐ Whether to plan now or to plan later

☐ The need for balanced plans

☐ The TSP detailed planning process

12.1   How Far Out Should Teams Plan?

The overall project plan should cover the entire commitment. For example, if the team has a job that will take five years to complete, its overall plan must cover the full five years. On the other hand, if the commitment is only for three months, the team need not plan beyond that point. Of course, if the three-month commitment is the first part of a bigger job, it would be a good idea to make an overall plan. Then the team could more intelligently discuss its plan with its customers and managers.

These long-term plans, however, are overall plans. It makes no sense to make a detailed plan for the distant future. Detailed plans should cover only the period that the team members can predict reasonably well. This is typically only a few months. Unless the team is doing very predictable work and it is work of a type that the team has done before, the members will not be able to make a detailed plan for more than a few months. With the TSP, detailed planning is done only for the next project phase or cycle, which will usually be for about two to four months. In general, the more complete the product's design, the more predictable the work and the further out the team should be able to plan. This suggests that requirements and design plans should be relatively short while implementation and testing plans could be for longer periods.

12.2   How Detailed Should Plans Be?

The more detailed the plan, the better guidance it provides for doing the work. Without detailed plans, developers must figure out what to do every time they finish a task. In doing this type of informal planning, they will generally talk to other team members or ask the team leader what to do next. This not only delays the other team members, it also likely results in uninformed and inefficient task assignments. With a detailed plan, this planning work has already been done and the developers merely need to follow their plans. This not only saves everybody time, it also produces more efficient task assignments.

The accuracy of plan tracking is governed by the precision of the plan. Thus, if you have only a high-level plan with two- to three-week tasks, you can only tell to within two to three weeks whether or not you are on schedule. The more detailed the plan, the more precisely these teams can track their projects and the better you can coach their work. More detail also means that the team members will gain earned value in smaller increments and will have a more precise, accurate, and continuous measure of their progress.

Another problem is the ability to make precise plans. The rule I suggest is, "The longer range the plan, the less detailed it should be." The further ahead the team members look, the less they will know about what they will be doing, and the less accurate their plans are likely to be. Thus, if teams make detailed plans for too far into the future, much of their detailed planning effort will be wasted. By the time they get there, the situation will almost certainly have changed. The general planning guideline is to break the planning horizon into three categories. As shown in Table 12.1, when planning for a week up to about 2 or 3 months, break the work into tasks of 8 to 10 hours or less. In looking from 3 months to about a year into the future, use the natural task size. This could be anywhere from tens to hundreds of hours. Beyond a year, do not make detailed plans.

12.3 How Plans Can Improve Efficiency

When teams work to detailed plans, their efficiency actually improves. For example, on one team, most of the tasks were planned for 20 or more task hours. Since the team members were only averaging 14 task hours per week, the developers often had no earned value to report. When the team held its relaunch, everyone wanted to make more detailed plans. Their principal reason was to earn value on

Table 12.1 Planning Horizon[a]

Planning Horizon	Task Detail
1 week to 3 months	8 to 10 hours maximum
1 to 12 months	Natural task times
Over 6 months	High-level plans

a. Note that the planning horizons overlap. This forces the team members to use their judgment.

a regular basis. The detailed plans they ultimately produced had all of the tasks under 10 hours and many were under 5 hours.

The developers were surprised to find that this level of detail improved their efficiency. They not only knew what to do every day, their task hours increased to over 16 hours per week. When they were partway through a task, they made an extra effort to finish it. They also resisted interruptions and were more likely to stick with a task to get it done. This modest change in behavior resulted in about a 15% improvement both in weekly task hours and in team productivity. Another reason for this team's improved task-hour performance was the improved quality of the plan. As teams gain experience, they see how to make plans that cover a higher proportion of their working time. When more of their time is planned, the developers waste less time deciding what to do, and their task hours increase.

12.4   Whether to Plan Now or to Plan Later

Team members should plan what they need to plan and defer the rest. Thus, when they are planning a large task but will not start the work for a month or so, there is no need to plan in detail right now. The general rule is to make detailed plans only when they are needed and to defer all other detailed planning until the team members are about to start on the work. Of course, they must have an overall plan for the next phase, and the plan must be in enough detail to schedule the tasks, balance the workload, and produce a quality plan.

For example, suppose a developer plans to develop 10 program modules, where each module is expected to have about 100 LOC. If the developer estimates productivity at about 10 LOC/hour, he or she could make one plan to cover the entire 100 hours. That would be like estimating the entire 10 modules as a single 1,000 LOC program. Alternatively, the developer could make detailed plans for each module, also taking a total of 100 hours. To save time during the launch and to defer planning until he or she knew more about the product, the developer could make one 1,000 LOC plan now and defer breaking out the 10 individual module plans until the time came to develop them. Then, the developer could make a detailed plan for each module before developing it.

The advantages of deferring the detailed planning for all but the most immediate tasks are that the detailed plans will be more accurate, and the developers will spend the minimum amount of time in detailed planning. However, this means that the developers will be updating their detailed plans almost every week. If the team members have been properly trained and have good tool support, though, this should not be a problem.

12.5   The Need for Balanced Plans

For any kind of work, some people will have less work to do and will finish their tasks faster than planned, while others will take longer. Although this is entirely normal, it causes unbalanced workload. With unbalanced workload, some team members will occasionally have nothing to do while others will be overloaded and delay the project. To minimize the project schedule, teams must keep everyone fully occupied. This is the purpose of workload balancing. With a balanced workload, every team member will always be productively working on tasks that must be done. Thus, those developers who finish their work early will know where and when to pitch in to help those who have more work left to do.

The importance of a balanced plan is illustrated in Figure 12.1. As shown by the unbalanced bars in the figure, the developers first produced personal plans for the next project phase. This phase was supposed to last 16 weeks but, as shown, one developer had less than one week of work to do and another's plan extended for 49 weeks. The workload for the other developers fell somewhere in between. After the developers balanced their workloads, their schedules were balanced as shown by the second set of bars. Here, the workload for all of the developers is reasonably even and the 16-week schedule looks much more realistic. The TSP

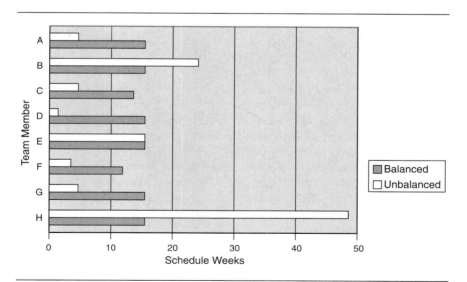

Figure 12.1 Balanced Team Workload

process helps you guide teams in producing balanced plans. Starting with an overall plan, they first produce detailed personal plans and then they balance these plans.

12.6   The TSP Detailed Planning Process

While there are many possible ways to make detailed and balanced plans, it is usually best to involve all of the team members. They will then be able to select tasks they are willing and able to handle. It also gives them a feeling of ownership for their personal plans.

The basic approach is for the team leader to lead the team in allocating the work in as balanced a way as possible. Depending on the team's knowledge of the tasks, the members should walk through the task allocation process. With detailed task knowledge, they should allocate tasks one week at a time, but with only a general idea of task size, they should allocate a month's work at a time. At each step, the members should keep track of the time they have committed compared to what they have available. When any member has no more time available, he or she should not agree to take additional tasks for that period. By ensuring that every developer is fully occupied all the time and that the priority tasks are handled in a logical order, this strategy will generally produce a reasonably balanced plan.

Once all of the work has been assigned, the developers produce their personal plans. Here each developer makes a plan for each of his or her assigned tasks. In doing this, they should follow the PROBE estimating method (Humphrey 2005). When they do not have personal data, they can use the times the team has already estimated for these tasks. Unless the team's estimates differ substantially from the developers' personal experience, the resulting plan should then also be nearly balanced. Since this balanced plan will likely have a somewhat longer schedule than the original overall plan, the team should update that plan so that the two have consistent dates.

While there are many possible ways to do workload balancing, this approach works and does not take much time. Once the team members know how to balance their workload, they can produce balanced plans quite quickly. This is most important for teams that work in a dynamic environment, since they will have to replan on a regular basis.

12.7   Summary

To produce accurate plans and to make realistic commitments, teams must plan in detail. With detailed plans, the developers will have clear and precise guidance for their work, and they will know precisely where their project stands. This chapter discusses the level of detail for planning and how far into the future teams should plan. It also discusses when to make detailed plans and the advisability of deferring detailed planning until the work is about to begin.

For any kind of work, some people will have less work to do and will finish their tasks before everyone else. Some developers will then be very busy, while others will have little to do. To minimize project schedules, teams must keep everyone fully occupied at all times. This is called balancing the workload. With a balanced workload, every team member will always be productively working on tasks that must be done. The TSP process guides teams in producing balanced plans.

Reference

Humphrey, Watts S. *PSP^SM: A Self-Improvement Process for Software Engineers.* Boston: Addison-Wesley. 2005.

13

Managing Risk

This chapter discusses risks and the issues to address in helping teams define and assess their project risks. It also reviews the principles of risk management, why risk management is important, and the TSP risk management process.

13.1   What Are Risks?

A **risk** is "a measure of the probability and severity of adverse effects" (Lawrence 1976). It is something that may or may not happen. If the event is certain to occur, it is an issue, not a risk. This is true regardless of the importance of the event. Issues are important, of course, but issues are things to address in the plan. However, with risks, there is a probability that the identified problem may not occur. While the team may wish to make advance preparations in case the risk actually materializes, the most effective way to manage most risks is to avoid them.

The TSP risk-management process starts with risk identification. The next step is determining the likelihood that the risk will actually occur. The third risk-management consideration is impact. That is, if the risk actually becomes a reality, what are its likely consequences? Thus, in considering a risk, you would like to know if it will cause serious problems. If a risk is highly likely but it would not have much impact, the team need not spend much time worrying about it. Similarly, if a risk would have a high impact but its likelihood of occurrence was very small, the team should not give it as high a priority as other more likely risks. The objective of risk management is to either prevent the risks from materializing or to devise mitigation actions to reduce the consequences of those risks that do occur. Finally, after the launch, the most important step is continuing risk management. The team must track its risks, take steps to avoid any risks that can be avoided and, where avoidance is not possible, initiate risk mitigation actions.

13.2   The Importance of Risk Management

Risk management is important for three reasons. First, many risks can be avoided. Thus, if you anticipate the risk and take appropriate actions in advance, there is a good chance that you can avoid significant problems. Second, the cost of recovering from a realized risk is almost always more than it would have cost to avoid the risk in the first place. In fact, the cost of later recovery is generally many times greater than the cost of more timely risk avoidance. Thus, by anticipating the risk and taking timely action to prevent it, you are likely to save the project substantial time and effort. Third, with few exceptions, most project disasters are known well in advance. Unfortunately, however, the people who know about the risks often fail to take the actions needed to avoid them. By ensuring that the right people are aware of the risks and that a team member is assigned responsibility for managing that risk, projects can generally avoid most of the problems that they anticipate. This is the objective of risk management.

13.3   The Principles of Risk Management

The five basic guidelines for TSP risk management are as follows.

1. **Learn from past mistakes.** Few risks are new. By knowing the most common problems with prior projects, teams can generally determine the principal risks for the next project. Even if they have never done a similar job, a thoughtful risk evaluation will generally identify the key exposures. Suggest that the team members talk to people on other similar projects or ask some experienced developers and managers for their opinions. Depending on the type of project, the customer might also have suggestions on important risks

to consider. You might also suggest that the team consult SEI's risk taxonomy for software-intensive projects (Carr 1993).

2. **Everyone on the team must manage risks.** The people working on the project are the ones who are most aware of the risks. By involving all of the members in risk management, teams can better anticipate potential problems and address them while they can still be prevented.

3. **Empower the team members to manage the risks.** To get the cooperation and involvement of working professionals in risk management, they must be treated as part of the management system. When people are merely doing what they are told and are not relied upon to be thinking professionals, they will not feel like project owners. Then they are not likely to think creatively about the project's risks or to take responsibility for identifying and managing them. That is why the TSP process assigns the key risks to team members.

4. **Every significant risk should be assigned an owner.** Organizations tend to ignore risks rather than address them. If a risk is not a current crisis, it is often hard to get anyone to take it seriously. Organizations are designed to handle the normal working routine and to resist unusual or nonstandard actions. So, a risk owner is needed who will insist that every important risk be addressed and that appropriate risk avoidance and mitigation actions be taken in time to prevent serious problems.

5. **Periodically review the risks.** After the team decides which risks are important enough to track, each risk owner is responsible for periodically reviewing his or her risks with the team. Review frequency should be based on risk severity and immediacy.

13.4 The TSP Risk Management Process

The TSP risk management process has two parts. The first part, *risk identification*, is handled during the TSP launch process. The second part, *risk tracking*, is covered later in this chapter.

13.5 Risk Identification

In launch meeting 7, start by explaining risk management to the team members, and then have the team leader walk everyone through the risk identification process.

Although there are several ways to do this, it is usually a good idea to use a brain-storming style to identify all of the potential risks.

The team should only evaluate the risks after they have all been identified. The reason for separating these steps is that thinking of new risks and evaluating identified risks are different activities. In identifying risks, the team members should think creatively about their prior experiences and visualize what could happen with this project. In risk evaluation, these same people should think criti-cally about the likelihood and impact of each risk.

The team leader leads the team in this brainstorming process and follows the guidelines described in Chapter 4 for involving all of the team members. During the brainstorming session, suggest that the team not list the typical risks of ordi-nary living. There are always risks of sickness, accident, and natural disaster, and these can cause problems for almost any project. While you don't want to ignore such problems, there is very little that the team can do to prevent them. Thus, in risk identification, coach the team to focus on the risks that are truly unique to the project. On the other hand, if the project is unusually dependent on one person or if a natural disaster is likely to have a unique impact on this project, then address those risks as well.

During brainstorming, the team leader should list each identified risk on a board or flip-chart, leaving room for the likelihood and impact evaluations, the team-member risk-tracking assignments, and the risk-management review dates. An example of an appropriate format for this chart is shown in Table 13.1.

Table 13.1 Risk Evaluation and Tracking

Risk Name and Description	Impact	Likelihood	Assignment	Review Date

13.6 Risk Evaluation

After the team members have identified all of the risks, the next step is to evaluate each one and to assign responsibility for tracking and managing it. In impact analysis, consider what would happen if this risk actually materialized. While there are lots of potential impacts, the easiest way to evaluate a risk's impact is in terms of its schedule consequences. The impact evaluation for a risk is H if it would have a high impact, M if the impact was expected to be medium, and L if the impact would be low.

Using schedule as a measure, a high-impact risk would normally delay the project by a few months to a year or more. Each such risk should have an H in the impact column. A medium-impact risk is likely to cause a delay of a few weeks to a month and is designated by an M. A low-impact risk is one that will delay the project by a few days. For these risks, the team leader should enter an L in the impact column. All of the team members should be involved in making these risk evaluations.

For very long or very short duration projects, the team should adjust the scale used for selecting risk ranges. For example, for a three-month project, a two- to four-week schedule impact should probably be considered as high impact. In special cases, the team might also want to consider other kinds of impacts, such as project cost, staff hours, or product quality.

It is a good idea to have the team evaluate each risk completely for both impact and likelihood before considering the next risk. Therefore, the likelihood evaluation should be made at the same time that the impact is being considered. Again, the evaluation is made using a scale of high, medium, and low. The evaluation for a risk is H if it is highly likely to occur, M if there is a medium likelihood, and L if the likelihood is low.

13.7 The Risk Evaluation Process

During the risk evaluation, suggest that the team leader challenge each H risk to ensure that it is really a risk and not an issue. Often, teams will view something as a risk even when it is certain to happen if no prevention steps are taken. For example, suppose the team identified a risk as missing the system testing schedule. During the evaluation discussion, however, the team concludes that the real concern is that a special system-test configuration had not been specified or ordered. If, for this project, this special test configuration was required for testing, this would be an issue that must be addressed in the plan.

Similarly, for the low-likelihood risks, suggest that the team leader challenge the team as to whether this is truly a risk or just a worry that isn't likely to happen. The world is full of worries and there is no point in tying up valuable team resources tracking them. The team's objective in the risk evaluation process is to identify and evaluate those few risks that are most likely to cause serious problems to the project. If the team members end up with more than about ten such risks, suggest that they reconsider their evaluations and attempt to reduce the list to six or eight of the ones they are most concerned about.

13.8   Assigning Risks

Once the team has evaluated each risk, the members should agree on who will track it. However, the team should focus only on those few risks it judges to be most significant. While the definition of significance can vary, suggest that the members assign only those risks that are judged to have a high or medium impact and a high or medium likelihood. Teams can generally ignore the low-impact or low-likelihood risks. Some of the high-likelihood and low-impact (HL) risks or low-likelihood and high-impact (LH) risks might also be assigned if they are particularly significant, but this is a matter of judgment. Even though every risk will not be tracked, the team should record all of them and then decide on those that are so minor that they can be dropped from the list.

The simplest way to make risk assignments is to use the team role assignments as a guide. It is often obvious which role should handle a risk. For example, the team leader should generally handle the resource-related and management-related issues, the customer interface manager should handle the requirements and customer-related issues, and so on. When the assignment is not obvious and no one volunteers, the team leader may have to persuade someone to take the assignment.

13.9   Risk Mitigation

Once the team has evaluated and assigned all of the risks, it should consider possible mitigation actions for the few most significant ones. The team leader might start by asking the risk owner for his or her ideas and then lead a general team discussion. For example, consider the risk that the customer might delay the project by taking too long to give approval after a design review. A possible mitigation action could be to raise this risk with the customer at the next management review meeting and to state that any approval delay beyond a certain date would mean a day-for-day slip in the schedule. This would also necessarily entail a corresponding increase in contract cost. An objective and factual discussion of this type will usually get the customer's and management's attention and enlist their help in avoiding or mitigating the risk.

The team should develop mitigation recommendations for the most significant risks. Since this is the one topic that senior management almost always asks about in the management meeting, the team leader should be ready with an answer, at least for the highest-priority risks. Also, if the team doesn't know how to handle a risk, the proposed mitigation action could be to raise the risk with management and to get their advice.

13.10   Risk Management Examples

While there are many examples of project risks, the following three give an idea of the range of exposures projects often face. An effective risk analysis and mitigation effort should consider the project in broad terms and provide management with a realistic view of the likely problems and the actions they should be prepared to take.

A Staffing Exposure

One team was given a very aggressive delivery date by management. When the developers made their plan, it showed that they could not finish on the required schedule with the current staffing. The team leader checked and found that the current plan was well within contract costs so he suggested that the team plan for five more developers starting in April. When they adjusted the plan, they found that if these developers were PSP-trained and on the job by April 1, the team could meet management's desired schedule. The project costs would also be within the contract funding.

The team made this alternate plan the base plan and listed project staffing delays as a high-impact and high-likelihood risk. The team leader was assigned to track this risk and, for the mitigation discussion, he had the planning manager generate three plans: one with the five additional developers, one with only two more, and one plan with just the current staff. The risk mitigation plan called for management approval at the end of the TSP launch followed by an immediate start on recruiting.

Based on these alternate plans, the team leader was able to show that the project costs would be essentially unchanged, whether they hired the new people and finished on schedule or if they did the job with the present staff and finished several months late. Since management needed to have the job finished on time and since the project costs were not affected by the new staffing, they approved the plan and the team leader immediately started recruiting.

Power Failures

This team worked in a laboratory near the U.S. 101 freeway south of San Jose, California. The team identified power failure as a major project risk. The laboratory power came from lines that ran alongside the freeway, and major freeway accidents frequently brought down the power lines that supplied the laboratory. Since an unanticipated power interruption could mean loss of important data and serious development disruption, the team judged this risk to be moderate impact and high likelihood. The risk was assigned to the support manager who proposed two possible mitigation actions. One was to have the laboratory install a backup power system and the other was to obtain an alternate power source from the power company. Management raised this problem with the power company and a backup feeder line was obtained that did not run alongside the freeway.

Late Changes

On another project, the developers felt that the customer did not really know what functions were needed in the product. Therefore, they expected several late requirements changes. The team judged this risk to be of high likelihood and high impact. The team assigned the risk to the customer interface manager. She suggested that the most effective mitigation action would be for the team to estimate the impact of every requirements change and to review their adjusted plan with management and the customer for approval before agreeing to make any changes.

Management agreed with the recommendation, and when the customer actually did request a major change, the team developed a new TSP plan and informed management that the change would extend the schedule by two months and increase the project costs. Management told the customer about the impact of the change and, after some negotiation, the customer agreed to adjust the contract.

13.11   Risk Tracking and Management

While it is helpful to identify and evaluate a project's risks, that is the simplest part of risk management. The most difficult and important part is tracking the risks and taking timely action to avoid or mitigate them. Have the team decide how often each risk should be reviewed and then establish a schedule to review it. The team member assigned to that risk should then set a follow-up schedule for reviewing the risk with the team. During this follow-up review, that team member should lead the team in deciding if an avoidance or mitigation action is required, when the next follow-up review should be held, or whether the risk should be dropped and no longer considered.

The role managers will be involved in tracking the risks the team identifies during the team launch, but they should also be involved in a continuing process of risk identification during the project. During launch meeting 7, only the team members participate in risk identification and evaluation. While this will likely identify many of the key risks, it will probably not identify them all. To identify the rest, it is essential to involve many if not all of the groups that will support or otherwise work with the team during the project.

Shortly after the launch, each of the role managers should meet with their respective support or other associated groups to identify and evaluate any risks that they view as significant. The team leader should meet with his or her immediate management, the process manager with the SEPG, the quality manager with quality assurance, and the like. The team leader, design manager, and implementation manager should also hold similar meetings with their counterparts on any associated development teams.

Any risks that are identified through this process should be reviewed by the entire team, assigned for tracking, and managed. This external risk search should be repeated at least at each project relaunch and occasionally in between relaunches if necessary.

13.12 Summary

This chapter discusses what risks are, why risk management is important, and the principles of risk management. A risk is something that may or may not happen. If the event is certain, it is an issue, not a risk. The TSP risk-management process includes a step for making likelihood and impact estimates for each risk.

Risk management is important because many risks can be avoided, and the cost of recovering from a risk is almost always more than it would have cost to avoid the risk in the first place. Since most project disasters are known well in advance, avoidance or mitigation actions are normally possible if they are initiated in time. The objectives of risk management are to identify the major project risks well in advance, to evaluate these risks for likelihood and impact, and to devise timely avoidance or mitigation actions.

The five basic guidelines for TSP risk management are that few risks are new, the people working on the project are the ones who are most aware of the risks, the working professionals should be involved in risk management, an owner should be assigned to every significant risk, and the risks should be periodically reviewed.

Risk identification is essentially a brainstorming process. After the team identifies all of the risks, the next step is to evaluate each risk and assign responsibility for tracking and managing it. In impact analysis, the team considers what would happen if this risk actually materialized. The risk is then assigned to a team member for tracking. The team then devises mitigation actions for the few most significant risks.

The final and most important risk management action is to track and periodically review the risks. Each risk should have a review schedule, and the responsible team member should review that risk with the team, agree on any needed avoidance or mitigation actions, decide when the risk should next be reviewed, or suggest that the risk be dropped if it is no longer significant.

References

Carr, Marvin J., et al. Taxonomy Based Risk Identification. *CMU/SEI 93-TR6.* Pittsburgh, PA. SEI, CMU, 1993, p. A2.

Lawrence, William W. *Of Acceptable Risk: Science and the Determination of Safety.* Los Altos, CA: William Kaufman. 1976.

14

The Management Meeting

The final management meeting is the most critical part of the TSP launch process. In launch meeting 1, management gives the team and team leader an aggressive schedule to meet. Now your job is to show the team members how to convince management that the plan they have produced is a responsible answer to that request.

Although the team's plan might meet management's desires, that is unlikely. Almost all TSP plans have longer schedules and cost more money than management wishes. This is not surprising, however, since management doesn't really expect the team to meet their date. Ideally, management would like to get the product now at zero cost. Since they know this is impossible, they have asked for the most aggressive date they think the team can meet. Now the team has to tell management that their date cannot be met, at least not for the resources provided.

If the team was able to meet the requested date, management would be surprised and would worry that they hadn't asked for a sufficiently aggressive schedule. Should they have asked for an earlier date? Or by some coincidence, did they happen to ask for precisely the best date the team could meet? The management meeting is where this issue must be addressed and, if the team handles the meeting properly, it will end up with a rational plan for doing the work and management's agreement to that plan.

This chapter discusses the management meeting and describes the steps teams must take to get management's agreement to their plan. It covers the following topics.

☐ Preparing for the management meeting

☐ Presenting the team's plan

☐ Alternative plans

☐ Risks

☐ Closing the meeting

☐ Presentation suggestions

14.1   Preparing for the Management Meeting

Meeting 8 is where the team prepares for the management meeting. Before launch meeting 8, suggest that the team leader take a little time to think about and decide on the material to present in the final management meeting. While the TSP process provides no prescribed format for this presentation, the following topics should generally be included.

Agenda and objectives. The team leader should start with a brief summary of the meeting's key points together with an agenda for the meeting.

Management overview. In a few charts, summarize what the product is, the development strategy the team plans to follow, and the critical schedule dates.

Overview of work done. The next step is to briefly describe what the team did during the launch, emphasizing the effort involved and the products produced.

Team goals and roles. This would be an appropriate time to introduce the team members and to describe the roles they each have selected. The team leader should also summarize the team's key goals and goal measures.

The team's plan. The team leader should briefly summarize the team's plan and compare its schedule to management's original request.

Alternate team plans. Where the team's plan did not meet management's original request, the team leader should describe the team's alternate plans and their expected costs and consequences.

Risks. The team leader should next review a few of the most significant risks the team has identified together with the team member assignments and planned avoidance or mitigation actions for these risks.

Questions and discussion. As the final meeting step, the team leader should ask for management's approval of the team's plan and invite questions and discussion.

14.2   Presenting the Team's Plan

In the final management meeting, the team leader reviews the team's plan with management. Since the team's preparation and the way it conducts this meeting will largely determine its success, it is important that the team leader and all of the team members be properly prepared for the meeting.

As noted in Chapter 6, the team's attitude in the opening and closing management meetings will largely determine how management reacts to the plan. If management perceives that the team really tried to meet their date but were unable to, they will be more receptive to the plan. It is also important for the entire team to clearly support the plan. If several of the team members can each make part of the plan presentation, this will be further evidence that this is the team's plan and not just the team leader's.

After the opening comments, the team leader should briefly describe the product and how the team plans to develop it. This discussion should be at a high level and in language that any executive would understand. The objective is to remind the audience about the project and its purpose. Executives have many responsibilities and it is important to make sure that there is no confusion about what project this is or why the team is doing it.

The next step is for the team leader to establish the team's credibility. One of the most effective ways to do this is to explain how much work the team has done in producing a thorough and complete plan. This description should cover the planning process, together with a description of the products the team has produced, including the overall project plan, estimates of product size and task time, and the data these estimates were based upon. It should also describe the quality plan and the developers' detailed plans for the next project phase. The team leader should point out that these next-phase plans show each developer's work for each week and that the tasks are detailed down to 10 task-hours each. This will permit precise project tracking and enable the team to report every week on exactly where the project stands against its plan.

The team leader should also explain that, to minimize the project schedule, the developers rebalanced their workload. In doing so, the team analyzed each developer's plan to see who would finish tasks early and who would be late. Then they adjusted each developer's workload to produce a balanced plan. In the final planning step, the team assessed the project risks and developed mitigation actions for the key items. The team leader could also mention that the team has produced a defined project process, identified the needed standards and procedures, and listed the required tools and support facilities. In deciding which items to discuss, the team should be prepared to provide backup on every item addressed. A common senior management tactic is to pick some unlikely topic and bore in to see if the team can support the team leader's story.

Now that the team leader has described what the team did and has presumably convinced management that they have done a thorough planning job, he or she should next restate management's goals. This is to answer management's implied question of "Did they hear me?" The presentation should repeat back what management said in the opening meeting and briefly summarize how the team's plan compares with management's goals. The presentation should also include the implied goals, together with any quantified objectives and measurement plans the team has developed.

14.3   Alternative Plans

In explaining the alternative plans, the team leader should present a Gantt chart showing the base plan and its key milestones. This should include a brief summary of the team's quality plan and what the committed quality level means in terms of shortened test time and reduced maintenance costs. Next come the alternate plans. These should show the schedule that the team can achieve with the currently available resources and what it could do with additional staffing. The team leader might even show several resource levels and, for each, the dates when the added developers must be PSP-trained and ready to start work.

As described in Chapter 10, there is an optimum staffing level for any project and it is important for the team to determine this level for its project. The plan should include at least one alternate plan that shows the team's current judgment on the optimum project staffing plan and the schedule that it would produce. After presenting these alternatives, the team leader can ask management for their preference among the plans. However, he or she should emphasize that staffing beyond the optimum project size is likely to add expense without commensurately reducing the schedule. It is also important to note that, while the development costs for all of the plans will be roughly the same, the optimum plan should be the least expensive.

14.4   Risks

After reviewing the alternate plans, the team leader should briefly review the risks the team has identified. This should be a summary of only a few of the key project risks, including their likelihood, impact, team-member assignments, and follow-up plans. The team leader should also mention the team's plans for mitigating these risks as well as any help that the team will need from management.

Management may comment on some of the risks, but as long as they see that their principal concerns are covered, that someone is assigned to track each risk, and that no immediate management actions are required, they will probably not have many questions.

14.5   Closing the Meeting

At this point, the team leader will have covered the meeting content and should ask for management's approval of the team's plan. While management will usually agree with the team's plans or one of its alternates, occasionally they will ask how long the project would take under some other set of conditions. Unless the team has already reviewed these specific cases, the team leader must not make up a response on the spot. This is the team's plan, and all of the team members must agree to any changes. The team leader should explain this to management and then ask for time to review the requested changes with the team and to produce a new alternate plan. This should generally be possible in a few hours to a day at most, depending on the size of the project and the magnitude of the requested changes.

After getting agreement to the plan, it is time to close the meeting. The team leader should end with a summary of the meeting's conclusions, any outstanding action items, who will handle each such item, and when.

14.6   Presentation Suggestions

The following paragraphs discuss how to prepare for and present the team's plan and how to make periodic customer and management status reports. This section also includes some general hints to use in guiding the team leader and team members in preparing for and making management presentations.

No Surprises

Give the conclusions first. Even if the result is really bad news, the team leader should get it on the table right away. The team must not lead management through a long meeting with a surprise punch line at the end. If it did, management would spend most of the meeting wondering what was coming and not know when to bore in and ask questions or when to relax and listen to what was being said. Ideally, the team leader should get a few moments with the senior manager some time after meeting 4 to explain what the plan looks like and the likely completion date. He or she might say, "After several days of work, the team has produced a comprehensive plan. Although we cannot precisely meet your requested date, in the meeting tomorrow we will describe the key risks in the plan and provide several alternate plans with different resources. One of these alternate plans comes quite close to your objectives for the project."

Now, the executive will know what is coming and can relax and listen to the story. In any event, the team leader should make this—or a similar—statement at the very beginning of the final management meeting. The objective is to tell everybody right up front where the team stands and what the presentation will cover. One way to do this is to have the team leader say during the agenda review, "Here is what we will be telling you, and the punch line is that we do not precisely meet your desired date. We will show you what we can do and present several alternate plans that come reasonably close to your needs."

Wherever possible, warn management before the meeting about the issues that the team leader will raise. Then they will know and have time to think about what is coming. You do not want to force senior managers to invent a response on the spot. This could embarrass them and might result in some guidance the team does not want. When management has time to think over the problems in advance, they are more likely to make rational decisions and the team is more likely to have a plan discussion that focuses on facts and data.

Remind Management of Open Action Items

There probably will not be follow-up items from the opening management meeting but, if issues were raised or if the team has received some prior direction on this project, this is the time for the team leader to list those items. He or she should have the meeting recorder read off the open issues. If you or the managers remember any other open items, get them recorded as well. A crisp and complete summary of the open action items, the person responsible for each, and the follow-up date will impress management and provide a positive start for the project.

Move Quickly

A common mistake many presenters make, particularly when they are developers presenting to senior management, is to take too long to make obvious points. This is not a classroom, and senior managers will understand with only a brief but complete explanation. Although the management team may not understand the technical details of the project, they will probably have had prior exposure to similar projects and have considerable background on the issues to be discussed.

It is wise for presenters to assume that the managers already know a great deal about the subjects being discussed and to cover the key points very quickly.

The guideline I suggest for presenters is to try to get management to ask them to slow down. They should treat it as a game and go over each topic very quickly, including all of the pertinent facts, but with absolutely nothing extra. Then the presenters should ask if there are any questions. As long as management has no questions, presenters should speed up to see if they can get management to ask questions on the next topic. In every case, however, it is essential to cover all of the pertinent facts. Any time management has to ask for a key item, they will think that the presenter overlooked it and may suspect that the team has done a superficial job.

Use Plain Language

The team members should check the presentation for any terms that are not in the dictionary or for any acronyms that are not generally understood. The team leader should either explain all such items in the presentation or replace them with plain language. If presenters cannot figure out how to do this, they should get help.

Be Crisp

Management presentations should be succinct and factual, with a clear summary of the key results and issues. One team member should act as the meeting recorder and track every action item and issue that comes up in the meeting. Then, at the end of the meeting, the team leader should briefly review these items with all the meeting attendees to make sure that the team understands them and that there is no disagreement on what is to be done, by whom, and when.

Stop When Management Accepts the Plan

In one meeting several years ago, a newly promoted executive was making a presentation to the senior management of IBM. After he had made his opening statement, the IBM chairman interrupted and said, "This sounds reasonable to me. Does anybody have any objections?" Nobody did, and the CEO was about to turn to the next matter.

At that point, however, this newly frocked executive plowed ahead with his presentation. He had prepared a 20-minute talk and was clearly disappointed to have only covered the first chart. The CEO was about to cut him off when he noticed something on the second chart and started to ask questions. Pretty soon, this poor clod was all tangled up in questions that he was not prepared to answer.

The subject was ultimately tabled until a more complete story could be prepared. It later turned out that the CEO's instincts were right and the proposal was eventually approved, but the newly promoted executive learned a painful lesson.

Once the team leader has made the sale, he or she should stop. There is nothing to gain by continuing, and by doing so it is always possible to lose the order. It is important for the presenter to make sure that the team really does have the order, then stop selling.

Make Sure the Team Knows What Management Wants

Above all, the team leader must not leave the meeting confused about what management said or what they want the team to do. If the team members are confused, others probably are as well, so it is essential to get clarification right now.

Bring Lots of Backup

It is usually a good idea to have a complete printout of the team's consolidated plan, the written goals, the team role assignments, the defined process, the size estimates, the overall task and schedule plans, the quality plan, and the risks. The team should not pass these items out at the beginning of the meeting because then everybody will be searching through the material to find the delivery schedule. Until they do, they will not listen to the presentation.

However, when the team leader gets to the alternate plan discussion, or if there are questions the back-up materials could answer, it is time to hand these materials out. In doing so, you can point out that the team has done a great deal of work and can support the plan with considerable detail. This is also a good place for some of the team members to answer questions. This gives the developers more management exposure and it demonstrates to management that the team knows what they are talking about. It will also make it clear that the developers support the plan.

14.7 Summary

The final management meeting is the most critical part of the TSP launch process. The team leader runs this meeting and should start by explaining the base plan and any alternative plans together with a brief summary of the team's quality plan. He or she should also explain what the committed quality level means in terms of shortened test time and reduced maintenance costs. Following a review of the alternate plans, the risks the team has identified should also be covered. It is also a good idea to have a complete printout of the team's plan, the written team goals, the team's role assignments, the size estimates, the overall task and schedule plans, the quality plan, and the risks.

Wherever possible, you or the team leader should warn management before the meeting about the issues to be raised. Then they will know what is coming and can be prepared. In the presentation, the team leader should cover the material briefly and concisely and have the recorder note every action item and key issue. Then, at the end of the meeting, the team leader should briefly review these items with management to ensure that they are understood and that there is no disagreement on what is to be done, by whom, and when. Although the team leader should make sure that he or she really has the order, it is important to stop selling once management has agreed to the team's plan.

15

The Launch Postmortem

This chapter covers the postmortem for both the launch and the relaunch, and it describes the key items to consider as you coach teams on this part of the launch process. The postmortem provides a structured learning vehicle for the team, the team leader, and the coach. It is where the team provides feedback on the launch process, on the effectiveness of each team member, and on the team leader's performance in helping the team through the launch process. It is also when the team members comment on the coach's style and effectiveness in guiding and supporting the launch or relaunch.

In the postmortem, experienced teams can consider how this launch worked compared to other launches in which they have participated. It is also where they can judge how this team leader and coach performed compared to others with whom they have worked. The postmortem provides a way for teams and team leaders to learn to be more effective in conducting launches, and it also provides a way for you to learn how your coaching style worked with this team and what you might do better the next time.

15.1   The Postmortem Attitude

The appropriate attitude for the team members to assume during the postmortem can be summarized as follows.

- ☐ There is always room for improvement.
- ☐ Improvement is generally achieved through many small changes.
- ☐ The users have the best improvement ideas.
- ☐ Everyone should be involved.
- ☐ Identify all the problems.
- ☐ Depersonalize and don't be defensive.
- ☐ Make people issues into process issues.

While books could be written about each of the seven aspects of the improvement attitude, the following paragraphs summarize the key ideas.

There Is Always Room for Improvement

It is easy to feel that you are doing something in the only possible way and that this is as good a way as it could be done. History has demonstrated, however, that whenever people feel this way, they are wrong. People's knowledge and capabilities evolve, new tools and methods are devised, and there are thousands of detailed steps, each of which could be performed better or more efficiently. While improvement takes effort, and it is almost impossible to think about changing your methods while you are in the middle of a job, it is important to occasionally stop and consider how to improve the way to do that job. This is the purpose of the postmortem.

Many Small Changes

Big process changes are occasionally possible, but that is rare and it usually happens only with processes that have not been widely used. However, for established processes, there are often a host of small details that could be adjusted and improved. Most process problems are minor details, but these details can make the difference between a convenient and efficient process and one that is confusing and hard to use.

Urge the teams you coach to think of the details they would like to see changed and to record their ideas in PIPs to submit to the team's process manager. However, since it is easy to forget such details, suggest that they keep blank

PIP forms on hand and make notes of the problems and improvements they think of when they think of them. Once the launch process is working well enough so the PIP process would not be distracting, have the team members do this after each launch meeting.

The Users Have the Best Improvement Ideas

Unless you actually use a process, it is hard to see where or how to improve it. That is why the postmortem is so important and why you should urge the teams you coach to record and act on their improvement ideas. Getting them to do this is important to you because you will use the launch process many times, while each team will only use it occasionally. Also, the teams you coach will not generally care much about process improvement. Their focus is on the project, and the launch is merely one step to help them do it. The launch postmortem is your opportunity to enlist the team's help in improving the launch process and in helping you do a better job the next time you launch or relaunch a TSP team.

Everyone Should Be Involved

As is true throughout the launch process, you want to get everyone's ideas. While some team members will be outspoken, others will not say very much. Often they will feel that their ideas are too minor to mention. If some team members have not said anything or if they started to speak and were drowned out by the others, try to get their ideas. Wait until the discussion slows down a bit and it appears that all of the ideas have been mentioned, then ask the quiet team members what they think. Often they will have valuable suggestions.

Identify All of the Problems

While it is important that everyone have a positive attitude and that the focus of the meeting be on improvement, you do not want to miss any significant problems. Once the discussion is properly focused on improvement ideas and when no one is being defensive, ask about any problems that have not been mentioned, even if the team members cannot think of improvements to address them.

Wait until the flow of suggestions has pretty much dried up before doing this. Then, for each of the problems that the team members raise, discuss possible improvement ideas to see what the group as a whole can think of. If no one can suggest how to address some problem, record it on a PIP so it is not forgotten and save it for review at the next launch postmortem. Then you can see if it is still a problem and if anyone has an idea for how to address it.

Depersonalize and Don't Be Defensive

It is easy to become defensive, particularly if the problems concern what you did or did not do. While some of the team members may feel this way, you and the team leader are more likely to get defensive since you will have led many of the discussions. Also, since you are a relatively safe target, the team members are likely to criticize you for problems that you did not cause. If you are objective about each of these issues and focus on what was done and how it might have been better handled, the others are more likely to behave in the same way.

This attitude is particularly important when the issues concern things the team leader did or did not do. Since many team members will be reluctant to criticize the team leader, it is important to keep these discussions objective and to focus on suggestions for how to better handle such situations in the future. If either you or the team leader appear defensive or angry, that is likely to inhibit further improvement discussions.

Make People Issues into Process Issues

Since processes guide people in doing their jobs, every process issue can be viewed as a personal problem by someone. Conversely, with few exceptions, people issues can be viewed as process problems. Either the process suggested an inappropriate action or the person didn't follow the process in the proper way. Since no reasonably sized process can possibly define every aspect of people's behavior, there are many ways to interpret any process. So if the discussion appears to be getting personal, whether about you or anyone else, try to state the problem in process terms and to consider how the process could be changed, how it might better be interpreted, or where the process users need more guidance in understanding how to use it.

15.2   The Postmortem Process

The mechanics of the postmortem process are much the same as for the other launch meetings. Start by getting volunteers for the timekeeper and recorder roles and then provide a brief meeting overview. The steps of the postmortem process are described in the following paragraphs.

Meeting Overview

In the meeting overview, describe the postmortem process and the results to be obtained at each step. While the meeting could consist of merely gathering facts and opinions, it should be much more. Postmortems are often ineffective because most people are reluctant to criticize others. They often see any effort to improve a process as an implied criticism of the coach, the team leader, or the other team members.

The principal point to impress upon all of the team members is that they should depersonalize their concerns and think in terms of objective process problems. While people will be involved in almost every issue, the team should focus on how people's behavior affected the process or on how the process affected the people's behavior. Emphasize that the purpose of the launch postmortem is to improve both the effectiveness and efficiency of the launch process. This can only be accomplished if everyone starts with an objective attitude.

Review Launch Data

The planning manager leads this part of the postmortem meeting. He or she reviews the data from the launch meetings and ensures that they are complete, accurate, and available. Also make sure that these materials are put into the team's project notebook. For an initial team launch, there will not generally be an existing project notebook, so you or the team leader should ask for a volunteer to set up the project notebook and to maintain it at least until the next team relaunch.

Prepare PIPs

You lead the next step of the postmortem script, and your job is to elicit comments and suggestions from all of the team members on how to improve the process. Process improvement is particularly difficult for programmers, since they are used to writing programs that are made up of predefined instructions. Processes are much like programs, however, so process improvement would be like programmers thinking about how to change the instruction set while they were writing a program. For programmers, this is a major attitude change and it will not happen quickly or easily.

There are many possible ways to lead the process improvement discussion. Your principal objective, however, is to get the team members talking and thinking about the process. For their first team launch, they will generally have nothing to compare this launch with and will not initially have many, if any, ideas or suggestions. If you ask leading questions and don't give up too quickly, that should start the team members thinking and talking. You will then likely get some helpful ideas. The final section of this chapter discusses various strategies for getting the team members to actively participate in the postmortem meeting.

Launch Evaluation

The launch evaluation is a relatively straightforward process of having the team leader and team members complete the launch process and coach evaluation forms for return to the SEI. These forms are used by the SEI to monitor the quality of the TSP launch process and to identify any areas where it should be changed or improved. They also provide a way to monitor coach performance and to ensure that the SEI's coach training and qualification processes reflect your and your teams' latest experiences and that they continue to be effective.

After the team leader and team members have completed these forms, ask them if completing the forms suggested any further ideas for process improvement. If so, briefly discuss and document their additional thoughts.

Launch Meeting Documentation

The final postmortem step is meeting documentation. This is particularly important for the postmortem phase because you want to ensure that all of the PIPs and other suggestions are properly recorded and that copies are provided to the person assigned to implement them. Every outstanding action item should be recorded on the team's issue tracking system and copies of all the meeting records and data should be entered into the project notebook.

15.3   Postmortem Coaching Strategies

While there are many ways to handle process improvement discussions, the following are some techniques that are generally effective for starting the discussion and for handling sensitive topics.

Since the team will probably not have thought about changing the process, start by focusing on specific process steps. First ask for suggestions about the launch preparations and then address each launch meeting. You could close this part of the discussion by asking if anyone had any overall issues or concerns about the process and how it was handled.

Next, ask the team members to think of any places where your coaching style might have been more effective. It is not generally a good idea to ask for comments about other people but, if you have previously discussed this subject with the team leader or any of the team members, hopefully they will ask the team for comments on how they handled their parts of the launch as well.

Another strategy to use if people start arguing about who did or said what is to ask the team members to focus on what they heard and felt, rather than what somebody else said or meant. After all, we are all experts on what we heard or felt and, if a particular situation made us angry or defensive, that is a valid concern. Then the team members should be able to objectively discuss that subject and figure out how to avoid such problems in the future.

15.4 Summary

This chapter reviews the launch postmortem and why it is particularly important to the coach. It also discusses the proper team member attitude for the launch meeting. The seven key attitude elements are: there is always room for improvement, improvement is generally achieved through many small changes, the users have the best improvement ideas, everyone should be involved, identify all the problems, depersonalize and avoid getting defensive, and make people issues into process issues.

The chapter suggests three strategies for coaching the postmortem meeting. First, focus the discussion on specific process activities. This should help people think about problems and remember issues that had troubled them during the launch. Second, suggest that the team leader ask the team members about his or her leadership style and where they see opportunities for improvement. Hopefully, with proper advance coaching, the team members will also ask such questions about their own performance. Finally, if the discussions become argumentative, suggest that the team members concentrate on what they themselves each heard, thought, and felt rather than on what somebody else said or did.

16

Relaunching a Team Project

This chapter describes the TSP team relaunch. The script for the TSP relaunch is shown in Table 16.1. The topics covered in this chapter are

☐ What is a relaunch?

☐ Why do a relaunch?

☐ When to relaunch

☐ How to do a relaunch

☐ The relaunch process

☐ Revising the quality plan

☐ Concluding the relaunch

TSP teams should be led through the TSP launch or relaunch process by a qualified TSP coach. After they have successfully completed several TSP launches and relaunches, some teams may think they can follow the TSP scripts to relaunch their own projects. Generally, however, this is not desirable—particularly with relatively new teams, large teams that have many new team members, or projects that are in trouble. Under these conditions, teams need the help of an experienced TSP coach. In fact, even very experienced teams find that they need coaching help to produce sound plans and to consistently reach team consensus on all of the key issues.

16.1   What Is a Relaunch?

A team relaunch is the same as a launch, except that it is done by a team that has already completed a launch. In a relaunch, the team members update their plans based on what they have done since the prior launch or relaunch. This means that some of the steps of the launch process need not be repeated in the relaunch.

The major difference between a launch and a relaunch is that the team members have already worked together on the project, know each other, and can better coordinate their planning. Another important difference is that the team has already committed to management what they intend to do and, if that commitment is unchanged, they need not repeat the management meetings. However, if the project has changed in any significant respect, the relaunch process should be treated as a new launch and should follow all of the steps described in Chapters 5 through 15. The relaunch is basically a team launch with a few steps omitted. This means that the material in the previous chapters applies to the relaunch.

Table 16.1 TSP Team Relaunch—Script REL

Purpose	To guide integrated teams in relaunching a software-intensive project		
Entry Criteria	<ul><li>The relaunch preparation work has been completed (PREPR, PREPT).</li><li>The team leader has prepared the project status report.</li><li>The team leader and team members are available for the entire relaunch.</li><li>An authorized TSP coach is on hand to lead the relaunch.</li><li>The updated project notebook is available.</li><li>Note: to meet aggressive schedules, the next phase may be relaunched before the postmortem for the current phase.</li></ul>		
General	Timing		

	Day	1	2	3
	Meeting	1, 2, and 3	4 and 5	6, 7, and PM

If there are significant project changes, follow script LAU.

Step	Activities	Description
1	Project Status and Objectives	Hold team relaunch meeting 1 (script REL1). <ul><li>Review the relaunch process and introduce new team members.</li><li>Review the project status to date.</li><li>Understand management's goals for the project.</li></ul>

Table 16.1 (continued)

Step	Activities	Description
2	Team Goals and Roles	Hold team relaunch meeting 2 (script LAU2). • Update and document the team's goals. • Allocate team roles among team members.
3	Project Strategy and Support	Hold team relaunch meeting 3 (script LAU3). • Update the system conceptual design, and, if needed, a fix list. • Update the development strategy and products to be produced. • Review and update the development process to be used. • Review and update the process and support plans.
4	Overall Plan	Hold team relaunch meeting 4 (script LAU4). • Develop or update the size estimates and overall plan.
5	Quality Plan	Hold team launch meeting 5 (script LAU5). • Update the quality plan.
6	Balanced Plan	Hold team relaunch meeting 6 (script LAU6). • Allocate work to team members. • Produce bottom-up next-phase plans for each team member. • Produce a balanced next-phase plan for the team and each team member.
7	Project Risk Analysis	Hold team relaunch meeting 7 (script LAU7). • Identify and evaluate any new project risks. • Define risk assessment checkpoints and responsibilities. • Propose mitigation actions for near-term, high-impact risks.
8	Launch Report Preparation	There is no relaunch meeting 8.
9	Management Review	There is no relaunch meeting 9.
PM	Launch Postmortem	Hold team launch postmortem meeting (script LAUPM). • Gather launch data and produce a launch report. • Put the launch report in the project notebook. • Assess the launch process and prepare PIPs.
Exit Criteria		• The relaunch is completed. • Team roles, goals, processes, responsibilities, and plans are defined. • The relaunch data are in the project notebook (specification NOTEBOOK).

16.2   Why Do a Relaunch?

There are several reasons for holding a relaunch. These reasons are

☐ The limited planning horizon

☐ Cycle completion

☐ Project changes

☐ Team changes

The Limited Planning Horizon

An important part of the TSP launch process is producing the detailed team and developer plans. These plans not only allow the team to balance its workload, but they guide the members on precisely what to do. Generally, teams can make accurate and detailed plans for only a few weeks or months into the future. Even when the project is stable and much like a prior project, few people can make detailed plans for more than about three or four months.

A relaunch is also needed because of the normal fluctuations in the work. For many reasons, some developers will generally be ahead of their plans and others will be behind. The team must periodically adjust its plans, both to properly guide the work and to rebalance the workload.

Cycle Completion

Often, a project phase or cycle will be only a few months long. Therefore, it might seem convenient to plan a relaunch at that time. While this might appear to simplify relaunch planning, it rarely does. Project phases are arbitrary periods that roughly correspond to one part of the team's work. While it may sound reasonable in theory for a phase to end at a point in time, all of a phase's activities are rarely completed simultaneously. This is true even in cyclic processes that release complete products in each cycle. Some work is always left over from the prior cycle, and some tasks from the next cycle will usually have been started. In setting the relaunch date, therefore, it is generally best to ignore the project phase or cycle schedules and to concentrate on the team members' needs. If many members feel that their current plans are no longer helpful and that they need new plans, then the team should hold a relaunch.

Project Changes

Projects change all of the time. It is not just that requirements change: markets change, the competitive situation changes, and teams learn more about the desired product. When the circumstances have changed enough to make the current plan obsolete, it is time to make a new plan. If the changes are significant enough to impact the team's commitments to its customers or management, it should hold an entire new launch. Otherwise a relaunch should suffice.

For example, in its initial launch, one team made an overall plan for the next eighteen months and a detailed plan for four months. Within two weeks, however, the customer had requested a major requirements change. This change was so significant that the team decided to make a completely new plan. While this is an extreme case, it is appropriate to replan, relaunch, or even hold another project launch when the situation has changed so much that the current plan is no longer useful—even if it is only one week after the prior launch.

Team Changes

An important element of teamwork is having a team that can work to a common plan and toward an agreed-upon commitment. When teams lose members, the work these members planned to do must be reallocated. Also, when teams gain new members, these new members must be integrated into the team. Until they understand the plan and share in the team's commitment, they will not be a fully productive part of the team. Whenever there have been substantial changes in team membership, the team should relaunch.

As the team's coach, you must be sensitive to the need for periodic teambuilding. While the team may have been a cohesive and productive unit right after the initial launch, any changes in personnel, the plan, the team's goals, or even an individual's personal life can disrupt the team's ability to work cooperatively together. A team relaunch can serve as a periodic teambuilding exercise and it can help to maintain the group's effectiveness.

16.3   When to Relaunch

There is no simple way to decide when to do a relaunch. The team should periodically review its current plan and thoughtfully balance the pros and cons of doing a relaunch. Then, it should decide on a target date for that relaunch. While there are several reasons to do a relaunch, there are also valid reasons for not doing one. The three major reasons for not relaunching too often are

☐ Relaunches take time

☐ The changes are minor

☐ The risk of "analysis paralysis"

Relaunches Take Time

While it generally only takes two or three days to relaunch a project, every day in the project schedule is important. So, before the team decides to do a full relaunch, it should consider the alternatives and weigh their costs and benefits. The principal alternatives to holding a relaunch are to delay the relaunch to a later date or to make individual plan adjustments.

Generally, if the team members believe that their current plan does not provide sufficient guidance for their work or that the strategy, process, overall plan, or risks should be completely reassessed, a relaunch is needed. If all that is required is a detailed plan update, then a one-day replanning session is often adequate. However, if many of the team members feel that a broader reassessment is needed, the team should plan for a full relaunch.

Minor Changes

While projects change all of the time, most changes will be relatively minor, and many will not have a significant impact on the plan. When these minor changes only affect one or a few developers, then those developers can make new plans and the rest of the team can continue as before. Of course, this may not be possible if any of the individual changes are so severe that the team's workload must be rebalanced. Then it may be necessary for the team to reevaluate the entire plan and to adjust everyone's workload accordingly. This will require a launch or relaunch.

One way to tell if a relaunch is needed is to ask the developers if their plans help them decide what to do next. Even if their plans contain tasks that are no longer needed, if the developers know what to do or can make minor plan adjustments to get this information, then make the minor plan adjustments and delay the relaunch. Of course, this assumes that none of the other reasons for holding a relaunch apply.

"Analysis Paralysis"

A bureaucratic way to avoid taking action is something called **analysis paralysis**. This is when teams spend so much time refining and perfecting their plans that they seriously delay starting on the work. While this is not a common problem with development projects, it does occasionally happen and it can waste a lot of time.

For example, after one software organization conducted a complete Capability Maturity Model (CMMI) assessment, management decided to start a process-improvement program (Chrissis 2003). They formed a task group of experienced developers and asked them to spend one afternoon each week developing the organization's process-improvement plan. When the team completed the first draft of the plan, they presented it to the laboratory director who asked them to make several changes. It took the developers another two months to make these changes but, by the time they returned, the laboratory had a new director. This new director didn't like the new plan and called for more changes.

By then, the team was disgusted and was not very diligent in updating the plan. It was nearly a year before these developers were called to a management meeting to review their revised plan. Again, however, management suggested several changes. This cycle continued through two more laboratory directors and three more years. Finally, a new director arrived who told the management team to stop planning and start doing.

Planning is important, and a sound plan can help teams do almost any job faster and more efficiently than they could without a plan, but excessive planning is counterproductive and actually delays the work. Until developers start doing the job, they cannot really understand it. They will learn a lot from the first plan, but thereafter they learn progressively less from each revision. Until developers have worked with a plan for some time and can see how that plan fits the work and where it needs adjustment, replanning is generally a mistake. So, urge the teams you coach to replan when they need to but not to fall into the "analysis paralysis" trap.

16.4   How to Do a Relaunch

As shown in Figure 16.1, the relaunch is much like a launch. The purpose for the TSP relaunch is to adjust the plan based on the work that the team has already done and to produce a detailed plan for the next cycle. Ideally, if the project has progressed exactly as originally planned, the overall plan will still apply and all the team needs to do is to produce and balance the detailed plan for the next period. However, since projects rarely proceed entirely according to plan, teams will often have to change their overall plans.

As in the launch, teams should start by assessing and updating their overall plans. Usually, they can do this by refining their prior plans. The suggested

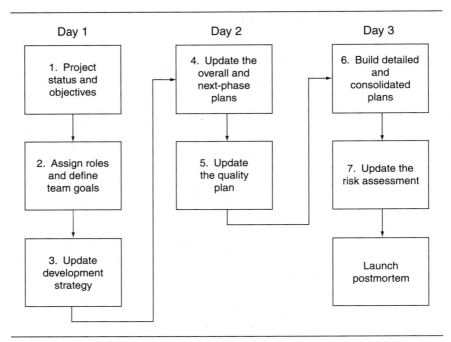

Figure 16.1 The TSP Relaunch Meetings

approach is to treat everything the team has done to date as history and to construct a new project plan starting at the relaunch point. This new plan should start at week number 1 with an initial earned value of zero. The new plan should include all of the work the team has to do from the relaunch point forward, regardless of the phase when that work was originally planned. For example, if any incomplete work remains from the prior planning period or phase, that work should be included in the new plan. The format of the TSP relaunch process is shown in Figure 16.1. It has no meetings 8 or 9 and a modified meeting 1.

16.5   The Relaunch Process

Except for the omitted meetings, the only places where the relaunch process differs from the launch process are in meetings 1 and 5. The following paragraphs review the relaunch process and describe the steps for revising the quality plan. The other relaunch steps are covered by the descriptions in the previous chapters on the launch meetings with the same numbers.

Project Status and Objectives—Relaunch Meeting 1

While there is no need for senior management to participate in the relaunch process, any interested managers or observers could attend meeting 1 for an update on the project's status. However, when management plans to attend this meeting, the team leader should present a full status review. Pages 1 and 2 of the TSP Status Specification in Table 16.2 suggest appropriate contents for this presentation. If management would like to review the team's final plan, add meetings 8 and 9 to the relaunch schedule and follow the guidelines given in Chapter 14 to prepare and present this plan.

In the relaunch, the first step is an overview of project status compared to plan. This will likely be the first time the team members and the coach have seen a comprehensive comparison of the project's progress against its plan. This review provides an opportunity for management and the team leader to congratulate the team on what it has done and to reemphasize the importance of the remaining work. The review also gives the coach a picture of project status and provides a comprehensive update for any managers or other interested observers. If the project notebook has been kept up to date, it should not take long to prepare this status presentation.

In concluding the status review, the team leader next reviews the team's progress against its goals, congratulates the team on what it has accomplished, and possibly adjusts the team's targets for the remaining goals.

Next, the team leader reviews any changes in management's goals for the project, describes why these changes were made, and explains how success will be measured. Then he or she answers any of the team's or coach's questions. Of course, if managers are present, they should also contribute answers where appropriate.

In closing relaunch meeting 1, the recorder reviews the outstanding action items with the participants and documents the meeting.

Table 16.2 TSP Project Status Report—Specification STATUS

Purpose	To guide the project in making accurate, complete, concise, and informative management status reports
General	• Frequent and informative management reports are essential to keep management informed of project status. • Management can most help the project when they thoroughly understand its status, risks, and issues.
Meeting Frequency	• Status meetings should be held weekly, biweekly, or monthly, as determined by management and the team. • If management even occasionally asks for project status information, increase report frequency.
Meeting Format	• Be guided by management's preferences and interests. • A consistent format saves preparation and meeting time.
Agenda and Problems	• Briefly cover the meeting agenda. • State at the outset any key issues or problems to be raised. • After a successful presentation, do not surprise management with a zinger at the end.
Project Overview	Unless **ALL** management attendees are familiar with the material, briefly summarize the project and its products.
Schedule Status	• Succinctly describe the project's status versus its plan. • Show cumulative and actual hours to date, and describe actions planned to address any resource problems. • Show earned value plan, actual, and projections, and describe actions planned to address any schedule problems.
Quality Status	• Briefly describe the quality plan. • Show data on quality performance versus plan, and describe actions planned to address any quality problems.
Risks and Issues	• Describe the principal project risks and issues and what is being done about them. • Describe where management's help is needed and precisely what you wish them to do. It helps to draft a list of actions needed from management in advance.
Prior Action Items	• Summarize the action item status from the last meeting. • Discuss **ALL** delinquent actions and needed next steps.
Current Action Items	• Review the action items from this meeting, including who, what, and when, and get agreement to the summary. • Review the decisions made in this meeting and who made them, and get agreement to the summary.
Meeting Report	• After the meeting, briefly summarize the meeting decisions and planned actions in a written report. • Distribute the report to all attendees and file a copy in the project notebook.

Table 16.2 (continued)

Purpose	• This page suggests specific STATUS report contents. • Some of the elements in these suggested report contents are described more fully on the previous page.
Suggested Approach	• Unless management suggests otherwise, present the basic report in management reviews. • Be prepared with the full report materials and present them only in response to questions.
Minimum Report Contents	At a minimum, the STATUS report must contain the following, • schedule status versus plan: use Gantt chart and EV formats • planned actions to resolve any schedule issues • any major risks and mitigation actions • any outstanding actions from prior meetings
Basic Report Contents	You should have a basic report ready to present at any time. The basic STATUS report should contain the following, • schedule status versus plan—use Gantt chart and EV formats • planned actions to resolve any schedule issues • planned versus actual weekly hours • staffing problems and needed actions • any major risks and mitigation actions • any outstanding actions from prior meetings
Standard Report Contents	Be prepared to present the standard report every week. The standard STATUS report should contain the following, • schedule status versus plan: use Gantt chart and EV formats • projected phase completion date • planned actions to resolve any schedule issues • planned versus actual weekly hours • staffing problems and needed actions • basic quality status (inspection rates, review rates, defect levels, and to-date yields versus the quality plan) • a review of all major risks and mitigation actions • the status of the actions from prior meetings
Full Report Contents	Be prepared to present the full report on request. The full STATUS report should contain the following, • schedule status versus plan: use Gantt chart and EV formats • projected phase and overall project completion dates • planned actions to resolve any schedule issues • planned versus actual weekly hours • staffing problems and needed actions • basic quality status (inspection rates, review rates, defect levels, and to-date yields versus the quality plan) • projected phase quality levels and PDF (defects per KLOC and percent defect free) • a review of all the major risks and mitigation actions • the status of the actions from prior meetings

16.6   Revising the Quality Plan

During the relaunch, teams use the same quality-planning process that they used for the launch. However, they only use historical injection and yield rates for the phases they have not yet started. The completed and partially completed phases are handled differently. Here, some or all of the defects removed will be known. The team will also have partial knowledge of the injected defects, but will not know the phases where some of the defects to be found in the future have already been injected.

To estimate how many defects were likely to have already been injected in each completed phase, use the actual data on the defect-removal phases the team has completed. For example, suppose that the team had conducted a requirements inspection and found nine major defects. If the developers knew the inspection yield, they could calculate the number of defects in the product before the inspection. Then they could estimate where these defects had been injected. A technique for estimating the yields of completed phases is described in Chapter 19.

When the team has both historical and current project defect data, it estimates phase yields by examining prior team data for similar inspections. The team first examines the developers' data for the completed reviews and inspections for this project and judges their yields. A higher rate would suggest a lower yield, and a lower rate would suggest a higher yield. Then, with these yield estimates and the known times for each completed project phase, the team can calculate the defect injection rates.

Once it has yield and injection rate estimates for all of the completed and future phases, the team can complete the quality plan in the normal way. It then reviews the planned number of defects injected and removed in each phase and, if the values look reasonable and are consistent with the actual numbers of defects found in the completed phases, the team has its revised quality plan. If the numbers do not look reasonable, the team should adjust the injection and yield numbers until the planned defects by phase look reasonable and are consistent with the team's actual defect data. Of course, this method will only work for teams that have consistently recorded all of their defect data.

16.7   A Quality Replanning Example

Suppose that a team had the actual and planned time and defect data shown in Table 16.3. How would it make a new quality plan? First, to simplify the example, only a few phases are shown. Second, in the example, the detailed design

(DLD), detailed-design reviews (DLDR), and detailed-design inspections (DLDI) are completed, but the coding, code review, and compiling phases are estimated to be 25% completed. Also, only about 8% of the code-inspection or unit-testing work has been done.

The following steps guide teams in making an updated quality plan. Using data from Table 16.3, the replanning results are shown in Table 16.4.

1. Use the actual times for the plan times of the completed phases and the estimated remaining times plus the actual times for the partially completed phases.

2. Using the available data for defects injected per hour, calculate the defects injected per phase. For coding, this would be 648.0*2 = 1,296.0.

3. Using the available data, estimate the yields of each defect-removal phase. Since all the DLD reviews were completed, DLDR yield would be 186.0/542.3 = 34.3%. For the code reviews, the plan shows 1,838.3 − 186 − 268 = 1,384.3 defects to be removed by the code reviews. Since 25% of the reviews have been done, the total that could have been found is 1,384.3*0.25 = 346.1. Since only 86 defects were found, that is an estimated yield of 86/346.1 = 24.9%.

4. Calculate the estimated numbers of defects injected and removed per phase. Using the 24.9% yield and the 1,384.3 defects from step 3 gives a total of 344 as the planned total defects to be removed in code reviews. This assumes that future code reviews will have the same yields as those already done.

5. If the team members plan to improve their review yields, they should commit to specific rates before adjusting the yields in the quality plan. They must, however, ensure that the planned defect numbers are consistent with the actual defects found in the completed and partially completed phases.

6. Since the detailed design reviews and inspections have been completed, the plan and actual numbers of defects removed should be equal.

7. If the team members do not plan to change their yields, the planned defects removed in code review and compile should be 4 times those actually removed to date in the same phases (since only 25% of this work has been completed). Also, for code inspection and unit test, the planned defects removed should be 12.5 times the actual numbers found to date (only 8% completed).

8. When done, examine the yield and defects-removed plans to see if the numbers appear reasonable. If not, make any needed adjustments.

The resulting quality plan is shown in Table 16.4. As you can see, the detailed design and code review yields are very low. Urge the team to set more aggressive yield objectives, adjust its quality plan accordingly, and take steps to actually achieve these higher yields.

Table 16.3 Sample Partial Quality Plan Data

Plan Summary Time in Phase (hours) Phases	Plan Times	Actual to Date	Percent Completed
Detailed Design	0	723.0	100
Detailed Design Review	0	116.0	100
Detailed Design Inspection	0	234.0	100
Coding	648.0	162.0	25
Code Review	85.8	28.6	25
Compile	40.5	13.5	25
Code Inspection	439.3	38.2	8
Unit Test	337.0	29.3	8
Total Time	1,550.6	1,344.6	
Defects Injected Phases	**Plan Total Defects**	**Actual to Date**	
Detailed Design	542.3	486	
Coding	1,296.0	220	
Total Defects Injected	1,838.3	706	
Defects Removed Phases	**Plan Total Defects**	**Actual to Date**	
Detailed Design Review	186	186	
Detailed Design Inspection	268	268	
Code Review	344	86	
Compile	504	126	
Code Inspection	325	26	
Unit Test	175	14	
Total Defects Removed	1,802	706	

Table 16.4 Sample Partial Quality Plan

Plan Summary Time in Phase (hours) Phases	Plan Times	Actual to Date	Plan Total Times	Percent Completed
Detailed Design	0	723.0	723.0	100
Detailed Design Review	0	116.0	116.0	100
Detailed Design Inspection	0	234.0	234.0	100
Coding	648.0	162.0	648.0	25
Code Review	85.8	28.6	114.4	25
Compile	40.5	13.5	54.0	25
Code Inspection	439.3	38.2	477.5	8
Unit Test	337.0	29.3	366.3	8
Total Time	1,550.6	1,344.6	2,733.2	

Defects Injected Phases	Plan Total Defects	Actual to Date		
Detailed Design	542.3	486		
Coding	1296.0	220		
Total Defects Injected	1838.3	706		

Defects Removed Phases	Plan Total Defects	Actual to Date	Scaled Up	To Be Removed
Detailed Design Review	186.0	186	186	542.3
Detailed Design Inspection	268.0	268	268	356.3
Code Review	344.0	86	344	1,384.3
Compile	504.0	126	504	1,040.3
Code Inspection	325	26	325	536.3
Unit Test	175	14	175	211.3
Total Defects Removed	1802	706		
Defects after Unit Test	36			

Table 16.4 (continued)

Defect Injection Rates Phases	Plan per Hour			
Detailed Design	0.75			
Coding	2.00			
Defect Removal Yield Phases	**Plan %**			
Detailed Design Review	34.3			
Detailed Design Inspection	75.2			
Code Review	24.9			
Compile	48.4			
Code Inspection	60.6			
Unit Test	82.8			

16.8   Concluding the Relaunch

Following quality planning, the team members produce and consolidate their detailed plans, balance their plans, reassess project risks, and conduct the relaunch postmortem. These steps are all described in Chapters 12, 13, and 15. If there are minor commitment changes, the team leader merely informs management and any other involved parties. However, if there are any significant schedule, risk, or other project changes, suggest that the team hold a meeting 9 with management. Then for that meeting, follow the pertinent parts of meetings 8 and 9 as described in Chapter 14.

16.9   Summary

This chapter describes the TSP relaunch process. A team relaunch is the same as a launch except that it is done by a team that has already done a launch. In a relaunch, the team members update and adjust their plans for what they have accomplished since the prior launch or relaunch. The TSP relaunch process is described as is the modified meeting 1 used in the relaunch. There are no meetings 8 or 9. Other than these changes, the relaunch process follows the TSP launch process described in Chapters 5 through 15.

A relaunch is needed when the circumstances have changed enough to make the current plan obsolete or when the team has completed much of the work in its current plan and needs a new plan for the next several months. Since the decision to do a relaunch is a matter of judgment, the team should periodically review its current plan and thoughtfully balance the pros and cons of doing a relaunch. One way to tell if a relaunch is needed is to ask the developers if their plans show them what to do next. If the developers' plans tell them what to do, there is generally no need for a relaunch.

Reference

Chrissis, Mary Beth, Mike Konrad, and Sandy Shrum. *CMMI: Guidelines for Process Integration and Process Improvement*. Boston: Addison-Wesley. 2003.

PART III

Coaching a TSP Project

Steve did a good job of coaching the team launch, and management bought the team's plan. Right after the launch, however, Steve had to be on the East Coast for several weeks. He did not get back to check up on the team for nearly a month, and by that time the members had run into so many problems that they quit using the TSP and refused to try it again.

Three of the seven-member team had been reluctant to use the TSP and one of them, Bret, was actively opposed. Right from the start, the team members all had trouble using the TSP support tool. Then they discovered that their plan didn't really fit the work they had to do. Bret argued that the TSP was designed for commercial work and wouldn't work for an embedded system like the one they were developing. Since Steve wasn't there and no one else could provide tool support or explain how to fix their plan, Bret talked the team into going back to their old way of working.

Even though this project turned out to be a disaster, and even though several other projects later used the TSP very successfully, Bret and the rest of this team never again agreed to use the TSP. First impressions are critical. If you can't coach a team for at least a full week right after the launch and provide at least weekly phone consultation for the next month or two, delay the launch until you or some other qualified TSP coach can do so. Without someone to answer questions, solve problems, and otherwise provide encouragement and support, teams often run into problems and are liable to quit using the TSP. This is unfortunate, since these problems are invariably easy to solve.

The four chapters in Part III deal with how to coach teams in properly using the TSP, maintaining their plans, doing quality work, and conducting periodic project postmortems. Chapter 17 discusses some of the most common issues and problems teams face right after their first TSP launch. They are frequently confused about how to record data, revise their plans, or manage their time. Without proper coaching in these first few weeks, few teams will be able to use the TSP process properly.

Chapter 18 addresses the problems of continuous planning. Once a team has developed its initial plan, the developers must maintain that plan. Right after the launch, first-time TSP teams often find that their detailed plans are incomplete and must be revised. Also, as they do their work, some will finish tasks earlier than planned and others will take longer. This chapter describes how to help teams adjust their plans and how to recognize and correct workload imbalance problems. Finally, the chapter discusses plan data and how teams can use these data to manage their projects and to conduct management status reviews.

Chapter 19 covers the responsibilities team members have for managing the quality of their personal work. It describes how to guide teams in measuring, tracking, and managing quality, and it discusses ways to support the team leader in ensuring that a quality product is produced. The principal issue is helping the team leader build and maintain the team members' personal commitment to quality.

Chapter 20 describes the project postmortem. While the project postmortem is similar to the launch postmortem covered in Chapter 15, there are some important differences. This chapter describes these differences, and it shows how you can help teams use the postmortem most effectively right before each project relaunch and at the end of the project. A properly run postmortem will help the team and its members improve their estimating, planning, and quality management performance.

17

Post-Launch Coaching

Once you have trained the managers and team members and have successfully launched a new TSP team, you may feel that the coaching job is done. This is not true. If you do not work closely with the team, at least for the first few weeks after the launch, the members almost certainly will not use the TSP properly, and they could even abandon it. Immediately after the launch is when teams most need the help and guidance of a qualified TSP coach. This chapter describes the steps required to coach a TSP team after the launch. This is also when you will first be able to assess the team leader's leadership skills. While this chapter deals primarily with coaching new teams, it also suggests ways to help experienced teams improve their TSP performance. For the leadership topics, consult Chapters 2, 25, and 26. The topics covered in this chapter are as follows.

- ☐ Starting new teams
- ☐ The coaching process
- ☐ The post-launch briefing
- ☐ The weekly team meeting
- ☐ The daily stand-up meeting
- ☐ The weekly status report
- ☐ Coaching inspections
- ☐ Coaching individuals

☐ Coaching role managers

☐ Coaching the team leader

☐ The project notebook

☐ The checkpoint review

☐ The coaching plan

17.1   Starting New Teams

When teams first use the TSP, they can easily become discouraged and revert to their pre-TSP habits. New teams usually have lots of problems and questions. The first few weeks after the TSP launch are critical and a qualified TSP coach must be available to answer the team's questions, help with tool issues, and ensure that the team properly follows its process and plan. If a qualified coach is not available, the team will almost certainly have problems and there is a good chance that the members will use the TSP incorrectly.

17.2   The Coaching Process

The TSP post-launch coaching activity starts during the launch and continues for the duration of the project. The initial team coaching can take a lot of time for a few weeks but, if you start out properly, the time demands will quickly abate. While it is most desirable to have a resident coach at the team's location, this is often impractical. If you are remote, arrange to be on-site for the first full week and for a day or two each week for the first month or two after the team launch. After that, consult with the team by phone every few days and visit at least once a month. The principal topics to address during this initial coaching period are covered in the rest of this chapter.

17.3   The Post-Launch Briefing

Before the team can properly record its time, size, and defect data, the members must know how to use their TSP support tool. With a little training and experience, TSP tools are not very hard to use. However, the TSP is a large and sophis-ticated process, and any properly designed TSP support tool will necessarily have many functions, options, and procedures. Building tool skills will therefore take a little time.

When teams are not guided through the basic TSP tool operations, they must learn how to enter data and modify their plans by themselves. It can take several days just to learn the basic tool operations through trial and error. To guard against tool and other problems, hold a post-launch briefing at the end of the launch to familiarize new team members with the TSP tool, the weekly meeting, and team inspections. The post-launch briefing takes a few hours, but it can save the team several days of frustration and false starts.

17.4 The Weekly Team Meeting

The weekly team meeting is one of the most important parts of the TSP process. It is where all of the team members review their status, resolve issues, and decide how to proceed. The weekly meeting is one of the things that differentiates TSP teams from typical software projects. In addition, many TSP teams have found that a brief stand-up meeting every day is an ideal way to keep the members focused on the top-priority tasks and to arrange for needed peer support. Nor-mally, on software teams, the members only interact socially or when their tasks require it, but not as a regular team activity. The stand-up and weekly meetings solve that problem. From a coaching perspective, your initial objectives for the weekly team meeting are as follows.

- ☐ Make sure that the team is holding weekly meetings and covering all of the required topics.
- ☐ Verify that the team members are following the defined meeting process or changing that process to suit their personal preferences. After using the TSP WEEK script for a while, teams often want to change the meeting agenda and process. This is perfectly acceptable as long as they update that script to represent the way that they actually conduct the meeting.
- ☐ Have the quality manager look at the team's weekly data to check that all of the members are gathering and reporting their size, time, and defect data, and verify that the planning manager is properly consolidating the team's weekly status.
- ☐ See if the team leader or planning manager is distributing the weekly meet-ing agenda in advance and if the meeting recorder is promptly documenting the meeting results.

Once the team is meeting these basic objectives, your next interests are as follows.

- ☐ The team is accurately assessing and reporting its status.
- ☐ The team members follow their plans or make timely plan changes to accurately reflect what they are doing.
- ☐ The role managers are performing their defined tasks and the team leader is using the role managers to provide appropriate team support.
- ☐ The team is tracking the key risks and establishing timely mitigation or avoidance actions.
- ☐ The team members are identifying and resolving issues and tracking the follow-up actions to completion.
- ☐ The team is properly concluding its meetings by reviewing open action items, completing the meeting minutes, and updating the project notebook.

Once the team members are properly conducting their weekly meetings, you need not attend every one. However, you should occasionally drop in to ensure that they continue to follow the process and to work cooperatively as a group.

17.5   The Daily Stand-Up Meeting

Because TSP team members often have a great many tasks in their detailed plans and because priorities change very rapidly in modern development work, each developer's priorities must also change. Since these changes will frequently involve several team members, and since all of the team members must understand their and everyone else's priorities to manage their own work, a daily kick-off meeting with the entire team can be very helpful.

This daily meeting is also the ideal time for the team leader to reemphasize the current top-priority tasks and check on the status of the work. To keep the meeting brief and to the point and to avoid the problems of arranging for conference rooms, it is often helpful to have the team leader and all of the members stand up during these meetings.

17.6   The Weekly Status Report

Part of the summary data from a team's typical weekly status report is shown in Figure 17.1. While various TSP support tools show many other weekly items, the basic data teams need to manage their work are each team member's and the entire team's planned and actual hours and earned value for each week and for the project cycle to date. One additional item that is generally very helpful is the hours each member and the total team planned to spend and have spent on the tasks completed to date. Note that in this example, the planned to-date hours for completed tasks of 238.1 are for the 14.9 EV of tasks completed to date. Since the 169.8 actual hours are for the same tasks, you can see that the completed work on this project was overestimated by about 40%.

This team of five members had been working for six weeks. Since several of the members had to spend part of their time testing the prior release, they all struggled to reach their planned total to-date task hours. By week 6, they had just made it. While the team appears to be 17% behind schedule, this is due primarily to partially completed tasks. In providing coaching guidance, some topics to discuss with the team are as follows.

1. The team has spent 295.5 task hours to date but has only spent 169.8 of the hours on completed tasks. This suggests that the members have spent a large amount of time (125.7 hours or 2.3 weeks of work) on tasks that have not been completed. While there are many possible explanations for this, a typical reason is poor task definition. Where task completion depends on someone else, a team member should split the task into at least two parts: one for before the other person's participation and one for their remaining work.

2. The completed tasks have only taken about 60% of the planned time. While this could indicate an overestimate, it could also be caused by team members not spending enough time on the design, review, and inspection tasks. If this is the case, the team members will likely have quality problems when they get into test.

3. The planned total project hours were 1,695 (100*295.0/17.4). Based on the project's current status, and assuming that the job really was overestimated by 40%, the total project hours will be 1,695*169.8/238.1=1,208.8 hours.

Weekly Data	Plan	Actual	Plan/ Actual
Project hours for this week	55.0	54.6	1.01
Project hours this cycle to date	295.0	295.5	1.00
Earned value for this week	3.9	3.8	1.03
Earned value this cycle to date	17.4	14.9	1.17
To-date hours for tasks completed	238.1	169.8	1.40

Figure 17.1 Weekly Team Summary Data

4. With 295.5 hours spent to date, there are 913.3 hours to go. At the current hourly rate of 54.6 hours, the remaining work will take 16.7 weeks. This means that the team would finish 8.3 weeks ahead of the 31-week schedule.

5. However, if the team continues to earn value at its average rate to date, it would earn 2.48 EV a week (14.9/6). At this rate, the job would take 34.3 more weeks and be 9.3 weeks late instead of 8.3 weeks early.

In coaching the team, review these data and find out exactly where the team stands. Then help the team leader and members develop a plan to deal with whatever problems this analysis uncovers.

17.7   Coaching Inspections

Once the team has started on its project and is beginning to produce work products, the members will soon start to conduct inspections. While the team's PSP training spent substantial time on personal reviews, it did not address team inspections. This is because an inspection is a team activity and cannot be done alone. Therefore, few if any of the team members will know how to conduct a TSP inspection.

To do quality work, TSP teams must do thorough personal reviews as well as complete team inspections. They should do reviews and inspections for all of their work products, starting with the initial requirements and continuing through to the final delivered code. The inspections should also include the various test and support products. For example, the requirements inspections should cover the system test plan and procedures. High-level design inspections should review the integration test plans and test cases. The detailed design inspections should examine the functional test plans and procedures. Finally, the code inspections should thoroughly examine the unit test plans and test cases.

While the inspection process involves many considerations, there is a great deal of literature about inspections and how they are done. The TSP inspection process is described in Appendix C of *Introduction to the Team Software Process*^{SM} (Humphrey 2000). If you are not familiar with this process, read this appendix before coaching a team inspection.

In coaching team inspections, consider the following guidelines.

☐ An inspection moderator must be available and prepared. Generally, the team's quality manager will serve as the inspection moderator.

☐ If the inspection team members are not properly prepared, the inspection moderator must defer the inspection meeting until everyone is ready.

☐ The inspection team members should follow the TSP inspection process when conducting the inspection.

☐ All inspection team members should properly record their inspection data.

☐ The moderator calculates the inspection yield and the estimated number of remaining defects.

☐ The moderator and all inspection team members understand the nature of the defect-remaining estimate and reach appropriate conclusions on further quality actions for the inspected product.

17.8 Coaching Individuals

Since the team members have all been trained in the PSP, they will be accustomed to having a coach review and comment on their data. To ensure that they continue to use the PSP practices and that they properly record and use all of their personal data, start by reviewing every developer's TSP data every week. If some developers do not properly record their data, check with them to understand the problems and then help them gather data correctly.

Generally, if the team members know that either you or the quality manager will review their data every week and that one of you will follow up whenever they do sloppy or incomplete work, they are more likely to record their data. Even after the members start properly recording their data, you must occasionally check to ensure that they continue to do so. Whenever you or the quality manager find that a member is not properly gathering the required data, make sure that the quality manager contacts that member as soon as possible and gets the problems fixed.

Occasionally, a team member will refuse to gather all of the required TSP data, regardless of anything you say. When this happens, review the situation with the team leader and decide how to handle it. The issue of handling team member problems is discussed further in Chapter 26.

17.9 Coaching Role Managers

The team-member roles are discussed in Chapter 8. While these role descriptions provide general guidance, each team member should think proactively about the responsibilities of his or her roles. Each team and team leader should evolve the specific set of role responsibilities and practices that best suit the situation, and they should feel free to adjust the role definitions to suit their personal preferences and skills.

The purpose of the TSP team roles is to help the team members take responsibility for managing their own project and working environment. Instead of waiting for someone else to handle a problem, team members should actively solve the problems by themselves. As you talk with the team members, discuss their assigned roles. While some role activities will concern current issues and problems, others should look further ahead. If the issues that the role managers anticipate are not reasonably imminent, they need not spend much time on them right now. However, they should identify the actions that will be needed in the future and enter them into their personal task plans. Once the members begin to anticipate problems, they will be more likely to take these role actions when the proper time comes. They will also be more likely to think ahead about other issues and deal with them in a timely way.

17.10   Coaching the Team Leader

To be most effective in coaching the team leader, your initial goal must be to build a trusting and cooperative mutual relationship. Once you have done this, you should be able to work together to build a productive and effective team. If you are unable to build this trusting and cooperative relationship, you almost certainly will have trouble coaching this team. To build this relationship, consider the following guidelines.

- ☐ Personally review your coaching plan with the team leader. If possible, do this before you review the plan with the team in launch meeting 8.

- ☐ Keep the team leader informed of your actions. Never surprise the team leader, and be the first to report your actions to him or her.

- ☐ Never, under any conditions, go to the team leader's management with any issue concerning this team or team leader without first reviewing your plans with the team leader.

- ☐ If the team leader disagrees with a proposed action, don't take the action without first resolving the issue with the team leader or escalating it to senior management for resolution. Remember, this is the team leader's team and you will be most effective if you and the team leader work cooperatively together.

- ☐ Finally, remember that your objective is to guide the team leader toward a coaching style of leadership. Ultimately, you want the team leader to take over most of your coaching activities. You can only accomplish this objective by working together cooperatively.

Coaching the team leader must be a top priority for, as pointed out in *TSP^SM—Leading a Development Team*, the team leader's performance is critical to the team's success (Humphrey 2006). However, in coaching team leaders, remember that their principal job is to do the following.

1. Deliver a quality product on its committed schedule and for its planned costs.
2. Ensure that the team does quality work.
3. Build and maintain the team as an effective working unit.

This is important because, if your coaching recommendations appear to conflict with team leader's top schedule and cost priorities, you will probably not get much cooperation. Therefore, whenever you have trouble working with a team leader, see if the team leader believes that your suggestions are likely to cause cost or schedule problems. If so, correct that misimpression or change your recommendations.

The principles behind the TSP process are that teams are most effective when properly managed and led, and that team leaders can best do their jobs by ensuring that their team members are efficiently and effectively following their defined processes and plans.

17.11   The Project Notebook

The project notebook is the official file for storing the team's plans, processes, and data. While the team members probably will not use the notebook extensively at first, they will need to use its historical data when making future plans, reporting project results, or demonstrating their team's performance. It provides an orderly, complete, and permanent reference for the team's data and results. By using these data, teams can set realistic but aggressive goals, improve their performance, protect themselves from overcommitments, and demonstrate their capabilities. Impress upon your teams the importance of establishing and maintaining their project notebooks, and ensure that they have assigned notebook maintenance responsibility to one of the team members. While the notebook could be assigned to any of the TSP roles, it most appropriately belongs with the process manager.

17.12   The Team-Member Notebook

Some team members may become so interested in the TSP process and so motivated to improve their personal performance that they start saving and using their

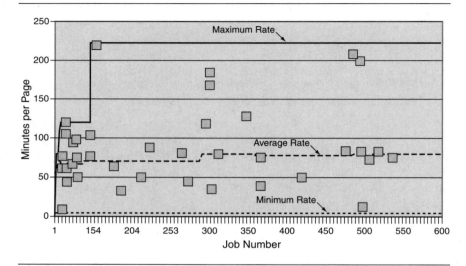

Figure 17.2 Sample Technical Report Productivity History

personal project data. When someone starts doing this, suggest that they consider establishing a personal project notebook. Such a notebook can be very helpful in planning by providing a ready reference to prior project data.

The two items that are most important for such a personal project notebook are a project plan summary for every completed project—with the planned and actual size, time, and defect data—and a summary of the size and time data for all projects in a category. This is useful in making PROBE estimates for future work. To facilitate using these data, it is also helpful to produce a summary scatter chart of productivity experience for prior projects of each type. One such chart is shown in Figure 17.2. Such charts are particularly helpful when task productivity varies widely, as it did in this example of report-writing tasks. Then, in planning a new project, it is easy to see the prior productivity range and judge where the new project will likely fall.

17.13   The Checkpoint Review

The TSP process calls for a checkpoint review about one to three months after the first team launch, and a second checkpoint after the first relaunch. If needed, follow-up checkpoints should be done again a month or two after each relaunch.

If there are problems in any of the areas covered by the checkpoint, these problems must be addressed promptly or the team's performance will suffer.

The primary purpose of the checkpoint is to help the team. Often, teams will have trouble gathering and managing their data, consolidating their team summaries, or generating progress reports. While these problems are usually easy to fix, they can waste a lot of team time and discourage the team.

The second purpose of the checkpoint is to assess the team's process fidelity. For this objective, it is necessary to examine data on every member's work and to see if everyone is following the process and gathering and reporting all of the required data. If there are data-gathering problems, it is important to fix them as soon as possible. Without good data, it is almost impossible to coach the team.

The third priority is to see if the team and all of the members are following the process. Are the developers' plans suitably detailed? Is the team leader holding weekly meetings? Are there weekly meeting agendas and reports? Also check on the role managers and see how they are handling their responsibilities. Do they understand what management wants them to do, and are they doing it?

Fourth, is the team properly using its data to assess and report on project status? This topic is covered in Chapter 18.

The fifth objective of the checkpoint concerns the use of the quality data. Are the members planning to do quality work and do their quality data indicate that they are succeeding? Does the quality manager monitor the quality of the team inspections and are inspections redone if inadequate? Finally, is the quality of every module examined before release to see if the quality goals were met and, if not, are remedial actions being taken?

While the checkpoint objectives are relatively straightforward and you might think that you could merely ask the team members about each item, this approach will not work. The first time I conducted a TSP checkpoint, I knew from the team's data that few of the members were properly recording their time or defect data. After introducing the checkpoint objectives and schedule in an opening management and team meeting, I met with each team member privately and asked about his or her data gathering. As I had found by examining the team's available data, nobody was doing a very good job of data recording. While everybody gave tool problems as an excuse, it was clear that nobody had tried very hard to gather the data.

When I reported my findings to management and the team members in the final meeting, the senior manager wanted to know why the members were not doing a better job of gathering their data. A few of them mentioned tool problems, but most said nothing. The team members were very defensive and clearly viewed the checkpoint exercise as a management audit, not as a way to help them to do a better job. On reflection, I realized that I had started with a negative attitude about the team's performance and was intent on "fixing it." Unfortunately, this attitude affected the way I ran the checkpoint.

The checkpoint process addresses this perception problem by following a procedure much like a process assessment (Humphrey 1989). The approach is to concentrate on asking open-ended questions and to not start with an "audit attitude." If you are convinced that the developers are not doing their jobs properly, they will sense your attitude and view the checkpoint as an audit. Your objective in conducting the checkpoint must be to learn what the team members think and to devise ways to help them address the problems they have. The fact that they may not recognize or understand all of their problems will almost certainly come out in the discussions. For example, if the topic of data gathering does not come up, you could ask a nondirective question such as, "What about data gathering?" This should at least get the members' concerns out in the open and provide you with some basis for dealing with them.

By concentrating on the team members' issues and concerns, you should be able to make the checkpoint a positive experience for them, as well as to help them address the issues that most concern them. If they are not yet concerned about data gathering, that means that they do not understand how data can help them to do a better job or how it can protect them from becoming overcommitted.

The power of TSP teams comes largely from the data, and team members must gather these data before they can use them to manage and improve the way they work. If it takes the team members time to understand the importance of data, be patient and plan for another checkpoint in a few months. In the meantime, concentrate your coaching efforts on convincing the team leader and the team members that they need to gather data to manage their process effectively. Then they will be more willing to gather the data. While you must mention the data gathering issue in the final findings review with management, do it in a way that does not imply criticism of the team or any team members and emphasize how useful the data will be for everyone.

The checkpoint is an excellent time to show the team how to address its problems. For example, one coach found that most of the members were upset about the volume of tasks that other groups were dumping on them. The coach showed them how to use their data to resist these demands, and the team's morale and performance quickly improved.

17.14   The Coaching Plan

During launch meeting 8, review your coaching plan with the team and provide the members with adequate time to comment on it and suggest changes. This is a good time to establish a hotline procedure for reaching you in emergencies. As part of this procedure, provide the team with access to an alternate coach who the team can reach when you are not available.

When the team members have problems and cannot get help, they are often in the middle of an important project task. If they can't immediately reach you or some other coach, they almost certainly will revert to their pre-TSP methods rather than waiting to hear from you. Then, once they do this, they will probably stop calling on you for help. So be available and, if you cannot be available for one or more days, arrange for an alternate coach to be "on call." The key measure of your initial success as a coach is your ability to answer all of the team members' questions promptly, preferably within a few minutes and certainly within an hour.

While there is no set format for the TSP coaching plan, several provisions are particularly important. As shown in the sample coaching plan in Table 17.1, the key plan provisions are as follows.

☐ For the first few weeks, ensure that you are available to answer the team's questions. If you cannot always be available in person, by phone, or via e-mail, arrange to have an alternate coach answer the team's questions.

☐ Participate in team meetings for a month or more, either in person or by conference phone call, to ensure that the meetings are properly and regularly conducted.

☐ Attend the first TSP team inspection and, if there are problems, attend subsequent inspections.

☐ Review the planning manager's initial data consolidation and promptly resolve any problems or issues.

☐ Have the team leader or planning manager provide you with copies of the team's consolidated data and each team member's data every week. Review these data and promptly discuss any problems with the relevant team members.

☐ In general, participate in any team activity the first time it is conducted. Examples would be project postmortems, inspections, and management reviews.

Draft the coaching plan before the team launch, revise it based on what happens during the launch, and then review it with the team leader before discussing it with the team in launch meeting 8. Then make any appropriate plan changes or additions suggested by the team. Also suggest that the team include a summary of the coaching plan in its meeting 9 report to management.

Table 17.1 Sample TSP Coaching Plan

Plan for John Doe to coach the TSP xy team at Acme Corporation	
Coach: John Doe	• Business phone: 123-456-7890 • Cell phone: 234-567-8901 • E-mail: jdoe@acme.com
Alternate coach: Jane Smith	• Business phone: 123-456-8863 • Cell phone: 234-567-0682 • E-mail: jsmith@acme.com
Week 1: September 1–5	• On site at Acme
• Meet with team members to answer questions and provide assistance on tool and process usage	
Week 2: September 8–13	• On site at Acme
• Assist the planning manager in consolidating the team's data • Review initial team data • Attend the first team meeting • Meet with team members to answer questions, provide assistance, and discuss their data	
Week 3: September 15–20	• Remote (by conference or personal phone)
• Review the team's data • Attend the team meeting • Discuss data questions with selected team members • Answer team members' questions as needed	
Week 4 and every week thereafter	• Remote or on-site, as appropriate
• Review the team's data • Attend the team meeting if needed • Discuss data questions with selected team members if needed • Participate in the first team inspection when held • Participate in subsequent team inspections as needed • Answer team members' questions as needed	

17.15   Summary

This chapter describes how to coach new TSP teams. Immediately after the team's first TSP launch, be available to answer team members' questions and to provide assistance as the team starts to use the TSP process. Without such support, first-time TSP teams generally have problems.

The principal steps required to prepare for TSP post-launch coaching are to prepare a coaching plan and to review that plan with the team leader and team members. Then, immediately after the launch, conduct a post-launch briefing to show the team members how to use the TSP support tool to gather data, how to hold weekly meetings, and how to conduct inspections. Finally, in the weeks following the launch, be available to answer the team members' questions, attend the team's weekly meetings, and discuss data gathering with the team members and team leader. As the project progresses, participate in one or more team inspections and provide guidance on how to properly conduct inspections and use the inspection data.

References

Humphrey, Watts S. *Managing the Software Process*. Reading, MA: Addison-Wesley. 1989.

Humphrey, Watts S. *Introduction to the Team Software Process^{SM}*. Boston: Addison-Wesley. 2000.

Humphrey, Watts S. *TSP^{SM}—Leading a Development Team*. Boston: Addison-Wesley. 2006.

18

Maintaining the Plan

Since few people can plan accurately, most of us should plan often. In fact, the best planning strategy is for teams to make new plans whenever their current plans are out of date. This chapter explains the nature of continuous planning and why teams need to periodically adjust and refine their plans.

This chapter assumes that the team members are doing a reasonable job of following their quality plans. If so, their plan data can be very helpful in determining project status and in understanding where and how to plan recovery actions. However, if they are not closely following their quality plan, they are probably building poor-quality products. Then their schedules will have a large and unpredictable amount of time in test, and it will then be impossible to accurately predict the project completion date.

As discussed in Chapters 9, 10, and 12, planning is an essential part of management. When teams do not make plans, they cannot make sound commitments and they cannot track and manage their work. Teams that work without plans not only have crisis-prone projects, they actually end up taking longer to do the job than they otherwise would. This chapter describes some of the key planning issues you will face in coaching TSP teams. The principal topics covered in the chapter are as follows.

☐ Plan types

☐ Plan dynamics

☐ Maintaining the team's plan

☐ A workload imbalance example

☐ Facing facts

☐ When to update the plan

☐ Updating individual plans

☐ Dynamic load balancing

☐ Interpreting plan data

☐ Management reporting

18.1   Plan Types

There are many types of plans and, unless you are precise, the teams you coach could easily become confused. The principal plan types used by TSP teams are the baseline or committed plan, the team plan, the detailed or personal plan, the overall plan, and the quality plan.

The Baseline Plan

The baseline plan is what the team committed to management in launch meeting 9. While it may be at any level of detail, it must identify the key project milestones and their dates. This plan defines the team's schedule commitments. Unless this plan is revised and the revisions are approved by management, it provides the baseline against which management will measure the team's and team leader's performance.

The Team Plan

The team plan is what teams use to guide their work. At launch meeting 9, it should contain the same milestone dates as the baseline plan. However, as the work progresses, these plans will diverge. During the job, teams will add unanticipated items to their plans and delete tasks that are no longer needed. The principal planning challenge for TSP teams is to continually ensure that their team plan continues to meet the commitments in the baseline plan.

Detailed Plans

The team members' detailed plans guide their work for the next few weeks or months. As the members learn more about the project, their plans must change to accurately represent what they currently plan to do. Early in development, these changes will happen almost every week. As teams consolidate their personal plans, the overall team plan will then change almost as often. This means that teams must regularly track their progress to ensure that their updated plans still meet the milestone commitments made in the baseline plan. As they make these plan changes, make sure that the team members continue planning for tasks of 10 hours duration or less.

The Overall Plan

The overall plan is what the team produced during launch meetings 3 and 4. This plan is used for making the quality plan and for guiding the team members in making their detailed plans. Once these detailed plans are consolidated, this consolidated plan becomes the next-phase team plan. The overall plan is then kept for reference but no longer used.

The Quality Plan

While the quality plan does not dynamically change the way the team and detailed plans do, it does provide the baseline against which to measure quality performance. This is fundamental, because unless teams come reasonably close to meeting their quality plans, their test times will increase and their project schedules will slip. Since these schedule slips can often be of many months, teams should establish realistic quality plans and then do their best to meet them. This subject is discussed in more detail in Chapter 19.

18.2   Plan Dynamics

Although planning is essential for well-run projects, detailed plans are generally accurate for only brief periods of time. As developers work, they learn more about the job and its many parts, and they see how long it takes to do various kinds of tasks. They also learn more about the product and have a better idea of how to develop it. Another factor affecting plans is that the developers' organizations and projects will change and evolve. Thus, even when projects are perfectly planned, changing conditions will often require plan adjustments. So, unless the members regularly adjust their plans, these plans will become less and less relevant to their work.

Even without external changes, the team's detailed plans will become inaccurate. Some developers will finish tasks ahead of their plans, and others will fall behind. There will also be estimating errors and overlooked tasks. The more detailed the plans and the longer they are used, the more inaccurate they will become. This is a problem because the team members' work must be synchronized. They must come together for design reviews, inspections, and management reviews. They must also coordinate to produce the team's products and to meet project milestones. As the workload becomes unbalanced, the schedule for these synchronization points will then be determined by the developers who are furthest behind. Periodic replanning is the easiest and quickest way to address this imbalance problem.

18.3   Maintaining the Team's Plan

Managers get nervous when developers update their plans. They intuitively expect that every replan will extend the schedule. However, once teams learn to make accurate plans and to work to these plans, they can replan without significantly changing their committed schedules. If the original plan was competently made, if it was based on historical size and task-hour data, and if there were no significant external changes, the baseline plan should be pretty accurate. Then, the team's plan changes will only involve the normal estimating fluctuations at the detailed level plus any resource and requirements variations.

At the detailed level, team plans must change on a regular basis. If the plans are based on average historical data, about half of the developers should finish their tasks early and the other half late. However, on average the team's overall plan will still be consistent with the baseline plan. The problem is that some developers will occasionally have several consecutive tasks that take longer than planned. They will then fall behind schedule and, unless their team reassigns some of their tasks, these normal workload fluctuations could lead to serious workload imbalances. Teams should regularly identify the members who are early and can handle additional workload and those who are behind and need tasks offloaded. If teams do not keep their detailed plans in balance, some members will eventually fall so far behind that they will delay the project.

18.4   A Workload Imbalance Example

To appreciate the imbalance problem, consider the hypothetical example of four developers who were developing a modest-sized product. The original size was estimated as about 12,000 LOC. After the requirements phase, the developers divided the product into 12 components of about 1,000 LOC each. They then assigned development of these components as shown in Table 18.1. They also estimated that they would implement these components at an average rate of 10 LOC per hour with 15 task hours per week. Based on this estimate, the four developers expected to take about 20 weeks to implement the 12,000 LOC.

After they had completed the work, the developers found that they had actually worked as shown in Table 18.2. Even though the job took almost twice as many weeks as planned, the original task-hour estimate was surprisingly accurate. The total 11,800 LOC was close to the originally estimated 12,000 LOC, and the developers actually did average about 15 task hours per week. They also produced an average of about 10 LOC per hour. The problem was that with the differing sizes and complexities of the components and, with the variations in productivity and task hours, the developers needed from 10 weeks to nearly 40 weeks to complete the job.

Had these developers been rebalancing their workload, Mary and Jeff would have offloaded some of Jim's tasks rather than starting on other projects. This would almost certainly have saved this project several weeks and, if the developers had completely balanced the team's workload, they would have finished the job in about 20 weeks instead of 37.5.

While it might seem unfair to give the fastest workers more work, developers intuitively understand that development times are influenced by many factors and that everybody will occasionally end up with tasks that take much longer than planned. With self-directed teams, this reassignment issue is not a problem.

18.5   Facing Facts

Teams sometimes find that even with workload balancing, they are falling behind schedule. Then they have several choices. First, if the exposure is small enough and the team feels it has a reasonable chance of recovering, there is no need to change the baseline plan. The team members should, however, update and rebalance their individual plans. Also suggest that the team develop a plan to recover the lost time and that the team leader tell management about their schedule exposure and recovery plan. If the team finds that it cannot meet its baseline commitments,

Table 18.1 An Example of Workload Imbalance—1

Component	Jeff	Mary	Beth	Jim	Team Total
A	1,000				1,000
B	1,000				1,000
C	1,000				1,000
D		1,000			1,000
E		1,000			1,000
F		1,000			1,000
G			1,000		1,000
H			1,000		1,000
I			1,000		1,000
J				1,000	1,000
K				1,000	1,000
L				1,000	1,000
Estimated LOC	3,000	3,000	3,000	3,000	12,000
Estimated LOC/hour	10.0	10.0	10.0	10.0	10.0
Estimated Hours	300	300	300	300	1,200
Estimated Hours/Week	15	15	15	15	
Estimated Weeks	20	20	20	20	20

Table 18.2 An Example of Workload Imbalance—2

Component	Jeff	Mary	Beth	Jim	Team Total
A	900				900
B	500				500
C	500				500
D		600			600
E		700			700
F		800			800
G			1,300		1,300
H			1,700		1,700
I			1,200		1,200
J				900	900
K				1,400	1,400
L				1,300	1,300
Actual LOC	1,900	2,100	4,200	3,600	11,800
Actual LOC/ hour	13.0	8.0	11.0	8.0	9.5
Actual Hours	146.2	262.5	381.8	450.0	1,240.5
Actual Hours/ Week	14	16	18	12	
Actual Weeks	10.4	16.4	21.2	37.5	37.5

it should make a new plan. If possible, it should also make one or more alternate plans with various combinations of additional resources and reduced functionality. Then the team leader should tell management that the schedule has slipped and describe the team's recovery plan together with any commitment or resource changes required to meet the schedule.

Schedule problems are normal in development work, and the team's job is to solve these problems and to meet its commitments. It should therefore not change the schedule prematurely. However, the team leader should warn management about schedule problems as soon as he or she can. When teams are open and honest about their problems, management can often help to solve them. However, when they hide their problems, the team will be blamed for any schedule delays. So, coach your teams to do their best to meet their commitments, but to be open and honest with management about their schedule problems.

18.6   When to Update the Plan

There are several reasons to update a plan. However, since it takes time to replan and since plan changes make it harder to track progress, it is important that teams do so only when they really need to. The pros and cons of replanning are essentially the same as those for relaunching. These reasons were discussed in Chapter 16.

The decision to update the plan should be based primarily on the team's needs. When the team members feel that their current plans no longer help them to do their work, they need new plans. When they make these new plans, they will revise their personal plans and rebalance their workload. If the new plans are not reasonably consistent with the baseline plan, they must meet with management and explain why they will miss their commitments and get management's agreement to a new baseline plan.

18.7   Updating Individual Plans

If every team member completed every task exactly as planned, workload balancing would not be needed. However, particularly with new TSP teams, the members' plans are often inaccurate and it is difficult for them to maintain a balanced workload. While they usually will start with little or no historical planning data, with proper coaching and guidance even new teams will soon gather enough data to improve their planning accuracy. The data they need are of three kinds.

☐ Weekly task hours

☐ Task productivity rates

☐ Frequency of unplanned tasks

Weekly Task Hours

In making personal plans, a helpful strategy is to use a weekly task-hour number that the team members are reasonably confident of achieving. For example, if the team had the weekly task-hour data shown in Table 18.3, its average weekly task

Table 18.3 Task-Hour Example

Week Number	Weekly Task Hours
1	84
2	93
3	91
4	87
5	84
6	93
7	85
8	90
9	84
10	87
11	95
12	93
13	85
14	86
15	98

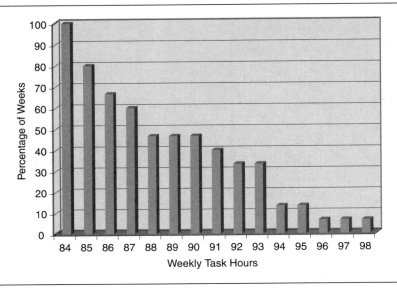

Figure 18.1 Percent of Weeks Achieving a Given Task-Hour Value

hours would be 89.0. However, since weekly task hours will fluctuate, the likelihood that a team will reach its average value will usually be less than 50%, often significantly less. For example, Figure 18.1 shows data for a team that only achieved the average 89 weekly task hours 46.7% of the time. However, the developers did achieve 87 or more task hours 60% of the time. Because of the normal fluctuation of its work, this team had a standard deviation of 4.43 hours around its average of 89 weekly task hours. By using data on the distribution of their weekly task hours, teams can make realistic weekly commitments.

Task Productivity Rates

For a good many years, I have kept a project notebook for all of my personal work. I track my weekly task hours and, for each job, I record the product size, job time, and job type. A job could be developing a program, producing a presentation, reviewing a paper, or even writing a complete book. The task times for these jobs range from a few hours to over 2,000 hours. Now when I plan a new job, I have historical data on over 500 jobs of 12 different types. I can examine the historical data on each job type, and I can estimate the time that this job will likely take. While my estimates vary considerably around the actual times, on average my estimates are quite accurate. When I make commitments, I allow a modest cushion to compensate for my normal estimate variation. As a result, I tend to finish most jobs slightly ahead of their committed schedules.

With the TSP, developers can keep such records for themselves. They can then estimate the size and time for each task before starting it, and they can track and record the actual size and time when the job is done. They can then use these data to make statistically sound estimates of the time required to do each task (Humphrey 2005). While their performance will necessarily fluctuate from task to task, on average they will be on or slightly ahead of schedule. As they gather more data, they can even calculate prediction intervals for their estimates and see how large a schedule cushion they need to consistently meet their commitments.

Frequency of Unplanned Tasks

This is the area that generally gives developers the most difficulty. Over time, they will learn how to make plans that accurately predict the time required to do their planned work. The unplanned work, however, will be more of a problem. Some examples of the typical unplanned tasks in development work are the following.

- ☐ A component that the team was enhancing turns out to have a major design defect that must be fixed before the enhancements can be made.
- ☐ The team finds that a required product feature involves several unestimated functions.
- ☐ An available test simulator is incapable of meeting the team's testing needs so a new one must be obtained or developed.
- ☐ A component's initial design is impractical and must be reworked.
- ☐ A module has so many inspection defects that it must be replaced and reinspected.

While requirements changes are frequently given as the cause for unplanned tasks, they should not be a problem. Requirements changes can generally be negotiated. The biggest cause of trouble is the changes that arise from a better understanding of the job the team has already committed to do.

A team member's level of unplanned activity is a function of the organization's process maturity, the team's knowledge of the project, and the member's planning ability (Chrissis 2003). Low-maturity organizations tend to have high levels of unplanned work, as do projects that are in the early requirements and design stages. However, as team members gain planning experience, they can learn to anticipate—or at least allow for—many of these activities.

Handling Unplanned Tasks

In handling unplanned tasks, the simplest approach is to insert new tasks into the task plan whenever they arise. This will give the team member a complete record of the work, and it keeps the task hours realistically related to the actual work. This also provides the task-productivity and weekly task-hour data needed to make accurate plans. However, this means that team members must regularly add new tasks to their task plans.

While there are several ways to allow for a high level of unplanned work, one approach that works well is to include rough estimates for any tasks the team members expect to do in the future. If they are slightly conservative with their task estimates and weekly task-hour plans, this strategy will minimize their unplanned work and allow them to almost always meet their commitments.

By tracking the level and type of unplanned work, team members can make progressively more accurate plans. They will insert new tasks whenever they need them and delete old tasks that are no longer required. They should also regularly check their schedule status to ensure that their plans are still meeting their commitments. If not, they should either rearrange some tasks to meet the commitments or work with their teammates to rebalance their workload. If this still does not meet the commitments, the team must renegotiate the baseline plan with management.

18.8   Dynamic Load Balancing

Workload balancing allows teams to most efficiently use their resources to do their work. The procedure for dynamic load balancing is the same as that used during the team launch. First, the members review their plans to see if they are still holding to the baseline plan. If not and the error is large enough to cause concern, they must rework their plans as described in Chapters 10 and 12.

If the baseline plan doesn't need to change, the team members produce and balance new detailed plans for the current phase. However, they must also take the additional step of keeping the new plan synchronized with the original plan. While the team's workload will likely change in detail and the times for many tasks will probably be substantially different, if the team's original plan was reasonably accurate, the overall workload should be approximately the same.

If this is the case and if the team's task hours were reasonably close to the plan, the team's overall earned value should also be reasonably close to the plan. If not, the next section of this chapter provides suggestions on how to help teams interpret their data. If they are close to the plan, review the developers' personal plans to see if they are reasonably in balance. If only one or two developers have workload problems, a few simple task reassignments will probably suffice. However, if the workload problem is more general, suggest that the entire team follow the workload balancing procedure described in Chapter 12.

18.9   Interpreting Plan Data

Assuming that the team is following its quality plan, there are two principal indicators of the teams' progress: earned value and weekly task hours. By examining these indicators, teams can learn a great deal about the quality of their plans, where they currently stand on the job, and what is likely to happen in the future. There are nine possible combinations of these plan data as shown in Table 18.4 and listed below.

1. Earned value is on plan and cumulative weekly task hours are on plan.
2. Earned value is on plan and cumulative weekly task hours are below plan.
3. Earned value is on plan and cumulative weekly task hours are above plan.
4. Earned value is below plan and cumulative weekly task hours are on plan.
5. Earned value is below plan and cumulative weekly task hours are below plan.
6. Earned value is below plan and cumulative weekly task hours are above plan.
7. Earned value is above plan and cumulative weekly task hours are on plan.
8. Earned value is above plan and cumulative weekly task hours are below plan.
9. Earned value is above plan and cumulative weekly task hours are above plan.

Table 18.4 Team Progress Indicators

		Earned Value (EV)		
		Below plan	On plan	Above plan
Task Hours (TH)	**Below plan**	5: EV and TH low	2: EV on plan, TH low	8: EV high, TH low
	On plan	4: EV low, TH on plan	1: EV and TH on plan	7: EV high, TH on plan
	Above plan	6: EV low, TH high	3: EV on plan, TH high	9: EV and TH high

These nine cases are discussed in the following paragraphs. In this discussion, it is assumed that the team has followed the guidance in Chapter 17 on interpreting weekly data. If the team has a significant number of task hours tied up in uncompleted tasks, it is very difficult to assess its schedule status. A few days of uncompleted tasks is normal, but if the number of task hours on uncompleted tasks is more that about a week's time, that problem must be fixed before the following analysis can be used.

1. **Earned value is on plan and task hours are on plan.** Things appear to be moving ahead as planned and there is no need to revise the plan or make any other changes.

2. **Earned value is on plan and task hours are below plan.** This condition has two possible causes. First, the team overestimated the job. That is, the members estimated that they would take more time to do the work than they actually spent. To avoid making similar mistakes in the future, determine if the plan is off because of a poor size estimate, a poor productivity estimate, or both. If that is the full explanation, the team need not do anything other than use its data to improve future estimates.

   The second and more serious cause for this condition is that the team is not spending enough time on some tasks. For example, the members might be spending inadequate time on inspections, reviews, or design work. This means that the team is not following its quality plan and that there will likely be problems in test. Depending on the areas where the work is inadequate, suggest that the team hold re-reviews or add some reinspections. The members should also start following their quality plan.

   Whenever the team's task hours are low, the members should determine the cause. It could be inadequate staffing or the staff not putting in enough hours. If management has not provided the required staffing or some members are being pulled off the job to help with other projects, urge the team leader to take a strong stand. Unless the planned resources are provided, the team cannot fulfill its plan. Providing the needed staffing is management's job, and the team leader should hold them to their resource commitments.

   When projects are fully staffed, the team's weekly task hours are a function of the organization's process maturity and the nature of the team's work. Low task hours could be caused by poor team morale, leadership problems, a poorly defined process, a disruptive working environment, or poor administrative support. If any of these areas are problems, suggest that the team address them promptly or these problems will almost certainly get worse.

3. **Earned value is on plan and task hours are above plan.** Since the team is holding schedule, it does not face a crisis. With task hours above plan, however, the team has underestimated the workload and the members are spending more hours doing the work than planned. This is an estimating problem

that the team should understand before making another plan. The team leader should also consider the team's ability to continue working at its current pace. While high task hours are desirable, there is a limit to how much time team members can work and still continue to be productive.

4. **Earned value is below plan and task hours are on plan.** This situation is serious. The team is falling behind schedule because it has underestimated the job. While the members need to understand the cause of the underestimate, their biggest problem is figuring out how to get back on schedule. This generally requires a major plan reassessment and a thorough review with management. Again, the team leader should not blow the whistle prematurely, but he or she should warn management about this problem as soon as possible.

5. **Earned value is below plan and task hours are below plan.** Here, the most likely problem is low task hours. While the team should consider the task hour points discussed in item 2, it is also useful to compare earned value status with task hour status. If, for example, the team is 15% below the planned value line and 25% behind the task hour plan, it is actually ahead of its plan. If it had been fully staffed, the team would be ahead of schedule. When projects have not been fully staffed or members have been pulled off the job to handle crises, teams can use this measure to explain to management that they are performing according to the plan but that the schedule problem is caused by understaffing. Team leaders can usually use this argument to get the needed additional staffing or management's agreement to schedule relief.

6. **Earned value is below plan and task hours are above plan.** As in point 4, this situation calls for an early plan reassessment and a comprehensive review with management. Suggest that the team do this as soon as possible. The earlier such problems are recognized, the easier they are to solve. Again, however, the team should understand the problem first and then prepare alternate plans to show management what it recommends.

One point of caution in replanning: during the early project phases, wide swings in estimated size and job scope are common. While it is always a good idea to keep management informed, the team should temper its concerns with a clear explanation of current job status. Teams must often complete the requirements and start on the design work before they can truly understand the scope of the job.

7. **Earned value is above plan and task hours are on plan.** The plan appears to be overestimated and the team has the necessary resources. Under these conditions, the team members should first make sure that the situation is real and not just a temporary variation. Also, they should review the considerations in item 2. If the members are not doing a thorough job of designing, reviewing, or inspecting, the job will likely be in trouble later, in spite of the positive earned value story. If the early schedule situation is real, the team

leader should go to management and ask if they want the team to finish the work early or to expand the job to include additional functions.

8. **Earned value is above plan and task hours are below plan.** This is much the same situation as that in 7. Again, the team should make sure that the work is being done properly and that the estimating problems are understood and addressed.

9. **Earned value is above plan and task hours are above plan.** This is much like case 1. The team is able to do more work than planned and it is ahead of schedule. The team members should enjoy this situation while they can!

18.10   Management Reporting

Coach your teams' leaders to hold periodic review meetings and to write frequent reports that keep management regularly informed about the project's status. They should only report the information that is most important to management, but do it clearly, completely, and concisely. If the team has accomplished something important, the report should state the facts and what this accomplishment means for the project and the business. Finally, in making these reports, they should avoid describing problems without either solutions or actions to develop solutions. Have them describe all of their serious problems and summarize what they are doing about them.

In making a report, if they have made prior reports, they should first briefly describe what they have accomplished since the last report. Next, they should address management's principal concerns. While these management concerns are usually about schedule, cost, and quality, there may also be other causes. For further information on management's perspective and the types of things they might worry about, see the book *Winning with Software* (Humphrey 2002). Third, suggest that the team members summarize where the project stands against its commitments and plan. If they are not on schedule, they should provide the following information.

☐ How late they are

☐ Why they are late

☐ What actions they are taking to get back on schedule

☐ How they plan to address the problems caused by the schedule delay

Finally, the team leader should describe any significant problems and what the team is doing about them. For further guidance on management reporting, suggest that the team leader consult *TSP^SM—Leading a Development Team* (Humphrey 2006).

18.11 Summary

This chapter explains the nature of continuous planning and how it can help teams be more efficient and better manage their workload. When teams do not make detailed and accurate plans, they cannot make sound commitments or manage and track their work. Then they actually end up taking longer to do the job than they otherwise would. The key coaching task for such teams is to help them gather and use the data they need to make detailed and accurate plans.

Detailed plans are only accurate for brief periods of time. If the original plan was competently made, if it was based on historical size and task-hour data, and if there were no significant external changes, the overall plan should be fairly accurate. However, in advanced technical work, this is rarely the case. Teams should update their plans when the members feel that their current plans are no longer helpful in guiding the work.

Team plans will change on a regular basis. If the plans are based on average historical data, however, about half the tasks should finish early and the other half late. Therefore, it is essential for teams to periodically rebalance their plans. In doing so, they should identify the members who are ahead of plan and can take on additional workload as well as those who are behind schedule and need to have some tasks offloaded. With a balanced workload, the team will make maximum progress against its plan.

In interpreting the plan data, teams have two principal indicators: earned value and task hours. By examining these indicators, they can learn a great deal about the quality of their plan, where the work currently stands, and what is likely to happen in the future. These indicators are only useful, however, if the team is following its quality plan. If not, no plan data can predict when the team will finish the job.

References

Chrissis, Mary Beth, Mike Konrad, and Sandy Shrum. *CMMI: Guidelines for Process Integration and Product Improvement.* Boston: Addison-Wesley. 2003.

Humphrey, Watts S. *Winning with Software: An Executive Strategy.* Boston: Addison-Wesley. 2002.

Humphrey, Watts S. *PSP[SM]: A Self-Improvement Process for Software Engineers.* Boston: Addison-Wesley. 2005.

Humphrey, Watts S. *TSP[SM]—Leading a Development Team.* Boston: Addison-Wesley. 2006.

19

Managing Quality

This chapter discusses the principles and methods for helping TSP teams do quality work. While it cannot possibly cover all aspects of software quality, it does address those issues that most affect a team's ability to produce quality products. The following topics are covered in this chapter.

- ☐ Principles of quality management
- ☐ Why manage quality?
- ☐ The quality journey
- ☐ The developer's responsibility for quality
- ☐ The team's responsibility for quality
- ☐ Quality management methods
- ☐ Interpreting quality data
- ☐ Reporting quality data
- ☐ Defect reporting considerations

19.1   Principles of Quality Management

The principles of software quality management are not new, and they come directly from general quality improvement principles. The basic principles of quality management have been used successfully in many other fields. They are as follows.

1. In any quality program, the team's primary focus must be on satisfying the customer. Therefore, if the customers do not demand quality work, they are not likely to get it. But even if the customer does not understand quality, the team's professional obligation is to do quality work. To ensure that its efforts are truly addressing customer needs, the team should, wherever possible, involve the customer in its quality-improvement efforts.

2. Management must make quality the top priority. Quality must be *the* top priority, not *a* top priority. Unless quality is at the very top of management's priority list, no team can maintain an effective quality program. Management must understand and support the principle that doing a quality job always pays, even if they cannot prove its value at the time.

3. The people doing the work must own the quality program. If the people who actually perform the work do not strive to build quality products, they almost certainly will not. To do quality work, all of the developers must feel that quality is important and the entire team must participate in the quality program. Since any defective part results in a defective system, everyone must strive to produce defect-free products.

4. To improve quality, the team must change its process. The quality of a product is determined by the quality of the process used to produce it. Just "trying harder" will not improve quality. If the process is wasteful or inefficient, product quality will ultimately suffer. The reason may not be obvious, but improving a wasteful or inefficient process will invariably result in better products.

5. Teams must measure quality. Without measurements, quality is just talk. Since quality is a complex topic, no single measure will be adequate and multiple quality measures are needed.

6. Doing the job right always costs less in the long run. When quality improvement increases costs, the team is doing something wrong. It costs less to do the job correctly than it does to fix the problems later, and it costs less to find and fix problems earlier rather than later. Since every defect represents an error, and errors are expensive to fix, no defect can be acceptable. Therefore, zero defects is the only rational and cost-effective quality goal.

As an example of principle 6, software managers often equate quality with testing. Then they argue that they can't afford to improve quality. These managers are not considering alternative and more effective ways to manage quality. While they can't afford to do more testing, they can afford to improve quality. In fact, they cannot afford not to improve quality.

Unfortunately, there is no simple way to prove that these principles are correct. This is why effective quality management is not more generally practiced. While the PSP-trained team members should agree with all of these points, the principal coaching challenge is to convince management to follow these principles and to require their teams to incorporate them into their development practices. By following these principles and gathering and analyzing the data on their work, teams can soon demonstrate the benefits of quality work.

19.2 Why Manage Quality?

In this book, **quality management** refers to managing the defect category of quality. The reason to manage defects is not just to produce better products, but because defects are essentially random in nature and the costs of finding and fixing these defects increases exponentially the later the developers find them. Defect management must have top development priority because the defect content of a software product will largely determine the team's ability to develop that product on a predictable schedule and for its planned costs.

All PSP-trained software developers know that it takes more time to find and fix defects in test than in reviews and inspections. They also know that they inject a lot of defects while developing programs. So, unless they manage the quality of their programs while writing them, they will have to spend a lot of time in testing. Poor quality management makes a developer's work unpredictable because defect fix times are highly variable. Therefore, defective products will have widely variable test times and both long and unpredictable test schedules.

Experience shows that software projects that do not manage defects have serious problems and that these problems are most severe during final testing and product use. It is then too late to do anything but test and fix. Also, as experience amply proves, fixing defective products in test or later takes a very long time. Thus, if the team doesn't manage its defects at the beginning of the project, those defects will manage the team at the end of the project. The team's work will also be highly unpredictable, and it will take much longer to do than it otherwise should. In short, the reason to manage defects is to permit the team to economically and predictably produce a quality product.

19.3 The Quality Journey

People often think of quality as a final result. It is not; it is a journey—a journey that never ends. As teams measure and manage quality, they learn more about quality management. Then each improvement step provides the knowledge, experience, and data to enable the next step. Even when team members understand PSP quality principles, they need regular reinforcement to consistently follow these principles. The coaching challenge is to recognize where each developer, manager, and executive is on the quality journey and to help everyone focus on the next improvement step. The steps in the quality journey are as follows.

1. **Test and fix.** The initial focus of most software groups is on getting their products to work. The team member's objective is to get the product into test as quickly as possible and to test and fix it until it works well enough to ship. The only quality challenge these groups generally recognize is improving testing effectiveness. Your challenge is to get them to move on to steps 2, 3, 4, and 5 of the quality journey as quickly as possible.

2. **Inspect.** The next step is when the team members start removing defects before test. This is usually done with various kinds of walkthroughs and inspections. The typical challenge in this step is to get the members to do high-quality inspections.

3. **Partial measurement.** As inspection programs mature, some groups begin to measure the inspection work and to use these data to identify and fix the most defective product elements. The challenge is to properly gather and use these data to improve the product.

4. **Quality ownership.** As they participate in inspections team members become more sensitive to their own mistakes. They start reviewing their personal work to eliminate defects before the team inspection. Once developers reach this point, product quality will quickly improve.

5. **Personal measurement.** Once team members are concerned about the quality of their personal work, they are ready for personal defect management. The challenge now is to get them to gather and use personal defect data.

6. **Design.** Once developers have mastered basic defect management, they are ready to focus on design quality. The coaching challenge now is to get them to use sound design practices for all of their programs—large and small—and to use sound design verification methods in all design inspections and personal design reviews.

7. **Defect prevention.** While defect measurement and improved design will prevent some defects, true defect prevention requires a structured way to

change the development process to eliminate the defect causes. The challenges here are to initiate a defect-prevention program, to make that program permanent, and then to broaden the defect-prevention focus to cover the entire product life cycle.

8. **User-based measurement.** Ultimately, the quality program should be driven by user-based measures. The challenges here are to understand the users, to define the quality characteristics that are most important to these users, and to measure and manage these quality characteristics in a way that is meaningful both to the team members and to the users.

The reason that the quality journey is never-ending is because, as long as technology advances and as long as it enables us to serve a broader spectrum of users, our users will continue to have new quality needs. This in turn requires that we develop new quality measures and plans. The principal message from this eight-fold quality journey is that it must be traveled in steps. Until the team members have made reasonable progress with step 5, they will not have the data to support steps 6, 7, and 8. So understand where your organization, your team, and each of the team members is in this quality journey and help them to focus on the next step. Then keep each of them moving forward on their personal quality journey.

19.4   The Developer's Responsibility for Quality

The team members must understand that they are personally responsible for the quality of the products they produce—it isn't the responsibility of the testers or of quality assurance. If the members do not strive to produce quality products, no one can do it for them. While defective software products can usually be patched and fixed in test, they will always be patched-up defective products. Fixing defective products costs time and money, delays projects, and increases the cost of the work. It always costs more to build and fix a defective product than it would have cost to build it properly in the first place.

The only way to economically and predictably produce quality products is for the team members to produce quality products from the beginning. They must know what quality products look like and they must know how to do quality work. Then they must take responsibility for the quality of their personal work, and they must act and feel responsible for achieving the team's quality goals. Only then will the team consistently produce quality products.

19.5   The Team's Responsibility for Quality

While the developers are personally responsible for the quality of the programs they produce, the team also has a responsibility. The team first establishes quality goals and a plan for meeting these goals. It does this in the TSP launch. The team next defines its quality methods. In doing this, the team members should consider their customer's and management's quality needs and decide on the quality methods that are appropriate. Finally, the team must support its members in following the quality methods it has selected.

This latter responsibility is much like that of a winning team in sports. In a hard-fought competition, all of the players must perform at their peak and several of them may even make spectacular plays. However, in the end, it is the *team* that wins. Just as in sports, a software team is more than just the sum of its members. Each member must do superior personal work and each must also back up and support the other team members.

In software as in sports, the team members are fallible human beings. They make mistakes, overlook defects, or have bad days. Here is where team support can be most valuable. When one team member makes a mistake or needs support, the other members can pitch in to ensure that the result is still a quality product. In sports, these backup plays and grandstand catches can be spectacular. In software, they are less visible but no less important.

There are many opportunities for software professionals to support each other. Each team member has a role, and a big part of every role responsibility is anticipating problems and seeing where members need help or support. Often, the members may not even know that they need support until a teammate offers to help.

An example of such support is the team inspection. Here, several members review a teammate's work. Their sole objective is to help their teammate produce a superior product. Another case would be where the quality manager finds potential problems in a team member's data. By examining the time and defect data on each product component, team members can often spot potential quality problems. They can then work with the developer to determine the nature of the problems and to figure out how to address them.

When teams follow the TSP process, the quality manager reviews the quality of all the product elements before they are inspected or released to testing. Make sure that any poor-quality work is identified before test. Then have the quality manager review the data with the responsible team members and show them how to address the problems. By the time a product component is ready for test, several team members will have been involved in its design and inspection. So, even though an individual team member has developed that poor-quality component, it is the team's responsibility to fix it.

Although management cannot evaluate individuals with personal defect data, they can evaluate teams. The team must monitor the quality of its work and refuse to accept any poor-quality components into the system. If the members fail to do this, management should hold the team, team leader, and team coach responsible.

One team was enhancing a COTS (commercial off-the-shelf) product that its company had acquired from a vendor. While the team had been told to clean up the product's existing defects, they were also given a very aggressive schedule. When management saw the initial test data, however, they realized that they had acquired a poor-quality product and refused to release it until its quality was improved. Then they told the team that they would have to figure out how to fix the COTS product so they could release it. The team used the system test data to devise a repair strategy. They decided to inspect those product modules that had been responsible for the most defects in integration and system testing. By inspecting the most defect-prone 10% of the code, the developers found and fixed over 300 defects in the next 4 weeks. Most of the problems were concentrated in less than 10% of the product's modules. After fixing these modules, the product was released and was quite successful.

With a COTS product, nobody will be defensive, because none of the team members injected any of the defects. When the team members have developed the code, this could be a problem. The quality manager should review the quality of each product element before it is inspected or tested. If data indicates a poor-quality product, the quality manager should not let the team waste time inspecting or testing it. Even though one team member has produced that poor-quality component, the team must not let it into the system until it is fixed. It is not a question of blame; it is just sound quality management.

19.6 Quality Management Methods

There are many ways to deal with quality problems, and they all relate to the use of TSP data. The following are some of the most useful TSP quality methods.

- ☐ Plan reviews
- ☐ Design methods
- ☐ Design review methods
- ☐ Inspection pre-reviews
- ☐ Capture-recapture defect estimates
- ☐ Estimating yield
- ☐ Quality profiles and quality criteria
- ☐ Test data analysis

The following paragraphs discuss these methods.

Plan Reviews

To ensure that the team is doing quality work, start by examining the team members' plans. If they have not planned to do quality work, they probably won't. As you coach the team, look at the members' plans and, if any look questionable, discuss the problems with those members to understand how they arrived at their plans and to see if they are truly striving to do a quality job.

In examining the plans, the principal topics to consider are the ratio of design time to coding time, the ratio of the time spent in design reviews to design time, and the ratio of the time spent in code reviews to coding time. Also look at the time planned for inspections. If any of these areas have problems, suggest that the team members fix their plans. Then look at these fixed plans to see if they are reasonable.

Most commonly, team members do not plan adequate time for design and code reviews. If they review at too high a rate, they will almost certainly have low review yields and poor-quality products. If you can convince them to plan an adequate amount of time for their reviews and inspections, and if they then follow these plans when they do the work, they will almost certainly produce high-quality products.

Design Methods

Even when developers are very experienced and do thorough code reviews and inspections, few produce defect-free programs. The reason is inadequate designs. With few exceptions, software developers do not take the time or make the effort to produce comprehensive and detailed designs. When developers produce only vague and cursory designs, they inevitably make many design mistakes. Often, these mistakes are subtle and exceedingly hard to find in test. Even with the best programming practices, the limit on the quality of the programs teams produce will be determined by the quality of the design methods they use. Thus, to produce quality software products, all of the team members must know and use sound design methods in all of their work.

One approach to guiding and monitoring design quality is for the design manager to define the team's design methods and standards. The team then reviews and agrees with these standards before adopting them. If any team members are not fluent with these methods, arrange for the training needed to bring them up to speed. Although design training can help with the fluency problem, it is rarely sufficient. It takes time to both learn sound design practices and it takes considerable guidance and support to get team members to consistently use the best methods they know.

Some years ago, I taught a graduate PSP course to experienced developers who had just completed a design course. Late in the course, I reviewed the students' defect data and noticed that they were all making design mistakes. On examination, I was surprised to find that no one had used the design methods they had just learned, and I asked them why. The developers said that the design methods they had learned were for large programs and were not appropriate for the small PSP exercises. That is nonsense. Since large programs are composed of many small programs, when the developers do not use sound design methods for writing small programs, they will not use these methods when writing large programs.

In coaching your teams, convince the members to use sound design methods, even for the smallest programs. One way to do this is to have the design manager examine each developer's work to ensure that he or she is properly using the selected design methods. If there are problems that the design manager cannot fix, those problems should be brought to you and to the team leader.

Design Review Methods

While design is important, design reviews are even more important. Since we are all fallible, the only way we can consistently produce quality designs is to consistently review these designs to find and fix our mistakes. Soundly performed design reviews can help teams to find and fix most of their design problems before they enter test. Design inspections also help, both to find more defects and to provide an added incentive for the team members to use the agreed design methods. When members know that their designs will be inspected and that they will have to produce complete designs to pass the inspection, they are likely to produce complete and high-quality designs.

A design review example. Doing design reviews and inspections can improve quality, but only if developers follow a defined design-review process to analyze their designs.

Sonya was an experienced software developer who had recently been assigned to a large development team. The project was to make a major modification to a large system that this team had developed and that the other developers were very familiar with. Sonya was not. However, when she participated in the team's design inspections, she was surprised to find that she was the only one who found many of the design defects.

When she discussed this situation with the other developers, she found that they reviewed their designs in the same way that they reviewed code: by reading it with a checklist. While Sonya also used a checklist for her design reviews, she knew that she could not find complex design problems by merely reading the design. She had to analyze it. She used trace tables and state-machine analyses to check all of the program's loops and complex structures.

Analyzing designs. Since team members usually want to start coding and testing as quickly as possible, they are likely to rush through their design work and spend little or no time in design reviews. However, unless they thoroughly analyze their designs, they will not find many complex design problems before test. Unfortunately, as the generally poor quality of modern programs demonstrates, they will also miss many of the design problems in unit testing.

Think of reviews in this way: in implementing the design, the programmer must read that design. Since he or she is likely to find many of the simple design defects during implementation, there is limited added benefit to just reading the design beforehand. Unless the developers review the design in a way that finds problems that the implementer will likely miss, merely reading the design will usually result in many of the design defects not being found until test or by the users.

Discuss design review methods with the teams you coach and show them how to do effective reviews and inspections. Then, when they do design reviews and inspections, check the work. If they are not using sound review methods, do your best to motivate them to use more effective review methods. For a discussion of design review methods, see Chapter 12 in *PSP*[SM]: *A Self-Improvement Process for Software Engineers* (Humphrey 2005).

Inspection Pre-reviews

One important part of the quality manager's responsibilities is moderating the team's inspections. In the TSP process, the inspection moderator first pre-reviews the product to see if it is ready for the inspection. If the developer (called the *producer* in inspections) has not reviewed the product and fixed the obvious mistakes, the product is not ready for an inspection. Discuss the purpose of pre-reviews with the team members to ensure that they all agree on how to implement the pre-review process. For the design inspection pre-review, the principal things to check are the following.

1. Did the producer create a reviewable design?
2. Did the producer follow the agreed design standards and are all of the required design elements included?
3. Has the producer provided copies of appropriate requirements, specifications, and standards?
4. Does the product design have many obvious oversights or mistakes?
5. Did the producer spend enough time in the design review? The moderator can determine this by examining the ratio of the member's design review time to design time and the design review rate. These rates and ratios should be reasonably consistent with the team's quality plan.
6. Did the producer find many defects in the design review and were any of them sophisticated design mistakes?
7. Has the producer done a sufficiently careful job to warrant the team's time to inspect this product? The moderator can determine this by comparing the developer's data with the team's quality goals.

For the code inspection, the inspection moderator should conduct a similar pre-review and examine similar data on the coding phase. Here, the principal items to review are the following.

1. Did the producer create a complete program? For example, did he or she follow the coding standards and include all of the required program elements?

2. Has the producer provided copies of the appropriate design and specification documents, pertinent standards, and reference materials?

3. Does the program have many obvious oversights or mistakes?

4. Did the producer spend enough time in the code review? The moderator can determine this from the ratio of code review to coding time and by the code review rate. These rates and ratios should be reasonably consistent with the team's quality plan.

5. Has the producer updated his or her personal code review checklist based on available data from the prior compiles, unit tests, and inspections?

6. How many defects were found in the code review? Was the number found in the review more than the number found during compiling? If more defects were found in compile than in code review, the code review was probably superficial and should be repeated with an up-to-date checklist.

7. When compared with the team's quality goals, did the producer do a sufficiently careful job to warrant the team's time to inspect this program?

Discuss these pre-reviews with the quality manager and meet with him or her every week to discuss the reviews done that week, what was found, and the actions that were taken. Continue holding these meetings until the quality manager is doing the inspection pre-reviews properly. The pre-reviews and inspections are the last times the team can monitor the product's quality before the focus shifts to finding and fixing defects in test.

Capture-Recapture Defect Estimates

When developers do inspections, there is a simple way to determine if the inspection was reasonably complete. It is called *capture-recapture*. This method is covered in the TSP inspection process script and is described in Appendix C of *Introduction to the Team Software Process*[SM] (Humphrey 2000).

To use this method, the quality manager first checks that each inspection was properly done. Since the quality manager moderates most of the team inspections, this should not be difficult. Again, discuss this topic with the quality manager to determine how well the inspections are being done and the yields achieved. Also discuss any inspections that were not adequate and the steps taken to remedy the problems. The following are suggested steps for checking the quality of the inspections.

1. The capture-recapture method is most useful when at least some of the developers have review yields of 50% or higher. With lower yields, capture-recapture estimates are often unreliable.

2. The capture-recapture method should be used only with major defects. These are defects that, when fixed, change the executable code.

3. Calculate the likely number of remaining defects and determine if a reinspection is warranted.

4. The capture-recapture method provides a general indication of the number of remaining defects. A useful rule of thumb is to look at the number of defects found by only one developer. If anyone found many defects that no one else found, the team should consider doing a reinspection.

If a program still appears to have quality problems after a reinspection, the team has several possible courses of action.

1. Continue to develop the program but watch its test data to see if it has many defects. If so, consider taking steps 2, 3, or 4.

2. Reinspect the program again before testing it.

3. Have the same or a different developer completely rework the program.

4. Scrap the program and have the same or a different developer develop a new one to replace it.

If the team chooses option number 1 and the program does have a substantial number of defects in test, it should have a different group of developers do another inspection, following the same procedure as above. Choice 4 is generally appropriate whenever a program has serious design problems. Coding problems can generally be fixed with reinspections and testing.

The choice of whether the same or a different team member should handle the rework or redevelop the program is largely up to the original developer. If he or she would like to do the program over and has ideas on how to produce a better design, that is usually the best choice. However, if the designer would like someone else to help or to even develop a completely new program, suggest that the team do that. Since the team member will usually have learned a great deal by producing the initial design, if he or she is not defensive and is motivated to do a better job the next time, that is almost always the best choice.

Estimating Yield

The best yield estimate for a development phase is to use actual yield data for that phase from prior similar projects. With no historical data, the team should assume a 50% yield for the latest defect-removal phase. It can then calculate the estimated yields for prior phases by assuming that the unfound defects were distributed in the same way as those that have already been found.

For example, suppose that a code inspection found 18 defects, 16 of which were injected in coding and 2 in detailed design. If the team assumes that this inspection had a 50% yield, that means that there are 18 more defects that were not found. The most reasonable assumption is that 16 of these unfound defects were injected in coding and 2 in detailed design. With that information, the team can calculate the yields of all the prior phases.

The same method would also work if the team had historical yield data. For example, suppose that historical data showed that code inspection yields averaged 66.67%. With 18 defects found in the inspection, a 66.67% yield would mean that 9 more defects were not found, with 8 of them injected in coding and 1 in detailed design.

While this approach will be reasonably accurate for the phase just completed, it will not be accurate for the yields of the design and requirements inspection phases. The defects that were missed in these inspections are not likely to be found in a code review or code inspection. Most of the missed requirements and design defects will probably be found in integration test, system test, or by the users. However, unless the team has historical data on the yields of all development phases, the above method is the best one available. For another example of how to estimate yield based on the team's data on the project currently under way, review the example in section 16.7 on quality planning during the team relaunch. This is an example of an alternate way to estimate yield with the team's available data.

Quality Profiles and Quality Criteria

The quality profile provides a graphical way to look at program quality data. These profiles represent the five key criteria for program quality that are used in quality planning. These quality criteria are defined as follows.

1. The time spent in detailed design is equal to or greater than the time spent in coding.
2. The time spent in detailed design reviews is equal to or greater than 50% of the time spent in detailed design.
3. The time spent in code reviews is equal to or greater than 50% of the time spent in coding.
4. The defects found in compile are fewer than 10 defects/KLOC.
5. The defects found in unit test are fewer than 5 defects/KLOC.

The program profile shown in Figure 19.1 is reasonably good. It indicates that few, if any, defects will likely be found in the product after unit test.

When the quality measure is equal to or better than the specified profile value, the profile value is 1.0 and is displayed at the outer edge of the pentagon.

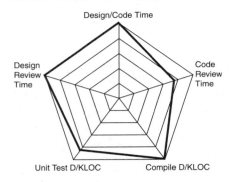

Figure 19.1 Component 3 Quality Profile

Values worse than the specified parameters are drawn toward the center of the pentagon. The values for the five profile dimensions are calculated as follows.

1. If detailed design time (DLDT) ≥ coding time (CT), P1 = 1.0.

If DLDT < CT, P1 = DLDT/CT.

2. If detailed design review time (DLDRT) ≥ 0.5 * DLDT, P2 = 1.0.

If DLDRT < 0.5 * DLDT, P2 = DLDRT/(0.5 * DLDT).

3. If code review time (CRT) ≥ 0.5 * CT, P3 = 1.0.

If CRT < 0.5 * CT, P3 = CRT/(0.5 * CT).

4. If compile defects (CD) ≤ 10 defects/KLOC, P4 = 1.0.

If CD > 10 defects/KLOC, P4 = 20/(10 + CD).

5. If unit test defects (UTD) ≤ 5 defects/KLOC, P5 = 1.0.

If UTD > 5 defects/KLOC, P5 = 10/(5 + UTD).

The reasons the quality profile is useful are as follows.

☐ When the quality profile indicates a high-quality program, that program is unlikely to have remaining defects.

☐ By examining the quality profiles for many programs, the team can quickly spot programs that are most likely to have quality problems.

☐ From the quality profile, the team can see which process steps are most troublesome. This can help the team members identify the source of the problem and take appropriate corrective action.

Examples of six quality profiles are shown in Figure 19.2. Of the six programs shown in the figure, components 1, 2, and 3 did not have subsequent defects,

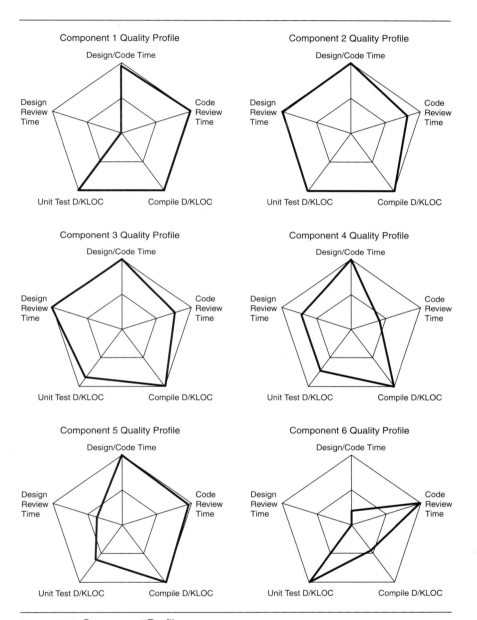

Figure 19.2 Component Profiles

whereas components 4, 5, and 6 did. Since testing does not generally find all of a program's defects, programs like component 1, which has a poor quality profile, may actually have no defects found in test. However, they probably still have undetected defects.

The simplest way to assess a quality profile is to see if all five of the profile dimensions are at or near the outer edge of the radar chart. The closer any measure is to the center of the profile, the more defects the program is likely to have. In interpreting the profiles, keep the following general principles in mind.

1. A good profile indicates that a program *is not likely to have* remaining defects.

2. A poor quality profile indicates that a program *may have* remaining defects.

3. The profiles are guides. When teams follow the TSP process and use proper methods, the profiles are reasonably reliable indicators of program quality.

For example, a good unit test value could indicate either a product with very few defects or a poor unit test. It could also indicate that the defect data are incomplete. Similarly, a good design to code ratio could indicate a good design, a developer who had a lot of design problems, or incomplete time data. In general, however, the combination of all five profile dimensions provides a reasonably comprehensive view of the development process. That is, when a program has high quality in all five profile dimensions, it is probably a high-quality program.

The quality manager can help you and the team leader monitor the team's data-gathering and ensure that all of the team members are properly reporting on their work. In your periodic meetings with the team leader, ask the quality manager to join you in reviewing the quality profiles for the programs that have completed unit test. If any profiles look troublesome, discuss the most effective remedial actions the team could take. The quality manager should also review these quality profiles with the team members involved and discuss what they should do to improve their quality performance. The team must also decide what to do with the programs that have poor profiles.

In these discussions, remind the quality manager and team leader that these reviews should not be seen as personal criticism of any team member. These are *process* problems. If quality is a problem, it is the team's problem and the team will have to fix it. The purpose of the reviews is to identify the problems and to work with the team to address them as early in the process as possible. The objective is to prevent a recurrence of similar problems in the future.

Test Data Analysis

The final quality management technique concerns test data analysis. Here, you coach the quality manager in examining the team's test data to identify any product elements that will likely have remaining defects. The guideline for this analysis is that the number of defects found in any test is the best indicator of the number likely to remain after that test. Thus, if a program has many defects in unit or integration test, it is likely to have many defects in system test and final use.

As complete data become available for any test phase, the quality manager should identify the few components with the lowest process quality index (PQI). PQI is calculated by multiplying the five component values of the quality profile. That is:

$$PQI = P1 * P2 * P3 * P4 * P5$$

When a component has a PQI value that is less than about 0.4, it is likely to have defects. The team should agree on a PQI threshold during launch meeting 5, and any component with a lower value should be reinspected and/or redeveloped. While this reinspection and redevelopment will take time, it will take a great deal less time than finding and fixing the defects in test. It will also produce a much higher quality product. The team should then use the data on the defects found to update their personal design and code review checklists.

19.7   Interpreting Quality Data

To maintain a consistent focus on quality, the team members must know how to analyze and report their defect data. The defect-removal profile provides the simplest and most effective vehicle for doing this. To provide consistent measures, planned program LOC can be used to calculate defects/KLOC in the early phases and then updated as actual data become available. Using the sample profile in Figure 19.3, the following paragraphs describe how to interpret these data.

1. When any of the early-phase defects/KLOC values are zero or near to zero, it either means that the team has not yet reached that phase, has spent little time in that phase, or that the members are not recording and reporting their defect data.

2. Until teams have data on similar completed projects, the requirements and high-level-design defect numbers will be difficult to interpret. However, if these numbers are very low (such as 1 or 2 defects/KLOC), it probably indicates low-yield inspections. In these cases, examine the review rates and discuss remedial actions with the team members.

3. When team members find very few defects in detailed design reviews, it either means that they are using sound design methods or that they are not doing effective reviews. You can usually tell by asking them to describe the analysis methods they used in the review. If they merely scanned the design

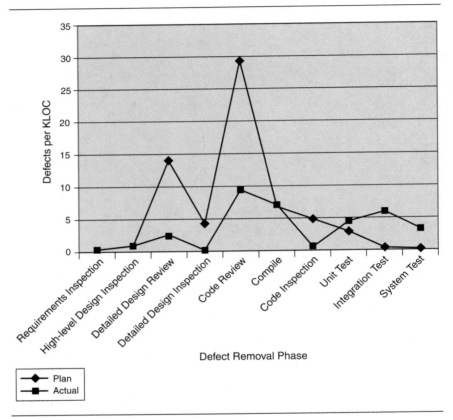

Figure 19.3 Defect Density Profile

with a checklist, they could not have found many sophisticated design problems. Show them how to do a careful design analysis. The detailed-design review should find more defects/KLOC than either the detailed-design inspection or unit testing. If not, the design review probably was not done properly.

4. The code review should find the most defects. If the code review defects/ KLOC is not substantially greater than the compile defects/KLOC, the code review was not done properly and the code probably has a substantial number of remaining defects. However, caution the team leader and quality manager to be careful in using this measure. Too strong a focus on defect counts could motivate some developers to stop recording their compile defects.

5. The compile defects/KLOC should generally be under 10. While this is an arbitrary number, it has generally indicated high-quality code. With experi-

ence, teams can develop reasonable target levels for their own environments and can use control charts to monitor performance against them (Florac 1999). The developers should learn to use their compile defect data, for they provide the only truly objective measure of code quality. If there are few compile defects, code quality is almost certainly good. Then, if there are many test defects, that would likely indicate design problems.

6. The code inspection defects should be quite low, generally well under the number found in compile or code review. After compiling, the code inspection should focus on those issues that the developer is likely to have missed, such as security, interfaces, timing, memory management, and the like. It is also a good time to check any of the loops or complex structures that were not checked in the design review or design inspection.

7. The unit test defects/KLOC should generally be below 5. As before, this is an arbitrary number that has generally indicated high-quality code. Also have the team develop its own target levels when it has the data and use control charts to monitor performance (Florac 1999). Generally, fewer defects should be found in unit test than in the code inspection, the detailed-design inspection, or the detailed-design review. If the unit test defects are higher than any of these prior reviews or inspections, a reinspection is called for.

8. If the prior criteria have been met, the integration and system test defects/ KLOC numbers should be very low. If not, the team should analyze the integration and system test defects to see which phases were troublesome and to decide what remedial actions are appropriate.

The defect-removal profile can be used with any program component or for an entire system. At the team level and for management reporting purposes, teams should focus at the system level. If any phases appear troublesome, they should then look at the individual component or module data to identify the problems. Then they can decide on appropriate remedial actions.

While teams' initial problems generally concern incomplete or inaccurate defect data, after the quality of their data improves and after they are consistently doing high-quality reviews, they can use the defect-removal profiles to quickly identify potential quality problems and take timely remedial action.

19.8 Reporting Quality Data

One of the most difficult problems for any TSP team is getting the members to consistently follow the process and to accurately report their data. By regularly reviewing quality data with the team and each member, you can greatly improve their process discipline. When these reviews are coupled with periodic management reports and reviews, members are most likely to follow the process. As described in Chapter 17, start these reviews immediately after the team launch and continue them until the team members are accurately and completely recording their data. Thereafter, check periodically to ensure that they continue to do so.

The basic quality report is the defect-density profile shown in Figure 19.3. Here, the plan data are shown, as well as the actual data by phase. While this profile is relatively easy to interpret at the end of the project, it is even more important to use it during development when there is time to fix the quality problems. For this purpose, the team should use charts that show the number of defects found per phase instead of defect densities. It is then easier to visualize the effect of partially completed phases. For example, when only half of the code has been inspected, the actual value for code-inspection defects should be about half of the planned value. Such a chart is shown in Figure 19.4.

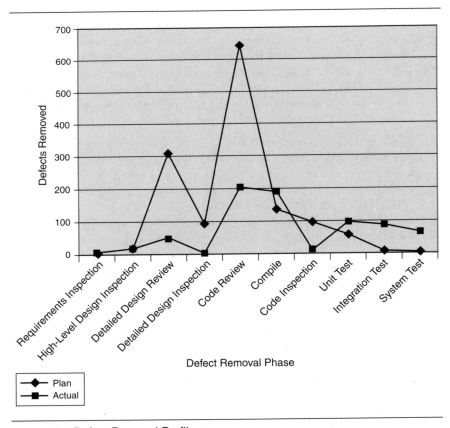

Figure 19.4 Defect-Removal Profile

Each week, as the team reviews its progress, the quality manager should show the defect profile with the total defects found so far in each phase. Point out that one cannot interpret the defect numbers for any phase without additional information. For example, a low number of defects could be either good or bad. To understand the data, the team must examine other process data for the phase being assessed. The following are some things to consider for each phase.

Requirements inspection. In the requirements inspection, only count the major defects and compare them with the plan. A major requirements defect is one that would, if not corrected, result in one or more product defects. Minor requirements defects typically concern document format, punctuation, and grammatical or spelling mistakes that do not affect the meaning of the requirements document. Wording mistakes could be major or minor defects depending on the specific case. Until teams have significant data on their requirements inspections, they cannot judge the adequacy of the inspection. They can only check that the inspection rates were reasonable and use the capture-recapture method described earlier in this chapter to estimate the number of defects remaining in the product.

High-level design inspection. While the situation with high-level design is similar to that for requirements inspections, the quality manager should also check on the design inspection methods. If the reviewers merely read the design, they will not likely have found many of the design problems. That would generally take a careful design analysis. If an adequate design analysis was not done, the team should do another inspection.

Detailed-design and code reviews. When teams get to the detailed-design and code review phases, they can quickly detect quality problems. For example, Figure 19.4 shows that there were few DLD review defects, no DLD inspection defects, and many fewer code review defects than planned. In these cases, the team can use process run charts like those shown in Figure 19.5 to better understand the data (Florac 1999).

In Figure 19.5, the review rate in LOC per hour is shown on the y-axis and the component number is given on the x-axis. The review rate target established in quality planning is shown by the solid line. This chart shows that components 1 and 7 had review rates that were close to the plan, components 2, 4, and 6 were reviewed far too quickly, and components 3, 5, and 8 were not reviewed. With these data, you can discuss the situation with the team members and guide them in deciding what to do about it. Clearly, the developers should all do reviews, and they should all review at close to the planned rates.

Compile. Even with PSP training, it is often hard to get developers to record the defects they find while compiling. The principal reason is that few developers understand how useful these data can be. The number of compile defects is the only truly objective measure for code quality. If a review or a test is poorly conducted, few defects will be found. However, few defects could also indicate a high-quality product. With compile defects, few defects always mean high-quality code and many defects always mean poor-quality code. As long as the defect data

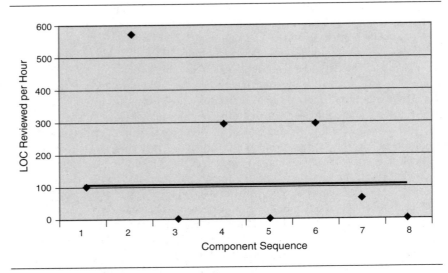

Figure 19.5 Code Review Rate Run Chart

are properly reported, no interpretation is required. Furthermore, there is a modest correlation between the number of defects found in compiling and the number found in testing. Therefore, the number of defects found in compiling is the first objective measure teams can get of the degree to which the members are producing quality programs.

From the compile run chart in Figure 19.6, components 2 and 6 had quality problems while components 1, 4, and 7 were close to or better than the team's goals. Components 3, 5, and 8 had no compile defects. This could indicate either that the members developing these components had produced high-quality code or that they had not recorded their compile defects. By comparing these compile data with the code review rate run chart in Figure 19.5, the team can see that components 3, 5, and 8 were not reviewed. This suggests that the developers had not gathered their compile defect data.

If the team members are not reviewing their code, their products will almost certainly have many defects in integration and system testing. If the team lets these components into test without thorough inspections and possibly even complete rework or replacement, the project will be exposed to many extra weeks of testing. It is not unusual to have teams spend as much time in testing as they did producing their designs and code, just because they did not take a few hours to do thorough reviews and inspections.

Code inspection and unit test. Teams can prepare run charts for the code inspection and unit test data in the same way that they do for code reviews and compiling. The data are also interpreted in the same way.

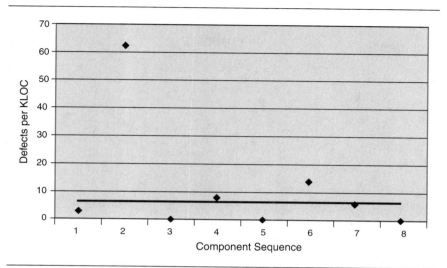

Figure 19.6 Compile Run Chart

Integration and system test. While integration and system test defect data can be presented in run chart form, it is then too late in the process to do anything but test and fix the product. To understand these phases, a chart like that in Figure 19.7 can be useful. This requires that the developers record every defect found after unit test and track it to the component where it was fixed. Teams often defer doing this until it is too late to do much to correct process problems. Emphasize that these test defect data can tell them where their development process is not working and suggest ways to fix it. The earlier they know this, the sooner they can fix their process.

The team should use these data to correct the process, to update their checklists, and to determine which components to re-review, reinspect, or redevelop. By quickly identifying and cleaning up poor quality components, teams can save significant test time, even after testing has started.

In analyzing the data in Figure 19.7, the following appears to be the case.

1. Components 1, 4, and 7 look pretty good.

2. Components 2 and 6 had excessive unit test defects. Component 2 should be reworked or replaced while 6 is marginally acceptable and should be watched.

3. Components 3, 5, and 8 had no unit test data and also should be reinspected, reworked, or possibly replaced.

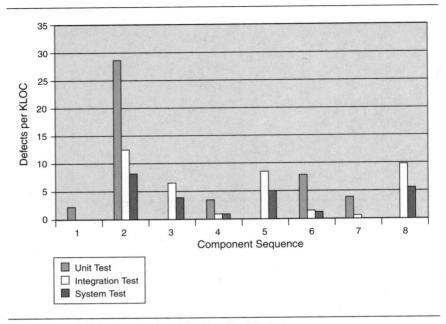

Figure 19.7 Unit, Integration, and System Test Defects

19.9   Defect Reporting Considerations

Teams must be careful in using defect data. If they press too hard to meet a defect goal, they are likely to bias the data. They should use the data to motivate their members to do better work, not to embarrass them. In coaching the team, never compare the members' data. The focus should be on the process and the product, with emphasis on improvement, complete data gathering, and thorough reviews and inspections. To consistently produce quality products, teams must resist the temptation to blame anyone for the problems they find. Since we all inject defects, defects must be seen as process problems, not as personal failings.

Many team members will object to recording compile defects. While PSP training demonstrates that this is not an onerous task, particularly when the members do thorough code reviews, the team leader should be flexible. If some members object, suggest that they start by keeping simple counts of the number of compile defects. As long as they count every defect they fix in reviews, inspections, compiling, and testing, they will have the data to evaluate the component quality profiles.

While this will not provide the data needed to update personal review checklists, it will provide a useful starting point for managing quality with data.

Finally, as your teams accumulate enough data for statistical analysis and as these data begin to stabilize, the team should consider using statistical control charts. XmR charts are generally the most useful for TSP data (Florac 1999). With the help of the control limits in these charts, the team can see when the various process phases have stabilized and where to concentrate on making further improvements.

19.10 Summary

This chapter discusses how to coach teams to produce quality products. The principles of software quality management are that first, the customer is key. Second, management must make quality the top priority, and third, the people doing the work must own the quality program. Fourth, to improve quality, teams must change their processes; and fifth, they must measure quality, because without measurements, quality is just talk. Finally, doing the job right always costs less in the long run. In fact, when quality improvement increases costs, it is a sure sign that the team is doing something wrong. Urge the team and team leader to consistently follow these six quality principles.

In this book, quality management refers to managing the defect category of quality. Defect management must have top development priority because the defect content of a product largely determines the team's ability to develop that product on a predictable schedule and for its planned costs. Quality management is a journey that never ends. As teams measure and manage quality, they gain the knowledge, experience, and data to take the next step in their quality journey.

The team members must understand that they are responsible for the quality of the products they produce. If they don't each strive to produce a quality product, no one else can do it for them. Although the members are personally responsible for the quality of the programs they each produce, the team as a whole also has overall quality responsibility.

By having the quality manager frequently review the defect-removal profile with the team and management, he or she can help the team members focus on quality and ensure that they consistently gather and report their defect data. Together with process run charts, the defect-removal profile will help teams recognize quality problems early in the process when they can devise timely corrective actions.

References

Florac, William A., and Anita D. Carleton. *Measuring the Software Process*: *Statistical Process Control for Software Process Improvement*. Reading, MA: Addison-Wesley. 1999.

Humphrey, Watts S. *PSP^{SM}: A Self-Improvement Process for Software Engineers*. Boston: Addison-Wesley. 2005.

Humphrey, Watts S. *Introduction to the Team Software Process^{SM}*. Boston: Addison-Wesley. 2000.

20

The Project Postmortem

The project cycle postmortem follows the same principles as the launch postmortem described in Chapter 15, so reread section 15.1 now and also reread it each time you prepare for a postmortem. TSP teams should hold a postmortem right before they relaunch the next project cycle. They should also hold another postmortem at the end of the job. The postmortem provides the data teams need to capitalize on their experiences, to improve their performance on this project, and to do better work on future projects. The topics covered in this chapter are as follows.

- ☐ The purpose of the postmortem
- ☐ The desired data
- ☐ Postmortem preparation
- ☐ The postmortem process
- ☐ The teamwork assessment
- ☐ Coaching and leadership assessment
- ☐ Coaching the postmortem
- ☐ The team-member postmortem

20.1   The Purpose of the Postmortem

At the end of each project or project cycle, TSP teams have a great deal of information on the accuracy of their estimates, the quality of their products, and how the process worked for them. However, this information is transient and, unless gathered and organized now when it is readily available, they will have trouble reconstructing it later. The TSP calls for a project postmortem at the end of every project cycle while the team members' experiences are fresh and they are likely to think of ways to do better work in the future.

While the TSP process calls for a postmortem at the end of each project cycle, teams do not generally hold cycle postmortems without some urging from management or the coach. They are in a hurry to start on to the next project cycle and do not recognize the importance of consolidating and recording their data, reviewing their personal and team performance, and updating their processes, checklists, and databases. This is also an ideal time to get feedback on your coaching performance and to ask for suggestions on how you could have been more helpful. If your teams do not regularly hold postmortems, urge them to do so and help them to hold thorough and complete ones.

20.2   The Desired Data

Before gathering data, it is important to consider how you intend to use that data. With the TSP, there is a great deal of potentially useful data, but without a plan, teams can waste a lot of time gathering data they will not use. For the postmortem, the principal interest is in the team's estimating accuracy, quality performance, and improvements the members could make to better guide them in their work. These topics are discussed in the following paragraphs.

Estimating Accuracy

Teams make the most accurate estimates when their members have historical data for the size and cost of similar work. The needed data concern estimated versus actual product size, estimated versus actual productivity, the to-date distribution of task time by week and by phase, and a database of planning parameters such as size to time correlation, linear regression parameters, and prediction intervals. The required data should be gathered for every process phase and for the smallest practical product elements. This will provide the maximum number of data points for future planning. Organizing and assembling these data is a principal purpose of the postmortem.

Quality Performance

Teams should gather data on the defects they injected during requirements, design, and coding. Then, in the postmortem, they can combine this information and their task-hour data to make preliminary defect injection estimates. The team must then update these estimates as more defects are discovered later. With a high-quality process, however, these later adjustments will generally be quite small.

Since defect injection rates and removal yields vary considerably with project type and team experience, quality data for the early project phases are particularly important. Where the team does not produce its own requirements and design documents, it is not possible to estimate defect injection rates. However, it is possible to make reasonably good estimates from historical data. For example, for requirements documents, a count of the major and minor defects per document page would generally indicate the number of issues the team should anticipate. In counting pages, only include those with substantive requirements data and don't count those with overview or summary material.

In general, when teams do work that injects defects, they should gather the data needed to calculate their injection rates. However, when they get work products from other groups, they will not generally have such data and must estimate the quality of these input materials from historical size, time, and defect data. They should also calculate the average requirement or design defect fix times and, where significant, the schedule delays normally involved in obtaining answers to requirements or design questions.

Other important quality data concern inspection and review yields and the defect data needed to update the team members' checklists. Actual yield data will not be available until the end of the project, but teams can make preliminary yield estimates. A method for doing this is described in Chapter 19. The data collected during the postmortem provides the basis for analyzing yield data and making accurate quality plans. Good quality plans are required to make accurate test-time estimates, and accurate test-time estimates are essential for making reliable team commitments.

Process Improvement

The required process improvement data concern the team member's experiences with the process. The team members should discuss the processes they used and consider how these processes could be improved. Ask how the various process scripts and forms worked and if anyone has suggestions for improving them. If some members did not use a particular process element, find out why. There could have been problems with that element, the team's plan might not have called for that type of work, or the team member might not have followed the team's defined process.

Review all of the process elements and give the team members time to discuss their experiences and opinions about each one. Since the team members will not know which problems were caused by the process and which were due to their personal mistakes or oversights, view every concern as a symptom of a real problem. Even then, it will usually take some effort on your part to get the team members to discuss process problems and to make change suggestions.

20.3 Postmortem Preparation

To make the postmortem most useful, the process manager must prepare for it in advance. Without advance preparation, the team members will not have the data to assess their performance or to obtain useful improvement guidance. Shortly before the postmortem, the process manager should ask the team members about the kinds of data they would like to discuss and then gather these data and make them available before the meeting. If the members have been diligent in gathering their data and if they have used a suitable TSP tool, data gathering should not be time consuming or onerous.

20.4 The Postmortem Process

Like all TSP meetings, the postmortem starts by establishing the meeting roles and reviewing the agenda. The following paragraphs review each of the subsequent steps in the team's project postmortem.

Baseline Evaluation

In this step, the support manager leads the team's review of the configuration management system. The principal questions to address in this review are the following.

1. How did the configuration management and change control processes work?
2. How many exceptions were made to the team's configuration management and change control processes and what were the reasons?
3. If there were any problems, what changes does the team suggest and who will produce the required PIPs?
4. What product elements were baselined in the cycle and on the project to date?

Plan Evaluation

In plan evaluation, the planning manager leads the team in reviewing its actual versus planned data for the size, resource, and schedule performance of the most recent project cycle and for the project to date. In this review, the principal questions concern estimating accuracy, productivity, and task time.

Quality Performance

The quality manager leads the team in assessing quality performance for the prior project cycles and for the project to date. The principal questions here concern defect injection and removal rates and defect removal yields. This review should cover a comparison of the team's quality performance with its goals and, if the goals were missed, an analysis of the causes for these results. If the yields for any phases are below the team's goals or if the defect injection rates are too high, the team should identify the reasons for these variances and agree on actions to improve performance in the future.

Planning Data

Based on the experiences in the prior cycles and on the data for all of the work done on the project to date, what have the team members learned that will help them make better estimates in the future? The final part of the planning data step is for the planning manager to lead a review of the planning guidelines and to update the productivity, rate, and percentage values to reflect the team's most recent data.

The team members should also discuss any opportunities they see for improving quality performance in the future and gather the data needed to take advantage of these ideas during the next team launch or relaunch. The final step in assessing the team's quality performance is for the quality manager to lead the team in reviewing the team's quality guidelines and making any needed updates to the quality criteria used in quality planning and in evaluating quality profiles (see section 19.6).

Process Evaluation

In this part of the postmortem meeting, the process manager leads the team through a review of all the team's activities to see where the team members followed the process and where they did not. Where they followed the process, they should consider how that process could be improved and then prepare and submit PIPs with suggested changes. Where they did not follow the defined process, they should reconsider the need for that process step in the future. Typically, if an activity is likely to be repeated more than a few times, teams should consider defining processes for it. This will permit them to measure, plan, and track their work. This, in turn, will quickly improve their estimating accuracy as well as the productivity and quality of their work. If any new or changed processes are called for, the team should prepare PIPs describing these changes and why they are needed.

Stakeholder Survey

The customer interface manager leads the team in a brief discussion of the stakeholder survey. The principal topics to be covered are the following.

1. What stakeholders should be contacted?
2. What information does the team need from each stakeholder?
3. How will the team use the information once it is obtained?
4. Who will take the actions required to gather the desired information, analyze the results, and prepare a summary report?

While formal surveys can be expensive and few organizations gather them, teams can usually conduct informal surveys relatively easily. Such surveys can be extremely useful in identifying problem areas, in maintaining a positive customer relationship, and in tracking the impact of process and product changes. Since, in the crisis-driven environment of most development organizations, successful performance is likely to be invisible, the survey results can also be used to demonstrate the significance and business value of the team's accomplishments.

Surveys are most useful after they have been used for long enough and on enough products for trends to be identified and analyzed. The SEPG or some other permanent group should have responsibility for accumulating and assessing these survey data. Also, since customer surveying is a highly specialized field, organizations should consider getting expert advice on constructing and administrating even simple surveys.

Goal Evaluation

In the next postmortem meeting step, the team leader guides the team through a discussion of the team's performance against the goals it established in launch meeting 2. The focus should be on any goals that were missed, why they were missed, and possible actions to improve future performance. Where the goals were met or nearly met, the team members should discuss how to both publicize and celebrate their successes. They should also consider what new and more challenging goals to set for the future.

Final Report Preparation

The last postmortem step is final report preparation. Here, the team leader and the postmortem meeting recorder gather all of the meeting data, check to ensure that they have complete data on the project, and produce the postmortem report. This report should have a brief cover page that summarizes the project's key results and the principal lessons learned. If any of the role managers have topics that should be included, suggest that they write a brief summary and then either include all the pertinent data or provide references to the data locations. The full report should then be filed in the project notebook, and a summary report circulated to interested management, project stakeholders, other TSP teams, and all of the team members.

20.5   Teamwork Assessment

Since the planning, quality, and process managers have already reviewed their activities in the previous postmortem steps, they may not have anything further to add at this point. However, if they or any of the team members would like to comment on the performance of these roles, this is an opportune time to do so. In addition, the other role managers should briefly comment on their activities during the cycle and ask the team for suggestions on how that role could have been more useful to the team or any of the team members.

In these evaluations, teams tend to concentrate on the negative aspects of the role manager job. However, it is also important to have them consider what was most helpful about each role. Make sure that this discussion does not turn into a complaint session, and emphasize that each role manager made a gift of his or her time and energy to help the team be more effective. Keep the discussion positive.

Teams are generally reluctant to discuss how their team performed as a team, and they are generally much more comfortable talking about impersonal topics like cost, schedule, or quality. However, a frank but positive discussion can help teams improve, so get the members talking about their teamwork. Instead of asking for criticism of any member or of the team leader, urge them to focus on what worked and what did not. Did the scripts help them work together and what additional information and support would have been useful?

Keep the discussion objective and avoid personality conflicts. Don't let this become an attack on anyone. Everyone has quirks and foibles and it is easy for people to get annoyed when they work under high pressure. It is always fair for someone to talk about how he or she felt, but it is almost always counterproductive for anyone to talk about what someone else did or said. We are all experts on what we heard and felt, but comments about what others said, did, or meant are usually counterproductive. Keep the session positive and keep the focus on what team members feel would have helped them.

20.6   Coaching and Leadership Assessment

The teamwork-assessment ground rules also apply to the coaching assessment. Ask the team members to comment on your coaching job, but have them focus on what could have been more helpful or where they didn't agree with something you said or did. When team members complain, as someone almost certainly will, don't get defensive, but ask them to suggest actions you could have taken or ways you could have been more helpful.

After this discussion, it would be appropriate for the team leader to ask for any comments or suggestions on his or her performance. However, do not ask for feedback on the team's leadership unless you have already discussed this with the team leader and agreed on how to handle the discussion. Depending on your agreement, it would be best to have the team leader lead this discussion with you being moderator. If, in the prior discussion, he or she was reluctant to do this, treat it as a question of trust. Suggest that the team leader trust the team to be constructive, and then do your best to run the meeting so that it is constructive and helpful to the team leader.

20.7   Coaching the Postmortem

In coaching the postmortem, your goal is to get the team members thinking about the data they would like to have when they next launch a team project. Then help them to gather as much of these data as they can from the records of the work they have just completed. If they have been diligent in recording their data, they will have almost everything they need at their fingertips. However, since few teams start with a clear understanding of the data they will need and why they will need it, the members will often be inconsistent in data gathering. Their time data will probably be fairly complete and their final product size data will be accurate. However, the size data for requirements pages, high-level design pages, or lines of detailed-design pseudocode are likely to be sketchy and inconsistent.

The defect data are also likely to be quite uneven, with a few members having complete data, some gathering data on a few project phases, and others with no defect data at all. While you should have caught and corrected these problems earlier in the project, it is likely that some will have escaped your and the team's notice. The key at this point is not to focus on blaming any of the team members. Assess the completeness of the team's data and objectively review what the team can learn from the available data and where there are gaps that make the data less useful. Then discuss these data gaps and focus on what data the team members would like to have at this point in their next project. With this need in mind, suggest that the team formulate data-gathering goals for the next project or next project cycle.

The objective of the postmortem is to help the team learn from its work and to prepare the members to capitalize on this learning when they start another cycle or project. Improved data gathering will most likely be the principal lesson for inexperienced teams. However, with your help and guidance, the members should soon get beyond this rudimentary stage and start addressing the truly challenging questions of improved quality management, better design practices, improved planning and tracking, and better teamwork. Software-intensive system development is a wonderfully challenging business, and the key is to interest teams in improving their performance with every successive project.

20.8 The Team-Member Postmortem

While postmortem data gathering and data analysis can be very useful at a team level, it can be even more useful at the individual level. Size to time correlations are generally quite poor for team data, but can be very high for individuals, as demonstrated by the PROBE method (Humphrey 2005). Similarly, using personal quality data can greatly improve review and inspection yields. The principal purpose of the team-member postmortem is to gather and analyze the data needed for process improvement. In a personal postmortem, the team members should follow roughly the same steps that the team followed in the project postmortem.

1. Review the available data and assess the adequacy of personal data-gathering practices.

2. Assess size and time estimating performance and see where they could be improved. Each team member should consider the correlations achieved and whether the proper PROBE methods were used.

3. Each developer should also examine his or her quality performance in each defect removal phase and see where review rates, review checklists, or review methods might be improved.

4. The developers should also consider the process phases their data showed to be most troublesome and ask other team members to suggest improvements. Have them prepare personal process scripts for any changed phases and get their teammates to review them.

At the conclusion of the personal postmortem, suggest that each team member prepare a brief summary report to put into his or her personal project notebook and possibly distribute to the other team members. This would also be the time to update the personal project notebook with any pertinent project or process results or conclusions.

20.9   Summary

The objective of a personal or a team project postmortem is to provide TSP teams with the data and insight to consistently improve their performance. A postmortem should be held at the end of every project cycle as well as at the end of the entire project.

In the postmortem, the team's and team members' focus should be on gathering data on estimating accuracy, quality performance, and process improvement. Since gathering these data will generally take time, the postmortem will be most effective if the process manager has first determined what team data are needed and then gathered and distributed these data to the team members before the meeting.

The postmortem meeting process includes an evaluation of the team's configuration management and change control system, a review of planning and quality results, and a discussion of process and goal performance. Teams should also conduct stakeholder surveys to determine how their performance measured up against their customers' and businesses' needs and to obtain the evidence to demonstrate the business significance of their efforts to management.

Your objective in the postmortem is to motivate your teams to gather the data they need to continue improving and to ensure that their data are properly reported in the project notebook and final project summary report.

Reference

Humphrey, Watts S. *PSP^{SM}: A Self-Improvement Process for Software Engineers.* Boston: Addison-Wesley. 2005.

PART IV

TSP Extensions

This was the biggest conference room they had, but it was jammed. All 52 team members were there as were the 5 subteam leaders, the program manager, and the company's entire senior management staff. The CEO had decided to personally kick off this team launch by describing the current business situation and why this product was critical to the company's future. He took about an hour to walk through the company's financial performance, the marketing situation, and the leading customers' priority needs. He then described what the competitors were offering and ended by describing their planned strategy for responding. The planned new product was the most critical element of this strategy.

While TSP teams are universally energized and excited by the launch process, this team was almost transformed. The CEO's story was a real eye-opener for everybody on the team, and their enthusiasm and energy level was greater than anything I have seen before or since. Being part of a motivated team is always exciting, but this was such a large group, it seemed like a corporate-wide commitment.

Since this team started on such a "high," I was concerned that the months of hard work that followed would be a letdown. I need not have worried. The team made a marvelous plan and then they delivered a quality product on schedule—a company first. The key was regular communication sessions, a factual and data-based management style, and the joy of being on a winning team.

The TSP supports several types of teams and provides guidance on the many ways to lead and coach these teams. For development teams, and particularly for teams involving a wide variety of specialties, teaming arrangements can become quite complex. This part of the book addresses various types of teams and provides guidelines to help you coach them. Since no book could possibly describe every situation or discuss every issue you will face, the emphasis of these chapters is on principles, together with suggestions for how to address the most common team problems.

The chapters in this section discuss the various categories of teams and some of the variations of the TSP process that have been designed to address these needs. However, since every team is different and since the specific needs of any given team will differ from the precise structure of any predefined TSP process, you will often have to make adjustments, either in the way the team is structured or in the way you guide the team's launch and subsequent work. Generally, by helping the team and its management in structuring the project and by properly interpreting the TSP process, you can address most team needs with one of the existing TSP process variants. The few TSP scripts shown in this book are only examples. While they reflect current TSP practice, there is a great deal to learn about teams and teamwork, and the TSP will evolve to incorporate this new knowledge.

Chapter 21 discusses team variations. That is, teams can be of either the project or the functional type, and their work can be composed of individual, subteam, or full-team tasks. Chapter 21 discusses these variations and how the TSP, the functional TSP strategy, and the multi-team TSP (TSPm) process variant address them.

Chapter 22 describes the functional team, what it is, and how it works. A functional team is one that is responsible for a set of relatively continuous activities. These functional teams may perform some organizational function like providing specialized support services, handling system maintenance and repair, or providing quality assurance. Chapter 22 describes how functional teams differ from project teams, and it outlines various ways the TSP process can be used to launch and run such teams.

Chapter 23 addresses distributed multi-teams. These are multiple teams that may be distributed among several locations. While the multi-team could be working on a single project or have a functional mission, its subteams are each large enough to function as full TSP teams. This chapter describes the special problems of coaching multiple teams and distributed multiple teams. It also describes the distributed multi-team launch and how this launch differs from the standard TSP launch.

Chapter 24 discusses large system-wide teams. These teams are generally much larger than standard TSPm multi-teams and include the many different skills normally required for large-scale systems development. Such teams typically have hundreds of members and generally include hardware and software developers, program management, systems engineers, requirements specialists, quality assurance and test personnel, manufacturing representatives, and possibly deployment, maintenance, or even customer participants. Since such large integrated teams are each unique, there is no standard TSP process to support them. However, this chapter describes the general principles that should guide development of the custom processes needed to support such teams.

21

Team Variations

Since there are many kinds of teams and many kinds of team projects, there must also be many possible variations of the TSP process. This chapter describes the principal variations in the kinds of work that teams do and the ways in which team structure and operation are typically adjusted to address these work variations. Starting with the various kinds of work teams must handle, the chapter reviews the primary dimensions of team variability and how those dimensions are addressed by the TSP. The following principal topics are covered in this chapter.

- ☐ Work perspectives
- ☐ Team structure
- ☐ Team communication
- ☐ Functional teams
- ☐ Distributed teams
- ☐ Multiple teams
- ☐ System-wide teams
- ☐ Coaching guidelines

21.1   Work Perspectives

Teams are typically established to accomplish some objective, be it to win a sports competition, engage in battle, or accomplish a workplace objective. Team effectiveness is largely determined by the capabilities of the team members, the quality of their leadership, the level of coaching provided, and the degree to which the team's structure and organization suits the work it is assigned to do.

While it is essential to have capable and qualified team members and to provide them with professional leadership and coaching, the team's structure and organization is also important. Without a properly formed and structured team and without an appropriate management system, effective teamwork is difficult. In fact, teams are more likely to fail for management reasons than for technical ones. Poorly structured teams are much less likely to be successful than ones that are properly formed and led. However, since projects come in all flavors and sizes, and since organizations can be structured in varying ways, you must adopt the TSP to whatever variations you face. This chapter deals with the principles involved, and subsequent chapters discuss more specific cases.

In structuring a team, it is important to consider the characteristics of the work to be done and to structure the team so its management system best fits its work assignment. In doing this, the key issues are the degree to which the team members' work can be separated into independent elements, the specialized skills required to do the work, and the size of the total effort. These can be viewed as the principal perspectives to consider in forming teams.

- ☐ Interdependence
- ☐ Specialization
- ☐ Size

Interdependence

In teamwork, the interactions among the members can vary enormously. At one extreme, the members can be completely independent, with few working interactions. One example is a small software team that supported a group of research scientists. When a scientist needed software support, he or she would call the team leader and explain what was needed. One of the team's developers was then assigned to support that scientist, and the developer worked with that scientist to develop the needed program. Each task might take from a few hours to a few weeks, but the tasks were completely independent and the developers had little or no need to interact with each other.

Another example might be a team developing a multicard embedded system, where each team member was assigned responsibility for developing one of the cards. To the extent that the design was well thought out and the card interfaces were completely and precisely specified, the team members could work almost entirely by themselves. They would, of course, have to interact when the time came to integrate their separate cards into the finished product.

At the other extreme are teams where the members never work by themselves. An example would be a design team for a communications system proposal. This team had three research scientists, three software developers, and two hardware developers. They were cloistered in a small house at the corner of the research laboratory campus. The entire team spent every day for two weeks hashing out the details of the system's design.

In most organizations and on most projects, the work is rarely at either of these extremes. There are occasional sessions involving the complete team and frequent small subgroup meetings to settle specific issues. There could also be a substantial amount of individual work. The degree of interaction among the team members depends on the kinds of work being done, the working style of the organization, and the preferences of the team members.

Since teams provide a powerful support structure for their members, and since well-formed and properly functioning teams provide a cohesive and intimate working environment, it is generally desirable to put all of the members of a common project on the same team. This common team environment then enables the kind of close cooperation and communication that builds truly superior products.

One fact that demonstrates the importance of team communication is that finished products are almost always structured like the organizations that built them. For example, if an organization's management sought a product that had multiple components that worked together smoothly and efficiently, they should form a single project team where the developers of these components worked together smoothly and efficiently. Conversely, if such a product were developed by separate teams that only communicated through some management structure, they would not likely produce components that worked together smoothly and efficiently.

Specialization

While the team's cohesion and level of interaction will depend on organizational structure, they also depend on the members' skills. With different specialties on the same team, the members will likely also have different goals and processes. Since the kind of work will dictate the required skill mix and the organization's structure will largely define the working environment, management will usually need your help in selecting the most appropriate team structure for the job at hand.

Projects may involve many different types of skills. For example, some development projects involve several different technologies. The items to be developed might include semiconductor circuits, power supplies, and software control systems. Conversely, some development teams consist entirely of one specialty. In such groups, any one member can often step in to help anyone else on almost any project task.

To be most effective, team members must have a common set of goals. If, in addition, they all work to a common process and plan, teamwork is even further enhanced. However, when a group has a common goal but the members follow different processes, it may still be structured as a single team. For example, when several people work together, some working on the system's requirements and others designing the software, they will almost certainly have quite different processes. Although such a group could be called a team, its members would not be as cohesive as a group with a common process. While this would not be ideal, it could still be the best choice.

While all of the members need not use a common process to be on the same team, when they share a process they can better support each other. They can then more flexibly balance their workload, interchange tasks, or otherwise provide help and assistance. This is much like the distinction between baseball and basketball teams. In basketball, the game is dynamic, with the players switching positions during the play. In baseball, the players may back each other up or pinch hit, but they have distinctly different and largely static personal roles.

While the sporting analogy is useful, it misses some of the rich variability of development teams. It would make no sense, for example, to have a baseball team composed entirely of first basemen, whereas a team composed entirely of circuit designers could be normal and natural. Also, in construction, teams of carpenters usually act as the overall generalists while teams of masons, plumbers, electricians, roofers, painters, and plasterers handle more specialized tasks. Depending on the size of the job, these teams could each range from part-time individuals to groups of many tradespersons. Development teams can have a similar mix of skills.

Size

Although there is no defined upper limit to team size, groups larger than about 15 or 20 members do not easily develop the close relationships needed for effective teamwork. This does not mean that all team members must be close friends, only that the members must understand each others' roles and plans and be able to support and assist one another. Thus, even if all members follow an identical process and have a common goal, a group of more than about 15 to 20 members should probably be divided into 2 or more unit teams within a larger multi-team structure. Subteams are called **unit teams** in the TSP.

At the other size extreme, there is a lower limit on team size. For example, to split a team into multiple groups, the subgroups should each be large enough to form coherent teams. For instance, if a project had one system requirements person, two software developers, one hardware developer, and one tester, these five people should form a single team. Even though the members follow different personal processes and have largely independent personal plans, there is no other coherent group to which they could belong. Thus, while their personal processes might be very different, the members all have a common team goal and should develop a common overall plan. They are then likely to form a reasonably cohesive working group. While they may not provide the dynamic support that a common process would allow, they can establish a common bond of team membership and a mutual commitment to an agreed-upon goal and plan.

21.2 Team Structure

Organizations have many constraints, and often it is not practical to have all of the members in the same location or even to assign them all to the same managerial unit. For example, a distributed team would have members at multiple physical locations. Although it might be possible to knit these distributed members into a coherent single team, it would be preferable to treat them as separate unit teams in a larger distributed multiple team. To do so, however, the groups at each geographic location should have at least three and preferably four or more members. Then the members would each have some degree of local team support and interaction.

Even when all of the team members are in the same physical location and share a common process, goal, and plan, there may still be managerial or political reasons to form them into separate working units. When that is the case, they should be treated as separate unit teams within a larger multiple team. There is no way to catalog all possible reasons for forming such structures, but examples would be jurisdictional disputes, specialized supervision needs, or representation issues. The problems can also be political or personal.

For example, George managed a small development department. He had been asked to contribute members to a high-priority company project that was being run by the central development group. While George could temporarily make Mack and his team available, he did not want his developers to be managed by the other department. He felt that his people would then likely disappear into this larger group and that he would have trouble getting them back. Therefore, Mack's group was set up as a separate team with its own team leader who reported both to George and to the program manager.

There are many situations where, for no clear technical or project-related reason, a group of closely related people must be grouped as two or more separate teams, each with a separate manager, goal, and workspace. Again, the best response to such situations is to create a multiple team, and then establish the relationships among the elements of this multiple team so that the total team can be effective.

Your job as coach is to help organizations establish the most appropriate team structure and process for each project and team. In doing this, remember that the team's structure need not mirror the organization structure and that the members need not have common managers, departments, or even skills. While management may initially pick a team structure that would not foster team cohesion, urge them to consider several alternate ways to structure the team before making a decision. Also remember that teams learn and grow throughout a project, and the structure that worked at the outset may not be best at a later point. An appropriate team structure can make a big difference.

21.3   Team Communication

Projects can be from one or two people up to hundreds or even thousands of individuals. While it would be most desirable to have one team handle every project, there are practical limits on team size. At the low end, the size limit is obviously two, since one person cannot be a team. At the upper end, however, the limits are not as clear. For example, when does a large group cease being a team and become an organization? One guideline is provided by the nature of the work. Teams tend to be transient and established to accomplish a specific objective, while organizations tend to have longer-term missions and to contain multiple subgroups with goals that are focused on project-like objectives.

With a small unit team of about 5 to 15 members, communication is not usually a problem because the team members know each other and can dynamically adjust their plans. For larger project teams, however, the overall job is generally subdivided into parts that can each be handled by a unit-sized team. Here, the problem is much the same as that for structuring systems into modular parts: maximize communication within the modules and minimize communication among them. If the team structure is not appropriate, the members of the unit teams will likely have excessive interactions with the members of other unit teams.

Since few jobs can be perfectly structured, there are often many unanticipated communication needs among the members of the various unit teams. In the multi-team TSP (TSPm), these communication links are handled through two mechanisms. First, a leadership team is formed of the leaders of each unit team and the overall project manager. This leadership team provides a clear and well-informed point for decision making and issue resolution.

The second mechanism is a network of role-manager teams. These teams consist of the role managers from the various unit teams. For example, all of the planning managers would form one team and the design managers would form another. These role-manager teams then meet at least weekly to coordinate the work of their unit teams and to identify issues to bring to the leadership team. These role-manager teams can also ensure that the work of all the unit teams is properly synchronized and guided.

21.4   Functional Teams

On most development projects, the nature of the job requires at least some interaction among the team members. This is because the product elements that each team member produces must be assembled into a single end product. As the members develop each product element, they must fit these elements together into a coherent total system. When a team works this way, we call that a **project team**. Interaction is required among the members to achieve the common goal of a single, integrated product.

The **functional team** has a functional, rather than a product, mission. While all of the members may do similar work, they do not develop a single product and their individual tasks are usually quite independent. For example, many software organizations have large numbers of one- and two-person projects that all use the same technology but are otherwise independent. Another example would be a maintenance group where each member handles the repair and enhancement of a product. While several of the members might occasionally work on elements to be integrated into a common release, they would usually work alone.

A third example could be a system-test group that uses a common test process to support many different products. Depending on the project, the test group might assign only one test engineer or, for larger jobs, it could use a small test team. While each test assignment would generally be planned to fit the test group's overall workload, these plans would also have to meet each of their project's schedule commitments.

Functional teams are teams in the same sense as track, swimming, and gymnastic teams. However, such teams do not have the same interdependent character as basketball, hockey, or product-development teams. This is important because, when teams have a common focus and set of goals, it helps them to jell. Without some common bond, groups generally fragment into relatively independent social clusters. While such groups may do good work, they do not have the same energy and enthusiasm as teams that strive to achieve a common goal.

In fact, the fundamental problem with functional teams is that they do not have a single, integrating goal that focuses all of the members' energies. There is no common team achievement and no last-minute crunch to get the product through system test and out the door. While functional teams do occasionally jell, they need a common bond, and it must generally involve some degree of exertion and stress.

21.5   Distributed Teams

A **distributed team** is one where the team members are not all in the same physical location. For example, most of the team members could be in the principal location with only one or two remote members. Alternately, the team could be evenly divided among two or more locations, or it could even consist of scattered individual members. There are also several types of distributed teams. They could be project or functional teams, or they could be single or multiple teams. In fact, it is common to have large teams distributed across several locations. While there are many special considerations in coaching distributed teams, these topics can generally be grouped as follows.

☐ Communication with team members

☐ Communication among team members

☐ Support

☐ Guidance, evaluation, and coaching

Communication with Team Members

Poor communication is one of the most frequent complaints of team members. In traditional hierarchically organized groups, the team members depend almost totally on the team leader for project status information, team decisions, task assignments, and performance evaluations. The TSPm process addresses this communication need through the launch process, the leadership team, the role-manager teams, and the weekly team meetings. The reason that distributed teams are a particular challenge for team leaders is that communication with the team members is much more difficult.

With a distributed team, the team leader must pay particular attention to the communication needs of each team member. The concepts of task and relationship maturity provide a useful way to think about these personal communication needs. For ideas on how to coach team leaders on this issue, see the discussion on task and relationship maturity in Chapter 16 of *TSP^SM—Leading a Development Team* (Humphrey 2006).

Communication Among Team Members

A second aspect of communication concerns the relationships among the team members. When team members do not interact frequently, they cannot maintain the rapport required for effective teamwork. There will be frequent misunderstandings, oversights, and disagreements that can easily lead to mistrust. The more closely these distributed team members depend on each other, the more likely they are to have problems. When they are remote, they cannot easily resolve these issues and are much more likely to have unresolvable disagreements. Over time, these disagreements can lead to downright antagonism. Such teams quickly become dysfunctional.

While there is no simple way to prevent interpersonal communication problems, one way to keep these problems under control is for the team to hold frequent meetings. Even if the meetings must be held by telephone or video conference, the team leader should hold a meeting of the entire team every week. In this meeting, the members review their work for the past week and their plans for the next week. They also discuss any issues or problems they face and ask for the team's help in resolving them. The members' issues are then either resolved or plans defined to resolve them. These issues are then recorded in the Issue Tracking Log (ITL) and tracked until they are resolved.

Support

If the team leader is sensitive to the special support needs of the remote members, the team should be able to support all of its members, whether they are remotely located or not. Typically, support comes in three varieties.

- ☐ Informal advice
- ☐ Reviews of draft work
- ☐ Sharing the work

While remoteness can cause serious inconvenience, all of the team members should be able to support each other, regardless of location. Work sharing is a natural consequence of team planning. When some team member is overloaded, others will offer to help. This not only helps the team to meet its commitments, it helps to build the team's cohesion. For example, when the team members know what everyone else is doing and when they are all familiar with each others' skills and abilities, it is easy to ask for advice, even on the phone or by e-mail. Similarly, most reviews are done by individuals examining a peer's work. If a team member knows that someone needs to have work reviewed, he or she can offer to help. Here, remoteness makes little or no difference, even when there are major time differences among the locations.

Guidance, Evaluation, and Coaching

The best general guideline for effectively managing creative technical people is daily management contact (Humphrey 1997, 71). In a multiyear study of 1,500 scientists and developers, Donald Pelz and Frank Andrews found a strong positive correlation between a professional's performance and the frequency of his or her management contact (Pelz 1966, 51). The most effective team leaders met and talked with their team members every day. When leading a distributed team, the team leader's ability to do this can be severely limited. Coach team leaders to adjust the frequency and nature of their interactions with remote team members based on that member's task and relationship maturity.

When members are remotely located, teams should arrange for frequent contact and discussion. While these remote interactions will not be as effective as face-to-face meetings, they are better than nothing, and they will show that the team and team leader are interested and care about what the remote members are doing.

21.6 Multiple Teams

By breaking the work into multiple team-sized jobs and establishing a communications structure among these unit teams, the TSPm process can handle projects of up to 100 to 200 or so team members. As described later in this chapter, much larger teams need a system-wide team process. However, even with modest-sized teams, there are many variations involving the team's locations and the functional nature of the work.

If you can, it is almost always preferable to do a job with a single team of 5 to 15 or so members. However, some jobs are just too big or require too many different specialties to be completed in a reasonable time by such a small group. Under these conditions, the project will require more people. Once management has decided to form such a larger group, then they must decide how to organize and manage it.

As teams get larger, their sheer size causes communication, coordination, and management problems. In addition to technical complexity, the mechanics of planning and tracking can become administratively complex. Also, since multiple teams generally develop large and complex products, the work of all the separate unit teams must somehow be related.

The traditional method for handling such problems is to break these large groups into multiple subgroups, each with its own leader. These unit team leaders then each guide the work of their own teams. The multi-team TSP process is designed to address the problems of such large development projects. While there are many possible problems, the two that must be addressed during team formation are selecting the team structure and team staffing.

Structural Issues

The first and most serious problem with large teams concerns the impact that team structure has on the work. Generally, large teams are formed through some managerial process that identifies the groups, selects the managers, and divides the work responsibilities among the teams. While this approach seems reasonable, it has one big problem: the work is allocated through a political process. As the groups decide on the precise boundaries for their work, the team leaders find themselves in a treaty-negotiation process. In other words, what should be a system design and architectural question has become a political one.

In the TSP, this problem is addressed during the pre-launch period. While no process can completely eliminate the political issues of work allocation, the TSPm process starts with a technical group producing a conceptual design for the overall system. Since it also defines the boundaries among the system components, the conceptual design provides the technical basis for allocating the work among the teams.

Staffing Issues

With any politically based process, there is always the danger of inefficiency. For example, the key resource in development organizations is skilled people. Since managers know that their success is largely determined by the qualities and capabilities of their people, hoarding is a common problem. This is where a manager tries to keep the people who were assigned to his or her project, even when they are not needed. While no process can entirely eliminate this problem, the detailed team members' plans, load balancing, and task-hour tracking used with the TSPm process can help.

21.7 System-Wide Teams

The TSPm communications structure can be very effective for TSP teams of up to about 100 to 200 or so members. Beyond that, the leadership and role-manager teams must be so large that their members are no longer intimately familiar with each other's work. They then lose the ability to identify and resolve the many interdependencies among the unit teams. While there is no entirely satisfactory way to resolve this problem, it can at least be partially addressed by forming multiple TSPm teams with multiple leadership and role-manager teams. The work of these multiple leadership and role-manager teams is then coordinated by an overall program management team with a role-manager coordination staff. However, since these very large teams generally have unique problems, each such team generally needs to use a customized TSP process.

With system-wide teams, the key communication issues are timely and precise reporting and identifying the communication needs among the unit teams. The objective is to establish the links to quickly and efficiently resolve issues and to make decisions at the working level. Since very large teams can have thousands or even millions of possible two-way communication links, these communication mechanisms must be easy to establish and effective at finding and resolving the issues that will inevitably arise among the unit teams. The lack of an efficient and effective technical communication and decision system is the source of many large-scale development problems.

21.8   Coaching Guidelines

While the TSP process provides an appropriate structure for launching and operating most project teams, there are many possible variations. For example, the team I work on at the Software Engineering Institute (SEI) has a central group in Pittsburgh with single remote members in Florida, New York, North Carolina, and Tennessee. We all come together in Pittsburgh every three months for a team relaunch and we hold weekly conference phone calls for our team meetings. By following the TSP process for distributed teams, we have managed to function effectively and maintain team cohesion.

Organizations typically have a mix of project and functional work. Again, for our SEI team, we have an overall functional structure with many tasks that involve individuals or small groups. When we do a team relaunch, we have found it best to keep the entire team together, even when planning the small subgroup tasks. We found that when we broke into separate unit teams, the planning work went no faster and we lost the feeling of team membership and involvement. By planning as an integrated team, everyone is thoroughly familiar with everyone else's work and load balancing is faster and easier.

The general guideline for running such varied team structures is to organize the work into project teams of 5 to 15 members wherever possible and to have all of the members work in a single location under one team leader. If the work must be distributed among multiple teams or at different locations, bring all of the team members together for each launch and relaunch. Where this is not possible, attempt to launch the unit teams at different times. With careful advance planning, this is often possible. Finally, if the launches must be done simultaneously at remote sites, arrange for frequent video conferences among the groups and have experienced TSP coaches available at each site. Also allow enough time for all of the unit teams to do their planning work. This will generally take substantially longer than a similar launch that is done at a single location.

21.9 Summary

This chapter describes the various ways that development teams can be structured and how the TSP process supports these structures. When you understand these variations and are familiar with the principal TSP process variants, you can help management form teams that have an efficient and effective team structure and that can be supported by a standard TSP version. When this is not possible, it should be relatively easy to adjust one or more of the existing TSP process variants to suit the particular organization's and team's needs.

Base your selection of the process for a team on the specific work the team is to do and its organizational context. Since teams face a wide variety of work assignments and environmental conditions, however, this chapter only describes the principles and perspectives involved. These are the integration of the work, the specialization of the members, and the size of the overall team.

Teams also generally face various management and physical constraints. For example, their members may come from multiple organizational units or be located in different physical locations. Wherever possible, form teams into individual units of 5 to 15 members and locate them in the same physical space. When this is not possible, try to bring the teams together in one location for the launches and relaunches.

The principal issues in handling large and distributed teams are the same as for smaller teams: communication among team members and with management. This chapter describes the structural, communication, and management issues involved in forming and staffing distributed teams, functional teams, and multiple teams. It also briefly describes the principles for handling very large development teams, which generally must be supported by uniquely customized versions of the TSP process. Subsequent chapters discuss the specifics of the relevant TSP processes.

References

Humphrey, Watts S. *Managing Technical People: Innovation, Teamwork, and the Software Process*. Reading MA: Addison-Wesley. 1997.

Humphrey, Watts S. *TSP^{SM}—Leading a Development Team*. Boston: Addison-Wesley. 2006.

Pelz, Donald C., and Frank M. Andrews. *Scientists in Organizations: Productive Climates for Research and Development*. New York: Wiley. 1966.

22

Functional Teams

This chapter addresses the special problems of launching and coaching functional teams. As described in Chapter 21, these are teams that have a functional, rather than a product, mission. When you coach a functional team, your principal challenges will be helping the team jell as a coherent group, and then guiding it in working as a cohesive unit to meet the team's goals. This chapter focuses on coaching issues, coaching principles, and coaching guidelines for functional teams. The following topics are covered.

- □ Why functional teams are needed
- □ The functional-team strategy
- □ Preparing for a functional-team launch
- □ Goal setting
- □ Launching functional teams
- □ Coaching a functional-team launch
- □ Coaching a functional team

22.1   Why Functional Teams Are Needed

There is a Swedish army proverb that says: "When the map and the terrain differ, believe the terrain." The same principle applies to processes. When the process doesn't fit the organization, team, or project, fix the process. Organizations come in all types and sizes, and projects can have almost any character, so we must adapt our processes to fit the actual situation for this project. Otherwise, our process will not be useful, and it probably will not be used.

Functional teams are needed because a lot of development work does not fit the normal working practices of project teams. Examples are maintenance groups, test departments, and support groups. Generally, these groups are collections of individuals who work individually or in groups of two or three to do small and relatively independent jobs. In maintenance work, for example, it is common to assign one developer to handle each problem report or group of reports.

Traditional TSP concepts apply perfectly well to these "functional" groups, but it is often hard to see how the traditional TSP project process should be applied when launching and coaching such groups. That is why special process tailorings may be needed when applying the TSP to functional teams. This chapter discusses the principles for using the TSP with functional teams and discusses some of the options to consider in launching and coaching a team with functional characteristics.

22.2   The Functional-Team Strategy

You can view the project and functional-team processes as extremes with the pure project process at one end and a fully functional operation at the opposite end. At the project extreme, the entire team works together throughout the launch, only breaking up to prepare personal plans in meeting 6. Conversely, the extreme of a functional team would have multiple unit teams of two, three, or more members that each hold separate parallel launches. These parallel launches would start with a common management meeting and end with a common meeting 9 for the plan presentation to management. Starting with launch meeting 2, the unit team members could then work as separate groups to plan their respective projects. The entire team would then periodically review launch status and coordinate the work of the unit teams. Most functional groups will also have some project work and fall somewhere in the middle of this spectrum. Special

TSP process adjustments may be needed to facilitate unit team launch activities when you need them.

While it might seem logical to run the functional launch as a parallel set of mini-launches, avoid doing this if you can. With new TSP teams or with small teams of less than about five or six members, treat the entire team as one group and work through the launch meetings together as a single team. Then, just like a TSP project team, the team members make their personal plans in meeting 6. Working as a single team could make the launch take a little longer than normal, but it will show the team members how to do a launch and will facilitate team-building. If a first-time TSP functional team is too big to keep together for unit team planning, consider either breaking it into two or more completely separate functional teams or having several coaches assist you. Then a coach would likely be needed to coach each of these smaller teams or unit teams with their separate launches.

The principal coaching challenge with a functional team is getting the members to act and feel like a team. When team members have relatively independent tasks, they do not have the integrating focus of a common product or mission. As a result, your coaching objective is to build a team with a cohesive spirit and energy. To do this, try to follow the general TSP launch strategy of having the team work as a unit in developing its goals, strategies, processes, and plans. Keeping the team together as a unit throughout the launch (except in meeting 6 when members make their individual plans) is natural for project teams. It is equally applicable when all of the team's tasks are handled by individuals. However, when the team has many tasks that involve two, three, or more members, it might seem more efficient to handle most of meetings 3 through 6 separately for each unit team.

If there is a team consensus to break into unit teams for any of the estimating or planning sessions, you could do so, but only do it for brief periods. Until the team members have a good deal of TSP experience, breaking into unit teams will generally take more time than staying together and having the entire team contribute to the unit team estimates. Even with experienced TSP teams, breaking into unit teams tends to fragment the group and lose much of the teambuilding benefit of the TSP launch.

When functional teams stay together for the entire launch, the members are usually surprised at the benefits. They benefit from the entire team's participation in each member's work, and they gain an appreciation of everybody else's work. They are also generally surprised to find that there are more opportunities for cooperative work than anyone suspected. By staying together, the team members can capitalize on each other's skills and knowledge, and they begin to feel more like a cohesive team with a common purpose.

22.3 Preparing for a Functional-Team Launch

Proper preparation is essential for a successful functional-team launch. The principal preparation activities are as follows.

☐ Team training

☐ Work identification and allocation

☐ Conceptual design

☐ Data preparation

Team Training

The training required for functional-team members and managers is the same as for the TSP. These needs are discussed in Chapter 5.

Work Identification and Allocation

The workload of functional teams can be highly variable. Since such teams generally have relatively small projects and many customers, the team members will normally face an almost continuous stream of requests to change their tasks and priorities. Also, because of the normally short job duration, such teams often have many simultaneous job assignments. The challenge for these teams is to maintain some level of control over their work and to provide both predictable and high-quality service to their customers.

While a functional team's ability to manage its workload will depend on its job responsibilities, it is likely that at least some of the team members will have been assigned specific customers and told to negotiate their own task assignments. Examples would be a level-of-service (LOS) contract to provide hourly advice or support services. If most of a team's work is of this variety, the team's planning would largely consist of allocating the customers and their committed tasks among the team members.

In general, however, a functional team's workload will be a mix of LOS and product-development tasks. Sample LOS activities would be teaching courses, providing technical assistance, and maintaining previously developed products. However, the team members might also spend part of their time on product development. The problem is that LOS work is generally viewed as the highest priority, is most visible, and is committed directly to the customers. As a consequence, development work is generally deferred whenever there are LOS demands.

Since deferring development work delays product deliverables, mixed LOS and product-development work frequently leads to dissatisfied managers and frustrated developers. This is why a common management concern with functional teams is their inability to meet committed product-development schedules. To address this problem, the team members must carefully manage their time and be highly disciplined in maintaining and adhering to their work priorities.

The final product of the work identification and allocation effort is a listing of the team's LOS and product-development commitments and an allocation of this work among the team members. Where some jobs are large or the work requires special skills, those tasks are assigned to small groups of team members. Each unit team and the team leader then agree on who will lead these unit teams and the unit teams then work together both during launch preparation and in the launch.

Conceptual Design

For product-development work, the unit teams should each create conceptual designs for their products before beginning the launch. These could be software or hardware products, documents, procedures, or almost any kind of product. These conceptual designs are just like the normal PSP conceptual designs, and they facilitate size estimating. Size estimates, in turn, help teams make accurate resources estimates and schedules. With unit teams, the unit team conceptual designs should be reviewed with the entire team during launch meeting 3.

Data Preparation

As they gain experience, TSP teams amass substantial amounts of data. Since these data help the members make accurate estimates, the team members should determine the kinds of data they will need during the launch and have these data available when they are making size and resource estimates.

22.4 Goal Setting

By working cooperatively during the launch, TSP teams generally jell as cohesive groups. To maintain its level of energy and commitment after the launch, each team needs a visible and compelling goal that will focus the members' efforts. These goals should be defined during the launch. Since few functional groups have clear and compelling goals, and since there are many types of functional teams, there can be many types of goals. However, functional group goals will generally fall into two broad categories: product-specific and functional. To properly serve all of its customers, a functional group must maintain a balance between its product-specific and LOS goals. It should also establish some overall goals that will guide its quality-of-service efforts. Then the team members should establish goal measures that are meaningful to them and to their customers.

Once a functional team's goals have been defined, it can proceed with the launch in much the same way as a standard TSP product team. When doing this, however, the team members and unit teams must address both the newly defined functional-team goals and the customer-specific team goals with their strategies and plans. While this goal-setting approach sounds reasonable in theory, there can be problems with multiple goals, vague or artificial goals, customer priorities, and goal definition. These topics are discussed next.

Multiple Goals

When fans cheer at a basketball game, they are urging their team to make a goal—not just any goal, but to put the ball through the opposing side's basket and get a score. The simplicity of the goal and the clarity with which teams achieve or miss their goals determines the motivating value of that goal. For maximum motivation, teams need one truly compelling goal to focus their energies and to integrate their efforts. While this is not always possible and while there may be other subordinate goals, one principal goal would provide the team motivation and energy.

When deciding on the goals for a functional team, the number one need is to identify a single and truly significant goal that everyone buys. This goal must consider the activities of each team member and relate all of these activities to this single goal. Then the entire team must agree that this is what they will strive to do. Finally, the team must measure performance against this goal and make progress visible to all of the members all of the time. Only then will the goal provide a motivating focus for the team.

While the team may agree on a single goal, it can't just be any goal. It must be important to the organization and compelling to the team. It needs to be a challenge but it also must be something that the team members think they can do. For example, Brad's team was responsible for providing database services to the rest of the department. The various team members had relatively independent jobs, such as obtaining service data, updating the database, performing statistical analyses, and advising users. In making the next year's plan, Brad challenged the team with one overriding goal: to provide superior service to the overall department. The developers struggled for several days to define what this challenge really meant. They finally concluded that superior service required a completely restructured operation. They would have to replace their current computer support, rework their procedures, and replace the obsolete department database.

The more the team members thought about this goal, the more excited they got. They would have to select and install a new database support system, convert the current database to the new system, establish new operating procedures, update the obsolete portions of the current database, and develop new analysis and reporting methods. They also realized that this work would involve everyone on the team, and that they would have to do it while continuing to support their current customers.

When the team reviewed this goal with the department director, he was equally excited and asked the team how long this work would take. The developers estimated that it was a full year of work. The director then said that he had to make the next department plan in nine months and would really like to use the new data analysis facilities then. While the team members did not know how to meet a nine-month schedule, they agreed to aim for it when they made their plans. Several weeks later, the team asked the director to attend their plan review. After selecting the new database support system and making their plans, they found that they could meet the nine-month schedule after all. The director was delighted and congratulated Brad and his team on their creative work. When the team later completed the job on schedule, the director attended the team's celebration party.

Although these support professionals had a *functional* mission, the goal of superior service helped them to become an integrated team and to develop the energy and enthusiasm needed to meet their nine-month schedule. When the members strive to do superior work, most groups can identify an overall integrating goal. It may not be as clear or comprehensive as Brad's goal, but the team members can usually come up with something that they agree is important.

Vague or Artificial Goals

Without proper guidance, teams often end up with vague or artificial goals. An artificial goal may sound like a plausible team objective but still not be motivating. For example, groups will often come up with general platitudes such as delighting the customer, cutting cycle time, or improving usability. While these goals are often worth pursuing, the team needs to make them specific and measurable before they will be meaningful. This does not mean just setting arbitrary numerical targets; the goals must be specific and operationally defined, and they should have a clear and compelling business logic like the nine-month date for Brad's team. Otherwise, the team members will not know when they have met the goal or where they stand along the way.

For example, the chief executive of a large corporation had established the goal of cutting development cycle time by ten times. When I talked to the managers of one of this company's laboratories, they described what they were doing to achieve this goal. While their general approach sounded plausible, I later met with several of the developers and found that management had never told them about the cycle-time goal or asked them to plan to meet it. Clearly, the developers did not understand the goal and were not motivated by it. No cycle-time measures had been defined, there was no current-performance baseline, and there was no plan. While the cycle-time goal may have had a valid business need, no one had explained that business need or translated it into the operational terms needed to motivate the developers.

In Brad's case, the goal of providing superior service also started as a vaguely defined goal. However, by making a plan, the team members made it very concrete. They first considered what superior service would mean to their customers and decided that they needed a new database facility. Then, by committing to deliver that capability in nine months, they converted a vague goal into a concrete one.

Artificial or arbitrary goals will not work. For Brad's team, the department director had a logical reason for his nine-month date and the team understood and respected it. They also established measures and a plan to meet that goal. While the goal provided the rationale for the plan, the plan provided the motivation for the team. A similar approach for a cycle-time reduction goal would have required defined measures and a specific improvement plan.

Finally, to be compelling, the team's goal should be challenging, simple, specific, and motivating to the team. The team members must all believe that the goal is important enough to strive for and they must believe that they have a reasonable chance of achieving it. While a 10 times cycle-time improvement in 10 years might seem unrealistic, a 25% improvement in 1 year would seem much more achievable. By improving 25% every year, however, the team would achieve a 9.3 times improvement in 10 years. That would be an extraordinary achievement and close enough to management's objective to be considered a success.

Customer Priorities

Functional teams typically have problems with customer priorities. This is because they generally have a large number of customers who each feel that their particular problems are the most important. When the customers are inside the organization, the TSP process can help teams deal with this problem by involving these customers in the opening and closing management meetings. While the customers' views of their priorities will not change, at least the team can expose them to the problems of multiple priorities and tell them the relative priority rankings the team is using to guide its planning. If the customers disagree with this assignment, the team should be willing to negotiate changes and revise the plan. If the customers and team cannot agree on a plan, the team must then ask management for help in resolving the issues.

When serving outside customers, however, this prioritizing strategy is not a good idea. Paying customers will not generally agree that any other customer has higher priority. The most practical strategy is to strive to meet every commitment, even if that involves additional resources and substantial team load balancing. To facilitate load balancing, it is helpful to keep the team together throughout the launch. Then, if meeting the team's commitments takes more resources than are available, the team can present several alternate strategies to management. Examples would be to rebalance the team's workload so that the customers all suffered similar delays or to focus most resources on the few highest-priority customers and defer work for the others. However, hold the trade-off discussions privately with management before reviewing the team's plan with the customers. It might also be a good idea to meet separately with each key customer and review only the parts of the plan that pertain to that customer.

Goal Definition

Before the launch, have the team leader and his or her immediate management establish customer priorities and define meaningful goals that would motivate the team. Goals are usually easy to define for product development since the cost, schedule, and quality objectives are usually clear. For functional teams, management can be most helpful by explaining how they evaluate the team's performance and where they would most like to see improvement. Then have management review these goals with the team in launch meeting 1.

22.5   Launching Functional Teams

With only a few changes, most of the TSP launch scripts can be used for the functional-team launch. If you plan any significant changes in the TSP process for the functional-team launch, produce tailored scripts to guide the launch.

Launch Meeting 1

Launch meeting 1 can follow the same script as the TSP. In meeting 1, management describes their goals for the entire team. If they do not state improvement objectives for the team, it will be hard for the team members to create their own goals. Ideally, the overarching management goal should be clearly connected to the objectives of the business. As with Brad's team, management may not be able to provide specific goals until the team members have thought through their goal-setting process. However, management should clearly define the kinds of goals that would be meaningful from a business perspective. While they should leave the specifics of the goal up to the team, they must enunciate what they want this team to accomplish and why. Otherwise, the team is not likely to accomplish what management wants. Also, since there may be several customer representatives attending the meeting, these representatives should each review their customers' needs.

Launch Meeting 2—Goals

In launch meeting 2, the team's goal setting should follow the defined TSP process script. However, the primary emphasis is on identifying, defining, and quantifying a primary team performance goal. One example of a primary team goal is one that the SEI team developing the TSP established. The team members had many more-or-less related tasks, but no single integrating focus. In the launch-planning meeting, they discussed the work to be done and concluded that the single most important task was to develop and announce a TSP coach-training course.

The team discussed this goal and agreed that the course should be announced at a major conference in eight months. While the team members knew that this was an aggressive goal, they all agreed that it was important and agreed to set this as the team's principal goal. This goal provided an integrating focus for the entire team. As they discussed the goal and how to meet it, the team members realized that most of their activities were in some way related to this one objective. In fact, the first draft of this book was written as the textbook for that course.

It is normal for teams to define many goals during meeting 2, but a large number of goals, even if measured and tracked, do not provide useful motivation. Try to get the team to identify one or two of its goals as key drivers for the plan. It could be a customer response-time target or an objective to cut the maintenance backlog by a given percentage. Make it a goal the team can measure and track, and then have the members establish a plan and define responsibilities for measuring and tracking it. Finally, in the meeting 9 management presentation, feature this goal, the measured baseline for the goal, and the team's tracking plan.

Launch Meeting 2—Roles

Role selection for TSP functional teams can also follow the same procedure as the TSP, except that the roles themselves could be somewhat different. For this reason, functional teams should generally start the role-selection process by deciding what roles they need and what responsibilities they want these role managers to have.

Although the functional-team planning, process, and support manager roles are much the same as for traditional TSP teams, the quality manager role may require some adjustment. If the team is developing or supporting software or hardware products, the quality manager role can be handled in much the same way as for a TSP project team. However, if the activities involve other kinds of products or substantial support activities, the team should discuss the quality question and decide as a group how to handle it. Suggest that the team figure out what quality characteristics are most important from a customer perspective, decide how to measure these characteristics, and then agree on how to manage them.

The customer interface manager role is also significantly different. With functional teams, there are usually many customers and the individual team members will likely be in close contact with them. Since customer contact is generally distributed across the team, the customer interface manager role should provide a focal point for handling general customer issues. Examples would be improving response time to customer requests and developing and conducting customer opinion surveys. It could also include maintaining summary data on customer status and activity. The responsibilities of the design, implementation, and test role managers will also depend on the types of work being done. Generally, however, whenever a team has development responsibilities, these development roles will be useful.

The suggested way to define team-member roles is to have the members first consider the kind of work the team is doing and then decide what roles are needed for that kind of work. Then the members should define what these role responsibilities should be. This could lead to establishing special roles for safety, security, documentation, packaging, or almost anything else. The team may also choose to drop some of the standard TSP roles if they do not believe that these roles would provide a useful function.

Launch Meeting 3

Launch meeting 3 either can follow the standard TSP script or a customized script, depending on whether the team is kept together for planning or broken into unit teams. The purpose of the standard TSP meeting 3 is to define the team's strategy and process, but functional teams usually have many diverse products and commitments and will likely need multiple strategies and processes. The team leader should first lead the team in listing all of its delivery commitments, establishing the commitment priorities, and identifying dependencies among these commitments. Next, the team should agree on which are the highest-priority commitments and identify any constraints or special problems that they expect to face in meeting these commitments. Finally, the team leader and team should agree on which team member will be responsible for each deliverable.

Since functional teams generally have continuing responsibilities, many of their jobs will have been underway before the launch and some of the team members will already have conceptual designs. For the new jobs, the team members should produce conceptual designs during launch preparation. They should then review these conceptual designs with the entire team in meeting 3. This informs the members about each other's work and enables them to identify where they could support each other. This will also make the team more efficient and further integrate the team as a cohesive group. Even for the existing projects, if all of the team members are not familiar with the work, the responsible members should briefly describe their conceptual designs to the entire team.

Following the conceptual design discussions, the team members focus on their operational or development strategies and the processes needed to support these strategies. Finally, the team considers its cross-team issues. Examples of these would be a common quality management strategy, a common inspection process, and deciding on common team support systems.

Where projects have unique process or support needs, these needs should be considered by each team member or unit team during meeting 3, either separately in unit teams or all together as a group.

Launch Meeting 4

In launch meeting 4, the team or each unit team produces its overall plan. Whether the team breaks into subgroups or works as a single unit, meeting 4 follows TSP's standard script.

Functional teams often have trouble using data to make estimates. For example, maintenance teams usually find that fix size is not useful for estimating fix time, and that most of the fix time involves investigating reported anomalies and little time is spent on writing and testing fixes. One team addressed this problem by listing all of their fix time data and then ordering it from the smallest to the largest item. While the times varied from less than 1 hour to over 700 hours, most fell between 18 and 187 hours. They also noticed that the data bunched up at the low values, suggesting that this was a log-normal rather than a normal distribution (George 2005). Then, using the procedure described in Box 5.1 in *PSP^{SM}: A Self-Improvement Process for Software Engineers* (Humphrey 2005, 79), they calculated the time ranges given in Table 22.1.

In using these data to make estimates, the team selected the likely time range for each anomaly based on the number of modules and any other product elements they felt would be involved in investigating and fixing that anomaly. While this did not yield as accurate a set of estimates as they would likely have gotten with size-based development estimates, it did cut the estimating error from almost 50% to about 25% (George 2005). While size data are most helpful in estimating development work, when such data are not available or are not applicable, the approach this team used could be applied to almost any kind of historical size or time data. First, however, the developers must gather the data needed to determine the various time or size ranges.

Table 22.1 Maintenance Fix Time Distribution

Range	Time (hours)
Very Small (VS)	6
Small (S)	18
Medium (M)	59
Large (L)	187
Very Large (VL)	596

Launch Meeting 5

If many team members develop or maintain software products, they should follow TSP's standard meeting 5 script to make their quality plans. Otherwise, the team should discuss its quality goals and decide which, if any, can be addressed with quality plans and quality measures. While the team should produce a quality plan, functional quality plans can be of many types, so there is no script for producing them.

If the team needs a quality plan for its nonsoftware products, it should devise its own quality measures and quality planning process. In doing this, help the members use the principles described in Chapters 11 and 19, and guide them in defining user-based and defect-based quality measures wherever possible. For example, if a maintenance group is developing a quality plan, it might establish target response times for delivering problem fixes and target goals for the percentage of defective fixes. Another example would be a test group that measured and managed test case quality, test-time estimating accuracy, defect discovery rates, and test yields.

Launch Meeting 6

In launch meeting 6, the team follows TSP's standard meeting 6 script to produce detailed personal plans, consolidate these plans into the unit team and team plans, and balance team workload. Workload rebalancing is performed by the team as a whole, also following the TSP script.

Launch Meeting 7

In launch meeting 7, the team follows the standard process to identify, evaluate, and assign the key risks.

Launch Meeting 8

In launch meeting 8, the entire team meets to review the team plan and prepare the management launch report for meeting 9. Meeting 8 follows TSP's standard meeting 8 script. The only time launch meeting 8 might differ from the standard TSP process is if the team broke into unit teams for planning. Then each unit team should briefly review its plan with the entire team. The team leader would then lead the entire team in deciding which unit team plans should be consolidated and which should be reported separately. The team then produces one common set of risk and mitigation actions and produces a consolidated resource summary showing the resource allocation by deliverable. Depending on the situation, management might also want to see consolidations by customer, project phase, product category, or something else.

Launch Meeting 9 and PM

The final two launch meetings follow the standard TSP scripts and are handled in the way described for standard TSP teams.

22.6   Coaching a Functional-Team Launch

While launching a functional team follows all the principles used in a project team launch, there are a few special considerations. The goal issue has already been discussed in this chapter, but three other issues concern team integration, team-member coaching, and launch meeting scheduling.

Team Integration

The principal concern when coaching a functional team is getting the members to feel like one coherent and interdependent group. If the team splits into unit teams for very much of the launch, the entire group will not spend much time together. The members are not then likely to build the trust and rapport needed to become a jelled team. This suggests that you keep the team together as much as possible. If the team does decide to split into unit teams for much of the launch, then the entire team should hold daily status review meetings, and the opening and closing management meetings would be particularly important. During the daily status meetings, coach the team and team leader to keep everyone involved and to consider everyone's views and opinions.

Team-Member Coaching

The second issue concerns team-member coaching. While individual team-member coaching for functional teams is much like that used for project teams, the dynamics of one-on-one coaching can be somewhat different. Now, instead of helping several team members solve a common problem, you will often work with only one or two members at a time. To avoid a lecture-like quality to your coaching, try to ask questions and suggest ideas rather than provide answers and specific direction.

   Another facet of the coaching issue is the problem of coach support. When teams break into multiple unit teams for many of the launch meetings, one coach will not be able to guide more than one unit team at a time. While this is not generally a problem for experienced TSP teams, new functional teams must either be launched as a single unit and take more time during the launch or have the support of several coaches.

Launch Meeting Scheduling

The third launch-coaching issue concerns scheduling. The problem here is that functional teams often have many simultaneous projects and many unit teams. They also often have support commitments that involve working varied shifts and responding to frequent calls for help. Because of the varied specialties among the team members and the continuing nature of many functional-team projects, each team member will likely belong to several unit teams. It would not be surprising, for example, for a ten-member team to have six or eight unit teams with two to four members on each. Scheduling the various launch meetings for all of these unit teams could be quite a challenge. This problem is obviated by keeping the team together for the entire launch. The launch process would then be much simpler and the team would end up with a better understood and agreed-to plan.

22.7   Coaching a Functional Team

The principal additional issues to consider when coaching a functional team concern tracking, status reporting, task priorities, and the weekly team meeting.

Tracking for Functional Teams

The standard TSP tracking methods work equally well for functional teams. In fact, the earned-value and task-time measures are particularly helpful, since they provide a common framework for measuring team progress. To provide each team member with a clear understanding of status, the planning manager should produce an updated chart of the team's status against all of its key milestones and then review this chart with the team at each weekly meeting. The chart should show the status of the major work packages and relate them to the team's key milestone commitments. This will help the members see where they stand and understand what they must do to meet the team's commitments.

Status Reporting for Functional Teams

Status reporting for functional teams is, if anything, more important than it is for project teams. Because they are generally not on a product-related critical path, management tends to ignore functional teams unless they have problems. This leads to the not uncommon view that functional teams are a necessary expense and not a major contributor to the organization's mission. To counteract this view, the team should periodically report status against its goals and describe how these goals support the organization's goals. One way to think of these reports is as periodic commercials that can help to maintain management's support for the functional team's work.

Task Priorities for Functional Teams

Task priority is a critical problem for functional teams. Since the members each typically have a large list of outstanding tasks and many workplace demands, it is easy for them to get distracted. For example, when members must travel for many of their customer-support activities, it is often difficult for them to schedule common times for team meetings and to handle their cross-team activities.

A different but related problem concerns the varying difficulty of team-member tasks. On a development team, the requirements and design work need concentrated thought and can be exhausting if done for extended periods. On the other hand, the coding, testing, and customer-support tasks are often less demanding and usually more fun. Therefore, whenever team members run into even minor roadblocks with design or requirements work, they will be tempted to switch to customer-support work or to start on other more relaxing development tasks.

Since all of the team-member's tasks are needed and since he or she will continue to be productively occupied, this might not seem like a serious problem. However, the team's commitments and deliverables have varying priorities and, unless these priorities are regularly managed, some of the team's most important work can be indefinitely delayed. With functional teams, the customer support work is typically done more or less on schedule and the development work tends to slide.

While there is no simple way to address this problem, one approach is to have every team member list his or her top priority tasks. Then, in the weekly team meeting, everyone should report on what they did on their top priority jobs in the past week and what they plan to do in the next week. This will keep the team's priorities visible, and should help to keep the individual members focused on their highest-priority tasks. Then, when product commitments start to slip, the team can either change the task priorities, rebalance resources, or adjust the schedule. It should never just ignore the problems and plow ahead. If this strategy does not work, suggest that the team leader hold daily stand-up meetings like those described in Chapter 17. These should be used to focus the team's priorities at the beginning of each working day.

The Weekly Meeting for Functional Teams

As should be clear from these last few paragraphs, most of the activities required to maintain a functional team's cohesion involve the weekly team meeting. This is when the team reviews its status, decides what to report, and reviews and updates its priorities. It is also where the team members discuss support needs, negotiate interdependencies, and resolve issues. As you coach the team and team leader, urge them to hold these team meetings every week if at all possible.

22.8 Summary

A functional team has a functional rather than a product mission. Without some common bond to hold them together, functional groups generally fragment into relatively independent social clusters. The TSP strategy for building and maintaining functional teams is to hold periodic relaunches and to conduct regular team meetings.

The TSP also uses the department's goals as an integrating focus. Teams need one truly compelling goal to focus their energies and integrate their efforts. To be an effective motivator, the goal must be important to the organization, compelling to the team, specific, measured, and visible. The more compelling the goal, the more likely it is to motivate the team and to help it jell into a cohesive working unit. The goal must also be reduced to a specific and measurable achievement and the team must have a believable plan to accomplish it.

With a few changes, the TSP launch scripts can be used for a functional-team launch. If you can keep the full team together for the entire launch, all of the launch meetings can follow the standard TSP launch meeting scripts. Where the team members feel the need to break into multiple unit teams and you agree that it would be helpful, the scripts for meetings 2 through 6 may need some tailoring. For software products, functional teams should follow script LAU5 to make quality plans. When teams develop hardware or other product types, they should still make quality plans but will likely need special guidance for defining their quality measures and goals.

In coaching a functional-team launch, consider the special issues relating to team integration, individual team-member coaching, and launch meeting scheduling. In coaching the team's operation, also give special attention to performance tracking, management status reporting, managing task priorities, and the weekly team meeting.

References

George, Ellen, and Steve Janiszewski. Applying Functional TSP to a Maintenance Project. *CrossTalk*. September 2005. www.stsc.hill.af.mil/crosstalk/2005/09/0509georgejanisweski.html.

Humphrey, Watts S. *PSP^SM: A Self-Improvement Process for Software Engineers.* Boston: Addison-Wesley. 2005.

23

Multiple Teams

When teams grow larger than 15 to 20 or so members, they should be divided into multiple smaller teams. These smaller or unit teams can maintain close relationships among their members and between these members and the team leader. Multiple teams, called multi-teams in the TSP, may also be needed to do a specific type of work or to meet organizational constraints. Examples are unit teams with different processes, large teams with members in multiple locations, and split team management. This chapter discusses multi-teams and it describes how to launch such teams. While this is a broad subject and one chapter cannot possibly cover all of its aspects, the objective is to acquaint you with the principles of launching and coaching such teams. The following topics are covered in this chapter.

- □ What is a multi-team?
- □ The TSP multi-team strategy
- □ Forming a multi-team
- □ The TSPm launch preparation process
- □ Launching a multi-team
- □ Coaching a multi-team launch
- □ Launching a distributed multi-team
- □ Coaching multi-teams
- □ Tracking and reporting on multi-teams

23.1   What Is a Multi-Team?

In the TSP, multi-teams can range in size from about 15 up to 200 or so members. The TSP defines a **multi-team** as any team that has more than one working unit. A **working unit** is a group that has a common plan, defined goals, and a set of role managers. The group also shares a common working space and has a single team leader. In the multi-team TSP (TSPm), the working units are called **unit teams** and each unit team has its own set of plans and team-member roles. While it is not generally desirable, two or more unit teams may share the same team leader but still be considered separate teams.

A TSPm multi-team is led by a leadership team that is composed of the project leader and the leaders of each unit team. This leadership team provides overall management coordination and guidance for the multi-team. To provide working level coordination among the teams, there are also role-manager teams with the unit-team role managers as members. There is one role-manager team for each TSP team role. These role-manager teams meet weekly to identify and resolve issues and to address any topics that the leadership team delegates to them.

23.2   The TSP Multi-Team Strategy

The TSP multi-team strategy follows the regular TSP strategy to build cohesive and self-directed teams. However, with a multi-team, the normal teambuilding and team-management issues are complicated by the larger size of the group and the need to coordinate the actions of the several unit teams. While each unit team can be self-directed within its defined scope, its scope must be defined by some higher authority. This higher authority is the leadership team.

With TSPm, the overall team is led by the leadership team. The members are the project manager and the leaders of the unit teams. Their responsibilities are to form the overall team and its units, allocate responsibilities and resources among the unit teams, lead the TSPm launch, and then lead the project. The team launch is coached by a coaching team with a lead coach who works with the leadership team. One coach is also required to coach each unit team.

The launch process runs in much the same way as a standard TSP launch. The principal difference is that some extra meetings are needed to coordinate the work of the unit teams and to resolve issues among them. During the launch, the leadership team meets with the entire team and senior management in both the opening and closing management meetings. It also meets with the lead coach at the end of each day to review launch status, handle issues, and provide any needed direction. When requested, the coaching team may participate in these leadership-team meetings to assist their respective unit team leaders in reporting launch status and handling issues.

The planning role-manager team is typically involved during the launch and, except for one quality-manager meeting, the other role-manager teams generally are not. However, they should all meet to get acquainted but not start work until shortly after the launch. By then the leadership team should have defined their roles and delegated specific tasks for them to handle. When developers first use the TSP, they are usually confused about the role-manager responsibilities. For these novice teams, it is generally best to delay forming the role-manager teams until the developers have used the TSP for long enough to be able to handle the added role-manager-team responsibilities. Then the team members will be more comfortable with their role responsibilities and able to be productive members of their role-manager teams.

23.3 Forming a Multi-Team

The process of forming a TSPm team has a somewhat circular character. On one hand, TSP teams make their own decisions about their processes and plans. They also decide which tasks to assign to which developer. When these decisions are made at the technical level, they are generally based on the technical nature of the work and on the interests and capabilities of the team members. The problem is that the team cannot produce a conceptual design or make work assignments until it has been formed and staffed. However, forming and staffing teams is a management responsibility.

In general, a TSP project is initiated by management based on the expectation that it will fill some business need on a desired schedule and for an expected cost. Management then allocates the needed funds and forms a team with what they believe to be an adequate number of developers. Then, during the TSP launch, the team makes its own plan and tells management whether or not it can do the job with the allocated resources and on the desired schedule.

The TSPm process resolves this resource allocation problem in the same way as the TSP. Management starts by making assumptions about the job so they can allocate the needed funds and staffing. However, with TSPm, the job is so large that a multi-team is needed. To staff the multi-team, management must first select the team leaders for the unit teams and then assign them the resources needed to launch the project. Once the team resources are identified, management can form the leadership team and prepare for the TSPm team launch.

In launch preparation, one of the leadership team's first actions is to allocate the planning work to the various unit teams. However, this requires a conceptual design and a technically informed estimate for the resources required by each unit team. The leadership team forms a design team from the members of the unit teams and asks it to produce the conceptual design and to recommend a strategy for doing the work. This design team then provides the technical basis for allocating the planning and development work among the unit teams. While this requires that the leadership team select the design team before the team members have chosen their roles, the team leaders should discuss these assignments with their teams and pick the members they all feel are most likely to become the design managers.

23.4   The TSPm Launch Preparation Process

Several steps are required to prepare for a multi-team launch. The leadership team is first formed and it then works under your guidance to prepare for the launch. This assumes that you are the lead coach for this multi-team and that you are qualified to coach a TSPm multi-team. The principal elements of launch preparation are described in the following paragraphs.

Purpose

During launch preparation, the leadership team defines the structure and responsibilities of the unit teams. This structure must be defined in sufficient detail so that the TSPm launch can be run as a parallel set of TSP unit team launches. However, since it is rarely possible to completely isolate the work of the unit teams, close coordination among the teams is required during the launch process.

Entry Criteria

The entry criteria for launch preparation are that the project be identified, the team leaders named, the team members selected, and all of the team members and managers properly trained. If many team members or managers have not been properly trained, the launch process will not work. While some final training requirements may be completed during launch preparation, the leadership team must ensure that all training is completed before the team launch. To avoid last minute problems, check launch preparation status with the leadership team every week for at least a month before the launch. If some managers or team members will not be trained in time, defer the launch until they are. For more information on TSP training requirements, see Chapter 5.

General

Every unit team will need its own authorized coach. It is also necessary to have an authorized multi-team coach coordinate and lead the entire launch process and guide the leadership team meetings. The unit teams should each have from 4 to about 15 members. In exceptional cases, this range can be extended down to 3 or up to about 20 members. More experienced teams can generally be larger than teams that are using the TSP for the first time.

Establish the Leadership Team

The leadership team consists of the project manager and the leaders of each unit team. If the project manager has a staff, one or two of these staff members may also be on the leadership team. However, it is important to keep the leadership team small enough to work together effectively and to discuss issues openly and frankly. While the leaders may wish to have some role managers or coaches attend selected meetings, the leadership team meetings should generally have no observers or visitors. As lead coach, you should participate in all of the leadership team meetings during the launch and in many of these meetings during the project.

Specify Team Membership

The leadership team's first task is to define the membership for each unit team. While this is not normally difficult, it does require that the team leaders ensure that all the members of each team are properly trained before the launch.

The Conceptual Design

The leadership team forms a design team from the team's best designers. They are then assigned the task of producing the product's conceptual design. If possible, at least one member from each unit team should participate in this design team. This conceptual design should be sufficiently detailed to guide work allocation among the unit teams and to facilitate size estimating for the overall system and its major components. While the conceptual design should define the system structure, it should only have a few dozen or so components. If some of the design team members wish to produce more detailed conceptual designs, suggest that they defer that level of detail until after the launch.

One team leader should be assigned to mentor the design team while it produces the conceptual design. He or she should also attend the design team's opening meeting and any other sessions where the group requests help. However, the conceptual design should be produced by a technical group and management should allow the members to do this work by themselves. The mentor should make it clear to the design team, however, that the leadership team is available to help whenever requested. To start this team off properly, you should also participate in the initial design-team's meetings and monitor its work thereafter.

The design team members should review their work with any of the other team members who are available and incorporate their ideas. These reviews will both familiarize the rest of the team with the design approach and take advantage of the combined knowledge of all of the team members.

The Project Strategy

The project strategy guides the unit teams in making their plans. For example, the strategy should specify whether the product will be developed in a single release or in multiple cyclic versions. It will also define the general content of each version. In general, cyclic development strategies have lower risk and a higher probability of success than single-shot strategies and should be used wherever possible. A cyclic strategy might have multiple cycles within a single phase or multiple phases within each cycle. Similarly, the cycles could cover only a few development phases or they could each extend from requirements through implementation, test, and customer use. Since there are many possible cyclic variations, the strategy selection should be based on the type of system being developed and the experiences of the team members with similar strategies. It should also consider anticipated development problems, user needs, and technical and business risks.

To ensure that all unit teams follow a consistent strategy, an overall project strategy is produced. The strategy should define whether prototypes are needed, the questions each prototype is to resolve, and how the prototype results will be used. The project strategy also defines how the team will identify and resolve the project's key risks. When these risks are identified early in the project, there is generally time to develop prototypes or to take other mitigation actions. A carefully designed strategy can facilitate risk mitigation and minimize the likelihood of late project problems. The leadership team may develop this strategy in conjunction with the design team or it may ask the design team to produce the strategy. In either case, the result should be consistent with the conceptual design and it must be supported by the entire leadership team.

Strategy development should also consider the relationships among the various specialty groups. For example, will the requirements, hardware, and software work be done separately or should there be joint activities with shared responsibilities? An example of a shared relationship would be a team to produce an early customer demonstration. This strategy might call for a minimum hardware model with enough software support to demonstrate basic functions.

Assign Product Elements to Unit Teams

Once the conceptual design and project strategy are available, it is relatively easy to allocate work to the unit teams. In doing this, however, the leadership team should keep highly interdependent activities within single unit teams. It should also maintain a balanced workload among the unit teams. When these considerations conflict, advise the team leaders to prefer a sound technical design, even if it means reallocating unit team resources or establishing unit teams with members from several different organizational groups or geographical locations.

Define Team Roles

The standard TSP team roles are usually adequate for TSPm, but additional roles may be needed. For example, a security manager, a safety manager, a privacy manager, a performance manager, or a configuration control manager could be added. If the leadership team believes that any new or modified roles are needed, they should specify these roles before the launch and briefly define what the new role managers are supposed to do. They should also decide if every unit team should have a role manager for each role or if some roles are to be covered by only some of the unit teams. However, every member of every unit team should have at least one role or alternate-role responsibility.

Assign Role-Team Mentors

In maintaining communication across the unit teams, all of the role managers for a given role form what is called a **role-manager team**. During the project, these role-manager teams should meet every week to discuss and manage the cross-team issues for their roles. The intent of these role-manager meetings is to coordinate the activities of all of the unit teams in the areas covered by their roles. These role-team weekly meetings are described in more detail later in this chapter.

The leadership team must also specify which of its members will be the mentor for each role-manager team. The mentor should meet with all of the members of his or her assigned role-manager teams during the launch to explain what the leadership team is relying on them to do. Where possible, and assuming that the leadership team mentor agrees, you or another coach should attend each of these meetings. For a description of some typical questions for these role-manager teams, see Chapter 8 or, for more detail, Appendix A of *TSP*^{SM}*—Leading a Development Team* (Humphrey 2006). The mentor also schedules a time after the launch when he or she will describe the tasks and responsibilities the leadership team has assigned to this role-manager team. This would also be the proper time for each role-manager team to organize its operations and to plan its work.

Prepare the Strategy Presentation

The final preparation step before the TSPm launch is for the leadership team to prepare a strategy presentation to all of the team members. This presentation is given during a special launch meeting 1A that is used with multi-team TSP launches to describe the strategy the project will follow and the roles and responsibilities of each unit team in that strategy. In their meeting 1A presentation, the leadership team explains the agreements reached with other groups, such as how the customer interface is to be handled with the marketing or requirements groups or how the quality manager's job is to relate to the quality assurance group. This presentation should also cover any other jurisdictional agreements that relate to the unit-team and role-manager responsibilities.

Preparation Review

To ensure that the launch preparation work is completed before the launch and that the leadership team is proceeding on schedule, meet with the leadership team at least every week to review preparation status. Do this for at least a month before the launch is scheduled to begin. These meetings could be in person or via telephone or video conference.

A Leadership Team Caution

Leadership teams often do too much during launch preparation. They may even prepare an overall project plan. When they do this, the unit teams are essentially given the leadership team's definition of the products each unit team is to develop, the resources for doing the work, and the dates when the work is to be completed. The unit teams will not then own their own plans and they will not be self-directed teams.

While some level of planning is required before the leadership team can assign resources to the unit teams and provide them with meaningful goals, the preparation focus should be on what the unit teams are to do and the resources allocated for the work. The actual task definition, size estimation, and schedule planning must be left to the unit teams. To protect against this over-specification problem, urge the leadership team to focus on goals, goal measures, and team direction and leave the planning for the unit teams to do during the launch.

23.5   Launching a Multi-Team

A multi-team TSPm launch normally takes five very full days rather than the four days for a typical single-team TSP launch. The additional time is required for the leadership and role manager meetings and to resolve cross-team issues. The standard TSP launch meetings are described in the chapters in Part II and are not repeated here. In addition, the leadership team meets with the coaches in the evenings to review launch status, settle any outstanding issues, and provide guidance to the team leaders and unit teams. In the following paragraphs, these and any other special meetings are labeled with a number and an *A, B,* or *C*. The number indicates the TSP launch meeting after which these special meetings should normally be held. The leadership-team meetings are labeled with an A and the planning role-manager-team meetings are designated with a B. The C meetings are for any other role-manager-team meetings.

Meeting 1A

Meeting 1A is held right after the traditional TSP launch meeting 1. It is when the leadership team presents the overall project strategy to the entire team and describes the unit team responsibility assignments. For relaunches, this is also when the leadership team reviews project status and progress against the goals established in the prior launch. If senior management is interested, the leadership team could invite them to meeting 1A or give the status and goals part of meeting 1A during meeting 1, if needed. Meetings 1A, 1, and 9 are the only ones that senior managers and outside observers can attend.

Meeting 2B

The planning manager role-manager team should meet with its leadership-team mentor as soon after launch meeting 2 as possible, and certainly before meeting 5. In this initial meeting, the leadership-team mentor describes what the planning-manager team is to do during the launch and when the leadership team needs their results.

If the leadership team decides to assign launch tasks to any other role-manager teams, those team's mentors should meet with their respective role-manager teams at this point and explain the assigned tasks and tell the team when the results are needed.

Meeting 5B

After meeting 5, the planning-manager team consolidates the overall team plan and identifies any issues or interdependencies among the teams. Where possible, it should identify the required dates and responsibilities for each unit-team dependency and ensure that these dependencies are logged in the team issue tracking logs (ITL) of all the involved unit teams. Where the planning managers see workload imbalances among the teams, they should inform the leadership team.

Meeting 5C

Shortly after TSP launch meeting 5, suggest that the leadership team ask the quality role-manager team to meet and to review the unit-teams' quality plans and to generate a composite quality analysis and plan summary for the overall multi-team. They should then report their results to the leadership team before launch meeting 7.

Meeting 6B

In meeting 6A, the planning managers join the leadership team to discuss and help to resolve any workload imbalances among the teams. If any other role-manager issues need attention, the involved role-manager teams should meet to either resolve these issues or bring them to the leadership team for resolution.

Meeting 7A

By the time of meeting 7A, the teams will have completed their plans and made their risk assessments. The leadership team reviews these risk assessments and generates a common set of project risks. It may assign responsibility for tracking any of these risks to one team for the entire project or it may choose to have the leadership team track that risk. Each team that is assigned risk responsibilities should produce mitigation plans for their highest priority risks.

Also in meeting 7A, the leadership team produces the agenda for the management presentation in meeting 9 and decides which team leaders will prepare and present each part of the presentation. It may also decide to have one or more role-manager teams prepare and give parts of the presentation. The leadership team also decides how and when to review the entire presentation prior to meeting 9.

The arrangements for meeting 9 will vary depending on the situation. For example, sometimes the project manager will have to act as the senior manager. This should be avoided if possible, for it shows a lack of senior-management appreciation for the developers' work. Whenever the project manager must act as the senior manager, launch meetings 1, 1A, and 9 merely become team informational meetings and not significant management events.

Where possible, have fairly senior managers attend launch meetings 1 and 9. In addition to reviewing and approving the team plan, the senior-management role in the opening and closing meetings is to reaffirm the importance of the project and to support the project manager in thanking the team members for their efforts.

The Leadership Team Status Meetings

The leadership team meets at the end of each launch day to review launch status and settle any outstanding issues among the unit teams. The role managers or team leaders bring any unresolved issues to these meetings for resolution, and the leadership team resolves any workload imbalance, resource, or schedule problems. It may also reconsider the resource and workload allocations among the teams or reassess the project strategy. The leadership team may also reassign or provide additional guidance to the role-manager-team mentors.

Role-Manager Meetings

At some point in the launch, the role-manager teams should all meet with their leadership team mentors for the first time. Particularly for distributed teams, this is often the first time that many of the TSP role managers will have met. It is essential that each of the role-manager teams meet, at least briefly, so the members can get to know each other and establish a working relationship. In these meetings, the mentors review the topics that the leadership team has asked their role-manager teams to address and help them plan how to handle these responsibilities. Some typical issues for role-manager teams to handle are described in Chapter 8 and in Appendix A of the book *TSP^SM—Leading a Development Team* (Humphrey 2006).

If the developers have had prior TSP experience, all of the role-manager teams should meet with their mentors at some point during the launch to discuss what their respective role-teams are supposed to do and how they plan to accomplish this work. The role managers should consider the overall project, any cross-team issues, and any tasks that could be performed by one team and reused by the others. A coach should attend the first of these role-manager-team meetings and should also attend other role-manager meetings occasionally to ensure that they are held and are productive.

For new TSP teams, it is generally wise to defer any effort to establish any but the planning and quality role-manager teams until the team members have used the TSP for at least a few weeks. When developers first use the TSP, they are often confused by the role assignments and need time to understand the standard TSP roles, what these role managers are supposed to do, and why the roles are important. Once they are familiar with the idea of team-member roles, they can better participate on the role-manager teams. Up until that point, unless the leadership team has specific assignments for the role-manager teams, it is best to defer initiating the role-manager teams and team meetings.

23.6   Coaching a Multi-Team Launch

Coaching the individual unit teams in a multi-team launch is much the same as coaching a single TSP team. However, the lead coach's job is substantially different. It involves coaching the leadership team and coordinating the launch activities of all of the individual unit teams. The principal coordination tasks are scheduling any required role-manager-team meetings and planning and facilitating the leadership team meetings. The lead coach may also assist in coaching any of the unit teams if needed.

Coordinating the Role-Manager Teams

The lead coach must coordinate the schedules for the initial role-manager-team meetings, and one of the coaches should attend each of these meetings if possible. Since the initial role-manager meetings must include the leadership team member who is mentoring that team as well as the role managers from all of the teams, the meetings must be scheduled at a convenient time for all of the unit teams. What has generally worked out best is to pick an arbitrary time for all of the role-manager-team meetings, such as during lunch on day 2, when all of the unit teams should have completed launch meeting 2. Since these meetings are to introduce the team members, disseminate information, and set a date for a future meeting, they should not take more than about 30 minutes.

Coordinating the Leadership Team

The leadership team should meet in the evenings of launch days 1, 2, 3, and 4 as well as when all of the teams have completed meeting 7. Since the unit teams will take different amounts of time to complete their work, one critical issue for each launch day is deciding on an appropriate point to break for the leadership-team meetings. To complete the launch in the allotted five days, the teams should all complete meeting 2 and parts of meeting 3 in day 1. They should also strive to complete meeting 4 on day 2 and meetings 5 and 6 on day 3. In addition to meetings 7 and 8, this then leaves day 4 for resolving issues, rebalancing workload, and producing alternate plans.

Since every team leader and several team members will be involved in the leadership and role-manager meetings, the lead coach will be busy with this coordination work. This involves monitoring the progress of each team launch, scheduling the attendance at each of the leadership-team meetings, and arranging for any needed role-manager-team meetings.

23.7   Launching a Distributed Multi-Team

Often, multi-teams will be geographically dispersed. As noted in Chapter 21, it is always preferable to have a team in one physical location. If that is not possible, it is easier to manage distributed teams with the TSPm than without it. In fact, if you have a distributed team, treat it as a multi-team if you can. When you have a distributed multi-team, there are a few special things to consider beyond those for local multi-teams. These concern building team relationships, launching a distributed team, guiding the distributed role-manager teams, and building the leadership team.

Building Team Relationships

In training the members of a distributed team, arrange for team training in a common location, if possible. When all team members take the PSP course together, they will get to know each other and start building the personal relationships needed for effective teamwork. The PSP course is particularly effective for this purpose since it represents a unique common experience for the team members.

If you cannot train the team as a single unit, look for opportunities for the team members to work together. For example, before the initial launch, consider forming small working groups that include the remote members. One such group would be the team to create the conceptual design. Another could select the team's design methods or define a common support system. Whether through training, working groups, or some other method, try to arrange activities to build the personal team-member relationships needed for effective teamwork. Regularly look for opportunities to build these relationships before, during, and after the team launch.

Launching a Distributed Team

As noted in Chapter 21, it is best to bring the distributed team together in one location for the team launch. If that can be done, the launch process would follow the standard process for launching a TSPm team. While it may be possible to bring all members of a small distributed team together for a week, this may not be practical for a large or multinational distributed team. Under these conditions, the distributed multi-team will have to be launched in a distributed way.

The first step in managing a distributed multi-team launch is multi-team launch preparation. For this, the leadership team must meet to start the preparatory work. The suggested approach is to have the leadership team initially meet in one location to plan launch preparation. At this planning session, the leadership team should also select the members of the overall multi-team who will be asked to produce the conceptual design and to participate in the leadership team's strategy development work. In doing this, however, remember the warning discussed in section 23.4: *Do not let the leadership team produce the team plan during launch preparation or during the launch!* Keep the leadership team focused on goals, goal measures, strategy, resource allocation, and team responsibilities. The process definition, estimating, and planning work should be left for the teams.

Once the launch preparation work has been completed, the preferred way to handle the distributed launch is to asynchronously launch the separate unit teams. That is, if possible, do not launch all of the unit teams at the same time. While it would seem desirable to synchronize the unit team launches, this is generally not necessary. If the preparation work has been handled properly, the unit teams will not have substantial interdependencies. While there will be cross-team issues, few of them will need to be settled in real time.

To do an asynchronous launch, the leadership team must decide on the order in which to launch the unit teams. Then the team leaders can arrange to make the materials from each prior launch available to each subsequent unit team for its launch. This allows coordination among the unit teams and helps the unit team leaders and role managers communicate and resolve issues. The leadership team must also meet regularly during this entire launch period to track launch progress, resolve issues, and provide guidance.

In handling a launch in this way, the first unit team does a more or less standard TSP launch. However, it must follow the conceptual design produced by the design team. During the second launch, the second team coordinates its work with the first team. Its members first review the conceptual design and the prior launch materials, and then pairs of team leaders and role managers from the two teams communicate with each other during the launch as needed. When the third team is launched, any needed coordination discussions would then be among three team leaders and groups of three role managers. These groups would again identify and resolve issues or bring these issues to the leadership team for resolution.

With this procedure, the first team sets the pace for everyone else. This is generally not a problem, however, as one team will normally take the lead for much of the multi-team's work. If the subsequent teams have problems with any of the prior team's plans, they can generally resolve them with those prior teams or bring the issues to the leadership team for resolution.

Guiding the Distributed Role-Manager Teams

On a distributed team, the role-manager teams are much more important than they are for local teams. Other than through the team leaders, there is almost no other way for the teams to coordinate their work. Because of the excessive travel required, the role managers for a distributed team will not generally be able to hold face-to-face meetings, but they can hold regular telephone or video conference meetings. Since these arrangements take preparation, however, these meetings will not generally happen without the guidance of the leadership team mentors.

Unless the leadership-team mentors actively support and guide their respective role-manager teams, these teams will not regularly meet or even communicate. Then, team communication will break down and the entire project could be seriously exposed. You or one of the other multi-team coaches should participate in these distributed role-manager-team meetings at the start and occasionally thereafter to ensure that they are being handled properly and are effective.

Building the Leadership Team

The leadership team is the critical integrating resource for a distributed multi-team. The members must work closely during launch preparation and they must all participate in the weekly launch-preparation conferences. Also, whenever possible, arrange for face-to-face meetings of the entire leadership team to review launch status, to make team-wide decisions, and to build and maintain team cohesion.

When a distributed multi-team is launched simultaneously, all of the teams in the various locations will be holding their launch meetings on the same days. Under these conditions, senior management and all of the leadership team members should either be together for launch meetings 1 and 9 or they should participate via video conference or teleconference, and all members of the leadership team should attend meeting 1A. The project manager should also participate in all of these meetings. If the distributed unit teams are not launched simultaneously, the project manager and leadership team should participate in each launch, even if only via video conference. This will emphasize the importance that management places on that unit team's contribution to the project, and it will help to convince each unit team member that his or her work is important to the organization.

While the leadership team will have to do a good deal of traveling or hold many video conference and teleconference meetings during a distributed project launch, this is the only way to ensure that all of the unit teams' plans are properly integrated and that all of the team leaders understand the project's overall plan and strategy.

23.8 Coaching Multi-Teams

While many of the coaching issues for multi-teams have already been covered, some additional discussion is needed for cross-team communication, role-manager-team weekly meetings, workload imbalance, and crowd control.

Cross-Team Communication

When a large team is composed of multiple work groups or unit teams, the members traditionally focus on their personal work and leave external team communication to the team leader. While the members can then concentrate on their technical tasks, this arrangement generally causes communication problems: the information the members need from the other groups must flow through the team leaders. For simple and well-structured jobs, this might be reasonably efficient, but when several interdependent teams develop large and complex systems, the team leaders will become a communication bottleneck. When that happens, the team leaders are likely to settle issues on a political rather than a technical basis.

The multi-team TSPm process addresses this problem by forming the role managers from all of the unit teams into several role-manager teams. Then these role-manager teams meet weekly to address common issues. When they cannot settle an issue, they take it to the leadership team. These role-manager teams provide the communication network among the unit teams and can often resolve cross-team issues at the level where they are best understood.

Role-Manager-Team Weekly Meetings

At first, the role managers will be confused about what they should do in their weekly meetings. The approach that has generally been most effective is to have the leadership team designate one of its members to act as a mentor for each role-manager team. This mentor can then explain the tasks the leadership team has delegated to that role-manager team and provide guidance on how to handle these tasks. The role-manager teams would then be asked to report periodically to the leadership team on their progress. For example, the leadership team might ask the support managers to recommend how product changes should be handled or have the test role managers work out a common testing plan with the test department.

In all of these cases, the principal objective is to ensure that technical decisions are made by the groups that are best informed and are most likely to make sound technical decisions.

Unbalanced Workload

Another common problem for large teams is that team workload will change during the job. While one unit team could have a heavy workload early in the project, others will have heavier workloads in later stages. Since unit teams are often treated as private fiefdoms, it is often hard to rebalance the workload across an entire multi-team project. The leadership team can address this issue in two ways.

First, during the team launch and subsequent relaunches, the leadership team reviews cross-team status and issues. When these plans show a workload imbalance, the leadership team can move people, adjust workload, or decide to obtain more team members. Second, during the project, the leadership team reviews project status in its weekly meetings. The team leaders can then see when one or more unit teams have problems and can make dynamic adjustments. Because the TSP process provides clear and explicit weekly status information, the leadership team can promptly detect workload problems and make timely adjustments to rebalance overall team workload.

Crowd Control

The larger the team, the more difficult it is to ensure that all of the members know what to do and how to do it. With non-TSP teams, the team leader commonly allocates the work among the team members. Since this command-type management style does not scale up gracefully, team size can be a problem. Development work is highly variable, and any directive work allocation process must be repeated every time a member finishes a task. With command-style management, the larger the team and the more dynamic and unpredictable its work, the longer the members will have to wait to get their assignments. Large team size also makes it harder for team leaders to understand all of the issues and to make optimum assignments. Thus, with a command style of management, productivity will decline as team size increases, and it will often decline very sharply.

The TSPm process addresses this issue by having each unit team make detailed plans for the immediate next project phase. Every member then has a detailed plan and knows what to do each week. Since these teams periodically rebalance their workload, the members will know what to do without being told. Further, when the situation changes and the members' plans are no longer useful guides, the team knows that it must make a new plan.

23.9   Tracking and Reporting on Multi-Teams

Tracking and reporting on a multi-team includes all of the normal tracking and reporting activities for a single TSP team plus reporting on the consolidated multi-team's status. While the volume of data will be substantially greater than for a single TSP team, the tracking and reporting issues for TSPm teams are identical to those for TSP teams. Of course, the leadership team must regularly review the results of each unit-team's and role-manager-team's work and consolidate and report on overall project status. It must also decide on what information to report to more senior management.

As noted in Chapter 21, the role-manager teams are a key resource for managing the multi-team and for providing the communication and technical coordination to hold the entire team together. They provide the information and insight the leadership team needs on technical issues and they help the leadership team anticipate serious problems. With a distributed team, the role-manager teams are particularly important. The leadership team must ensure that each such team has an appropriate leadership team mentor, and that this mentor is being effective in guiding and supporting his or her assigned role-manager teams.

Remember, however, that until the team members understand and are properly managing their role-manager responsibilities, many of them will not be prepared to participate constructively in the role-manager teams. While you should not try to start the role-manager teams before the team members are capable of handling these responsibilities, don't delay too long. With proper coaching and an effective leadership team mentor, the role-manager teams should be able to function fairly early in the project. The objective is to have the role-manager teams participate in all the important cross-team technical decisions on the project.

23.10   Summary

When teams grow larger than a dozen or so members, they should generally be divided into multi-teams. Large TSP teams are called TSPm multi-teams, and they can range in size from about 15 up to 200 or more members. Multi-teams are needed when unit team groups have different processes and goals, when team size is greater than is reasonable for a single team, when a large team is in multiple locations, or when team management must be split. The multi-team TSP process (TSPm) is designed to launch and guide the operation of large development projects.

The leadership team is the critical integrating resource for TSPm multi-teams. It consists of the project manager and the leaders of each unit team. With the TSPm, the role-manager teams provide the communication network among the unit teams and they resolve cross-team issues at the working level.

To prepare for a multi-team launch, the leadership team defines the membership, structure, and responsibilities of each unit team. The leadership team also arranges for a design group to produce the product conceptual design. The leadership team and all the unit teams are guided by this design in developing the product strategy, allocating work, and making plans. However, you should ensure that the leadership team does not do too much during launch preparation. Restrict its focus to goals, goal measures, strategy, resource allocation, and responsibilities, and leave the estimating and planning for the unit teams to do during the launch.

Every unit team launch requires an authorized coach, and there must be an authorized multi-team coach to orchestrate the entire launch. It typically takes five very full days to launch a TSPm team instead of the four days for a single TSP team launch. The additional time is required for leadership and role manager meetings, to coordinate the unit team launches, and to resolve issues among the unit teams.

Often, multi-teams will be geographically dispersed. While it is always preferable to have a team in one physical location, it is easier to manage a distributed team with the TSPm than without it. It is also preferable to treat a distributed team as a multi-team if possible. The special considerations for multiple distributed teams concern building and coaching the leadership team, launching a distributed multi-team, and guiding the distributed role-manager teams. For a distributed multi-team, the leadership team provides overall project coordination and the role-manager teams are even more important than they are for local teams.

Reference

Humphrey, Watts S. *TSP^SM—Leading a Development Team*. Boston: Addison-Wesley. 2006.

24

Integrated Development Teams

Teaming concepts can be used to launch and run very big development programs. Examples include a large project to design and build a computer operating system and a multilaboratory effort to develop a line of computer products. More broadly, multicompany teaming methods could be used to manage the development of entire weapon's systems such as an army battle tank or a military aircraft. There are many kinds of large-scale development programs, and there can be just as many kinds of large-scale development teams.

While there is no standard way to define a process for such a program-wide team, the first step is to determine the precise needs of the specific development program, and then customize an overall program process, using whatever process elements are available and have been proven effective on prior projects. Most large programs are collections of related smaller projects with an overall coordinating management structure. The overall program development process will then likely be composed of collections of smaller team processes with a customized overall coordinating management process. There is now considerable experience with team-based processes and a substantial body of available process elements. This background and these resources can be used to develop a customized process for any given large-scale integrated development program.

Since every integrated development team will likely be different, this chapter concentrates on the principles for developing a large-scale system-wide process and suggests some guidelines and strategies. While no standard process could possibly work for these very large teams, and since these processes are likely to be very large and have many elements, available standard process elements should be used in building each such process wherever possible. Examples of such available process elements are as follows.

- [ ] Team launch and relaunch processes
- [ ] Team management processes
- [ ] Role-manager definitions
- [ ] Management reporting standards and procedures

Some items that would likely have to be customized for each program would be the following.

- [ ] The structure and content of the leadership team
- [ ] The reporting structure for the unit teams
- [ ] The program management structure
- [ ] The role-manager-team structure and mentoring process

This chapter discusses these topics in the following sections.

- [ ] Process principles for large-scale teams
- [ ] The program-initiation team
- [ ] The program-management problem
- [ ] Program launching and coaching strategies
- [ ] The role-manager teams
- [ ] Program monitoring and reporting

24.1   Process Principles for Large-Scale Teams

There are seven principles to consider in developing a large-scale system development process.

- [ ] Use sound engineering methods at all levels
- [ ] Manage daily workload changes
- [ ] Define standard reporting measures
- [ ] Encourage team-level decision making
- [ ] Enforce architectural discipline
- [ ] Manage the system's emergent properties
- [ ] Employ quantitative quality management

Use Sound Engineering Methods at All Levels

This principle states that, to effectively manage an overall program, all of the parts of that program must be properly managed. This further means that, to properly manage all of the parts of a program, the teams developing each of these parts must also all be properly managed. And finally, it means that, to manage all of the teams properly, all of each team's developers must properly manage themselves. To meet these conditions, all of the individual developers must personally follow disciplined engineering principles in their work. These principles have three dimensions and are taught in PSP courses (Humphrey 2005).

- ☐ Accurate scheduling
- ☐ Precise change management
- ☐ Disciplined quality control

The principles of accurate scheduling are defined as follows.

- ☐ To have predictable schedules, developers must plan their personal work.
- ☐ To make accurate plans, the developers must base their plans on historical data.
- ☐ To have the data needed for accurate planning, the developers must all use defined and measured personal processes.

The change-management principles are as follows.

- ☐ Development work involves innovation and discovery.
- ☐ Such work typically has frequent surprises.
- ☐ With few exceptions, every surprise involves plan changes.
- ☐ Every plan change generally requires more work than was originally planned.
- ☐ To meet their commitments, the developers must constantly reprioritize their work.
- ☐ To hold to their schedules, development teams must regularly rebalance their resources.

The quality-control principles are as follows.

- ☐ Test time is generally long and inherently unpredictable, so for predictable, timely, and cost effective development work, the developers must minimize test time.
- ☐ To minimize test time, the developers must produce quality products.
- ☐ To produce quality products, the developers must measure and manage the quality of their personal work.
- ☐ To consistently do this, the development teams must track and manage the quality of every member's work.

For the developers and their teams to consistently work in this way, their organizations must follow TSP principles (Humphrey 2002; Humphrey 2006). These organizations must

☐ Give their teams aggressive development goals

☐ Require these teams to make their own development plans

☐ Have the teams negotiate their commitments with management

Finally, for the teams to track their plans and measure and manage the quality of their work, all development teams must be properly led and competently coached.

While following these principles will not guarantee program success, by having all of the teams in a program define and follow their own processes and do disciplined and high-quality work, the program will have the best chance of being successful.

Manage Daily Workload Changes

Surprises are normal in development work, and every surprise always seems to involve additional work. Therefore, every team in every large multi-team program is in a constant fight to recover lost time and to compensate for the newly added or discovered workload. While each added task is usually small and may only take a few hours, there are generally so many small changes that, unless they are managed on a daily basis, their cumulative impact will soon threaten the team's schedule.

While an occasional change may be so severe that it impacts the overall program, with sound team practices, schedule problems can be recognized and addressed in time for the individual development teams to contain most changes to within their committed schedules. However, to do this, they must know precisely where their work stands and understand the impact of each added task on each member's workload. Then the team can rebalance the work and maintain its schedule. For each team to work in this way, its plans must be sufficiently detailed to show each developer's daily tasks and project tracking must be sufficiently precise to identify even a one-day schedule slip.

Define Standard Reporting Measures

If all the unit teams in a large program could be relied upon to manage their own plans and to consistently meet their schedules, no higher-level management reporting would be needed. However, even when the unit teams have sufficiently detailed plans, and even when they can precisely measure their status and rebalance their workload, they will periodically encounter issues that are too substantial or have too broad an impact to be handled locally. This is when the rebalancing and recovery actions must involve multiple teams or even the entire program.

However, for program-wide workload rebalancing, the tracking and reporting for all of the unit teams must be sufficiently precise to show the impact of each small change, and it must be sufficiently consistent across all of the teams to permit program-wide workload rebalancing. Conversely, if every unit team has its own measurement and reporting system, senior management will find it hard to precisely compare team status, pinpoint problems, or adjust workload. Unless they can do all of these things, the overall program schedule will be unmanageable.

Encourage Team-Level Decision Making

As programs grow larger, program management becomes progressively further removed from the technical details of the work. Furthermore, with large-scale integrated development programs, there are typically many technical specialties that involve complex and often arcane topics, and each topic usually has a unique and often subtle influence on overall system and program performance. Just as with large-scale political systems, too much centralized control saps the creativity and initiative of the working-level professionals. This frequently leads to poor decisions and to generally unsatisfactory results.

To avoid the inherent problems of authoritarian management behavior on a development program, it is essential to force technical decisions to the lowest practical levels. This calls for a management policy and an overall defined process that establishes the criteria and responsibilities for decision making at each management level. This process must provide coordination mechanisms to ensure that the best technical skills are employed in making each technical decision. There must also be a process requirement that each such decision and its supporting rationale be properly documented. These decision records must then be made available to the entire program.

Enforce Architectural Discipline

While local decision making is important, these decisions must be made within a coherent, sound, and well understood overall program context. Documented management goals and policies provide the overall management decision-making context, and the development plan and schedule provides more specific daily direction. However, this level of coordination is only sufficient for those cases where the technical work of each development group is independent of the work of the other groups.

In large programs, this level of independence is rare and there are generally many interdependencies. While some of these interdependencies can be negotiated among the one or two involved unit teams, there are usually system-wide considerations that require consistent choices by all involved groups. Examples are

- interface definitions
- file structures
- naming standards
- power, weight, or performance specifications
- message standards
- error and recovery conventions
- design and implementation standards
- test standards

To have any hope of producing a properly functioning and usable system, all of these standards and conventions must be established and documented at the system level, distributed to and coordinated with the individual unit teams, reviewed to ensure that they are technically sound and feasible, and based on a sound system design concept. This typically requires a competent architectural definition and design capability as well as architectural resolution and control procedures that are defined and enforced.

Manage the System's Emergent Properties

While large systems are generally composed of many smaller component parts, the system produces behaviors that are not available from any of the system's individual pieces. These system-wide properties are called **emergent properties** and, while no single system component can be relied upon to supply any emergent property, many and often most of the system's components must participate in providing these properties. Examples of such emergent properties are

- security
- performance
- safety
- usability
- availability
- maintainability

These and other emergent properties must be given special attention during system development. Since responsibility for these emergent properties cannot be delegated to the unit teams developing any of the system's component parts, the overall program management process must include provisions for defining, maintaining, measuring, evaluating, and controlling the system's emergent properties. This process must define the relationship between the architectural control mechanism previously discussed and the means for managing the system's emergent properties.

Employ Quantitative Quality Management

The system's emergent properties have one very special characteristic. That is, while no one system component can provide any one of the system's emergent properties, many if not all of the system's components could, if improperly implemented, damage or even destroy the system's ability to provide that property. For example, for a system to be secure, all of its component parts must be secure. Any single insecure component could destroy the system's security and negate all of the security precautions taken with all of the other system components.

To ensure that all the system's emergent properties are properly addressed by every development team, the unit teams must all have clearly defined goals and responsibilities for each such property, and each goal and responsibility for tracking performance against these goals must be assigned to a role manager on each unit team. There must also be process provisions to ensure that these role managers track and report on their team's performance against its emergent-property goals and responsibilities, and the program management team must have available resources, facilities, and skills to evaluate these reports and take corrective action whenever needed.

24.2   The Program-Initiation Team

All of the massive programs I have ever been associated with started with a small core of experts who defined the program concept and requirements, established the program goals and strategy, and convinced management to sponsor and launch the development effort. Wherever a program has such a program-initiation team, this team should follow the TSP teaming strategy and methods from the very beginning. It should then use these TSP methods to launch and guide the program-initiation work and follow the TSP principles in defining the major program elements.

When the program-initiation team identifies groups to develop each of the system's principal parts, it should promptly involve those groups in all of the subsequent program planning and design work relating to that area of responsibility. Since many groups could be involved in launching a large program, the program-initiation team could rapidly become large and unwieldy. For this reason, one of the first things the program-initiation team must do is establish its scale-up strategy.

The Scale-Up Strategy

Initially, as long as the program-initiation team can be kept smaller than about 15 to 20 members, individual members of the development teams should be appended to the program-initiation team. However, for large programs, this strategy will probably not work for very long and may not even be feasible at the outset. A multi-team structure should then be used, following the standard TSP multi-team process described in Chapter 23.

When using the TSP multi-team structure, there is still the question of unit-team composition. Generally, the recommended approach is to form unit teams of about 8 to 15 members with similar goals, skills, and processes. For example, the groupings could be by such specialties as application requirements, system design, product development, manufacturing, and so forth. As the program-initiation staff grows further, these initial unit teams could be further subdivided by organizational entity, technical specialty, and location. In general, in forming unit teams, the criteria to consider in determining membership in general priority order, are as follows.

1. Common product development goals and commitments
2. Common technologies and processes
3. Common geographical location
4. Common organizational reporting

For example, suppose two development groups, group A and group B, worked on two products, product X and product Y, and some of the A group worked on the X product and some on Y, while some of the B group also worked on the X product and some on Y. In this case, it is best to form X and Y teams rather than A and B teams. This would even be true if the A and B groups were in different locations or even in different companies. Common product goals should be the top priority in forming unit teams, followed by technology and process, and then by location and management reporting structure.

As long as the program-initiation team can be held to about 100 to 150 members, it is desirable to continue using the multi-team TSP process described in Chapter 23. However, as soon as it is clear that the program will grow beyond this point, special process provisions should be defined for:

☐ Overall program management and staff
☐ The program launch and the relaunches
☐ The role-manager teams
☐ Program monitoring and reporting

These topics are discussed in the following sections of this chapter.

24.3   The Program-Management Problem

Before describing how to handle large program-development teams, it is first important to discuss the management problems we are trying to solve. The principal concern is how to structure a large development operation into manageable working groups. The two principal structural issues concern span of control and leadership team size.

With a traditional hands-on management style, it is rarely possible for a single manager to control more than 5 to 10 subordinate groups. However, with self-directed teams, spans of control of 15 to 20 or more unit teams could be practical. Therefore, with TSP teams, the problem is no longer one of management span of control; it is with the size of the leadership team. Since it is difficult to develop a cohesive management team that has more than 10 to 15 members, this suggests that the maximum span of control should be about 15 unit teams but preferably fewer than 10. When groups get larger than this, the program-management leadership team must have members who themselves lead multi-teams.

For example, a moderately sized development program could likely get by with one unit team for requirements, another for systems design and architecture, and a further one for the program management staff. Then the development groups would all be assigned to one overall development manager who would lead a multi-team with its own leadership team. As the program grew even more, there might be several development multi-teams, and the requirements and systems groups might also grow large enough to require a multi-team structure. As the program grew even further, some of these multi-teams would grow beyond the realistic limit for a single multi-team, requiring additional management layers.

While this strategy of adding management levels would seem extendable almost indefinitely, a host of problems will soon arise. These problems are in three general categories.

1. How to define comprehensive yet reasonably unique responsibilities for these management layers.

2. How to make program-wide decisions.

3. How to maintain program-wide communications.

Management Responsibilities

To illustrate the responsibility problem, I was once made director of a large development laboratory with four major technical groups and a total staff of several thousand professionals. When I first examined the organization, I found that some of the major departments had five or six levels of management between me and the working-level professionals. The problem this structure caused was one of responsibilities. It was easy to see what the lowest-level professionals did to develop products, run tests, provide technical support, and handle administrative tasks. At the top, it was also easy to understand the key managers' responsibilities. They handled the major development issues, ran the test and support groups, or managed administrative operations. But what about the 2, 3, or 4 levels of managers in between? What were their responsibilities and what decisions could they make?

This is the essence of the middle-level management problem in most organizations. Competent and often very successful professionals get promoted to levels above where they should make the technical decisions but not high enough to have responsibility for resources, program strategy, or much else. Because managers are typically held responsible for everything their people do, and to keep busy and feel productive, these managers generally get involved in almost everything their teams bring to them. Their people must get their approval before going to higher management, they generally require justification before passing requests upstairs, and they rarely even let their people talk to senior management. They prefer the personal visibility of taking each issue upstairs themselves.

This means that every level of intermediate management must learn about the problems and agree with their teams' recommended solutions before taking any action. It also means that when and if a complex issue gets to senior management for decision, it has been filtered through so many layers of management that the story is often garbled beyond recognition. This management escalation process takes time, adds little if any new intelligence, and often presents such a confusing story that senior management either makes a poor decision or sends the issue back downstairs for more work.

This is the nature of the management responsibility problem. If large development organizations are not structured properly with responsibilities clearly delineated, the middle management problem can seriously limit program efficiency, delay development progress, and inhibit communication and sound decision making.

Matrix Management

One common way to address this middle-management problem is through matrix management. Here, instead of structuring the development work in a people-management hierarchy, it is established according to the project work-breakdown structure. Since this could leave the developers without any career guidance or management, the technical people are typically administered by resource departments that handle training, salaries, appraisals, and the like but do not get involved in project decisions. The development management structure then has responsibilities that are defined by the product assignments of their groups.

While this approach has its own problems, it does work reasonably well, particularly for very large projects and organizations. The common problems with matrix-management structures are of two kinds. First, the developers have two managers: one for personnel needs and the other to direct the day-to-day project work. The typical problems here concern professional development and training. The career managers will generally support training and professional development, but they may not have the required funds and they are generally unable to pull the developers off the projects to attend courses. Conversely, the project managers could direct the developers to attend courses but, because it is generally hard to show that a course would immediately benefit a project, product managers rarely support training programs.

The second problem concerns system design and architectural control. When the management hierarchy follows the product structure, the successively higher levels of product managers often see themselves as responsible for the overall design of the products their people are developing. Since organizational structures are rarely designed by competent systems architects, this leads to a natural conflict.

As this discussion should make clear, there is no perfect organizational structure. Therefore, the process definition should include provisions to address the natural conflicts in whatever structure is employed, and the senior managers should be shown how to use the process to produce superior products regardless of the organizational structure used.

Making Program-Wide Decisions

While the previously described decision-making problem can be partially addressed by matrix management, this structure does not provide a complete solution. The remaining problems concern knowledge and responsibility. Who really understands the problem? Who has the requisite knowledge to make a sound decision? And who has the responsibility and authority to make the decision? The problem for large organizations is that these three "people" are likely different and may not even be three individuals. Often, on large projects, the requisite knowledge is shared by many people. Therefore, instead of getting two or three people to agree on a proper course of action, dozens or even hundreds of people might be involved.

A good example of the problem of involving all of the right people in a decision is the effort to find the wreckage of the nuclear submarine *Scorpion* somewhere in the eastern Atlantic Ocean under about five miles of water (Humphrey 2006). The team assembled for this purpose by the U.S. Navy included experts from all relevant technologies and activities. The results of their combined inputs directed the search party to start looking only a couple of hundred yards from where the wreckage was actually found. To get this kind of extraordinary technical decision, all of the right people must be involved, and they must all thoughtfully and cooperatively contribute to the solution. In devising a process and an organizational structure that will help to ensure that decisions are made properly, the following three issues must be addressed.

1. Management responsibilities (discussed in the previous section)
2. Program-wide communications (discussed in the next section)
3. Making program-wide decisions (discussed here)

Management's attitude about decision making is a style issue. This problem is complicated in many technical organizations by the fact that most of the managers have been developers themselves. Since they typically enjoy technical work but don't often get a chance to do any, they generally leap at the chance to get involved in a technical issue. They are also likely to make any required technical decisions, even when they are not the most qualified people to do so.

One of the best examples I know of this decision problem is a situation that developed shortly after I was made IBM's Director of Programming. Our two largest locations were in Poughkeepsie, New York and San Jose, California. Because the Poughkeepsie group had grown to nearly 1,000 developers and because it still needed many more people to handle its committed work, we had decided to move the data-management mission from Poughkeepsie to San Jose. The problem was that the interface between the Poughkeepsie operating system work and the San Jose data management products had not been defined. The resulting design disagreements were seriously delaying the development work.

We had told the two groups to agree on the interface definition and to come to me if they could not. Unfortunately, the interface definition had become a highly contentious issue with no clearly best answer, and the two groups were unable to agree. One morning, the two laboratory managers with about thirty of their best technical people showed up in my office with two competing proposals. Although I knew less about this subject than anyone else in the room, I ended up designing the interface. I told the groups to either make my definition work or to agree on a better solution and to let me know what they agreed on. They never came back.

This was a management failure. The problem had started many months before when what should have been a technical issue had become highly political. Then the technical experts were essentially forced to defend their management's positions rather than carefully considering the pros and cons of the various alternate ways to design the interface. We therefore ended up making a political decision on a technical issue.

While the way I handled this interface problem was clearly a management failure, what was the specific failing, and what should I have done differently? In retrospect, I believe that the problem was caused by differing goals and objectives. The Poughkeepsie manager was the OS/360 project manager while the San Jose manager was a laboratory manager with multiple projects, one of which was the

OS/360 data management work. Therefore, they had no common basis for agreeing on what was the best solution. Rather than making an instant decision, I should have made these two groups resolve the problem properly.

The proper approach would have been to start with the goals to be met by the decision. That was a topic where I, as the senior manager, could have made a real contribution. Then, after reaching agreement on the goals to be met by the interface decision, we should have addressed the criteria for making the decision. After settling the goal and criteria questions, I should then have sent the groups off to make the decision themselves and asked them to either report their conclusion and rationale to me or to come back if they needed further help. In summary, the management style issue is as follows.

1. Do managers rush to make the decisions themselves?
2. Do they thoughtfully consider who the best people are to make the decision?
3. Do they then guide these people in making the decision properly?

Program-Wide Communications

In large development programs, there are three types of communication problems.

1. Communicating the technical information needed to properly make technical decisions.
2. Communicating the project information needed to properly manage the business.
3. Communicating the technical, project, and business information needed to maintain the morale, energy, and efficiency of the working professionals.

Point 1 was covered in the previous section of this chapter and point 2 is covered in section 24.6. Point 3 is the feedback problem. To maintain team energy and efficiency, the developers must know where they stand at all times and see clear evidence that they are making progress. When developers are in the dark and are just slogging away doing whatever they think they are supposed to do, they soon lose their energy and enthusiasm. To ensure that all the unit teams in a large development program have the energy and enthusiasm to do superior work, the organizational structure and the process definitions must ensure that all developers are regularly appraised of program status, are kept aware of the key management decisions, and understand the impact of their personal work on the overall program and business.

The TSP weekly team meeting is the first and most important step in accomplishing this objective. However, for larger programs, additional provisions are needed to communicate program-wide information. One common method is to periodically issue a program-wide newsletter. This is a small step in the required direction, but management must also hold frequent meetings with the technical staff, periodically hold video conferences with the entire development program, regularly visit and talk to the working teams, and ensure that outstanding individual and team work is promptly and properly recognized.

24.4 Program Launching and Coaching Strategies

A reasonably large number of dedicated coaches are needed to launch and coach any large program. These coaches will each typically be assigned to parts of the overall organization with at least one being responsible for coaching the program-level leadership team. However, the coaches must also work together to ensure that the unit teams function smoothly and produce a beautifully designed, well-integrated, and efficiently performing product. Unless the program's teamwork is well integrated and efficient, it is unlikely to produce products that are well-integrated and efficient.

Achieving this kind of result requires that the coaches form a program-wide coaching team and that this team be represented on the program-management level leadership team. While the team coaching activities must generally be focused on the individual team members and leaders of each unit team, the coaches must also watch for any program-wide issues and help the one or more leadership teams involved address these issues in a timely way.

One of the first issues this coaching team will have to address is designing and leading the initial program launch, and designing and leading each subsequent relaunch. If the program starts out using the TSP, then the launch for the program-initiation team described in section 24.2 will probably be a standard TSP or TSPm launch. However, as the program scales up or if the TSP is not introduced at the outset, special launch and relaunch provisions will be needed for the overall program. In designing and conducting the program launch and relaunches, keep the following principles in mind.

1. Start with an overall program-management presentation to the entire development staff. If possible, this should be in person with all of the members of the entire program present. For larger distributed teams, however, it may be necessary to hold this meeting via video conference.

2. Hold such program-wide meetings at least once a year, preferably in conjunction with a program relaunch. In the meeting, have management reemphasize the program's goals, communicate all key decisions and changes, and recognize outstanding work.

3. Where possible, hold the initial program launch in one location with the program manager and all team members attending meetings 1 and 9.

4. For larger distributed programs where a single-site meeting 1 is not practical, hold a program-wide video conference for meeting 1. For the remainder of the launch meetings for a large distributed program, follow the phased-launch or relaunch strategy as next described.

The phased-launch steps are as follows.

1. Identify and initially launch the pacing teams that define the overall program structure and development context. These groups typically include the requirements, system design, and architectural teams and their work typically establishes the overall "pace" or rate at which the program proceeds. Where appropriate, they might also include one or more of the testing, verification, and validation, and quality assurance activities.

2. As part of the TSP multi-team meeting 1A for the pacing teams, have the leaders and key technical representatives of the remaining groups present their requirements. These groups are the customers for the pacing teams, and they should specify the order, content, and priority of the pacing group products. These customer groups should also provide contact points and available participants/consultants to assist the pacing teams when and if they have questions or problems. This 1A meeting is intended to emphasize that the remaining development teams are the customers for the products produced by the pacing teams and that, by producing these products in the proper order, the overall program schedule can be accelerated.

3. At the end of the pacing-team launches, the pacing teams hold a preliminary meeting 9 with the meeting 1A participants. In this meeting, the attendees review the pacing-team plans and either accept their work as a proper foundation for the subsequent launches or request changes.

4. Following the pacing-team launches and resolution of the outstanding issues from step 3, launch the remaining development teams either simultaneously or in phased groups, depending on their interdependencies.

5. At the launch conclusion, hold a program-wide meeting 9, either in person or via video conference, to review the overall program plan.

6. Throughout this phased launch process, keep the leadership team or teams appraised of launch status and results. This will help ensure that the final launch meeting 9 result is consistent with management's needs and priorities.

24.5 The Role-Manager Teams

As long as there are fewer than 10 to 15 or so unit teams, the standard TSPm role-manager-team approach should work. However, as program size grows beyond this point, the role-manager teams would have too many members to form cohesive groups or to work efficiently. At this point, establish a multi-team structure for the role-manager teams. However, because the program-level role-manager function would involve too much work to be handled as a part-time job by a development team member, the program manager must establish a technical staff with members responsible for monitoring, guiding, and supporting the role-manager teams.

These role-manager staffs then participate in all of the role-manager-team meetings for their assigned roles, ensure that the work of all of the role-manager teams is properly coordinated across the program, and make sure that any role-manager issues are promptly escalated to the leadership team. Depending on program size, these role-manager staff members could be members of the program management leadership team or report to a staff head who is a member of that team.

24.6   Program Monitoring and Reporting

While program monitoring and reporting is critically important for large programs, the TSP framework and measures greatly simplify and improve the reporting process. As long as the coaching staff can assure the leadership team that all of the unit teams are properly reporting their data, the leadership team can be confident that the unit-team and multi-team weekly reports accurately portray program status and reliably project milestone and program completion dates. While the specific report content and format must generally be established for each program, the growing set of available standard TSP report formats can be used in defining the reporting process.

24.7   Summary

While no standard process will generally be adequate for a very large integrated development program, the TSP teaming concepts and process elements are entirely applicable and should be used wherever possible. The principles to consider in forming and coaching such programs and in defining the program's process are to use sound engineering methods for all development work, to rigorously manage all changes, and to define standard reporting and decision-making methods. Architectural design, system performance control, and quality management are also critically important.

When initiating a large development program, it is common to start with a relatively small program-initiation team. Where possible, use the TSP process with this team. This will provide early experience with the process and facilitate later scale-up. Whether or not the TSP is used initially, a scale-up strategy should be defined and followed in supporting program growth and evolution. During scale-up, special process provisions are generally needed for the program management staff, the launch and relaunch processes, the role-manager teams, and program tracking and reporting.

In launching and coaching large integrated development programs, several TSP coaches are needed. While each coach can probably support several teams, every team must have an assigned coach and one coach must be available to support the program-management team and staff. As described in Chapter 27, these coaches should also work together as a coaching team.

Other than these special considerations, the TSP and TSPm multi-team processes should be adequate to support the program's smaller development elements under an overall program-wide customized TSP integrated team process.

References

Humphrey, Watts S. *Winning with Software: An Executive Strategy.* Boston: Addison-Wesley. 2002.

Humphrey, Watts S. *PSP^{SM}: A Self-Improvement Process for Software Engineers.* Boston: Addison-Wesley. 2005.

Humphrey, Watts S. *TSP^{SM}—Leading a Development Team.* Boston: Addison-Wesley. 2006.

PART V

Maintaining a TSP Team

This was an established team of 12 developers, and they were partway through their first TSP launch. The job was a major functional enhancement for the product this team had been working on for several years. While the launch had gone smoothly through meeting 5, Joan, the team leader, was worried about load balancing. If the work was perfectly balanced, the team would finish in 26 weeks. While this date was later than management wanted, she was confident that she could convince them to buy it. The problem was that in the past, the team members had resisted working on any modules they had not personally developed. She thought they would also resist her efforts to balance the team's workload.

When she discussed her concerns with Adam, the team's coach, he suggested that she was looking at the problem in the wrong way. She was acting as if load-balancing was her problem. Suppose, instead, she treated it as the team's problem; might that change the team's attitude? Joan wasn't sure but was willing to give it a try. She and Adam worked out a plan for handling the problem if it came up.

Sure enough, after the team members had made their plans in meeting 6, the team's workload was badly out of balance. One member finished in 4 weeks, a few more took less than 15 weeks, and the work for two of them stretched out to 56 weeks. Everybody else was somewhere in between. When the members finished telling their story, Adam looked at Joan and said; "It looks like the team has a big problem. Is it acceptable to finish in 56 weeks with some people idle most of that time?" Joan smiled and said, "I think this is the team's problem. Why don't we go get a snack and come back in a while to see what they have figured out?"

When they came back in 30 minutes, the room was in "happy chaos." Everybody was involved as they worked in several small groups to figure out who could pick up what tasks, what skills they lacked, and where they might need training or mentoring. After another 40 minutes, they had the plan as balanced as they could get it with the workload ranging from 22 to 29 weeks. Since they could still see ways to fine-tune the schedule, the team agreed to a 27-week commitment.

Teams can do amazing things when they are properly motivated and when they "own" a problem. The final part of this book discusses some common issues in coaching teams. The four chapters in Part V provide guidance on how to handle many of these issues and outline some principles to follow when you encounter ones that have not been covered.

Chapter 25 describes the problems and challenges of developing teamwork and how to help the team members, the team leader, and the organization's management build and effectively use their development teams.

Chapter 26 concerns coaching ethics. It addresses the coach's responsibilities to management, team leaders, and team members. It also addresses the problems of measuring people, the sensitivity of personal data, and your responsibility for protecting and respecting the privacy of all the people with whom you work.

Chapter 27 is about teams of coaches. When you work in even a moderate-sized organization that is introducing and using the TSP, you will work with several coaches. TSP coaches have a lot to do, and to efficiently and predictably train, launch, and support your teams, you and your associates must have a plan. This chapter describes how the TSP can help you manage your coaching work.

Chapter 28 covers the TSP coach's role, what the coach does, and how the coaching role changes as teams, team leadership, and management gain experience. The chapter also discusses how, as a TSP coach, you can manage and improve your personal coaching skills.

Being a team coach is a truly marvelous job: guiding people to improve their personal performance and helping them to work more effectively in teams. Coaching is one of the most rewarding and enjoyable things you can do.

25

Developing Teamwork

This chapter discusses several aspects of teambuilding and describes your role as team coach in ensuring that the team, the team leader, and the organization's management properly handle these issues. As you and they work to build an effective and productive team, there are many topics to consider. While some of these items have been discussed in prior chapters, this chapter addresses the people-related issues to consider when working with managers, team leaders, and their teams. These topics concern the many aspects of building a close-knit and smoothly functioning team.

Teams are enormously varied, and each one can have a wide variety of problems and issues. While some problems are fairly common, there are some special people-related topics to consider in coaching a TSP team. They concern measuring and evaluating people, and ensuring that the team members' personal concerns do not inhibit their ability to work cooperatively with their teammates. Anything that separates people or raises concerns about their personal situations will distract them from focusing on team success. Additional people-related topics are covered in Chapter 26. The principal topics discussed in this chapter are as follows.

- ☐ Team-member communication
- ☐ Principled negotiation

353

□ The TSP communication strategy

□ Maintaining team communication

□ Process discipline

25.1 Team-Member Communication

Communication involves the flow of information. On TSP teams, communication concerns the way the team members interact with each other, with management, with the team leader, and with you. Without good communication, teams cannot jell.

In the TSP launch, the team is together for every meeting, and all team members participate in every launch step. Your principal responsibility as the team coach is to ensure that everyone is involved, that everyone contributes to the launch process, and that there is complete communication among all of the team members. After the launch is over, your job is to help the team and team leader maintain this level of communication.

Real communication is more than just an information transfer; it takes interaction to achieve full understanding and agreement. This requires feedback. When one party makes a statement, the other reacts, and then the first responds. This give-and-take continues until the parties know that they have reached agreement. Unfortunately, however, not all communication is interactive or complete. Other kinds of communication include

□ Broadcasting (or informing)

□ Persuading

□ Negotiating

□ Listening

At the top of this list, the communication focus is on pure transmission with no interaction, while the bottom largely concerns reception, again with no interaction. In the middle, the communication is interactive, at least to some degree. These various ways to communicate are shown in Table 25.1. At one extreme, with *broadcasting*, management merely informs the team of their position. Next is *persuasion*, which can range from simple debate to coercion or even threats. The third communication item involves give-and-take and compromise: interactive *negotiations*. Finally, at the end, in *listening*, management might be receiving information from the team.

Table 25.1 Communication Types

	Broadcasting	Persuading	Negotiating	Listening
Participants	Speaker Listeners	Manager Subordinates	All participants equally important	Listener and speakers
Goal	Disseminate information	Acceptance	Agreement	Understanding
Approach	Clear statements	Discover and build on convictions	Separate the people from the problem	Listen and ask questions when not clear
Trust	Be open and honest	Trust others	Proceed independent of trust	Trust the speaker
Focus	Provide information and opportunity for clarification	Change positions based on reactions	Focus on interests, not positions; explore interests	Gather information
Bottom line	Provide rationale for the stated position	Disclose *your* bottom line	Avoid having a bottom line	Understand *their* bottom line
Options	Present options if there are any	Accept one-sided agreements	Invent options that everyone will accept	Understand options provided
Deciding	Accept inputs and report back later if decisions are affected	Search for the single answer: the one *they* will accept	Develop multiple options to choose from; decide later	Raise issues to provide clarification
Criteria	Clarity	Agreement	Develop mutually acceptable criteria	Accept all inputs
Will	Explain message, expect acceptance	Try to avoid a contest of wills	Try to reach a result based on standards independent of will	Listen to message and refrain from challenges
Pressure	Overt pressure	Subtle pressure	Yield to principle, not pressure	Minimize pressure

Broadcasting and Informing

Broadcasting and informing are used when the objective is to provide information. Where the material is easily understood and there is no need for feedback or interpretation, a simple announcement or publication is sufficient. Although broadcasting is an efficient and necessary way to disseminate information, it does not replace the need for interactive communication. One of your principal concerns is to ensure that the team leader and senior managers interact with the team in two-way dialogs and not purely through broadcasting or listening.

Persuading

In persuading, management wants the team members to understand and agree with what they propose. While this form of communication involves participation, it is clearly intended to obtain the team members' agreement with what management has already decided. In attempting to convince the team members to accept a proposal or decision, management explains what they believe and, almost as an afterthought, seeks the team's agreement.

Negotiating

In informing and persuading, the managers usually form their own views and then try to get the team to follow along. However, this team is needed because management cannot develop the product by themselves. They need more than mere involvement; they need this team to turn the initial market concept into a finished product. This requires creativity and imagination, and it takes the intellectual involvement of all of the team members. This level of agreement cannot be mandated; it requires negotiation.

Listening

In the listening mode, management relies on the team's creativity and ideas. Most launches start with management telling the team members what they want. At the end, however, the members tell management about the plan they have produced. A similar transformation occurs during the project. As development proceeds, management's communication style gradually evolves from broadcasting to listening.

Just as management's communication style evolves, so too does that of the team members. At the beginning, they not only must learn from management about the desired product, they must also capitalize on management's knowledge of what is wanted and why. As the project proceeds, they will want management's feedback on their performance and on the products they create. So, all types of communication are important to the proper functioning of the team. Help your team members and their management use the most appropriate communication style for each of their workplace interactions.

Moderating

Another aspect of communication is called **moderating**. This is almost the inverse of persuading. In moderating, an independent party, such as yourself, helps management and the team members communicate effectively. Moderating focuses on the communication process and not on the end result. As long as all of the parties agree, you don't much care what they agree upon. Moderating is the most appropriate communication style to use when you are helping team members resolve issues among themselves and with management. Your objective is to guide the communicating parties through an effective negotiation process, relying on them to arrive at an appropriate outcome.

25.2   Principled Negotiation

One particular kind of negotiation is called **principled negotiation** (Fisher 1981; Humphrey 2000). In principled negotiation, the parties' objectives are balanced. You want an outcome that the team will agree with and accept. Only with all of the team members' agreement can you be sure of their full participation and support. The following discussion uses the negotiation topics listed in Table 25.1 to explain principled negotiation.

Goal. In principled negotiation, the objective is to solve a problem in a way that all team members will accept.

Participants. If everyone is to agree with the outcome, everyone must participate and everyone's views must be heard and respected.

Approach. Human beings are almost unfailingly competitive, and they often get emotionally involved when decisions are made with which they disagree. When team members become emotional, point out that this issue is only a small part of the overall job and that it will not seem as significant when the project is completed. Allow the developers time to calm down and to see the issue from a broader perspective. One way to do this is to look for facts on which to base decisions. That will help the team to objectively consider the available alternatives.

Trust. By considering facts and using sound criteria for making decisions, the negotiators can separate themselves from the problem. In essence, they end up trusting both the facts *and* the people with whom they are negotiating.

Focus. Concentrate on interests. What do the parties truly want, and what do they think is important? Help them to discuss all points of view and to reach consensus on as many aspects as possible. Then, with the issues narrowed, it is generally easier to agree on a conclusion.

Bottom line. On any contentious issue, keep the parties from taking pro or con positions, at least at the start. Once people publicly take positions, negotiation becomes much more difficult. Positions are like ultimatums and they generally elicit nonnegotiable counterultimatums from the other side. This will make it harder—if not impossible—to reach an agreement.

Options. Ultimately, the team members must end up with a position that will allow them to proceed with the job. Ask them to identify options that address the principal interests of all the members. Once everyone understands everyone else's interests, you can generally find an option that all the parties will accept. While everyone may not agree that this is the best conclusion, if it is accepted as workable by everyone, the team will probably be able to proceed with its work.

Deciding. While action-oriented developers and managers want to make decisions quickly, help the team to concentrate on options and criteria, at least until you sense a team consensus. It is appropriate to be in a hurry, but too much haste will only waste time if the team is not ready to decide. It is also a mistake to let decisions drag out too long. Coach the team members to gather the relevant facts, review the options, get everyone's views, and then urge them to decide.

Criteria. One of the best ways to defuse a contentious topic is to ask the team members to describe *how* to settle the issue. What criteria should they use? What facts and data should they consider in the decision? Surprisingly often, a discussion of objective criteria causes a team member to say, "Oh, now I see what you mean." Once you see these flashes of insight, expect early agreement.

Will and pressure. Keep the negotiation focused on interests, facts, and criteria and avoid tests of will, threats, or pressure. Unless you do this, some team members will likely feel coerced.

25.3   The TSP Communication Strategy

The TSP launch process provides several examples of the various types of communication. The launch can be viewed as a series of communications exercises. In meeting 1, management essentially tells the team what they want and the team members generally say very little. This is an example of informing.

In meeting 2, you and the team leader strive to get the team involved. First, you guide the developers through a series of steps to set goals. They start with what management wants, but end up with agreement on a set of team goals and measures. Although the objective of meeting 2 is to hold a negotiation, the members of most newly formed teams are unsure about how to behave. Therefore, goal-setting in meeting 2 is generally more an example of persuading than negotiating. Although you would like the team and team leader to negotiate, most new TSP team members are not ready to fully participate at this point in the team-building process.

When the team members select their roles in the second part of meeting 2, they are better able to negotiate. Now they are dealing with a topic that they understand and feel more qualified to discuss. However, when selecting the roles, the negotiations should be among the team members themselves, with you and the team leader acting as moderators. Your objective is to get the team members to agree on each role assignment. You should accept almost any outcome, as long as all of the team members agree.

Most launch meetings (3 through 8) are examples of negotiation, where the team leader and the team negotiate the plan. There should be lots of give and take, with everyone participating and giving opinions. The final objective is a consensus plan on which the team leader and all of the team members agree. Your job as the moderator is to facilitate this process and to ensure that there is complete and frank communication among all the members and the team leader.

Meeting 9 illustrates several communication modes. The team leader is the team's spokesperson seeking to persuade management that the team's plan meets their stated business needs. If the plan does not meet the business objectives, management is likely to have many questions. However, the team has the facts, and management must learn from the team members what they plan to do and why. Because the team now knows a great deal more about the project than management, the meeting starts with management listening to the team. Then, as they learn enough about the team's plans, they can move to a more interactive communication style to negotiate a plan agreement with the team.

In the final postmortem meeting, you and the team leader switch to the listening mode. You are seeking to learn from the team how the launch worked, and how you could do a better job in the future.

25.4 Maintaining Team Communication

Communication among team members is the single most important element of both building and maintaining teams. To become a close-knit group, every member must understand what every other member thinks, believes, and feels. This level of intimacy can be achieved only if all of the members communicate freely and often. The TSP launch will usually establish open and full communication among team members, and then that level of communication must be fostered and maintained as the team does its work. The following techniques can help to do this.

- ☐ Sharing a common workspace
- ☐ Holding frequent team meetings
- ☐ Concentrating on facts and data
- ☐ Getting everything on the table

Sharing a Common Workspace

When the team members share a common working space, they are in frequent contact and can easily interact with and support one another. A shared working space allows them to meet often, discuss ideas, and review and comment on each other's work. This enables each team member to understand what every other member is doing and to see when anyone needs help.

A shared working space is indispensable for jelled teams. Once the members learn to communicate freely and to trust and rely on each other, it might seem feasible to disperse the team physically. However, this is risky because teams are rarely static; new members come and old members leave. As the membership mix changes, the remote members may become outsiders and no longer feel a part of the close-knit group. So, wherever possible, urge management to keep teams together and to maintain a common workspace where the members can meet informally in pairs, small groups, or as an entire team.

Holding Frequent Team Meetings

The weekly team meeting is an important part of maintaining team communication. Even though this meeting takes only a modest amount of time, it is an essential part of maintaining a cohesive group. The weekly team meeting also provides the feedback that the members need to feel that they are contributing and progressing. Think of this feedback in sporting terms. Knowing the score—knowing precisely where the team stands—is essential to maintaining the team's energy and motivation. While uninformed development groups can plod through their projects, they won't have the energy or enthusiasm to produce creative or exciting products.

When properly run, team meetings need not take very long, but they can provide the team members with a sense of membership and the feedback they need on the team's progress. Because the team meeting is such a crucial part of maintaining the team's cohesion and commitment, urge the team leader to hold a team meeting every week.

Concentrating on Facts and Data

A good way to minimize team contention and disagreement is for management to insist that decisions be based on facts and data. When people look at the relevant data, it is surprising how often a seemingly obvious position will be directly contradicted by the available facts. The team leader should set an example by looking at and, wherever possible, using team data in the weekly meetings to identify problems, assess team status, or make decisions. Urge the team members to do so as well.

Getting Everything on the Table

Once groups have worked together for a while, they occasionally develop special hang-ups and problems. For example, one member may refuse to work with another, there could be serious disagreements about design or other methods, or someone might regularly fail to meet his or her commitments to the team.

While these problems are normal, they can make it hard for the team members to maintain open and honest communication. When you sense that a team has such problems, talk to the members privately to understand the problems and what lies behind them. Then, if you can get all of the involved parties to agree, hold a team meeting to get the issues on the table and to help the team resolve them.

Treat these issues cautiously, however, as they are occasionally very difficult and your intervention could even make matters worse. Sometimes, the underlying problems are so deep-seated and sensitive that even a trained therapist would have trouble resolving them, so be careful how you proceed and make sure that everyone is really willing to discuss the issues before you hold any resolution meetings. On the other hand, if you cannot get the team to resolve these issues, it will probably have trouble jelling as a motivated and productive working group.

25.5   Process Discipline

In process terms, **discipline** refers to the fidelity with which teams follow their defined processes. Highly disciplined teams thoroughly plan their work, rigorously follow their processes, and consistently gather and analyze their data. Undisciplined teams, however, will be less thorough in some or all of these areas. Usually, the first sign of a discipline problem is poor data-gathering. Undisciplined teams generally also ignore their data and continue making intuitive decisions.

The Importance of Discipline

While there are many definitions of discipline, the most pertinent one for software work is "a regimen that develops or improves skill" (Random House 1983). Thus, the focus of discipline is on improving performance and, in process terms, it concerns the fidelity with which a defined process is actually followed. Developers may argue that some process is too complex, has too many steps, or requires too much data, but these are not discipline issues. Even if the points are valid, they concern process *definition*, not process *fidelity*. If the process is not appropriate, change it. Ask the members who object to the process to prepare PIPs describing their proposed changes and provide the evidence to support them. Whenever a team member takes the trouble to prepare a PIP, the process manager should review it and suggest to the team what changes to make. However, once the team members have picked a process and agreed to use it, they should use it. In short, team discipline deals with a single issue: working the way that the team members have decided to work.

Discipline is particularly important to TSP teams. As has been demonstrated by many teams, when the team members are disciplined in their work, they are more productive, their work is more predictable, and they produce higher-quality products. Such teams are highly respected by their peers and highly valued by their employers. Ultimately, this is the recognition that most professionals seek.

Establishing Process Discipline

The first and most important discipline challenge is to get the team members to gather time, size, and defect data on their work. The first step in doing this is PSP training (Humphrey 2005). If the team members have been properly trained, they will have gathered complete data on the programs they wrote in the PSP course. They should also have seen that these data were not hard to gather and that they provided very powerful insights into their work.

Gathering data, however, requires constant attention. It is easy to forget to record data when struggling with a difficult design problem. This is normal. If the developers forget to record some data, urge them to record their best estimates for these data as soon as they can. While their data may not be very accurate, it will at least be a start.

The best way to motivate team members to accurately gather data is for you to regularly review their data with them. Coach them on gradually improving their data-gathering practices and show them how to use the data they gather. As long as they are trying to gather their data properly, you have a good chance of gradually getting them to improve their process discipline.

When some developers do not improve or refuse to gather data, discuss this problem with the team leader. This issue is discussed further in the section of Chapter 26 on handling difficult team members.

Maintaining Process Discipline

One part of maintaining a team's process discipline is for you and the team leader to regularly emphasize the importance of complete and accurate data and the need for every team member to be disciplined in gathering those data. While this is essential, it alone is not enough. You must also work with the team and team leader to show them how to use the data to continue improving productivity and product quality.

While there are many ways to do this, they all involve getting people interested in and excited about their data. You can best do this by being interested in and getting excited about the team's data yourself and then by showing the team leader and team members what they can do with these data. You can also make a regular practice of working with the team leader to identify some team achievement, explaining its importance in business terms, and then telling higher management about it. This will not only help to sustain management's support of the TSP, it will build the team's pride in its achievements.

Responsibilities for Team Discipline

Discipline is like quality: Everyone must be responsible for the discipline of their own work. However, team discipline is more than just the composite of team-member discipline—it concerns overall team behavior. The team leader must be responsible for his or her personal process discipline as well as for the team's discipline. In fulfilling this responsibility, the team leader should ask the quality manager to ensure that all team members properly gather and use their data and to report any problems. When there are problems, the team leader should then talk to the involved team members and encourage them to follow the process. If they won't, the team leader must then consider this to be a personnel issue. The final section of Chapter 26 on handling difficult team members discusses what to do then.

Finally, management and the team leader need to hold you responsible for periodically reviewing the team's data and for ensuring that both the quality manager and team leader are properly doing their jobs. When you find problems, review them with the team member and team leader first and then, if necessary, take them to higher management. Remember, you are the team coach, and you are responsible for ensuring that the teams you coach do quality work. This requires that they be disciplined in following their processes.

25.6 Summary

Communication is an important aspect of teamwork. It is not just a way to tell team members what to do and to describe events in the organization, it is also a way for management to show respect for the team and to enlist the members' minds and energies in achieving management's goals. Real communication is more than just a one-way street; it takes interaction and feedback. The various modes of communication include broadcasting (or informing), persuading, negotiating, and listening. Broadcasting is pure transmission, while listening is almost entirely reception. Persuading and negotiating must be interactive. The team and management will use all of the modes of communication during the team launch and during the team's subsequent project. In team communication, the coach's role is to act as the team facilitator or moderator. Effective communication among team members is the single most important element of both building and maintaining effective teamwork.

In process terms, discipline refers to the fidelity with which a team follows its defined processes. In development work, discipline is a regimen that develops or improves skill. Discipline deals with a single issue: following the process the team has decided to follow. The first and only important principle of process discipline is for the team leader and coach to demand discipline and not to accept any arguments or excuses. Process discipline is important because it determines the quality of the process that is used, and the quality of the process determines the quality of the products created. Product quality, in turn, determines the effectiveness of the project at meeting its cost and schedule objectives.

References

Fisher, Roger, and William Ury. *Getting to Yes: Negotiating Agreement Without Giving In*. Boston: Houghton Mifflin. 1981, 13.

Humphrey, Watts S. *Introduction to the Team Software Process*^{SM}. Boston: Addison-Wesley. 2000.

Humphrey, Watts S. *PSP*^{SM}: *A Self-Improvement Process for Software Engineers*. Boston: Addison-Wesley. 2005.

The Random House Dictionary of the English Language. New York: Random House. 1983.

26

Coaching Ethics

Ethics is an enormous subject, and we as professionals have an obligation to follow the codes of ethics established by our professions. The IEEE, for example, has a code of ethics that defines the basics of ethical engineering behavior (IEEE 1990). While ethical behavior might seem simple in principle, we rarely face black-and-white choices; when dealing with people, most situations are too complex for simplistic answers. The source of many ethical problems, however, is self-interest: People can become so preoccupied with their personal needs and interests that they literally cannot visualize how some action would impact others. A helpful guideline in such cases is to completely eliminate your self-interest from the decision process. Once you have decided on the ethical course of action, consider your personal needs in deciding how to proceed.

This chapter focuses only on those portions of applied ethics that can guide our work as coaches. The general principles of moral and honest behavior are excellent guides to most coaching situations, but there will be cases where the most appropriate behavior is not obvious, or where our loyalties to the team and our responsibilities to management conflict. As a team coach, you will have obligations to the team members, the team leader, management, and yourself, and these different obligations can conflict. This chapter outlines some general principles for addressing the typical conflicts coaches often face. The following topics are covered.

- ☐ The coach's responsibilities
- ☐ The coaching commitment
- ☐ Handling team and individual data
- ☐ Measuring people
- ☐ Relating to management
- ☐ Handling difficult team members

26.1   The Coach's Responsibilities

Your principal responsibility as a coach is to management. They are paying you to do this job, and you have presumably agreed to do it. So your objective must be to do at least a competent, and hopefully superior, job of handling the assignment. Within this broad guideline, you will have many choices to make, but your principal guidepost must be your commitment to management.

Next comes your commitment to the team leader. Presumably this team leader asked you to coach this team or at least agreed to you being the coach. Your obligation to the team leader is to do your utmost to help this team do its job successfully. Since what you and the team leader believe to be success may differ, you may not always agree on how to handle specific situations. Since the team leader is responsible to management for this team's performance, any conflicts you have with the team leader must be viewed as critical, and should be amicably settled if at all possible.

Third is your obligation to the team members. To effectively coach developers, you must have their trust, and you must know a great deal about them. Since much of what you know will be private, and since the team members will generally not want that information known to others, you must respect the privacy of all the confidential information you have about the team members. If you don't, you won't keep their trust, and you will no longer be an effective coach.

Next comes your obligation to yourself. We all have personal standards and seek to perform our jobs with distinction. We also generally try to improve our capability to do the jobs we will be assigned in the future. The real obligation here is the responsibility to respect ourselves. This means that we need to stick to our principles, even in difficult situations. Your primary concern here must be with avoiding situations where your obligations to your various constituencies will likely conflict, and where you might be forced to do something that you feel is dishonest or unethical. An example would be being forced to give management a team member's personal data.

26.2 The Coaching Commitment

The best time to avoid conflicts of interest is before you take a coaching job. Chapter 27 discusses one aspect of this problem: getting committed to more than you can do. The aspect covered here concerns getting into impossible situations. These generally concern cases where management, the team leader, or some of the team members do not agree with the principles of the TSP but were somehow forced to use it anyway. Your principal leverage in these situations is before you take the coaching assignment.

Before agreeing to a coaching job, satisfy yourself that it is likely to be successful, and don't take on troublesome cases if you can help it. There are four categories of troublesome cases, and there are steps you can take to fix or avoid each of these situations. The principal cases are

- ☐ Troublesome management
- ☐ Troublesome team leaders
- ☐ Troublesome team members
- ☐ Hopeless projects

Troublesome Management

When the team leader's manager or any higher-level manager does not appreciate the importance of sound development methods, he or she would be a troublesome manager. Such managers are usually focused on getting the product out the door. They do not understand the impact of poor-quality work, and they have no appreciation for the benefits of sound planning. This is a question of standards.

Some managers may have high standards in their own fields, but no appreciation for development standards. Often, these managers are not familiar with the kind of development work the team is doing and do not appreciate the benefits of using disciplined methods in that work. If that is the case, try to convince them that the TSP will pay off on the very first job that uses it. If a manager does not buy the TSP principles before the launch, however, do not coach any project that this manager controls.

Even managers who have development backgrounds may not appreciate the need for high-quality products and the necessity of following a disciplined process. Most modern systems are software intensive and much larger now than in the past. They are also increasingly complex and sophisticated. Software-intensive applications are also more demanding and they are used under progressively more sensitive conditions.

The danger is that, when the troublesome manager makes decisions about this project, his or her decisions will be based on short-term schedule pressures rather than on sound engineering principles. Such decisions generally undermine disciplined teamwork and often destroy or seriously damage the project. Take the time to convince the manager of the importance of process discipline or think twice about launching or coaching any team that reports to this manager.

Handling Management Problems

Once management agrees to introduce the TSP, they will generally support the TSP principles and agree to have the team make its own plan. However, you will occasionally find troublesome managers. Unfortunately, these troublesome managers are often fairly senior and generally inaccessible. This makes them particularly difficult to deal with, not only because they won't attend the opening or closing launch meetings, but because they won't even meet with you.

One such manager was the vice president of a large electronics company. Tammy was director of one of the company's laboratories, and she had been told to finish this software project by the time the planned hardware was completed. This was the vice president's top priority, and Tammy pushed her team to make that date. While Tammy wanted the project to use the TSP, she also realized that if her team submitted a schedule that the VP did not accept, there would be a new laboratory director. Therefore, Tammy decided not to introduce the TSP. The project schedule debates were deferred until the project was in trouble and it was clear that the date would be missed. Although Tammy kept her job for another year, once it was obvious that the team would not meet the VP's date, she was replaced.

Under these conditions, laboratory directors will probably lose their jobs no matter what they do. However, they will have a better chance of surviving if they insist that all of their projects have sound plans. Just continuing in the hope that things will work out is always a mistake; things never work out by themselves. In coaching these managers, point out that they have a better chance of surviving if they do the job properly. In development management, the gamblers *always* lose.

Troublesome Team Leaders

One common problem with team leaders is training. Many will argue that they do not have the time to get properly trained before launching a TSP team. Managers in most development organizations are busy, but people can always find the time to do what they know must be done. If the leader has not been properly trained, that leader does not believe that training is important. After all, TSP management training only takes a few days, so this manager must have the TSP pretty far down on his or her priority list.

When a team leader is not trained, that leader will not understand the methods his or her team will be using. Such leaders either do not think the methods are important, or they don't care how the team members do their work. In either case, such leaders are not good candidates to lead TSP teams, and you should avoid them.

Another way to tell if the team leader will be troublesome concerns team-member training. If the team members have not all been PSP-trained before the team launch, that should be a warning signal. The TSP training needs are well-known and they clearly state that all team members must be PSP-trained before they can properly use the TSP process. So, ask the team leader why the developers are not trained.

The team leader's answer should tell you whether or not you want to coach this team. If the team leader explains that one member had been ill or had a last-minute family crisis and will finish the training by some specified date, that is reasonable. If, however, the leader claims that there was not time for the training, that the developers didn't want to take the PSP training, or that they will do it later when they have more time, don't work with this team leader. He or she is either unable to motivate the developers to finish their training or does not believe the training is important. Generally, these team leaders are using the TSP because they were told to do so by senior management. Do your best to explain the TSP process and what it can do for them, but if you cannot change their attitudes, expect to have trouble with such team leaders.

Troublesome Team Members

If senior management and the team leader support the TSP and the team members have all been trained, you will not generally have problems with the team members. While one or two may not accept the PSP and TSP methods even after training, they can usually be handled by the team leader. If, however, more than one or two of the developers do not want to use the PSP and TSP, there is usually a deeper problem. In general, such problems stem from an earlier failed PSP or TSP introduction or from a poor management strategy for introducing the TSP.

Against the advice of the PSP instructor, management in one laboratory decided to train all of the developers in the PSP and delay TSP introduction until PSP training had been completed. After nearly a year of training, they started looking into the TSP. Many of the developers had not used the PSP since their training nearly a year earlier. They had largely forgotten the PSP methods and had lost their initial enthusiasm for using it.

This problem was exacerbated by one developer who argued that the PSP methods would not work for their kind of business. Since nobody knew any better, it was soon generally accepted that the PSP would not work for systems programming. Since many TSP teams have successfully developed various types of control programs, this argument was clearly nonsense. Even though all of the developers had been PSP trained, unless the coach could change their attitudes, such a team would be nearly impossible to launch or coach.

Another common problem is top-down management directives to introduce the TSP at flank speed. In one case, management wanted to introduce the TSP as rapidly as possible, so they sent out a directive to train the first team. Unfortunately, management never took the time to explain why TSP was important or to convince the developers to take the PSP course. The first team was told on Friday that they were to start PSP class on the next Monday. They were also given a 350-page book and told to read the first 7 chapters. Not surprisingly, they didn't think the course would help them so they set out to prove that it was a waste of time. The course was not a success and the TSP introduction failed. If the TSP introduction is not reasonably well planned, don't agree to participate.

Hopeless Projects

If senior management, the team leader, and the team are all prepared for the TSP launch, the project almost doesn't matter. Even if management's desired schedule is hopelessly unrealistic, as long as these managers will support the team in following a sound process and conducting a full TSP launch, they are likely to deal rationally with the plan the team produces. Under these conditions, the TSP is probably the best way for this team to proceed, almost regardless of the project's problems. Thus, when the people are prepared, the customer is reasonable, and management is supportive, you will rarely find hopeless projects.

26.3   Handling Team and Individual Data

Managers should never use TSP data to evaluate their people. What makes the data privacy issue so complex is that if management properly uses the team's data, most developers will not object to sharing it with them. They will then not bias or otherwise fake their data to show anything but the objective truth. However, there are a small number of team members who will object to gathering data, regardless of how management uses it.

There can be many reasons for team members refusing to gather data, but the ones who object will usually have stories about how much time data-gathering takes or how management misused their data in the past. Furthermore, these members can almost never be relied upon to accurately and completely gather process data. Thus, the members who object the most are also the ones you and the team leader need to worry about the most. This is what makes the handling of personal data so challenging.

If someone on the team is truly opposed to gathering TSP data, try to understand why. See if there is some way to address these concerns while still getting the required data. You will generally find that the arguments concern the time to gather the data or the use that management will make of these data.

While these arguments may sound plausible, they are usually just excuses to justify or disguise the member's real objections. These objections are usually of two kinds. First, these members may truly believe that they do such superior work that the TSP process and data will not help them. Unfortunately, this contention is usually hard to refute until you have integration and system test data on the member's work. Second, these members may know that they do poor work and are afraid that their data will make their poor performance obvious.

The Costs of Data Gathering

While the time needed to gather data is a major concern for some team members, data-gathering, when properly done, takes very little time. If the member is truly concerned, however, discuss his or her data-gathering methods. Generally, some modest tool training or support assistance will make data gathering more comfortable and natural. While adequate tools can be a big help, consistent data gathering still takes a considerable amount of personal discipline. The real key to data gathering is doing it long enough and regularly enough so that it becomes routine. Then, the members will usually accept data gathering as a necessary part of doing professional work.

If a member continues to argue, there is probably some other problem which he or she is not revealing. If you get to this point, ask the member to measure his or her data-gathering activity and to review these data with you. In reviewing these data, if the member says that recording any item takes more than a few seconds to a minute, get that member to demonstrate what takes so long. A defect report should not take more than about 20 to 60 seconds at most, and logging time should take no more than about one percent of a team member's time. With proper tool support, weekly data reporting should only take a few minutes once a week.

The time it takes for team members to do their tasks is a management issue. After the member has measured his or her data-gathering time and reviewed these data with you and the team leader, you will know the costs and benefits of data gathering. If management decides that the benefits are worth the costs, the member is paid to spend the time and produce the results that management directs. So, although the member may believe that the data-gathering time is excessive, once management has reviewed the data and decided that the value of the data was worth the cost, the argument should be over. If the member still objects to gathering data, refer to section 26.6 on the handling of difficult people and to the discussion in Chapter 16 in *TSP^{SM}—Leading a Development Team* (Humphrey 2006).

Management Review of Data

The second objection that members generally have to gathering data is that they do not want management to see their data. There are two common reasons for this. First, they do not want to change the way they work and cannot think of another reason that management would accept. Second, they are afraid that management will use the data to justify a negative evaluation of them.

Here, the argument can be quite short. In general, no manager needs to see a team member's personal data. Your job as the team coach is to make sure that the members are properly gathering and using their data. As long as the managers are assured that this is the case, they have no need to look at anyone's personal data. However, if you find that the data are not being properly gathered and used, you will have to convince the team member to change or you will have to inform management. Then, to understand the problems, management may have to look at the member's data. After all, the managers are responsible for managing how their people work, and by objecting to gathering data, the member has made data gathering a major issue when it need not have been an issue at all.

The Team Member's Personal Data

While the members' personal *data* are private, their *performance* is not. Don't get into protracted debates about what data should be public or private. The basic principle is that developers are paid to do a job, so the amount of time they spend, the tasks they perform, and the products they produce are valid management concerns and these data should be public. However, defect data and the detailed time and defect logs are much more personal, and there is generally no need for management to see them.

Team members are paid to produce results, and their cost, schedule, and quality performance are serious management concerns. If some member's work products take excessive time in test or are highly defective in customer use, management must be concerned. Then it would be appropriate for them to ask the member to explain what he or she did and why the quality of his or her work was so poor.

If the member was actually following the team's process and had data to prove it, that data would provide clear evidence on how he or she did the work. It could also help the member explain why testing took so long or why the product had so many defects. Otherwise, with no supporting data, management might properly suspect that the member was not really trying to do a quality job and consider him or her to be a personnel problem.

When a member is not gathering time, size, or defect data, it is often obvious from the team's overall data. If only one member of a large team is not gathering data, that is hard for management to detect, but the team would know. Then, even if management never looks at that member's data, the other team members will almost certainly complain.

If the members are disciplined about gathering their data, management will have no reason to look at it. However, if the members are not gathering their data, they are almost certainly not producing quality products and cannot accurately plan or report on their work. Under these conditions, management should ask them about their poor performance. Then, the members may want to use their personal data, if only for self-protection.

26.4   Measuring People

Management must not measure or evaluate any of the team members on the defect data they report. If management even implies that they blame any of the developers for their defects, they will destroy the team's commitment to quality. The developers know that everyone makes mistakes, and they know that no one intentionally leaves defects in their programs. If management were to judge the developers by their personal defect data, they would no longer be able to trust that data. Defect data would have become threatening and no one would report it. Without the team's data, you cannot coach the team, and management cannot track, manage, or improve the quality of its development work.

The basic rule to remember is: Managers must not use TSP data—or any other data—to evaluate their people. They should not even hint that the value of any measure will affect how they evaluate their people's performance. Even if the managers do not use TSP measures to evaluate their people, if the members merely suspect that they do, there will almost certainly be problems.

Proper Use of Data

While this last discussion about never using data might seem inconsistent with the prior comments about team members who do poor-quality work, it really is not. When individuals or teams produce poor-quality products, that fact should be obvious from system-test and customer-reported defect data. These data should then alert management that there is a quality problem. The proper management reaction then is to investigate the cause of this quality problem. If they find that, in spite of paying to train the developers in proper quality methods, the developers are not using these methods, that would be cause for disciplinary action. Note, however, that the data used in this case are gathered by the test and service groups and not provided by the developers. Note also that management did not act on the basis of the data. Their actions were based on what they found by investigating the quality problem.

Misuse of Data

Personal data are sensitive and, depending on how managers use the data, they could get very different results from what they expect. The topic of people measurement and the problems of misusing data are described in a book by Robert Austin entitled *Measuring and Managing Performance in Organizations* (Austin 1996). This is a large subject and Austin's book is worth reading. I cover some of the highlights here.

The essential issue in misusing data concerns motivation. What makes team members want to do a good job? Are they motivated by the team's goals? Do they want to support their teammates? Or are they just trying to get a raise or a promotion? When people are driven by goals or team spirit, management has nothing to worry about. Measurement will not be a problem as long as the measurements do not relate to their personal goals. However, if the members work hard principally because they want their managers to recommend them for a raise or a promotion, there will likely be problems.

While salary increases and bonuses are supposed to encourage good work, the real issue is not how managers evaluate their people, but how these people *think* they are being evaluated. If they think their evaluations are based on some numerical measures and that management has specific targets for these measures, they will do their utmost to meet those targets, almost regardless of how their actions impact any other objectives. On the other hand, if the members believe that their evaluations will be based on how they perform as team members or on the degree to which they contributed to the team's success, they will not be concerned about the value of some numerical measure.

Measurement Limitations

No simple measures can possibly capture all aspects of what management wants their people to do. If teams feel that their evaluations will be in any way influenced by the numerical value of some measure, they will maximize that measure, and the unmeasured aspects of their work will likely be ignored. If the work is simple and if all management cares about is widgets per hour, then they might safely measure their people on widgets per hour. But if they care about the quality of those widgets, or whether the widgets' feature mix meets market needs, or any other unmeasured characteristic, simplistic measures would likely produce less-than-optimum results. Unless every important characteristic is measured and included in the evaluation in exactly the proportion management desires, they will not get the results they want.

However, the team members will always have an unconscious concern that, in spite of everything you or the team leader say, management will still consider some numeric measures, particularly if their values were poor. Therefore, when some member has a poor result, emphasize to that person that management is most interested in superior team results and not in some numbers. Urge the member to learn from what happened and then to forget it. The proper attitude is to strive to do better work the next time. Point out that every job is different, and that development performance varies enormously from one job to the next. Not only are there variations in the work, but performance varies from day to day and even from hour to hour. The objective is to learn from what we do and to try not to repeat the same mistakes.

26.5 Relating to Management

A fundamental cause of coaching conflicts is balancing management's need to understand their peoples' capabilities and your commitment to protect the team members' personal data. Since this is rarely a problem when management has been properly trained, the cautions described in section 26.2 should take care of many of these cases. Unfortunately, however, managers frequently change jobs, and the new managers are often not TSP trained. In this case, your only recourse is to meet with the new manager, if you can, and arrange for the appropriate training. If the TSP has already been widely used in the organization, this should not be a problem. However, when the TSP is relatively new, these replacement managers are often untrained and unwilling to get trained.

Since untrained managers will not generally understand the TSP or appreciate the value of the team's data, you will not likely get pressed for any of the team members' private data. If you are, you can almost certainly get by with providing composite team data and explaining that this is what you have available. If you don't mention the personal data, it will probably not be requested.

As long as you can protect the team's data, your principal problems will concern lack of management support for process discipline and management's likely efforts to move people on and off the team regardless of their training status. If you and the team leader cannot protect the team from such destructive actions, stop coaching this manager's teams and concentrate on supporting the more receptive managers.

26.6 Handling Difficult Team Members

Handling difficult people is a large subject and there are an almost infinite variety of cases. However, there are two general principles to follow in dealing with problem people. First, everyone is different, and many seemingly difficult people are merely confused or not yet comfortable working with their managers and teammates. They could be having family problems or facing stresses that have nothing to do with their jobs. You and the team leader should take the time to listen to and understand these people and to establish a degree of personal rapport. When you understand their problems, you will be able to help them get the help they need. Once they get help, their initial team-working difficulties will usually disappear and they will become productive team members.

Second, if there are continuing problems in productively using an employee on the team, this is an issue that the team leader must handle with his or her management. Since personnel problems can become exceedingly messy, you should stay out of them unless explicitly invited by management. Even then, be careful not to get so involved that the other team members view you as part of management. Then your ability to function effectively as a couch will be seriously damaged. However, if some team member is troublesome and disrupts the team, and if the team leader is doing nothing about it, first discuss the situation with the team leader. Then, if his or her actions are not effective, you may have to raise this issue with higher management. Be very careful how you do this, however, or you could antagonize the team leader. That is likely to destroy your ability to continue functioning effectively as that team's coach. For further information on handling of difficult team members, see Chapter 16, pages 208 to 213, in *TSP^{SM}—Leading a Development Team* (Humphrey 2006).

26.7   Summary

The principal ethical issues in coaching concern your responsibilities to management, the team leader, the team members, and yourself. Since you work for management and have agreed to do this job, that responsibility must be your first priority. Within this broad framework, your other obligations are to support the team leader, to coach the team members, and to be true to your own personal values and ideals.

Before agreeing to do a coaching job, satisfy yourself that this job can actually be done and that you are capable of doing it. If possible, avoid coaching teams for managers or team leaders who do not believe in or support the TSP. Also avoid coaching teams where any significant number of members are actively opposed to using PSP and TSP methods.

Team-member data can also be a significant ethical issue. The concerns here relate to the process discipline required to gather these data, the proper use of these data, and your obligation to protect every team member's personal data.

Management must not use the data that people gather to evaluate or otherwise reward or punish them. The team members who object the most to data gathering are usually the ones you and the team leader need to worry about the most, and they may require additional counseling and monitoring to ensure their cooperation.

If any team members are difficult to work with or refuse to follow the team's agreed-upon process, they will almost certainly disrupt the team and damage its effectiveness. Although you must alert management to such problems, these are typically personnel issues, and other than making sure they are being addressed by the right people, you should not get involved unless explicitly requested to by the team leader or management.

References

Austin, Robert D. *Measuring and Managing Performance in Organizations.* New York: Dorset House Publishing. 1996.

Humphrey, Watts S. *TSP^{SM}—Leading a Development Team.* Boston: Addison-Wesley. 2006.

The Institute of Electrical and Electronic Engineers, Inc. IEEE Code of Ethics. 1990. www.ieee.org/portal/pages/about/whatis/code.html.

27

The Coaching Team

Whether you are a coach or a developer, you need to make plans, track your work, and regularly report on your progress. Similarly, when you work with a group of coaches, you should work together as a TSP team, using TSP principles and methods on the job. This will set an example for the developers and managers, and it will help you to do a better job. You will also find the work more rewarding. So whether you are the only coach in your organization or part of a coaching team, use the TSP and PSP methods to plan and manage your work. This chapter addresses some issues to consider in building, launching, and working on a coaching team.

27.1 Coaching in Organizations

Most organizations, when initiating a TSP effort, find that they need several coaches. They are embarking on a challenging job, and it will take many months or even years to transition the TSP into widespread use. TSP transition requires a substantial amount of work, and most of this work must be done by qualified TSP coaches. Just as with a development project, to do a quality job on an acceptable schedule, you must have enough qualified and capable team members to do the work.

While the TSP works consistently when it is properly used, it is not magic, and like any transition effort, it can be screwed up if not properly managed and supported. The coaches' job is to make sure this transition work is properly handled and that it is successful. As with any significant job, this work should be planned, tracked, and managed. Since the TSP coaches must do this work and perform the bulk of the tasks, they should work as a team to plan the work, to implement the plan, and to track and report on their progress. And, most important, in doing this work, they should use the TSP process and methods.

While there are many other ways that groups of coaches could work as teams, this chapter concentrates on teams that are transitioning the TSP into general use. However, the principles described in this chapter will work equally well for teams of people coaching any kind of work. The topics covered in this chapter are

☐ Why use a coaching team?

☐ Forming a coaching team

☐ Launching a coaching team

☐ Managing and tracking coaching teams

☐ Coaching a coaching team

☐ Being on a coaching team

27.2   Why Use a Coaching Team?

Some years ago, a moderate-sized software organization had completed two TSP pilot projects, and senior management decided that the results were so good they should use TSP throughout the organization. They told Carl, director of the process department, to put TSP into place in one year. Carl developed a plan in a couple of days and presented it to the VP of development. The VP, however, had many questions that Carl could not answer, so he told Carl to make a more complete plan and to come back in a week.

When Carl discussed this assignment with his staff, one of the coaches suggested that they form a team of the four trained coaches and have them make the plan. Carl agreed, and they started preparing for the team launch. They even got an experienced coach from another organization to lead the coaching team's launch. The VP also agreed to attend launch meetings 1 and 9 and to explain to the team what he wanted and why.

Even though this organization had more than 1,000 developers in several countries, the coaching team produced the plan in four days. In meeting 9, the coaches could answer all of the VP's questions. He then accepted the team's plan, even though the planned transition took a little over 2 years instead of his originally desired 12 months.

Launching and coaching a coaching team is a marvelous experience, and this opportunity will give you an initial sense of what it will be like when all of your teams and team members are properly trained and have used the TSP. While TSP teams can do outstanding work, TSP coaching teams can produce truly amazing results. They are not magicians, but these people know what they are doing, are committed to doing great work, and are comfortable with themselves and their roles on their team. Their energies are entirely focused on doing a great job. Coaching teams are a pleasure to work with.

27.3   Forming a Coaching Team

Like any other team, a coaching team needs a leader and a coach. But a coaching team is more than just a group of TSP coaches working together as a team to perform some task. All of the team members must be trained as TSP coaches. This equips them to efficiently do all of the tasks in a team launch, to communicate clearly, and to support each other. There will be no debates about why to make a plan, how to make estimates, or the need for load balancing.

One of the first questions you will face in forming such a team is training. Suppose you have some job to do that involves a couple of trained TSP coaches and two or three untrained candidate coaches. Why not form this group into a team, even though they are not all yet trained as TSP coaches? If these candidate coaches are PSP trained, they truly will do this job, and if the group does not include observers or other political representatives, then it would be a good idea to use the TSP to form, launch, coach, and support this team. However, this would be a standard TSP team and not the kind of coaching team discussed in this chapter.

The reason this is important is that coaching teams are truly special. The members all understand the TSP process, agree with the TSP principles, and know how to perform all of the tasks required to make teams truly effective and efficient. They come right to the point, identify key issues, and suggest creative solutions.

One of the team-member coaches will probably be the team leader, but you will also need a coach. If you can get an independent coach from some other organization to serve in that role, that would be desirable. Otherwise, one of the team members could act as the coach or the team could decide to rotate the coaching assignment among the team members.

27.4   Launching a Coaching Team

As illustrated by the example in section 27.2, meeting 1 is critically important for all teams, particularly for coaching teams. Don't try to form the coaching team or hold a team launch until you have senior management's agreement to participate in meetings 1 and 9 and to describe what they want and why they want it. While the launch process will be pretty standard with the normal goal, plan, and risk discussions, three points deserve special attention: resource commitments, alternate plans, and the minimum schedule.

Resource Commitments

While the team members will all understand the importance of clear and firm resource commitments, their managers probably will not. The time the coaches need for the launch will probably not be a problem, but the time needed to actually do the planned work almost certainly will. Until they have considerable experience with TSP teams and plans, few managers will appreciate the time commitment required for coaching. They could then look on this as a relatively low-priority part-time job.

With proper launch preparation, the coaches will have management agreement on their available task times, but at least some of them will likely have trouble putting in those committed hours. The most common reason will be that their managers have simultaneously committed them to doing development work, and the development work will have management's highest priority. It is therefore essential to stress the coaching resource issue during launch preparation, in meeting 1, and in meeting 9. It is also important for the team members to base their personal plans on several different resource levels and to establish the likelihood of achieving each level. Suggested levels are

- ☐ What management has agreed to
- ☐ The level the coaches are confident they can achieve
- ☐ The worst-case risk level they think is likely

The team should then use these risk levels to establish alternate plans and to describe these plans in meeting 9. If the coaches come from several different departments, it is also essential to have all of their managers attend launch meetings 1 and 9. If any of these managers do not attend at least meeting 9 and agree with their coaches' commitments and plan, expect these coaches to have trouble putting in their planned task hours.

Alternate Plans

For most development projects, alternate plans are typically based on the number of team members and the product's functional content. For a TSP transition effort, the principal variables will be the number of available and planned coaches and the number of parallel organizational units that are simultaneously training and launching new TSP teams. In making the plan, the coaching team should also consider the resource risk-level discussion in the previous section and base its commitments on management's commitments for available coaching time.

The first alternate plan should be for the coaching time that the managers have agreed you and your teammates can commit. Then the team should define alternates for several lower-resource risk levels with cumulative task-hour and EV plots for each. These plots will then be the task-time reference to review with management during subsequent reviews. While these alternate plans might not convince management to change their initial resource commitments, they will highlight any resource problems and pinpoint the actions required to meet the original committed schedule.

The Minimum Schedule

For any development project, there is some minimum achievable schedule, regardless of resources. If teams try to plan for earlier dates, they will get unachievable plans and waste a lot of resources. With development work, there are many things that contribute to these schedule limits, but they generally concern such things as learning time, scheduling conflicts, and long-lead items. For TSP introduction, the limiting items are related but different. The key limiting item is the time required for managers and team members to learn the TSP methods and to become sufficiently practiced to use them properly even in new or unanticipated situations.

This lead-time problem is important for the developers, but it is even more important for the team leaders, managers, and coaches. This is why you should plan a bootstrap-like transition strategy. Start with a few teams and build their management and coaching experience. Then gradually expand the number of teams while you correspondingly increase the number of newly trained managers and coaches. Limit the growth rate so that experienced coaches are always available to guide the new managers and coaches.

While new coaches and managers can learn very quickly, they need time to do so. The new coaches should not attempt to support more than one or two projects until they have guided and supported at least one successful team. Similarly, the new managers should at least have managed one or two successful TSP projects before significantly expanding the TSP efforts in their departments. In reviewing the coaching team's alternate plans, stress this schedule issue and emphasize that time is required to build skills at every level, even for the intermediate and senior managers.

27.5   Managing and Tracking Coaching Teams

While most of the leadership, management, and training problems for coaching teams are similar to those of other teams, the principal difference concerns senior-management involvement. The major issue here is resources and priorities. It also relates to the middle-management issue discussed in Chapter 24. The problem is that most transition efforts fail or take much longer than planned because of middle-management problems.

While senior management and the working level managers and developers will usually support TSP introduction once they understand it, the middle managers often will not. It is not that these managers are actively opposed, but that they usually have a large number of high-priority senior-management-directed action items with little or no guidance on which ones are most important. Not surprisingly, they then put most emphasis on those areas they understand the best and tend to defer the others.

So when the transition effort is in trouble, the problems usually concern middle-management support, and these problems will typically focus on the availability of resources. For coaching teams, this will result in the coaches not even having the time required to do the coaching work they have committed to do. Generally, the only way to fix this problem is to have senior management clarify the priority of the TSP transition effort.

Sometimes, the proper action will be to have middle management commit more resources. However, the more practical solution will often be to initially concentrate the transition effort on the areas that already have middle-management support. Then, as the coaching team gains experience, and as the management and business benefits of the TSP become clearer, it will be easier to increase senior management's priority for TSP transition. This will quickly increase the level of middle-management interest and support.

To accomplish these objectives and to ensure that the TSP transition status reports are not blocked by those middle managers who do not support the effort, establish periodic senior-management quarterly reviews. Each review should cover the performance of each group that is piloting the TSP or transitioning it into practice. In these reviews, assuming that coaching resources is the principal problem, present the alternate plan charts described in the previous section and compare current performance with these plans. This should make the resource problem clear and lead the senior executive to ask the intermediate managers how they intend to address this issue. Generally, this will resolve the resource problem.

27.6 Coaching a Coaching Team

While the knowledge and experience of the coaching team members is a big help, it can also cause problems. The principal problem is that the team members know the process so well that they can follow it without reading the scripts. They are then likely to stop following their process scripts while doing the work. While this will not cause problems if they continue to follow the defined process, this is not what generally happens.

As they use a process, most people will see small ways to change and improve it, and they will typically make these small changes as they perform the process. They will then continue to make these small changes whenever they use the process. However, because they are typically busy, they will defer updating the process and probably not even document the changes in PIPs. After a while, the process these people are using will no longer resemble the process script and the team will not really be following any defined process.

While some delay in updating the process is understandable and acceptable, get the coaching team to concentrate on following their defined process scripts. Then, whenever the script does not reflect how they now want to work, have them submit a PIP. As soon as the script diverges sufficiently from the way they work so that following the script is no longer helpful, have the process manager update the process to reflect the outstanding PIPs.

The key to getting development teams to work this way is to have their coaches work this way. While it is not easy, it is the only way to continue improving a team's or an organization's processes.

27.7 Being on a Coaching Team

The key issue in being on a coaching team is what I call the "All-Star" problem. Could you imagine Lance Armstrong being a support rider for George Hincapie in the Tour de France? While George is obviously a great rider, it is hard to imagine him as leader and Lance Armstrong as a follower or supporter.

This "Star" issue is a problem for the outstanding performers as well as for their team members. Leaders are leaders because they have followers, and they have followers because they act like leaders. But suppose you had a team of leaders—how could any of them act like followers? This is also a potential problem for coaching teams. While it is often not as big an issue as it would be for star athletes, it is hard to get experienced and highly qualified coaches to stop being coaches and to let someone else coach and lead them on a team.

When you are a member of a coaching team, try to act like a team member and play the role of a support rider. Your job is to help these people be great coaches and leaders. While you should actively participate and offer changes and suggestions whenever appropriate, give the team leader and coach the room to do their jobs they way they want to. There are many almost equally effective ways to lead and coach any team, so let your team leader and coach do their jobs their way. If you see potential issues or problems, discuss these privately with the team leader or coach. Even then, only try to help when you feel that the problems are serious or when you are asked.

The key to doing this is to treat every team experience as an opportunity to learn. If some style, strategy, or action doesn't work out very well, try to see why. Or if something works exceptionally well, remember what happened and incorporate it into your personal coaching practices. The dynamics of coaching teams can be fascinating, and being on such a team is a marvelous learning opportunity.

27.8 Summary

Coaching teams are teams of TSP coaches and they are a pleasure to work with. While such teams can be very effective and produce truly amazing results, there are a few special issues to consider in forming and coaching such groups. The principal issues concern training, the launch, and coaching.

While any group of PSP-trained professionals could form a TSP team, all the members of a coaching team must be trained as TSP coaches. If some are only PSP trained, you would have a normal TSP team and not the kind of coaching team discussed in this chapter.

The principal issue to consider in launching a coaching team is resources. Until organizations have considerable experience with the TSP, management will probably not appreciate the importance of the coaching job or the time it takes. They will then typically treat coaching as a part-time job and simultaneously assign the coaches to development work. Emphasize this issue in launch preparation and again in launch meetings 1 and 9.

The coaching issues of most concern during the job are two: the "All-Star" problem and process fidelity. Since all the members of a coaching team are TSP coaches, they often need help in working and acting like team members. Also, because they know the TSP process so well, they are likely to stop following the process scripts. Their actual process will then soon diverge from the defined process and they could end up following no defined process at all.

28

Being a Team Coach

Coaching teams is both challenging and exciting. It is challenging because it concerns people, their skills, their interests, and their motivation. I have found that motivating people is the most fascinating part of working with development teams. It is also the area where coaches, managers, and team leaders generally need the most help.

Coaching is exciting because motivating people is exciting. It is an enormous challenge to get people to try their very hardest and to consistently do superior work. They must be excited about what they are doing, and they must believe that good work is important to them, to their teammates, and to their managers. As you learn to motivate people to do great work, you will get excited too. It is unbelievably rewarding to see what people can do when they are highly motivated to do it. This chapter concerns the nature of coaching, why coaching teams is so rewarding, and some things to think about as you coach development teams. The following topics are covered.

☐ Building understanding and motivation
☐ Building a coaching team
☐ Reporting to management
☐ Coaching yourself

28.1   Building Understanding and Motivation

Have you ever taught a child to read? The process is instructive. My wife and I have seven children, and they all learned to read before they finished first grade. One of them learned to read even before she started school. We didn't try to teach them to read, all we did was read to them. We read to them every day, and reading became a fun thing for us all to do. Soon reading became a habit.

There are three keys to learning to read: fun, reward, and habit, and these learning keys also apply to the TSP, only with an interesting twist. This twist is illustrated by how I learned to read as a child. I didn't read until I was nine years old. While my family regularly read to me and my brothers, I was dyslexic. This made reading very difficult. I had to sound out each word phonically until I could hear and understand the words that I could not recognize. While I still can't spell or punctuate, reading is now rewarding, but the reward is not so much the pleasure of reading as much as all the other fun and rewarding things reading enables me to do.

What makes this like the TSP is the struggle that people have in learning good development methods and learning them so well that they become habits. While it would be hard to argue that taking the PSP course is fun, practicing the PSP methods on a team is rewarding and, if consistently used, these methods will ultimately become habits. The fun part of the TSP comes from working on a team and seeing the benefits of all the effort and struggle required to do truly superior work.

What developers find truly rewarding about the TSP is discovering the power they have when they use the methods they have learned. Now they can predictably create quality products, their products work when they enter test, and they regularly deliver these products on time. While the fun and reward of doing good work is important, the impact this has on their work performance is truly amazing. The developers now know how to make commitments and they can successfully negotiate with management. Now management will listen to them and agree to realistic plans and schedules.

The true excitement of the TSP is learning how discipline gives us the control to run our own lives. When we predictably do quality work, our peers and our managers will respect us and will trust us to make realistic but aggressive plans and commitments. When developers work this way, they discover that developing complex systems is really as much fun as they thought it would be. Also, as one developer told me, "Now I can have a family life too!"

28.2   Building a Coaching Team

As you introduce the PSP and TSP into your organization, you are likely to have other TSP coaches working with you. Now, as described in Chapter 27, you can form a coaching team and plan and track your coaching work. You can use the same PSP and TSP methods that you teach to help you do a better coaching job. This coaching team will provide a support structure, and it will help you to anticipate and resolve problems while learning and benefiting from the support of your peers. When you work with a team of coaches, you will see better ways to help and guide your development teams, to help them build on each other's successes, and to share and benefit from each other's data.

Finally, as you launch and relaunch your coaching team, you will develop strategies and plans for integrating the TSP work into your organization's other operations. For example, you might interest the quality group in the TSP quality data. Suggest that they work with your teams to develop statistically sound quality planning guidelines that are based on data from your own organization's teams. You could interest the testing group in projecting test and post-test defects from development data and in establishing test estimating, test tracking, and defect projection techniques. As they see the value of the TSP data, other groups might develop improved support tools, better reporting methods, administrative and clerical support opportunities, or innovative marketing strategies. By thinking strategically, your coaching team will see many opportunities where the TSP methods and data could be used to improve the organization's business performance. These data can also be used to improve the overall working environment and to make everyone's work more rewarding.

28.3   Success Is Invisible

One of the most frustrating aspects of quality work is that success is invisible and often unrewarded. One TSP team completed development on schedule and their product completed system test with no defects. Instead of being praised and rewarded, however, management merely thanked the developers and gave them another job to do. At about the same time, a non-TSP team was late getting into test and worked day and night for several more months to fix the many test defects. When they were finished, this team got a big party with a cake and management thanked them profusely.

Not surprisingly, the TSP team thought this was unfair and blamed management for not appreciating their work. While I don't know exactly what happened, I suspect that management knew little or nothing about what either team did. The celebration was proposed by this team's leader. He made a big deal out of the team's hard work and arranged for management to come to the party and thank everyone for what they did.

When one of your teams does good work, make sure everyone knows about it. Help the team leader arrange a party. Make sure that management knows why this was such a good job and what it means to the business. Then have the managers tell the team how much they appreciate the good work. In many organizations, management knows little or nothing about the technical details of the products, and often they don't even understand what's involved in development work. You and the team leaders must tell them, and you must tell them at every opportunity you can get.

When your TSP teams deliver products on schedule and have very few test defects, most managers will not be impressed. After all, this is just what the developers said they would do. The key is for you and the team leaders to find opportunities to brag about your team's work. Put the team's results in the cost, schedule, and customer response terms that management will understand. Be brief and factual, and compare the team's results with prior organizational performance or with other groups in other organizations. Help the team explain the business and technical significance of the achievement.

28.4   Reporting to Management

Whenever possible, have the team leaders present their own team's results, while you provide comparative trends and data. Some typical reporting opportunities are the following.

- ☐ Give management presentations at PSP course completion. When you review class results, explain what they mean in business terms.

- ☐ After each team launch or relaunch, write a brief summary report and make a management presentation comparing this team's plan with prior teams and other projects. Show goals, trends, and business consequences.

- ☐ After every checkpoint review or major project milestone, summarize the team's accomplishments and describe what they mean to the business.

- ☐ After a team has completed several consecutive TSP projects, have the members produce a longitudinal study that shows how much they have improved and what these improvements mean in business terms.

Excerpts from some typical reports are shown in Tables 28.1, 28.2, 28.3, 28.4, and 28.5. In Table 28.1, several points can be made about the business significance of the class results. By focusing on the quality of their work from the beginning of each job, the developers reduced their compile and test defects per KLOC from 82 to 17 and cut their percent of development time spent in compile and test from 32% to 16%. By reducing their compile and test defects by 4.8 times, these developers actually cut their compile and testing time in half. Furthermore, while cutting testing time and improving quality, the developers actually improved their productivity by 23.2%.

Table 28.1 Summary of PSP Class Results

Measure	Starting Value	End Value
Percent of development time in compile	9%	2%
Percent of time spent in design	10%	17%
Percent of time spent in unit test	23%	14%
Compile defect density	51 defects/KLOC	9 defects/KLOC
Unit test defect density	31 defects/KLOC	8 defects/KLOC
Yield before compile	5%	55%
Productivity	43 LOC/hour	53 LOC/hour

Table 28.2 shows an early progress report on a TSP team. The important message is that the developers on this job spent a lot of time fixing the test defects from a prior product that was not developed with the TSP. This not only delayed the delivery of that product, it also delayed the products that these developers were supposed to develop now. Poor product quality has a lasting impact. Product shipments are delayed by excessive test time, and all subsequent products are delayed because the developers are busy fixing test defects and can't develop new products.

Table 28.2 Sample Project Status Report

- Interim report after 4 weeks of work
- Initial project estimate
    - Base size of 54 KLOC
    - Added and modified size of 14 KLOC
    - Total estimated hours of 2,050
    - Delivery to test in July 2006
- High-impact risk during launch
    - Developers pulled off project to fix defects in prior non-TSP project
- The risk has so far been realized
    - Team delayed to support prior product release
    - Team now about 20% behind in task hours

Table 28.3 Average Team Task-Hour Results

Time Period	Plan	Actual
Weeks 1 through 14	12	11.25
Weeks 15 through 31	14	15.44

Table 28.3 shows one team's task-hour data. While the numbers may not look impressive, the business message is that by improving their task time from 11.25 to 15.44 task hours per week, these developers spent 37.2% more hours per week working on project tasks. This is a direct productivity increase that cost no additional money.

Table 28.4 shows the extraordinary impact of quality work on a team's business performance. The two TSP teams each produced relatively large programs with about one year of development time and approximately three months of final testing time. Another much smaller product team did not use the TSP. It finished development in about three months but spent over ten months in test. In fact, this smaller program had substantially more test defects than the two larger programs combined. Explain to management that if these developers had used the TSP, their short-term need for training might have cost a couple of weeks but they would have saved nine months of testing time.

Table 28.5 shows the benefits of keeping teams together and treating them as assets to be coached and improved. After first using the TSP on one project, this team completed three more projects to further enhance the same product. Compared to the prior non-TSP release, the TSP team reduced system and acceptance test defects by 99.1%. Since the data on release 2 were not complete, the developers calculated their productivity improvement from release 3 to release 5. It was 81.1%. Release 1 was developed by a different team that did not use the TSP.

Table 28.4 Quality Results for Three Products

Product	TSP Used	Size KLOC	Months in Development	Months in Test	Test Defects
X	Yes	91	12.3	3.0	78
Y	Yes	116	11.6	2.5	56
Z	No	31	3.0	10.8	189

Table 28.5 One Team's Longitudinal Study of One Product

Release Number	1	2	3	4	5
System and Acceptance Test Defects per KLOC	14.11	2.48	0.81	0.97	0.12
Relative Productivity: LOC/hour	N.A.	N.A.	1.00	1.40	1.81
TSP Used	No	Yes	Yes	Yes	Yes

28.5 Coaching Yourself

Being an effective coach is a challenging job. You must know how to do the work you are coaching, and you must also know how to be a coach. This requires interpersonal skills, high performance standards, and a willingness to stand up for what you believe in. Doing all of this is quite a challenge, particularly when you must do it by yourself. While there may be other coaches in your organization and they may be helpful and supportive, when you coach a team, you coach it by yourself with no other coach to help you, offer advice, or provide support.

While this is challenging, it is not hard. Your teams will have smart and dedicated members who are highly motivated to help you succeed. However, your teams can't be of much help in assessing and improving your performance as a coach. While they will generally sense whether you have done a good or a poor coaching job, they will not know the difference between good and poor coaching. And, even if they do, they will be reluctant to criticize you or to offer advice, even when you ask for it in the postmortem meetings.

Your teams will be focused on their own work and not thinking about how you are doing or how they could help to make you a better coach. The job of managing your personal improvement is almost entirely up to you. In addressing this challenge, consider assessing yourself. Periodically review your own performance and identify areas where you could improve. Think about specific ways to change what you do and then concentrate on making these changes over the next several weeks. Don't pick more than one or two improvement actions at a time, and try to adopt them as regular practices before you tackle the next improvement topic.

Some questions to consider in a coaching self-assessment are shown in the sample questionnaire in Table 28.6. While you may want to use these questions as a starter, you will almost certainly think of other areas and questions to consider. Add some questions to address the improvements you plan as well as the

Table 28.6 Coaching Self-Assessment Questionnaire

Topics	Ratings		
PSP Training	**A**	**B**	**C**
Was everyone properly notified and ready for the course?			
Did you use a checklist to promptly grade and return every assignment?			
Did you provide prompt feedback to each student on his or her work?			
Except for the first day, did you show class results every day?			
Did everyone finish the course?			
Did the course results meet normal improvement expectations?			
Did you review PSP course results with management?			
Did you submit the course data to the SEI?			
Improvement ideas			
TSP Preparation	**A**	**B**	**C**
Did you hold four weekly preparation reviews before the launch?			
Was everyone properly trained before the launch?			
Was management prepared for meetings 1 and 9?			
Did the team prepare a conceptual design in advance?			
Was the team prepared to bring historical data to the launch?			
Were the launch facilities suitable?			
Did everyone who was supposed to attend actually attend?			
Improvement ideas			
TSP Launch	**A**	**B**	**C**
If people were missing, late, or ill prepared, did you take proper action?			
Did you effectively facilitate the launch meetings?			
Did you follow the scripts in conducting the launch?			
Did you gather and submit launch data to the SEI?			
Did the team produce a complete plan, including suitable alternates?			

Table 28.6 (continued)

Topics	Ratings		
TSP Launch (continued)	**A**	**B**	**C**
Did you prepare a post-launch coaching plan and review it with the team?			
Did the team present a complete and effective report in meeting 9?			
Did the team include the coaching plan in their meeting 9 presentation?			
Did the team provide useful feedback in the launch postmortem?			
Did the team leader tell management the launch results before meeting 9?			
Improvement ideas			
TSP Post-Launch Coaching	**A**	**B**	**C**
Did you hold a post-launch briefing for the team?			
Were you available to help the team after the launch?			
Did you ensure that the weekly team meetings were properly conducted?			
Did you ensure that the team inspections were properly conducted?			
Did you monitor the quality of every team-member's data?			
If members did not properly gather data, did you effectively coach them?			
If members refused to gather data, did the team leader resolve the problem?			
Did you faithfully follow your post-launch coaching plan?			
Did your teams and team members conduct a postmortem for each project?			
Did your teams and team members keep complete project notebooks?			
Have the team leaders regularly celebrated their teams' successes?			
Do the team leaders report their team's achievements to management?			
Do you regularly inform management about team progress and success?			
Improvement ideas			

ones you have already made. Then, when you use the questionnaire, treat it as a checklist to remind yourself about what to do and how to do it.

If you regularly assess your performance and make one or two little behavior changes with each assessment, your coaching performance will gradually improve. Then your coaching results will also improve. You will also find that coaching is more fun and much more rewarding.

28.6 Summary

This chapter describes the nature of the coaching job and what makes it so rewarding. It also describes why PSP-trained developers get so excited about the TSP. When teams are excited about their work, they create better products on shorter schedules than they otherwise could. The members of such teams are more productive, do better work, and have more fun. The coach's job is to help their teams have a truly rewarding team experience.

After discussing the challenges of building the team's interest and excitement about its work, this chapter covers the opportunities coaches have for building coaching teams. As organizations introduce the TSP, all but the smallest will have several TSP coaches. This provides the coaches with an opportunity to form their own teams and to use the TSP methods to guide and support these teams in doing the coaching job.

One problem with doing quality work is that it looks so easy. Managers and executives who do not understand development work will not generally know how difficult it is to produce quality software-intensive products and to do so on aggressive and predictable schedules. An important part of the coach's job is to help the team leaders keep their management informed about their teams' achievements. This will also help the coaches retain management's support for their work and for their efforts in coaching the TSP teams.

Finally, the TSP coach is in many ways alone. There may be other coaches in the organization, but you do the coaching job essentially by yourself. That is, you will work with a team and team leader but will not generally have another coach there to provide help and to support you. You must therefore be responsible for improving your own performance as a coach. This in turn means that you should periodically conduct a self-assessment of your coaching performance. Then, based on the results of this assessment, establish and implement a personal improvement plan.

As the team coach, you have the opportunity to guide and support some of the smartest people on the planet. If these people are properly motivated and guided, they can perform truly extraordinary work. You will find that helping people to perform at their best is one of the most rewarding things you have ever done.

INDEX

TSP communication, 358
waterfall, 118, 120
Structural issues, large teams, 291
Structure
    large projects, 286
    large teams, 291
    support, 283
    team, 285, 292
Style
    management, 345
    team, 25
Subcontract manager, 110
Success
    celebrate, 37, 390
    focus on, 36
    invisibility of, 389
    rewards of, 390
Successful teams, 49
Suggestions
    coaching, 20, 21, 23, 24, 32
    management presentation, 175
Summary data, weekly report, 213
Support
    manager, 109
    management, example, 65
    plans, 123
    remote team members, 289
    structure, team, 283
    team member, 289
    tool, TSP, 74
Surprising management, 175
Surveys
    opinion, 90
    stakeholder, 274
Synchronous group, 27
System
    complex, 6
    emergent properties, 338
    kernel, 120
    test defects, 141–143
    -wide teams, 291

Talents
    building, 36
    mix of, 7
Targets, task-hour, 132
Task
    hours, 31, 131, 233, 238
        definition, 31
        edicts, 31
        example, 32, 233

target, 132
weekly, 233
maturity, 288
priorities, functional team, 310
productivity, 234
project, 129
unplanned, 235, 236
versus earned value, 238
Team
    baseball, 9
    basketball, 9
    behavior, 17
    building, see Teambuilding
    charter, 79
    coach, being a, 387
    coaching, 314, 379
    cohesion, 11, 37
    communication, 11, 283, 286
        importance of, 283
        links, 286
        maintaining, 359
        within, 288, 354
    coordination, 10
    credibility, establishing, 173
    data, handling, 370
    definition, 8
    development, 5, 9
    distributed, 288, 325–328
    effectiveness, 282
    establishing credibility, 173
    experienced, coaching, 69
    failure, 28
    feedback, 12, 87
    final report, 275
    formation phases, 18
    goals, 85, 172
        why needed, 86
    how launch builds, 51
    huge, 10, 291, 333
    ineffective, 28
    inspection, 248
    integrated, 69, 333
    jelled, 8, 49
    kinds of teams, 9
    large, 10, 291, 333
    launch, why, 37
    leader,
        coaching, 40–46, 61, 216
        role, 14, 15
        troublesome, 40–46
    leadership, see Leadership team

Watts Humphrey Is the Definitive Voice on Software Process!

"An informative book for any business person (not just technologists) who has ever been involved with a software development effort and thought 'there must be a better way!' Watts has provided that better way—the PSP/TSP, and a great book."
—Roy Kinkaid, EBS Dealing Resources

Watts Humphrey, drawing on his own extensive executive and management experience, shows corporate executives and senior managers why software is both a business problem and a business opportunity, and the critical importance of software to nearly every business, large and small.

ISBN 0-201-77639-1

The First Step in Software Process Improvement
This book describes and documents the Personal Software Process (PSP[SM]) for individual software developers, and introduces them to the Team Software Process (TSP[SM]) for teams.

ISBN 0-321-30549-3

The Essential Guide to Leading Teams of Software Engineers Trained in the PSP
Whether you are a new or experienced team leader, Humphrey provides invaluable examples, guidelines, and suggestions on how to motivate your team to handle the many issues you and your team face together.

ISBN 0-321-34962-8

Invaluable Examples and Guidelines You Need to Get Started and Keep Developing as a Team Coach
The team coach monitors team performance and assists the team members to improve. Using real-world examples and situations, this book shows coaches how to cooperatively support the team leader and how to work with the leader to build, guide, and motivate the entire team.

ISBN 0-201-73113-4

For more information on these and other books in the SEI Series in Software Engineering, please visit www.awprofessional.com/seiseries

The SEI Series in Software Engineering

ISBN 0-321-18613-3

ISBN 0-321-22876-6

ISBN 0-321-11886-3

ISBN 0-201-73723-X

ISBN 0-321-15495-9

ISBN 0-321-17935-8

ISBN 0-201-54664-7

ISBN 0-321-15496-7

ISBN 0-201-70372-6

ISBN 0-201-70482-X

ISBN 0-201-70332-7

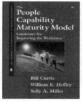
ISBN 0-201-60445-0

ISBN 0-201-60444-2

ISBN 0-201-52577-1

ISBN 0-201-25592-8

ISBN 0-201-54597-7

ISBN 0-201-54809-7

ISBN 0-321-30549-3

ISBN 0-201-18095-2

ISBN 0-201-54610-8

ISBN 0-201-47719-X

ISBN 0-321-34962-8

ISBN 0-201-77639-1

ISBN 0-201-73-1134

ISBN 0-201-61626-2

ISBN 0-201-70454-4

ISBN 0-201-73409-5

ISBN 0-201-85-4805

ISBN 0-321-11884-7

ISBN 0-321-33572-4

ISBN 0-201-70312-2

ISBN 0-201-70-0646

ISBN 0-201-17782-X

Please see our web site at www.awprofessional.com for more information on these titles.

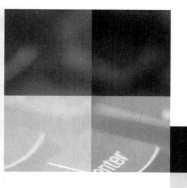